Kafka Translated

Kafka Translated

How Translators have Shaped our Reading of Kafka

Michelle Woods

BLOOMSBURY
NEW YORK • LONDON • NEW DELHI • SYDNEY

Bloomsbury Academic
An imprint of Bloomsbury Publishing Inc

1385 Broadway	50 Bedford Square
New York	London
NY 10018	WC1B 3DP
USA	UK

www.bloomsbury.com

Bloomsbury is a registered trademark of Bloomsbury Plc

First published 2014

© Michelle Woods, 2014

All rights reserved. No part of this publication may be reproduced or transmitted in any form or by any means, electronic or mechanical, including photocopying, recording, or any information storage or retrieval system, without prior permission in writing from the publishers.

No responsibility for loss caused to any individual or organization acting on or refraining from action as a result of the material in this publication can be accepted by Bloomsbury or the author.

Library of Congress Cataloging-in-Publication Data
Woods, Michelle, 1972-
Kafka Translated : How Translators have Shaped our Reading of Kafka / Michelle Woods.
pages cm
Includes bibliographical references and index.
ISBN 978-1-4411-9771-9 (pbk. : alk. paper)– ISBN 978-1-4411-4991-6 (hardback : alk. paper) 1. Kafka, Franz, 1883-1924–Translations–History and criticism. 2. Translating and interpreting. I. Title.
PT2621.A26Z9858 2013
833'.912–dc23
2013029972

ISBN: HB: 978-1-4411-4991-6
PB: 978-1-4411-9771-9
ePDF: 978-1-4411-3344-1
ePub: 978-1-4411-3195-9

Typeset by Fakenham Prepress Solutions, Fakenham, Norfolk NR21 8NN
Printed and bound in the United States of America

And so there I was on the platform, under a warm, pale-blue sky, wearing a thick woolen scarf, a cloth cap, and a new autumn coat I had just bought in order to look respectable in Armenia. Muscovite experts in sartorial matters had looked me up and down and said, "Well, it's hardly chic, but it'll do for a translator."

Vasily Grossman

I hear the voice, my voice! […] I don't know how it happens, after all I only read it with my eyes, so how did my blood find out so quickly, so quickly that my veins are already hot from circulating its words?

Kafka, on receiving a translation of his work from Milena Jesenská

*For my mother,
Yvonna Woods.*

Contents

Acknowledgements		ix
Introduction		1
1	Translating Kafka	13
	Milena Jesenská	13
	Willa Muir	44
	Mark Harman	79
	Michael Hofmann	104
2	Kafka Translating	129
3	Adapting Kafka	191
4	Interpreting Kafka	241
Bibliography		265
Index		277

Acknowledgements

While spending four years in Kafka's company was mostly a delight, I was glad to do it with the company and support of so many. A huge thanks to my editor, Haaris Naqvi, whose interest and patience allowed the project to develop. I am completely indebted to Mark Harman and Michael Hofmann, who were both so gracious, kind and interesting. I'd like to thank the Provost's Office and CRAL at SUNY New Paltz for an award to pursue research at St. Andrews University's Willa Muir Archive and I would like to thank the librarians at St. Andrews for their help. I am very grateful also to the Ústav pro českou literaturu for a stipendium that enabled me to pursue research on Milena Jesenská in Prague. I would like to thank Professor Gerald Sorin and the Resnick Lecture series for a chance to try out my material on František Soukup. Parts of the book have appeared in different form elsewhere: "Reassessing Willa Muir: Her Role and Influence in the Franz Kafka Translations." *Translation Studies*. 4:1 (2011) 58–71; "The 'Factional' Translator: Willa Muir." *Transfiction and beyond*, edited by Klaus Kaindl and Karlheinz Spitzl. Amsterdam: John Benjamins, 2013; and "Translator, Writer and Wronged: Milena Jesenská Unconstructed." *Translation Right and Wrong*, edited by Susana Bayó Belenguer, Eileán Ní Chuilleanáin, and Cormac Ó Chuilleanáin. Dublin: Four Courts Press, 2013. Thank you to the wonderful English Department at New Paltz and to my students and their discussions in three classes I taught over the last few years at New Paltz: Horror and Humor in European Fiction, and my two Major Authors: Kafka classes. A special thanks to my student research assistant, Mike Herrera.

None of this would be possible without the love and support of my husband, Michael Reisman, who has only occasionally seen me – like Kafka's Poseidon – peek out from a desk full of papers in the last few months.

Introduction

"Read it sucka," Walon (Steve Earle) says to Bubbles (Andre Royo) in *The Wire*, and hands him one of Franz Kafka's aphorisms, which Bubbles reads out loud:

> You can hold back from the suffering of the world, you have free permission to do so, and it is in accordance with your nature, but perhaps this very holding back is the one suffering you could have avoided (Kafka quoted in Simon 2008).[1]

It is a beautiful aphorism, at once pulsating with meaning and somehow intangible. "We obscurely feel, we bet, we practically *know* there is something more going on in a story," Michael Hofmann writes, "something probably to do with sex or violence or families or metaphysics, but we're damned if we know what it is" (Hofmann 2008: x). It is this "over-plus of meaning on Kafka's side" that "gives rise to the profusion of interpretations," he adds (x). Bubble squints at the aphorism Walon has handed him: "Fonzie Kafka. Who he?" Bubbles asks. "Some writer," Walon says. "Read his books?" "Fuck no." Bubbles is perplexed. "What it mean to you?" he asks. "I dunno, Bubs," Walon says. "What's it mean to you?" (Simon 2008).

The lure of interpreting Kafka's work is in this perplexed refrain: "What it mean to you?" "I dunno, Bubs. What's it mean to you?" As Adorno famously wrote: "Each sentence says 'interpret me,' and none will permit it" (Adorno 1981: 246), something Peter Heller also argues: that, in Kafka's work, "the subjection to the experience of not understanding seems to me to be *the* or at least *a* major point of reading Kafka. He is drawn into, and draws the reader into, the dramatization of the – guilty – failure to arrive, to communicate, to understand" (Heller 1977: 382). Heller questions – as he believes Kafka's work does – what we actually mean by "understanding": "Apparently," he writes, "to interpret, to translate the unfamiliar into terms familiar and hence reassuring and meaningful" (386). But this does not mean that such interpretations or translations are true, and it is because we have a sense that these "rationalizations" are just that (386), that Kafka's work continues to intrigue us, because we "recognize very well what Kafka is saying, for he scratches the wounds of our lives where they

---

[1] David Simon used the same aphorism as an epigraph for his non-fiction book *The Corner*, published in 1997.

itch" (385). We don't understand life, in other words, and are constantly, and finally, ineffectively, looking to translate it into answers. Reading Kafka is a re-enactment of that sense of failure and misunderstanding. Adorno describes the effect in cinematic terms:

> the contemplative relation between text and reader is shaken to its very roots. His texts are designed not to sustain a constant distance between themselves and their victim but rather to agitate his feelings to a point where he fears that the narrative will shoot towards him like a locomotive in a three-dimensional film (Adorno 1981: 246).

The place of understanding, however, is in the language; "Kafka's authority is textual," Adorno writes. "Only fidelity to the letter, not oriented understanding, can be of help. In an art that is constantly obscuring and revoking itself, ever determinate statement counterbalances the general proviso of indeterminateness" (247). If we consider again the aphorism Walon gives Bubbles through two different translations, we can begin to understand what Adorno argued:

> **Du** kannst **D**ich *zurückhalten* von **d**en *Leiden* **d**er **W**elt, **d**as ist **D**ir freigestellt und entspricht **D**einer Natur, aber vielleicht ist gerade **d**ieses *Zurückhalten* **d**as **ei**nzige *Leid*, **d**as **D**u vermei**d**en könntest.

> You can hold back from the suffering of the world, you have free permission to do so, and it is in accordance with your nature, but perhaps this very holding back is the one suffering you could have avoided (Kafka 1960: 305).

> You can withdraw from the sufferings of the world – that possibility is open to you and accords with your nature – but perhaps that withdrawal is the only suffering you might be able to avoid (Kafka 2006: 102).

Here, Kafka makes a statement about "suffering"/"Leid" and "withdrawal"/ "zurückhalten," two melancholic words that are repeated twice: "You can hold back from the suffering of the world"; "this very holding back is the one suffering," around the fulcrum of "but perhaps"/"aber vielleicht." Contrapuntal to the emotion being described, however, is the muscular sound of the language in German; the repetitions of the "d" "k" "v" "ei" "r" and "g" sounds through the aphorism. Kafka's lexicon is not poetic but the way it is used is, and this use complicates the sentiment of the aphorism; as Adorno adds, "by avoiding all musical effects, his brittle prose functions like music" (Adorno 1981: 264). Both the Muirs and Hofmann are thinking about that rhythm and music; so although the Muirs's choice of "free permission" seems a stretch at first to translate "freistellen" – "das ist Dir freigestellt" – it makes more sense when thinking about the sound: "**f**rom the **suff**ering **of** the world, you have **f**ree permission to do so" where we see an attempt to approximate the consonance of the German. Hofmann takes the same approach but with some different sounds: "withdraw from the sufferings of the world – that possibility is open to you." The texture of the two translations is different: the Muirs choose to translate "zurückhalten" as "hold back" which is a very literal translation but it also – with the cluster of plosives "can hold back" – effects a strong euphony at the beginning of the aphorism. Hofmann opts for a softer sound, the "w" and "s," and lures you into the plosives: "possibility is open." The propulsive sound of the aphorism makes this melancholy aphorism exuberant.

We read Kafka in translation. Not only, as we might imagine, in a linguistic form of translation, but also in a network of translation: a translation of the man, Franz Kafka, into an icon, a critical translation of his works into various schools of theory, a commercial translation of the man and his work, and popular – screen translations – of his work and himself. All of these function, to some extent, together, and help form our sense of Kafka and his work even before we might have read any Kafka. It has been a sense shot through with loss and tragedy and suffering: the loss of Kafka at the age of 41 from tuberculosis, the loss of his texts – not all burned per his request, but unfinished and tinkered with by his friend Max Brod; the loss of the culture from which he arose, Prague German Jewry, and a loss of the language that preceded the assimilated culture Kafka was born into: Yiddish; and finally, anxieties about the loss of meaning in translation – if Kafka wrote in a language inflected by the loss of other languages (Prague German, Yiddish) then how can that be conveyed into English? The loss of meaning itself seems to cradle Kafka's work, a loss read so nihilistically after the war and after the Holocaust, then ludically in the era of poststructuralism, but perhaps now, finally, may be read as something that is tragically funny: "What it mean to you?" "I dunno, Bubs. What's it mean to you?"

At the heart of translation is recovery, Walter Benjamin's "afterlife," a living-on of meaning that eschews the hunt for original meaning, but opens it up and interrogates it. Kafka is a "world celebrity" (Gross 2010: 411) because of translation, not only because he was discovered for the English-speaking world by two Scots translators, Willa and Edwin Muir, in the late 1920s, but because the import of his work became translated into the intellectual needs and currents of the times into which his work was translated, specifically in the immediate post-World War II era. The Muirs's long-serving translations of Kafka's work are currently being superseded – they are regarded as being faulty, too domesticated, too in sync with Max Brod's Messianic vision of the texts (and with his resultant editing practices), and too lacking in humor. It is an exciting moment in Kafka translation in English, as multiple re-translations by different translators and publishers are being made in order to recover what was felt to be lost: pieces of text (since the scholarly re-ediing of Kafka's work in the late 1970s and early 1980s), the ambiguity and strangeness of the language and the subsequent humor of it. "The power of Kafka's text," his translator of *Der Prozeß/The Trial*, Breon Mitchell, writes, "lies in the language ... in a closely woven web of linguistic motifs that must be rendered consistently to achieve their full impact" (Mitchell 1998: xviii). For him, despite "the virtues of their translation," the Muirs's translation "fell far short, for in attempting to create a readable and stylistically refined version of Kafka's *Trial*, they consistently overlooked or deliberately varied the repetitions or interconnections that echo so meaningfully in the ear of every attentive reader of the German text" (xviii).

What the recent re-translations have brought to the fore are the stylistics of the work because they can: Kafka – unlike when the Muirs translated him – is now an iconic writer, having influenced a swathe of modern, postmodern, and contemporary literature. We are now ready, perhaps paradoxically, to reread his work through our readings of those he influenced. The new translations have been heralded (and sometimes dismissed) as foreignizing translations that attempt to convey the "simplicity" of Kafka's vocabulary, the repetitions, and his sometimes loose punctuation and "long sentences in which main clauses are linked only by commas" (Robertson 2012: xxx). As Breon Mitchell writes, paraphrasing Malcolm Pasley: "as Kafka becomes more engrossed in the writing process his punctuation tended to loosen, periods turning into semicolons or commas, and commas themselves disappearing, as if a bird were lifting off in flight" (Mitchell 1998: xvi–xvii).

These repetitions, motifs, modes of punctuation, long paragraphs effect what another Kafka translator, Mark Harman (following Samuel Beckett's judgment on Kafka), describes as the "steamroller-like quality of Kafka's prose" (Harman 1998b: 180). They are innately tied into the beauty and humor of the prose, something that is not always obvious except when the text is heard out loud. As Malcolm Pasley points out – with regard to the unusual punctuation of *Das Schloß/The Castle*, we have the version of the text (unfinished) that Kafka used to read out loud. He did so to the great amusement of his friends – they "laughed quite immoderately" when Kafka read the opening chapter of *The Trial* aloud, and "he himself laughed so much that there were moments when he couldn't read any further" (Brod 1992: 178).

In his essay on Kafka translations, "A Sentence," Milan Kundera shows the importance of recognizing the effect of the repeated words, euphony, punctuation, and long paragraphs on the beauty and humor of the work; something which Kundera feels has been misunderstood and effectively lost in translation and its requirements for a "good style" in the target language. Unlike Deleuze and Guattari, he does not regard Kafka's "bareness of vocabulary" as a result of Kafka's suffering and alienation from language, but as "Kafka's *aesthetic intention* ... one of the distinctive marks of the *beauty* of his prose" (Kundera 1996: 110). The repetitions and unusual punctuation are central to Kafka's prose, the "*author's personal style*" that inevitably, with great authors (thus providing the newness of great literature), "*transgresses* against 'good style'" (110, all italics are Kundera's). Kafka's transgressions, he implies, are not as obvious as exuberant stylists like Joyce or Faulkner, but are central to the mechanism and meaning of the work.

Kundera blames the translators for domesticating the Kafka texts, arguing that they introduce synonyms, for example, to break up these repetitions in order to show off "their own mastery and competence" (109) and to "invest the text with his own creativity" (108); the translators after all can only be judged by the "good style" of the receiving, or target, culture. Kundera is being slightly disingenuous here; in his own experience, the problems clearly lay not with the translators but with his editors who would systematically cross out repetitions and shorten sentences in Kundera's novels after the translations had been completed to make them more acceptable to English-language norms for explicitly commercial reasons (Woods 2006: 27–41). With this caveat in mind, Kundera's essay points out the resistance to and the possibilities of translation: the translators have to negotiate with the cultural norms and practices they translate into while also being what Mark Harman calls "slow readers," or intimate readers, of the text – absolutely aware of the mechanisms of Kafka's style (Harman, personal communication). What is important about Kundera's essay is that it points out what translators already know: that the stylistic elements of the text can be the most translatable element of it, if material conditions in the target culture accept them. As Michael Hofmann points out, when he has translated Kafka's work, that he tried to "translate the surface" of the work rather than to provide a hermeneutic re-encoding of it; in other words, he was interested in what the language *does* – in translating what it does, the possibility is left open to read and reread what it may mean (Hofmann, personal communication).

The resistance that both Harman and Hofmann have encountered – J.M. Coetzee, for instance, fretting that this was a new, boring Kafka that, if he were less famous, one might be tempted to "silently" fix up (Coetzee 2001: 82) – speaks to the domestic pressures facing translators, especially of iconic writers whom we, to paraphrase Hofmann, "practically know." Coetzee, as his example of boringness, quotes a passage from *The Castle* that is actually (as I hope I show) very funny because of its length and register (legal reasoning from the mouth of a child) and its inclusion in a novel all about how narrative and story-telling detain and distract us. "But ... does the story bore you?" the endlessly bureaucratic Council Chairman asks K. (interrupting his own pages-long disquisition). "No ... it amuses me," K. answers (Kafka 1998a: 63). The set-up of this joke is long and tortuous, the reader feels the work s/he has to put in to get through the pages, but in the end, as Harman points out with another novel, the narrator "occasionally winks to the reader over the hero's head" (Harman 2008: xxviii). The translators, though, have to have a thick skin, as the reviews have shown, since some readers want an easier Kafka, a more familiar one. Yet, in doing so, they miss exactly what makes Kafka a great writer.

It must be said, before their translations are completely superseded, that the Muirs did recognize how Kafka's style worked, and in many cases managed to translate it. Their general domestication of the texts was not, as has been argued to date, due to misreading or fundamentally not understanding a modernist writer, but, as I argue here in Willa Muir's case, a reaction to material and cultural pressures. Her case is a vital one to reassess because it gives an example of how a wider understanding of the translator's context can elevate translation reviewing and criticism from what Mark Harman calls its "gotcha" mentality – look at the mistakes! – to a more self-reflexive understanding of what we expect from translations and translators, given the conditions in which they translate. Muir was not a native English speaker – she grew up speaking Shetlandic, then mainland Scots; she was a first-wave, outspoken feminist; and she was a modernist novelist. Both her public – but even more so, her private – writing indicate that when it came to translation she and her husband (who grew up as an Orcadian Scots speaker) were intimately aware of the imperative to domesticate texts, because of the hegemony of an English literary culture that would only accept these two Scots and this woman if they acceded to the rules of the game. Dependent on their income from translation in the inter-war years, the Muirs actively repressed their identities to produce normalizing translations, literally in the case of Willa Muir, who claimed – only in private – that she in fact was "THE translator" of the majority of the Kafka translations but that "patriarchal society" would never accept the fact, would "sweep it into oblivion" (St. Andrews MS 38466/5/5: August 20, 1953). Muir needs to be swept back from that oblivion, from a kind of "gender censorship" in translation (Woods 2012: 75–6), to enable us not to understand so much the product but the process of translation and the importance of the translator as a holistic, gendered, and literary being.

The first translator considered in this book was Kafka's first translator ever, and was also a woman (and, in practice, a feminist): Milena Jesenská. There would seem to be no need for recovery here, no story about loss, since numerous biographies have been written about her, novels too, even songs. She was immortalized in Kafka's *Letters to Milena*: the love letters written to her by Kafka, a love affair ignited by her request to translate his story, "Der Heizer"/"The Stoker." The fact that she was the first translator of Kafka's work – into the other major language of his homeland, and one that he spoke: Czech – is always mentioned, but no one has actually examined those translations, which have tended to be dismissed immediately on little or no evidential basis – Jacqueline Raoul-David in her recent and bestselling part-fictionalization of Kafka's love life, *Kafka in Love*, informs us that "Milena's" translations were full of "egregious mistranslations" despite not having read them and, it seems, not speaking or reading Czech (Raoul-David 2012: 177). It is a throwaway remark for what is regarded as a throwaway art. Jesenská has been translated into an icon herself, referred to almost always as "Milena" and as Kafka's lover, but she was a successful translator and journalist. Kafka was not only aware of this; he fictionalized her and her work in his writing – to some extent in the *Letters*, but also in *The Castle* (specifically an article of hers called "The Café").

Kafka's beautiful, funny, self-deprecating *Letters to Milena* have been read and reread as insights into Kafka's thinking, but never as a discourse on translation which the letters so clearly are: the two fall in love talking about translation as an intellectual, visceral, and sensual enterprise. Kafka, who lived a life involving daily acts of translation and who was an inveterate language learner, knew what was involved; he understood the limits and possibilities of the act, of the inevitability of untranslatablity, of the intense and tough labor involved, and was acceptant and excited about the idea of the new life translation could bring to the original version of the work. He wanted to see Jesenská's hands on his work, partly because he was falling in love with her but also because he was falling in love with her work. His one worry was that she was too faithful – not to the meaning of the words, as he (living it) understood the issues of untranslatability between German and Czech, but to his style. What is so interesting about Jesenská's literary milieu, however, was that the avant-garde press in which her translations were published was eager for experimental work and corresponding experimental translations: it was a much more acceptant target culture than the English-speaking one, then and now. When she published that first translation – of "Topič"/"The Stoker" – in 1920 (four years before Kafka's death), the socialist newspaper, *Kmen*, unusually devoted the whole issue to the story in recognition of its literary worth. Kafka, belying the Kafka myth, was becoming known in German avant-garde literary circles while he was alive, but also, thanks to Jesenská, in Czech circles.

Despite the "ocean of Kafka exegesis" (Heller 1977: 380) on Kafka's work, remarkably little has been written, in English, about the translations and translators. I focus here on four of his translators: Milena Jesenská; Willa Muir; and two contemporary translators, Mark Harman and Michael Hofmann, in order to discuss the importance of translators and translation to the dissemination of Kafka's work but also to an understanding of it. The resistances to them and their work actually open up issues of reading Kafka and points of resistance in the texts themselves, what I call, in the final chapter, "transreading." A way out is needed for the impasse in traditional translation reviewing (Venuti 2008: 1–8) which tends to compare and contrast translations in an attempt to adjudicate worth and, ultimately, an impossible fidelity. Instead, if we look at how different translators approach the text, with a fuller knowledge of their backgrounds and literary identities, we can see how these differences bring us back ultimately to what is important and difficult and interesting about what language does in Kafka's work.

There is a very contested critical terrain about what Kafka's language actually is: Gilles Deleuze and Félix Guattari dominated Kafka studies for some years with their insistence that, stripped of Yiddish and speaking a deterritorialized and marginalized variant of German, namely Prague German, Kafka was moved to write in "his own *patois*, his own third world, his own desert" (Deleuze and Guattari 1986: 18). The critical sense now is that their case for Kafka writing in a minor language or dialect is a misreading, that Kafka in fact wrote in a fairly normative High German (Corngold 2004: 273). What is unusual about his language, however, is not what he wrote in, but how he wrote – what any great writer does with language: stretching it, defamiliarizing it, interrogating it. This interrogation is informed by what Claire Kramsch calls "the wager of multilingualism" (2008: 331), because as Marek Nekula has so impressively shown, Kafka lived in – and was not, as previously thought, alienated from – a multilingual milieu, learning, if imperfectly, Czech as well as German (Nekula 2003). The question of language and Kafka has often been portrayed as one of suffering and loss – a generation removed from Yiddish because of assimilation, worries about an ethnic accent (i.e. a *mauscheln* German (Anderson 1992: 197)) in a society intolerant of it, being forced to speak in a form of German alien to his daily Prague German, isolated from the Czech-speaking majority, and so on.

However, if we look at Kafka's writing, especially his fictionalization of translation (something that has not previously been examined), a wry, funny narrative appears – a narrative written by someone who lived daily with the pitfalls of translating between languages and cultures. In *The Trial*, Josef K. is asked to translate for a visiting Italian businessman but finds he cannot understand a word the man says because the Italian's moustache is getting in the way and K. is strangely attracted to that moustache, wanting to go up and sniff it. He runs off and tries to memorize words from his Italian dictionary but gets bored quickly, finding it a difficult and tedious task. Kafka – who worked as a lawyer for an Italian insurance company – tried to learn the language and used his lessons as an excuse for his tardiness, a habit that drove Max Brod: "I am only simply unpunctual through my Italian industry [his lessons]," he wrote to Brod, "but you through your lust for pleasure" (Brod 1992: 70). Brod, in his biography of Kafka, conveys a picture of Kafka and languages as one invested with humor and joy. They cemented their friendship reading Plato's *Protagoras* in the original, "with the aid of translations and our school dictionary – often with a great deal of difficulty" (53). What kept them going was the humor in it, the "vivid and scurrilous description of the life of the Sophists, and the Plato-Socratic irony" (53). Kafka insisted they read Flaubert in the original, something, Brod almost groans, that took "years" (53). Kafka learned Hebrew "with special zeal" toward the end of his life; "of the papers he left behind" after his death, Brod writes, "the papers filled with Hebrew exercises are not much fewer than those covered with literary works in German" (197).

As young men they came up with an idea to financially support their writing. They produced travel guides called "On the Cheap." Since it was "impossible to learn a foreign language properly" they decided to insert dictionaries of bad tourist versions of each language on the basis that they would "prefer to teach it to you badly straightaway. This gives you less trouble, and is quite enough for making yourself understood. It is a kind of Esperanto, bad French or bad English, invented by us." These dictionaries, made them laugh themselves "sick" because they "contained of course an undercurrent of irony, which was directed at our own shortcomings – we neither of us had any talent for languages" (121). Brod's rather saintly and pious portrayal of Kafka that gave birth, Milan Kundera argues, to the cult of suffering and loss, "Kafkology" (Kundera 1996: 42), does, however, show Kafka laughing and joking and being industrious when it came to all sorts of languages. Importantly, it also shows him negotiating with those languages, and thinking about and enacting translation.

He was also aware of the issue of language hegemony and the cultural implications of language, but showed himself open to viewing this rather serious subject with humor. In 1912 he gave a short public lecture, before a recitation of Yiddish poems, about the Yiddish language, in which he teased his audience: "many of you are so frightened of Yiddish," he said, "that one can almost see it in your faces" (Anderson 1989: 263). He warned them that it was this "dread of Yiddish" that made them unable to understand it, a "dread mingled with a fundamental distaste" because of the perceived inferiority of the language (263). He directly confronted why it was "a despised language" because it seemed to be a bastardized tongue, borrowing from numerous languages, and because it was associated with Jewishness, but pointed out that it was this very "linguistic medley" that might make it a lingua *franca*, an "international language," a notion that seemed "obvious" but impossible given its status (264). Kafka's spirited and humorous defense of the language – especially its untranslatability into German when it was "torn to shreds" because of the apparent likeness of the two – seemed not only to directly contradict notions of his embarrassment about or alienation from the language, but also showed his wry humor about, and interest in, it.

Kafka gave his audience a brief précis of the three Yiddish poems they would hear, assuming that his audience would deliberately not understand the Yiddish because of their "dread" and "distaste" but immediately made fun of his own explanations and the possibility of any literary explication. "Do not expect any help from the explanation of the poems," he said, "At best you will understand the explanation and become aware that something difficult is about to follow. ... Straight-jacketed in these explanations, when you hear the poems you will try to make out what you know already, and you will miss what is already there" (265). He reassured them that if they spoke German they would be "also capable of understanding Yiddish" (265). Kafka's deliberate act of, and involvement in, non-translation gets to the heart of his own work: the ironic acknowledgment of non-understanding and mis-understandings; the pleasure and humor readers might get in acknowledging this; and the demand on readers to put away their dread, distaste and prior prejudices.

This is not the Kafka we are used to and maybe not even the Kafka we want, because we are used to an iconicized Kafka, a translated Kafka (if we allow the religious sense of "translation" here). Brod – through grief, I argue in Chapter 4 – spawned, as Milan Kundera articulated it "Kafkology," the science of reducing Kafka's work to a solipsistic sainthood (Kundera 1996). Yet in his biography of Kafka there is a lot of humor and humanness; in fact, it is also postwar readings of Brod's biography that excise this human side of Kafka, that turn him into a sanctified genius with no precedent and no peers and, most importantly, with no humor. Much of this has to do with timing: the Muirs's translations of Kafka's work were well reviewed in the 1930s and 1940s, but during and after World War II his work suddenly seemed prescient of this bleak new age. That post-Holocaust, nuclear, Cold War age translated Kafka into its own parameters that defined him and his work for readers and students in the twentieth and into the twenty-first century, as Stephen Dowden has so excellently shown (in the case of *The Castle*) (Dowden 1995). In some ways, to read Kafka we have to strip back layers of critical and cultural translations, read the work past the icon.

Jesse Pinkman (Aaron Paul) in the TV series *Breaking Bad*, in an episode entitled "Kafkaesque," sums up the reading (describing his work life in the Gus Fring/Walter White meth lab): "Lots of red tape. My boss is a dick. The owner – super dick. I'm not worthy or whatever to meet him, but I guess everybody's scared of the dude. The place is full of dead-eyed douchebags, the hours suck, nobody knows what's going on." "Sounds kind of Kafkaesque," his drug rehab leader says. Jesse has no idea what he's talking about: "Totally Kafkaesque," he answers (Gilligan et al. 2010).

The screenwriters here mine the humor of Kafka's iconicization with the cheap currency of the term "Kafkaesque" that sums up so much and so little; its seeming universal applicability and the emptiness at the heart of it. On closer reading, what makes this demotic dialogue funny is what the language does (the repetition of "dick"; the alliterative refrain with "dude" and "dead-eyed douchebags"; the pairing of "dick" and "suck"; "everybody" and "nobody"; the assonance "nobody knows what's going on"; the consonance "kind of Kafkaesque" and then the beat, and the two-word dactylic riposte: "Totally Kafkaesque"). The sentiment is funny, the situation is funny, but what makes it great is that it *sounds* funny: the language is dynamic, euphonically effecting meaning.

I am not suggesting Gilligan and his co-writers are sitting around thinking about including consonance and dactyls in their dialogue, but it is why the language sounds right and the mechanism through which a tragic situation is undercut with humor: it is in fact quite similar to what language does in Kafka's work. Going back to these mechanisms, thinking about how language works in his prose via translatorial decisions brings us back, past the icon and suffering to the exhilaration of writing, to thinking about how the texts *do* communicate, even though they circulate endlessly around the metaphysics of incommunicability.

Screen translations can help. Although film adaptations of Kafka's work have generally been seen as failures and even purveyors of the "Totally Kafkaesque," they can also serve as ways back into the work and a means by which we might understand how we read Kafka, or rather, how we reflexively – rather than self-reflexively – read Kafka. Steven Soderbergh and Peter Capaldi deconstruct Kafka the icon in quite interesting ways in their films *Kafka* (1991) and *Kafka's It's a Wonderful Life* (1993), but the critical response to the films says as much about how we read Kafka as do the films. Orson Welles, Michael Haneke, and Federico Fellini all made films based on Kafka's work that are unmistakably centered on their auteur identities, but all three of them question the notion of filmic authority as they appropriate Kafka's work. Fellini's *Intervista/Interview* (1987) seems the most flagrantly unfaithful adaptation, or translation, of Kafka's work (specifically, his novel *Amerika*) but on close viewing, I argue, is an intricate reading of the work, an "inter-view" of it, that opens up motifs and characters in the novel. As Lawrence Venuti argues (2007), in thinking about film adaptation we should move away from the parameters of fidelity and betrayal and look at how the films and their source texts interact with an especial awareness of what expectations we, the critics, come armed with. The visual language of film – explored also in Vladimir Michálek's 1994 *Amerika*, the first Czech film, post-communism, to adapt Kafka's work – is a means by which we can return to the question of motif and textual language in Kafka, especially with an awareness of how Kafka himself was responding to the new technology and visuals of film in his narrative (especially *Der Verschollene/Amerika*).

Kafka was also a literary adaptor. We see him "translating" others' work into his own, something that has been very much understated in Kafka criticism (although this is changing). Kundera argues that "Kafkology" has prevented intertextual readings of Kafka, because of its insistence on the *sui generis* nature of his work, and thus its genius, but that Kafka should be studied as one of a "generation of great innovators – Stravinsky, Webern, Bartók, Apollinaire, Musil, Joyce, Picasso, Braque – all born, like him, between 1880 and 1883" (Kundera 1996: 44). Whatever the reasons, Kafka's "translations" of others' work into his own is revelatory about how his texts work and what the innovations of them are; how he translates David Copperfield's box and Frantisek Soukup's socialist travelogue, *Amerika: řada obrazů amerického života*, into *Amerika* or Homer's *Odyssey*, Jonathan Swift's *Battle of the Books*, and Jesenská's "The Café" into *The Castle* allows us to understand his aesthetic and his humor, as well as what his language does.

Kafka Translated clearly deals with different ideas of what "translation" is – linguistic translation, cultural translation, untranslatability, screen adaptation, iconization, literary rewriting and adaptation, critical interpretation – but, in doing so, suggests that these translations are part and parcel of each other, that a multivalent translation process is going on all at the same time. In other words, that we cannot just speak about translation as a simple comparison between a source and target text, but need to be at least aware of all these issues and, especially, aware of the translator as an embodied agent. In fact, an awareness of these translators and translations allows us a keen and illuminating re-entry into the textual Kafka, a Kafka thinking in language and about translation; a Kafka, like translation, not solely about suffering and loss.

1

Translating Kafka

Milena Jesenská

washerwoman of other people's joys
refugee from life
Milena Jesenská, you with the ancient name from the execution grounds.
Marie Pujmanová, "To Milena Jesenská"

In 1945, Jana Černá still refused to believe her mother was dead. Incarcerated in Ravensbrück concentration camp, Černá's mother, the journalist and translator Milena Jesenská, had died a year earlier of kidney failure. It took a visit from a woman who had been interned with Jesenská to persuade Černá of the fact; the woman brought with her an "irreplaceable relic" that Černá knew she could not live with. She stored it in a safe place and never found it again. "On the table before my eyes lay a piece of her body," Černá wrote in her memoir of her mother, "a segment of her smile, a part of the mouth that had once talked to me" (Černá 1998: 17). All that was left of Milena Jesenská was a tooth.

The physical metonymy of that tooth is perhaps emblematic of the remnants of Jesenská's translatorial legacy, constructed mainly from silence; she is mostly remembered by Franz Kafka's *Letters to Milena*, first published in 1952, a correspondence charting a mostly epistolary love affair through a few months in 1920, of which only the letters *from* Kafka survive. The correspondence began because of translation; Jesenská was the first translator of Kafka's work, initially approaching him with her translation of "The Stoker"/"Topič" (the short story that became the beginning of the novel *Amerika*). Her translation ignited the love affair, but inevitably, in the several books on Jesenská, the love affair supersedes the acts of translation. Although she is always referred to, rightly, as the first-ever translator of Kafka's work, the actual translations, and discourse around them – both Kafka's and Jesenská's – are barely acknowledged. And yet, both of their writings reveal a sense of translation as being a means of grasping the self and others, however momentarily.

Her cruel and untimely death at the age of 46, and the absence of Jesenská's letters, seems to herald the vanishing of the "mouth that had once talked," to Kafka and others, but her translations of his work – alongside the journalism that made her famous – still exist. The lack of critical interest in them perhaps speaks to an undervaluation of translation as genuine literary work, as well as perhaps to a sense that a silent "Milena" suits critical perceptions of Kafka and his apparently troubled relationships with women. Kafka, critics argue, "treats Milena as an inner aspect of himself" and, in doing so, "Kafka refused Milena a voice" (Boa 1996: 87–8). His letters to Jesenská should "be regarded more as a highly condensed association between Kafka and his inner objects than as an act of genuine communication," writes Harmut Böhme, adding that the "real, rarely seen, distant Milena is the projection screen for K's narcissistic neurosis" (Böhme 1977: 84, 88). She represents the "narcissistic longing for an archaic mother": "Mother Milena," he writes, is "nothing more, silence, deep forest" (88). But Kafka was receiving the letters we do not see from an actual woman he met; a "textual intercourse" (Boa 1996: 62) heightened by her re-imagining of his writing in one of the other languages of his homeland. The ludic passion of his letters enunciates a wry skepticism about idealization, while at the same time considering the regenerative possibilities of love through language, and through her translations of his work.

Jesenská's translations are important for a variety of reasons. Her translations are products of a new generation of educated and emancipated women entering the Czech literary world; "translation work" was a duty "for the Czechoslovak nation" (Florian 1993: 23). Translating contemporary world literature was regarded as a means of introducing a cosmopolitan view to the writing of the new Czechoslovak Republic (founded in 1918), and women were at the forefront of the respected profession. There was a leftist bent to much of the avant-garde scene, with a real interest in socialism and communism – the revolution in artistic form was connected to social change. Jesenská's first translation of his work, "The Stoker"/"Topič," in all its experimental glory, was published in a socialist periodical. Translations in Czechoslovakia during this period often emphasized the modernist aesthetics of the translated texts rather than trying to neutralize or domesticate experimentation. Her translations of Kafka's work are, as he said of them, "faithful" because they are faithful to the form, tone, and seemingly eccentric sentence and paragraph length (i.e. to what Milan Kundera calls the "author's personal style" (Kundera 1996: 110)). Czech writing engaged with this translated experimentation, and there is some correlation between Kafka's work and Jesenská's journalism, in tone, style, and content. Their common interest in language and miscommunication, so evident in Kafka's *Letters*, may also be seen in her work and her translation of Kafka's work. Importantly, Jesenská's translations show that Kafka understood Czech and was, in however small a way, part of the Czech language literary scene while he was still alive. In her obituary of Kafka in the Czech newspaper *Národní listy* on June 6, 1924, Jesenská wrote that though "Few people knew him … he has written the most significant books of German literature" (Kafka 1990: 271). But the few people who did know of him were the readers of the avant-garde journals in which her translations were printed – likely other Czech-language writers and those interested in the artistic scene. Thanks to Jesenská, there were connections between Kafka and the other major language and cultural life of his homeland.

Jesenská initiated the correspondence with Kafka in April 1920 from Vienna. She had begun translating as a means of survival; "material poverty and want of all support gave rise to her first literary experiment," her daughter wrote.

> She herself had a low opinion of her efforts – they did not live up to her own expectations [but] at last a letter arrived from Prague [...] they would [...] print her translations. Milena was prouder than she had ever been in her life. Her first fee as a writer and her name in print filled her with a sense of achievement she had never known before
>
> (Černá 1988: 66–7).

As a journalist, Jesenská wrote movingly and with humour about her hardscrabble existence in postwar Vienna; in a 1921 article, "My Friend" (referring to her concierge Mrs. Kohler), she wrote how

> cut off from our homelands [...] I from Bohemia and she from Hungary, we sat for months without a heller, our stomachs rumbling, on the box of ashes in her hole in the cellar by the flickering light of the kerosene lamp and racked our brains for a way to get money. [...] Hunger is a terrible thing, and a foreign city can be cruel
>
> (Jesenská 2003: 88).

She tells her readers about her suicide attempt and how Kohler brings her back to life by stuffing "a large, black dumpling into my mouth ... because I had dreamed of them aloud ... [she has] ... a sentimental notion of what Czech dumplings were" (Jesenská 2003: 88). "I think I will never poison myself again," she adds. "Not because I am afraid of death, but [...] because I am afraid of more of Mrs. Kohler's dumplings" (88).

Born into a wealthy Prague family in 1896, Jesenská had eloped to Vienna with the German-speaking Jewish writer, Ernst Pollak, but it was an increasingly unhappy marriage due to his neglect and philandering. Times were so hard, the myth goes, that Jesenská was forced to work as a porter in a Vienna train station. Her friend Staša Jílovská suggested she translate and write for a Prague literary journal, *Tribuna*, to help mitigate the poverty (Černá 1988: 66). Jílovská and Jesenská had been friends since attending the Minerva gymnasium in Prague, the first girl's grammar school to be founded in the Austro-Hungarian empire, where students could sit the *abitur*, and Jesenská and Jílovská were among the first women in Bohemia to go to university. The fervor for women's education was partly nationalist: "for a Czech renaissance, the emancipation of women was part of the fight for the emancipation of the nation" (Wagnerová 1996: 34).[1] Austro-Hungarian remonstrations against this advanced education for women was "regarded as another example of discrimination against the Czech nation" (35).

Jílovská was herself a translator (she translated, among other books, *Orlando* in 1929 and, in 1930, *A Portrait of the Artist as a Young Man*); she had been encouraged

---

[1] All quotes from the books on Jesenská by Alena Wagnerová (1996), Marie Jirásková (1996), Marta Marková-Kotyková (1993), and Jaroslava Vondráčková (1991) are in my translation, as are the quotes from Josef Florian's correspondence (1993), and František Kautman's "Kafka a Milena" (1968).

into the profession by the publisher Josef Florian, who saw translation as a service to the newly independent (since 1918) Czechoslovakia. Jílovská was more realistic about the translating profession. "I don't want to work for nothing," she wrote to Florian in 1919, "I certainly do not work from some calling and even less can I live from it … I would live very badly just translating" (Florian 1993: 14). However, translation provided some independent income and also an entrée into the literary world for women. Female translators such as Jesenská, Jílovská, and Jarmila Fastrová (one of the translators of *Ulysses*) were at the margins of the vibrant avant-garde circles, translating modernist work that was influential in creating and sustaining post-independence Czech literature.

During the period of her correspondence with Kafka (1920–3), Jesenská published the first Czech translations of: "The Stoker" ("Topič"); selections from the 1913 story collection *Contemplation*, including "Being Unhappy" ("Nešťastný"); "The Sudden Walk" ("Náhle procházka"); "The Excursion into the Mountains" ("Výlet do hor"); "The Plight of the Bachelor" ("Neštěstí mládence"); "The Businessman" ("Kupec"); "The Way Home" ("Cesta domů"); "The Men Running Past" ("Ti, kteří běží mimo"); as well as "A Report to an Academy" ("Zpráva pro akademii"); and "The Judgment" ("Soud").[2] She also translated *The Trial* and *Metamorphosis* and intended to publish these, alongside *Contemplation* and "The Stoker," in a book in S.K. Neumann's imprint Edice Červen, but the publication never transpired. She had asked Max Brod to write an introduction, and insisted on her translatorial ability, assuring him that "The translation *is* good" (Brod 1992: 236).

Brod was skeptical of her linguistic ability, asserting in his biography that her German was "imperfect," though acknowledging that she was an "excellent writer" (222) and "a truly great woman" (219). Kafka was much more complimentary about her ability to speak German and, in one of his first letters, insists that any imperfections in her German language only add to the impact of her writing:

> most of the time [your German] is amazing and on those occasions when it does falter, the German language becomes pliant just for you, of its own accord, and then it is particularly beautiful, something even a German doesn't hope for; a German wouldn't dare write so personally (Kafka 1990: 8).

> Sie beherrschen es meistens erstaunlich und wenn Sie es einmal nich beherrschen, beugt es sich vor Ihnen freiwillig, das ist dann besonders schön; das wagt nämlich ein Deutscher von seiner Sprache gar nicht zu erhoffen, so persönlich wagt er nich zu schreiben (Kafka 1952: 15).

However, he does so while begging her to write to him in Czech, "because, after all, you do belong to that language, because only there can Milena be found in her entirety (the translation confirms this)" (Kafka 1990: 8)/"weil Sie ihm doch angehhören, weil doch nur dort die ganze Milena ist (die Übersetzung bestätigt es)" (Kafka 1952: 15). Yet, even when she begins writing in Czech, the letters (now missing) are only ever a

---

[2] *Kmen*, April 22, 1920: 61–72; *Tribuna*, July 16, 1920: 1–2; *Kmen*, September 9, 1920: 308–10; *Tribuna*, September 26, 1920: 1–4; *Cesta*, December/January 1923: 369–72.

stand-in for the physical Milena, for Milena in her entirety, and though the translation confirms a sense of her entire identity, for Kafka, and is a physical artifact of hers sent to him, it is also not quite her: "When I pulled the translation out of the large envelope," Kafka writes in the same letter, "I was almost disappointed. I wanted to hear from you and not from the voice of the old grave" (Kafka 1990: 7)/"Als ich das Heft aus dem großen Kouvert zog, war ich fast enttäuscht. Ich wollte von Ihnen hören und nicht die allzu gut bekannte Stimme aus dem alten Grabe" (Kafka 1952: 14). Kafka is disappointed in hearing only his writing, "the voice I know only too well" (Kafka 1990: 7), in Milena's tongue, rather than her own words, but he realizes that it is his writing that has brought them together: "Why did it have to come between us? Then I realized that this same voice had also come between us, as a mediator" (Kafka 1990: 7)/"Warum mischte sie sich zwischen uns vermittelt hatte? Bis mir dann einfiel, daß sie auch zwischen uns vermittelt hatte" (Kafka 1952: 14).

Almost immediately in the correspondence, Kafka's language concerning the translations carries intimations of a love relationship, here the almost clichéd cry of thwarted love ("Why did it have to come between us?") turned on its head to an affirmation of the translation coming between them as a physical link. Kafka plays quite cheerfully and wryly with the proximate meanings of translation and love, notably with the question of fidelity, right at the beginning of their relationship. "I am moved by your faithfulness toward every little sentence," he writes, "a faithfulness I would not have thought possible to achieve in Czech, let alone with the beautiful natural authority you attain" (Kafka 1990: 7–8)/"… und tief rührend, mit welcher Treue Sie es getan haben, Sätzchen auf und ab, einer Treue, deren Möglichkeit und schöne natürlich Berechtigung, mit der Sie sie üben, ich in der tschechischen Sprache nicht vermutet habe" (Kafka 1952: 14–15), and, adding in another letter:

> I just don't know whether Czechs will hold its very faithfulness against you, which for me is the nicest part of the translation (not because of the story but for my own sake); my feel for Czech – I have one too – is fully satisfied, but it is extremely biased. In any case, if someone should attack you on this point, try to balance the offense with my gratitude (Kafka 1990: 13).

> Nur weiß es nicht, ob nicht Tschechen Ihnen die Treue, das was mir das Liebste an der Übersetzung ist (nicht einmal der Geschichte wegen sondern meinetwegen), worwerfen; mein tschechisches Sprachgefühl, ich habe auch eines, ist voll befriedigt, aber es ist äußerst voreingenommen. Jedenfalls, wenn es Ihnen jemand vorwerfen sollte, suchen Sie die Kränkung mit meiner Dankbarkeit auszugleichen (Kafka 1952: 22).

The question of theorizing fidelity in translation has been a gendered one; translations seen as the passive, feminized text which "like women, should either be beautiful or faithful" (Simon 1996: 10); and, on the face of it, given the quick intimacy of the letters, Kafka's approval of literary fidelity may seem to convey a stereotypical male positioning that resonates through to their growing personal relationship. Yet it is interesting that Kafka immediately recognizes the potential literary demerit of

Jesenská's fidelity to his text; that, rather than being praised for her fidelity (the traditional gauge of the quality of a translation), she might be "attacked". His concern may partly emanate from an anxiety about his own text; that he feels her translation will be attacked because of the content of the original story. Second, there is a sense that in bringing her Czech version so close to the German version, as a translator, she is enacting some form of betrayal of the Czech language. He closes his first comment on her fidelity with a query: "German and Czech so close to each other?" (Kafka 1990: 8)/"So nahe deutsch und tschechisch?" (Kafka 1952: 15), suggesting both the impossibility of this proximity and also the possibilities for it. In real terms Jesenská had already crossed the cultural lines by running off with a German-speaking Jew, and here she was, through her translation work, once again on the cusp of a possible cultural betrayal, both in literary and physical terms.

Kafka also, very flirtatiously, plays with a sexual subversion of the notion of fidelity. While the concept of a faithful copy may represent a feminized and passive text, Kafka knows Jesenská will baulk at fidelity so described, and again turns the notion on its head; he turns her potential reaction into a fantasy suggestive of sexual dominance: "go ahead and scold me on account of this 'faithful'," he writes:

> I know you can do everything but maybe you scold best of all, I'd like to be your pupil just so you would constantly scold me; I'm sitting at my desk, scarcely daring to look up, you are bent over me and your index finger is glittering in the air, finding fault, isn't this the way it is?) (Kafka 1990: 20).

> (zanken Sie mich nur wegen des "treu" aus, Sie können alles, aber zanken können Sie vielleicht am besten, ich wollte Ihr Schüler sein und immerfort Fehler machen, um nur immerfort von Ihnen ausgezankt werden zu dürfen; man sitzt auf der Schulbank, wagt kaum aufzuschauen, Sie sind über einen gebeugt und immerfort flimmert oben Ihr Zeigefinger, mit dem Sie Aussetzungen machen, ist es so?) (Kafka 1952: 47).

The sexual teasing may also assert his own dominance (in that he can project his own fantasy on her) but it is ambiguous, and this kind of ambivalence toward fidelity may be seen in another passage when he again asserts that "your translation is faithful" (Kafka 1990: 20)/"sie 'treu' ist" (Kafka 1952: 47), and writes of himself leading her through his own text: "I have the feeling that I'm taking you by the hand through the story's subterranean passages" (Kafka 1990: 20)/"ich das Gefühl habe, als führte ich Sie an der Hand hinter mir durch die unterirdischen [...] Gänge der Geschichte" (Kafka 1952: 47–8). The sense of dominance, of Kafka controlling her passage through his text, "by the hand," is, however, then subverted first by his ambivalence and humor toward his own work and then by a suggestion that Jesenská will eventually exert some control over it:

> I have the feeling that I'm taking you by the hand through the story's subterranean passages, gloomy, low, ugly, almost endless (that's why the sentences are almost endless, didn't you realize that?), almost endless (only two months, you say?). (Kafka 1990: 20)

ich das Gefühl habe, als führte ich Sie an der Hand hinter mir durch die unterirdischen, finstern, niedrigen, häßlichen Gänge der Geschichte, fast endlos (deshalb sind die Sätze endlos, haben Sie das nicht erkannt?) fast endlos (zwei Monate nur, sagen Sie?) (Kafka 1952: 47–8).

Here, Kafka gets to the heart of his stylistic aesthetic; namely his use of long, looping sentences and paragraphs to convey tone and meaning in his work, but he does so with humor, adding the parantheses to lengthen his thought as a kind of pastiche both of his work and his falling in love (the wry, heartsick "only two months, you say," being the length of their relationship to date). He then adds that he guides her through the text "hopefully in order to have the good sense to disappear into the daylight at the exit" (Kafka 1990: 20–1)/"um dann beim Ausgang im hellen Tag hoffentlich den Verstand zu haben, zu verschwinden" (Kafka 1952: 48); it is as if her translation is bringing his work out of the cave (in which case her translation might be an illumination of his work), or up from the underworld, with Kafka as a Tiresias figure and Jesenská as Odysseus (in which case her translation might be a homecoming of sorts; Kafka's German text made Czech).

While Kafka professes himself thankful for the fact that Jesenská has taken on his work, he also feels guilty because he sees translation as a task. This is partly out of real concern; he knows from Jesenská's letters that she is in need of funds and that translation is a job that can provide some money for her. He worries that Jesenská is tiring herself out on this "troublesome task" (Kafka 1990: 7); he writes, "You are toiling over the translation in the middle of the dreary Vienna world. Somehow I am both moved and ashamed" (Kafka 1990: 4–5)/"Sie mühn sich mit der Übersetzung inmitten der trüben Wiener Welt. Es ist irgendwie rührend und beschämend für mich" (Kafka 1952: 10). Again, though, he approaches this with some humor: "If you waste as much as one minute of your sleep on the translation," he writes, "it will be as if you were cursing me" (Kafka 1990: 7), adding:

> For if it ever comes to a trial there will be no further investigations; they will simply establish the fact: he robbed her of her sleep. With that I shall be condemned and justly so. Thus I am fighting for myself when I ask you to stop (Kafka 1990: 7).
>
> Wenn Sie auch nur eine Minute Ihres Schlafes für Übersetzungsarbeit verwenden, so ist es so, wie wenn Sie mich verfluchen würden. Denn wenn es einmal zu einem Gericht kommt, wird man sich nicht in weitere Untersuchungen einlassen, sondern einfach festellen: er hat sie um den Schlaf gebracht. Damit bin ich gerichtet und mit Recht. Ich kämpfe also für mich, wenn ich Sie bitte, das nicht mehr zu tun (Kafka 1952: 14).

Kafka, in fact, had written with great humor about translation as a task, and a skilled one at that, in his novel *The Trial*. Josef K, increasingly suspicious he is being sent out of the office so that his clients will be stolen from him, is asked to show an Italian client around Prague, because he has some knowledge of the language. He stays up half the night reading his Italian grammar and stuffs a dictionary in his pocket for the meeting. But when it comes to it he finds that "he understood only bits and pieces of what the Italian was saying" and only when the man spoke "slowly" but those moments of comprehension "were rare exceptions" (Kafka 1998b: 202); he cannot watch the Italian's lips for clues because they were camouflaged by a moustache, so bushy and perfumed that "one was almost tempted to draw near and sniff it" (202). The sense of physical proximity in the act of translation is also brought into his letters to Jesenská, and here the promise of escape from labor is sexualized. Referring to her stint as a railway porter in Vienna, Kafka writes, "I would like to kiss your hand so long, that you would never be able to use it again for translating or for carrying luggage from the station" (Kafka 1990: 117)/"ich Dir so lange die Hand küssen wollte, daß Du in diesem Leben nicht mehr dazu kämest zu übersetzen oder Gepäck von der Bahn zu tragen" (Kafka 1952: 125). In another letter, he again imagines himself as physically and sexually present with her in connection with her work: "I see you bent over your work," he writes:

> your neck is bare, I stand you behind you, you aren't aware of it – please don't be frightened if you feel my lips on the back of your neck (Kafka 1990: 123).
>
> ich sehe Dich über die Arbeit gebeugt, der Hals ist frei, ich stehe hinter Dir, Du weißt es nicht – bitte erschrick nicht, wenn Du meine Lippen am Nacken fühlst (Kafka 1952: 173–4).

The faintly vampiric imagery of Kafka leaning over toward her neck, unseen, again subverts the notion of the translator somehow feeding off the original work; here, the author needs the translator, both sexually, but also suggestively in literary terms – the translation is the new blood of the work. Kafka uses this imagery himself; finally reading her translation of "Unhappiness," he writes:

> I'm not even concerned about what's inside, but I hear the voice, my voice! […]
> I don't know how it happens, after all I only read it with my eyes, so how did my blood find out so quickly, so quickly that my veins are already hot from circulating its words? (Kafka 1990: 129).

Also suggestive is Kafka's recurrent use of the mouth and the hand as visceral images of mediation – the mouth linked as a sexual and a linguistic means of communication, and the hand as a connection; both further linked by written texts: "Please send the translation," he writes in another letter, referring to her translation of "Unhappiness," "I can't hold enough of you in my hands" (Kafka 1990: 108)/"Die Übersetzung schicke mir bitte, ich kann doch nicht genug von Dir in Händen halten" (Kafka 1952: 127).

Kafka and Jesenská met only twice as lovers; once in Vienna and once at Gmünd, on the border between Austria and Czechoslovakia. They had met briefly in Prague, in a café, probably in the Café Arco, among the German-speaking literary circle the *Prager Kreis*, or the "Arconauts," a meeting Kafka refers to in a postscript to his second letter to Jesenská. "It occurs to me," he writes:

> that I can't really remember your face in any precise detail. Only the way you walked away through the tables in the café, your figure, your dress, that I still see (Kafka 1990: 4).

> Es fällt mir ein, daß ich mich an Ihr Gesicht eigentlich in keener bestimmten Einzelheit erinnern kann. Nur wie Sie dann zwischen den Kaffeehaustischen weggingen, Ihre Gestalt, Ihr Kleid, das sehe ich noch (Kafka 1952: 9–10).

The sudden intimacy of this comment seems at first glance to indicate the making of a fantasy with the deliberate elision of Jesenská's face and the focus on her body, "Ihre Gestalt, Ihr Kleid." But the ghostliness of the Magritte-like image of the human cored from the dress and figure also suggests a sly commentary on this objectification, Kafka making fun of his own propensity to mythologize this, until now, unknown female; "that I see still" he ends, the lingering after-effect of that fantasy undercut by the reality of the woman writing to him, a body constructed at least in text. Her letters and her translations, her writing in Czech, bring him a physical sense of her; the language itself a kind of portal to intimacy and to identity. "I have never lived among German people," Kafka writes.

> German is my mother tongue and therefore natural to me, but Czech feels to me far more intimate, which is why your letter dispels many an uncertainty, I see you clearer, the movements of your body, your hands, so quick, so determined, it's almost a meeting (Kafka 1990: 14).

> ich habe niemals unter deutschem Volk gelebt, Deutsch ist meine Muttersprache und deshalb mir natürlich, aber das Tschechische ist mir viel herzlicher, deshalb zerreißt Ihr Brief manche Unsicherheiten, ich sehe Sie deutlicher, die Bewegungen des Körpers, der Hände, so schnell, so entschlossen, es ist fast eine Begegnung (Kafka 1952: 22).

Kafka's reference to his own unstable identity – as a German-speaking Jew in a newly Czech-speaking capital – and to Jesenská's – a Czech speaker writing from a old German-speaking capital, married to a Jew – allows a common ground in writing, where there is "almost a meeting." The two of them, in other words, are already living translated lives; living in one language, *writing in one language*, and surviving in another. Jesenská, for Kafka, is only fully present in Czech, but even then her identity is elusive: "almost a meeting," he writes, "although when I try to raise my eyes to your face, then in the flow of the letter – what a story! – fire breaks out and I see nothing but fire!" (Kafka 1990: 14)/"es ist fast eine Begegnung, allerdings wenn ich dann die Augen bis zu Ihrem Gesicht heben will, bricht dann im Verlauf des Breifes – was für eine Geschichte! – Feuer aus und ich sehe nichts als Feuer" (Kafka 1952: 22–3).

Jesenská's facial invisibility could certainly be read as a metaphor for the translator's invisibility and the silencing of the translator by a literary culture intent upon the supremacy of the author's vision and importance, and doubly so as a woman on the edges of the Vienna literary circles of the 1920s, where she was viewed as "lost," "foreign," "on the periphery" (Wagnerová 1996: 75), but Kafka, rather than trying to erase or dominate her identity, her face, seems unsure both of what it looks like and of his own attempts to imagine it himself. As with his "almost endless" sentences, Kafka defers meeting Jesenská and knows exactly why – a hyphenated feeling of what he calls, in Czech (though writing primarily to Jesenská in German), "strachtouha"/"fear-longing." In an article about Kafka's letters, Julian Preece writes:

Kafka often appeared to prefer the disembodied act of communication by letter to an encounter in the flesh, however. Seeing Milena Jesenská for a second time was a drab but anticipated disappointment, which he had struggled to put off. It is the turning point (for the worse) of their epistolary relationship which had held out the prospect of happiness (Preece 2002: 113).

However, while their second physical meeting at the border seemed a disappointment, from the letters, Kafka seems more critical of himself than of Jesenská. It is not Jesenská in all her reality that he fears, but, in fact, the reality of Kafka. Speaking in the third person about himself he writes: "You can be sure your actual presence will no longer blind her. Is this why you don't want to go, tender soul, because that is what you actually fear?" (Kafka 1990: 28). Kafka's inability to capture a precise image of Jesenská while longing for her is deliberate; he is aware of the mechanisms of imposing identity and it is instructive that he refuses to do so.

Throughout the correspondence he wants to hear her voice: begging her to write in Czech; disappointed at first that the translations seem only to be versions of his voice, but then seeing her in them; and asking her to send her own work, namely her journalism. In other words, language is where her identity resides, where he can find her: "I'm just walking around here between the lines," he writes, "underneath the light of your eyes, in the breath of your mouth like in some beautiful happy day, which stays beautiful and happy" (Kafka 1990: 26)/"ich gehe nur hier zwischen den Zeilen herum, unter dem Licht Ihrer Augen, im Atem Ihres Mundes wie in einem schönen glücklichen Tag, der schön und glücklich bleibt" (Kafka 1952: 39).

He repeats some of her Czech words back to her, and in an interesting passage connects her question about his identity and her incomprehension of him with the physicality of her Czech words:

> Milena is still going on about anxiety, striking my chest or asking: *jste žid*? [are you a Jew?] which in Czech has the same movement and sound. Don't you see how the fist is pulled back at the word "jste," so as to gain muscle power? And then in the word "žid" the happy blow, flying unerringly forward? The Czech language often produces such side effects on the German ear. For example you once asked how it happened that I made my stay here dependent on one letter, and then you immediately answered your own question: *nechápu* [I don't understand]. A strange word in Czech and even in your mouth it is so severe, so callous, cold-eyed, stingy, and most of all like a nutcracker, pronouncing it requires three consecutive cracks of the jaw or, more exactly, the first syllable makes an attempt at holding the nut, in vain, the second syllable then tears the mouth wide open, the nut now fits inside, where it is finally cracked by the third syllable, can you hear the teeth? (Kafka 1990: 21).

> Und dann redet noch Milena von Ängstlichkeit, gibt mir einen Stoß vor die Brust oder fragt, was im Tschechischen an Bewegung und Klang ganz dasselbe ist: *Jste žid*? Sehen Sie nicht, wie im "*Jste*" die Faust zurückgezogen wird, um Muskelkraft anzusammeln? Und dann im "*žid*" den freudigen, unfehlbaren,

vorwärts fliegenden Stoß? Solche Nebenwirkungen hat für das deutsche Ohr die tschechische Sprache öfters. Sie fragten zum Beispiel einmal, wie es komme, daß ich meinen hiesigen Aufenthalt von einem Brief abhängig mache und antworteten gleich selbst: *nechapu*. Ein fremdartiges Wort im Tschechischen, und gar in Ihrer Sprache, es ist so streng, teilnahmslos, kaltäugig, sparsam und vor allem nußknackerhaft, dreimal krachen im Wort die Kiefer aufeinander oder richtiger: die erste Silbe macht einen Versuch, die Nuß zu fassen, es geht nicht, dann reißt die zweite Silbe den Mund ganz groß auf, nun paßt schon die Nuß hinein und die dritte Selbe endlich knackt, hören Sie die Zähne? (Kafka 1952: 48–9).

Again, the image of the mouth appears, along with Kafka's fears that "this final, absolute closing of the lips at the end prohibits the other person from expressing anything to the contrary, which is actually quite good at times, for instance when the other person is babbling as much as I am now" (Kafka 1990: 21–2)/"Besonders dieses endgiltige Schließen der Lippen am Schluß verbietet dem andern jede andere weitere gegenteilige Erklärung, was ja allerdings manchmal recht gut ist, zum Beispiel, wenn der andere so schwätzt wie jetzt ich" (Kafka 1952: 49). Kafka does not see Jesenská inhabiting the traditional female or translatorial role; he does not want his voice or the voice of his work canceling out hers. At one point, he describes a nightmare he's had, "I was very unhappy [in the dream]," he writes to Jesenská, "because I was treating you like some mute woman ignoring the voice that was speaking out of you directly to me" (Kafka 1990: 50)/"Ich war sehr unglücklich … ich Dich behandelte wie eine beliebige stumme Frau und die Stimme überhörte, die aus Dir sprach und gerade zu mir sprach" (Kafka 1952: 66).

Of course, we no longer have Jesenská's reply; she asked Max Brod to burn her letters when Kafka died (Brod 1992: 239), and it seems, in this case, that he or Kafka's family followed the request. Brod, however, quotes in full some of her letters to him, in his biography of Kafka. Kafka ended the relationship, asking her not to write to him any more, because, according to Brod, it had become clear that she would not leave her husband for him (231). In a letter to Brod following the breakup, she writes:

> I am as lonely as the mute are lonely, and if I speak to you of myself as I do, it is because I am vomiting out the words; they rush forth entirely against my will, because I can no longer keep silent. Forgive me.
>
> I shall not write to Frank, not a line, and I do not know what is going to come of it all [...] And if you write to me how he is from time to time – I cannot cure myself of the habit of going to the post office daily – I should be very glad (235).

Just underneath, she adds:

> One more request, a ridiculous one. My translation of the books *The Trial*, *Metamorphosis*, *The Stoker*, *Contemplation* will be published by Neumann. [...] Now that I am finished with it – in these last months it devoured my heart and brain; it was ghastly, to be so abandoned and to work on his books – but Neumann wants me to write "a few words to introduce him to the Czech reading public." Jesus Christ, am I to write about him for people? [...] The translation *is* good [...]

I would like to appear before the eyes of the world with this book as perfect as it is possible to make it – you know, I have the feeling that I must defend something, justify something. So please.

And say nothing to F. We will surprise him – all right? Perhaps – perhaps it will give him a little pleasure (235–6).

These translations were never published.

From the outset Kafka was in no doubt that Jesenská was a good translator of his work; that, when it came to his work she had a "magic hand" (Kafka 1990: 174)/"Zauberhaften Hand" (Kafka 1952: 214), because she had understood it on a profound level; "the truth of your translation is obvious," he writes about her translation of "The Stoker"; "hardly a single misunderstanding; which wouldn't mean so much in itself, but I find there is a constant powerful and decisive understanding as well" (Kafka 1990: 13)/"die wie selbsrverständliche Wahrheit der Übersetzung ist mir, wenn ich das Selbstverständliche von mir abschüttle ... kaum ein Mißverständnis, das ware ja noch gar nicht so viel, aber immer kräftiges und entsclossenes Verstehn" (Kafka 1952: 22). She was one of the first Czech readers, indeed readers worldwide, to understand the importance of his work, and intended her translations to widen the audience for it via her translations. Jesenská wrote an obituary of Kafka in the newspaper *Národní listy* on June 6, 1924, writing that though "Few people knew him here ... he has written the most significant books of German literature" (Kafka 1990: 271).

In explaining why they were so significant, she added, "All his books paint the horror of secret misunderstandings, of innocent guilt between people" (Kafka 1990: 271–2). On one level, this could describe their epistolary relationship; Preece argues that Kafka had a "pained sense that real communication by letter was impossible – because the gap between what he meant and what he could say (in language, on paper) was too wide ... The letter writer ... knows his missive can fall into the wrong hands or get lost in the post ..." (Preece 2002: 112–13). But perhaps this explains exactly why he chose this method of conducting a relationship; "We are indeed beginning to misunderstand one other, Milena" Kafka writes (Kafka 1990: 58), as if this is the real start of their relationship. For Kafka, and perhaps Jesenská, it is how the world works.

"The Stoker"

"Když 16letý Karel Rosman, který byl svými chudými rodiči poslán do Ameriky, poněvadž ho svedla služka a měla s nim dítě" (Kafka 1920: 61). So began Jesenská's first translation, published in *Kmen* in April 1920, of Franz Kafka's story "The Stoker." It is likely that Jesenská met *Kmen*'s publisher S. K. Neumann during a trip back to Prague in 1919 (and this is possibly when she briefly met Kafka); *Kmen* was a socialist paper, through which Neumann explicitly wanted to "press the ideas of proletarian culture" (Cabada 2010: 70); one that would "represent not only the revival of the socialist struggle, but also a new literary and artistic life, and will concern itself primarily with the question of proletkult [proletarian culture]" (Neumann 1921: 587, my translation).

"The Stoker" seemed to fit into this remit, with the immigrant Karl identifying with the proletarian stoker, defending his rights, only to be co-opted by the forces of capitalism in the guise of his uncle. Jesenská "cannily sold" the story to Neumann "on the strength of its credentials as a story about the oppression of a worker" (Hockaday 1997: 47). Neumann, "an energetic socialist of broad tastes" (47), was clearly impressed by the story; in a highly unusual move for the paper, he devoted the entire issue to the story, adding an editor's note at the end:

> The story, with which we filled this whole issue, belongs to the best of modern German stories. We decided it would be better if we did not serialize it, but present it whole to our readers as an unusual but pleasant exception (Neumann 1920: 72, my translation).

Neumann's note belies the given assumption that Kafka was ignored and unknown in his own lifetime by Czech readers; not only was he translated and published, but his work was also presented as among "the best of modern German stories" – "Topič"/"The Stoker" came with a guarantee from one of the leading lights of the new Czech literary scene and as part of the debate on avant-garde writing and socialist possibilities.

Kafka was also known in Vienna, and this is possibly how Jesenská was inspired to translate his work. Her husband, Pollak, was "one of the biggest admirers of Kafka's work and often spoke of him in the Herrenhof and at home" (Wagnerová 1996: 85). Jesenská's friend, Jaroslava Vondráčková, also suggests that the café literary circles influenced Jesenská's choice: "'That Kafka is doing really good things; Milena, you could translate them,' they said at the Central. So she translated" (Vondráčková 1991: 32). But Jesenská also had an "independent" taste for good literature and "recognized the quality and unusualness of Kafka's prose" (Wagnerová 1996: 85). Jesenská was also beginning to be influenced by politics and would go on to translate explicitly socialist writers, such as Rosa Luxemburg.

Apart from a financial motive, the opening of the story may also give a clue as to why Jesenská decided to translate Kafka. "The Stoker" begins with the portrait of a teenager forced to emigrate by his "unfortunate parents" because he was seduced by a maid and got her pregnant, a passive past that seems to gear up toward an active future in the new world, one lorded over by a Statue of Liberty with a sword in her hand. The strange, ordered, but also anarchic world Karl meets on the ship as it enters New York harbor is seen through his slightly suspect innocent eyes; he navigates a world he simply does not understand.

Jesenská was 23 years old when she translated the story in Vienna; her emigration to Austria was partly encouraged by her father to mitigate public scandal over her socially unacceptable liaison (and her aborted pregnancy) with Pollak. On a thematic level, it seems to parallel her story with its familial shame over an unacceptable relationship and the promise of a new life underwritten by a certain fear and strangeness. But Kafka's use of language too, the wryness and optimism of its tone (in Rossman's camaraderie with strangers, his legal defense of the stoker, the apparently lucky adoption by his uncle), however doomed, generates the ambivalences of meaning and comprehension that Jesenská was living with, in her daily life, and in the act of translation.

Kafka's one memory of her speaking at their first meeting in Prague, probably at the Café Arco in 1919, a "half-silent meeting," was her remark that she enjoyed the foreignness of Vienna; "but do you also enjoy foreignness for its own sake?" he asks in his first letter to her, adding that this might be "a bad sign by the way, a sign that such enjoyment should not exist" (Kafka 1990: 3). For him the rain in Meran is "bearable" because he is "in a foreign country here, admittedly only slightly foreign, but it does the heart good" (3). The notion that pain or trouble is easier abroad because of a sense of newness and possibility is connected with a sense of finally understanding the normalcy, abroad, of isolation and miscomprehension. For Kafka, Jesenská "belong[s]" to Czech, "only there can Milena be found in her entirety (the translation confirms this)" (8), but it is Czech re-approached through Jesenská's exile.

Kafka's delight in receiving the copy of *Kmen* with her translation is obvious, as is his ability to judge whether or not it is a good translation. He sends her notes after the fact, but writes that there "is nothing for page after page" to correct or question, not simply because of a linguistic ability, but because of her "constant powerful and decisive understanding" of the story (13). The three surviving notes (in *Letters to Milena*) all highlight the difficulties of translation as a skill, but also the interpretive choices that the translator has to make when translating a story.

From the second line of her translation, Kafka notes that "arm" in "armen Eltern," translated by Jesenská as "chudymi rodici/(by his) poor parents" (Kafka 1920: 61): "here also has the secondary meaning: pitiable, but without any special emphasis of feeling, a sympathy without understanding that Karl has with his parents as well, perhaps *ubozí*" (13). English translators have translated it as both "poor" (Kafka 2008a: 3; Kafka 1992: 48) and "unfortunate" (Kafka 2002a: 3), both of which choices are valid. Kafka's explication, and the suggestion of *ubozí* (pitiable, wretched), places emphasis on the "sympathy without understanding" that only really becomes clearer as we read through *Amerika* (rather than the story that would become its beginning). Kafka knows what he means, but "arm" contains these nuanced differences in meaning.

His second comment concerns the end of the first paragraph and the movement of wind around the Statue of Liberty: "und um ihre Gestalt wehten die freien Lüfte" (Kafka 1994: 9), which Jesenská translates as "a kolem její postavy vanul volný vzduch" (Kafka 1920: 61) – Mark Harman's 2008 English translation is similar: "and about her figure blew the free winds" (Kafka 2008a: 3). Kafka writes to Jesenská that "*freie Lüfte* is a little more grand [than *volný vzduch*] but there's probably no alternative" (Kafka 1990: 13). The more lyrical connotations, for Kafka, in German, seem difficult to translate, because the same phrase does not necessarily have the same connotations in Czech (or English; though Michael Hofmann translates it more lyrically and with grandeur as "unchained winds" (Kafka 2002a: 3)). What Jesenská's choice does do, also, is introduce alliteration – "*vanul volný vzduch*" – that does not exist in the German sentence, but does in the next clause: "'So hoch', sagte er sich und wurde, wie er so gar nicht an das Weggehn dachte" (9), thus introducing a lyrical tone in an alternative way.

In his final comment, he asks that she remove part of the sentence from her translation: "'z dobré nálady a poněvadž byl silný chlapec' from 'Jsem přece již hotov,' řekl Karel usmívaje se, a zdvihl z dobré nálady a poněvadž byl silný chlapec, kufr na ramena" (Kafka 1920: 61). This was not an addition by Jesenská, but a part of the sentence in the original; Kafka is clearly second-guessing himself, rereading his original through the translation and wanting to re-edit and rewrite (although it remains in the German editions of his novel). Kafka's notes suggest a sensitivity toward the task of the translator; there are elements he would have changed, but he realizes the difficulty in doing so, owing to issues of linguistic and cultural untranslatability. He does not suggest that these are mistakes or professional errors; they simply point to the complexity of the act.

His fear, as we have seen, is that she is too faithful to the German original. Yet his comment that he doesn't "know whether Czechs won't hold its very faithfulness against you" (Kafka 1990: 13) is not a reference to an impossible linguistic fidelity, but to what Milan Kundera calls (in reference to Kafka) fidelity to "the *author's personal style*" (Kundera 1996: 110). Kundera argues, through the lens of three French translations of a sentence from *The Castle*, that translators hew to the "*conventional version*" of good French (110), rather than allowing the transgressions of the original text to be translated (in Kafka's case the repetitions of keywords, the sentence length, and the paragraph length). But he argues, "every author of some value *transgresses* against "good style," and in that transgression lies the originality (and hence the raison d'être) of his art. The translator's primary effort should be to understand that transgression" (110).

Often translators do "understand that transgression"; the problem tends to lie with editors and publishers requiring more domesticated, and thus commercially viable, texts, as happened in Kundera's own case (Woods 2006). In Jesenská's case it is clear that she did "understand that transgression" and that this is the fidelity to which Kafka refers; she was fortunate also to be translating in a place and era in which these transgressions were actively sought out for their perceived enunciation of the potential for aesthetic, and with it social, change.

An example from "The Stoker," and Jesenská's translation, "Topič," is Karl's reminiscences about the maid, Johanna Brummer. Instead of the usual portrayal of a bourgeois hero impregnating the maid, Kafka describes a funny, subversive account of non-will and non-intent. He does so not only through a description of Johanna Brummer's gradual seduction of Karl, but also through the repetition of "Sometimes" which precedes each step of the seduction – the passage ends with an explosive "once," describing Brummer's actual seduction of Karl (in German, "manchmal" and "einmal"). The rhythm of the passage through this repetition suggests the buildup of intercourse itself, but cheekily, subverting the stereotypically male progress to orgasm, with a more recursive and arguably female rhythm:

> Actually, Karl had no feelings for the girl. In the crush of an ever-receding past, she was sitting in the **kitchen**, with one elbow propped on the **kitchen** dresser. She would look at him when he went into the **kitchen** for a glass of water for his father,

or to do an errand for his mother. **Sometimes** she would be sitting in her strange position by the dresser, writing a letter, and drawing inspiration from Karl's face. **Sometimes** she would be covering her eyes with her ***hand***, then it was impossible to speak to her. **Sometimes** she would be kneeling in her ***little room*** off the ***kitchen***, praying to a wooden cross, and Karl would shyly watch her through the open ***door*** as he passed. **Sometimes** she would be rushing about the ***kitchen***, and spin around, laughing like a witch whenever Karl got in her way. **Sometimes** she would shut the ***kitchen door*** when Karl came in, and hold the ***door***knob in her ***hand*** until he asked her to let him out. **Sometimes** she would bring him things he hadn't asked for, and silently press them into his ***hands***. **Once**, though, she said "Karl!" and led him – still astonished at the unexpected address – sighing and grimacing into her ***little room***, and bolted it (Kafka 2002a: 21).

Karel neměl však žádných pocitů k onomu děvčeti. V návalu stále vice se vzdalující minulosti seděla ve své ***kuchyni*** u ***kuchyňské*** skříně, kde se opírala lokty. Dívala e na něj, přišel-li tu a tam do ***kuchyně***, aby přinesl sklenici vody pro otce nebo vyřídil matčin rozkaz. **Někdy** psala dopis v propadlé poloze stranou od skříně, a čerpala vnuknutí z Karlova obličeje. **Někdy** měla oči ***rukou*** zakryty, a tu se k ní neprodralo žádné oslovení. **Někdy** klečela ve svém úzkém ***pokojíku*** vedle ***kuchyně*** a modlila se k dřevěnému kříži. Tehdy ji Karel pozoroval jen v chůzi mezerou pootevřených ***dveří***. **Někdy** honila se po ***kuchyni*** a, přišel-li jí Karel do cesty, uskočila zpět, smějíc se jako čarodějnice. **Někdy**, když Karel vešel, zavřela ***kuchyňské dveře*** a podržela kliku tak dlouho v ***ruce***, až žádal, aby mohl odejíti. **Někdy** přinášela věci, kterých vůbec nechtěl a vtlačila my je mlčky do ***rukou***. **Jednou** však řekla: „Karle" a s posuňky, grimasami a vzdychajíc vedla jej, udiveného neočekávaným oslovením, do svého ***pokojíku***, který zavřela (Kafka 1920: 69).

This passage not only provides a humorous mimesis of the sexual act through the repetition of "sometimes" ending in "once" (and the orgasmic "Karl!") and its syntactical pace, but the passage is also a latticework of repetitions and resonance: kitchen, hand, little room, door. Jesenská is faithful to the style of the passage, its aesthetic intent, understanding that the repetitions are central to the meaning of the piece. The passage may not necessarily represent what was seen as a "good style" of the era, which is why Kafka warns her that she will be blamed for its quiet challenge to that good style. Jesenská was fortunate in working in this place and era, since the profusion of avant-garde publications in the inter-war era were serious about introducing experimental and revolutionary narrative styles into the domestic sphere. There was a real excitement about the possibility that translations of experimental work (such as Karel Čapek's influential translation of Apollinaire's "Zone") would influence the development of Czech-language literature.

Almost nothing has been written about Jesenská's translations, even among Czech critics. Two of her Czech biographers make only one – and the same – comment about the quality of the Kafka translations: that she mistranslated "Das Urteil"/"The Judgment" as "Soud"/"Court" rather than "Rozsudek"/"The Judgment"

(Marková-Kotyková 1993: 52; Wagnerová 1996: 101). Marta Marková-Kotyková claims that Jesenská made many mistakes in the translations, including her mistranslation of this title, and that Kafka's silence on the translations indicates that he found them wanting (52–3). However, it seems that Marková-Kotyková relies on an earlier edition of *Letters to Milena*, in which Kafka's favorable comments on the translations were not published. In addition, even if Jesenská's German was weak, "das Urteil" is not an unusual or demotic noun; it is highly unlikely that she would not have known or checked it. Wagnerová writes that "Perhaps her linguistic sense rather than a lack of knowledge of the language led her to translate the title" as "Soud" (Wagnerová 1996: 101). Neither suggests that perhaps it was a translatorial decision, a specific interpretation of the *mise-en-scène* of the story, reading both Georg's room and his father's room as courts, in which they judge others. She clearly recognizes the term when it is used in a variant verbal form; when Georg's father judges him: "Ich verurteile dich jetzt zum Tode des Ertrinkens!" (Kafka 1946: 67)/"I sentence you to death by drowning!" (Hofmann 2008: 49), Jesenská translates this as "odsuzují tě k smrti utopením!" (Kafka 1923: 372).

Jesenská had a dramatically difficult relationship with her father, whose judgment placed her in a psychiatric hospital and then in exile in Vienna (because of her choice of a Jewish lover). She told Margerete Buber-Neumann that she saw herself as Gregor Samsa, rejected and injured by his family; it is possible to read these bedrooms as courts – the father's dark, hot bedroom as the place of expulsion and Georg's room, where he judges his friend in Petersburg as incapable of returning home (given that Jesenská was still in exile in Vienna). "What could you say to a man like that," Georg thinks as he tries to write to him, "who had obviously lost his way, whom you might sympathize with, but could do nothing to help?" In the paragraph that follows, the words "home," "friend," "return," and "abroad" are repeated, articulating not only Georg's apparent concern for his friend, who may no longer fit in, but also emphasizing his own belief in the stability of his home. Kafka has already lured us into a relatively normal portrait of this house that, once Georg travels down the passage to his father's bedroom, is blown apart, whether through Georg's unreliability or his father's senility.

Jesenská heightens the tension and emotion in this paragraph in two ways: she adds punctuation at the beginning of the paragraph, shortening the sentences and adding question marks and the repetition of "aby"/"in order for" or "so that." These initial short sentences are then a strong springboard into a long, anxious sentence. Second, she heightens the euphony in the language, especially the emphasis on the plosive "p" and "př," i.e. from, among other words, the repeated "pomoc"/"help" and "přátele"/"friends":

> Co je možno **p**sáti takovému člověku, který se zřejmě ukvapil a kterého lze litovati, ale jemuž nelze **pomoci**? Snad mu poradili, **aby** se **vrátil domů**? **Aby** svoji existenci **p**řesadil sem? **Aby** navázal opět staré **p**řátelské vztahy, pro co by **p**řece nebylo **p**řekážky – a **aby** se **s**polehl na **pomoc přátel**? To **by** však neznamenalo nic jiného, než mu současně okázati, čím šetrněji, tím bolestněji – že jeho dosavadní

pokusy se ne**po**dařily a že **by** konečně měl od nich **u**pustiti, že je nutno, **aby** se **vrátil** a **aby** se nechal ode všech udiveně okukovati jako někdo, kdo se **vrátil p**ro vždy, že jen jeho **přátelé** něčemu rozumí a on že je staré děcko, které **by** mělo své **přátele**, úspěchy bohatší, **p**rostě **po**slechnout (Kafka 1923: 369).

In "Das Urteil" those first four questions are two sentences, and there is only one question mark at the end of the second sentence which makes the tone more resigned and less urgent (Hofmann's translation has a question mark on the first statement, but the length of the two sentences is similar; a rough translation of Jesenská's translation is given below Hofmann's):

Was wollte man einem solchen Manne schreiben, der sich offenbar verrannt hatte, den man bedauern, dem man aber nicht helfen konnte. Sollte man ihm vielleicht raten, wieder nach Hause zu kommen, seine Existenz hierherzuverlegen, alle die alten freundschaftlichen Beziehungen wiederaufzunehmen – wofür ja kein Hindernis bestand – und im übrigen auf die Hilfe der Freunde zu vertrauern? (Kafka 1946: 53–4)

What could you say to a man like that, who had obviously lost his way, whom you might sympathize with, but could do nothing to help? Should you advise him to come home, to take up his old life here, pick up the threads of his former friendships – there was no reason why he shouldn't – and look to the support of his friends in other ways too? (Kafka 2008b: 37–8).

What could you write to a man like that, who was obviously rash and whom you might be sorry for, but you could not help? Perhaps advise him to return home? To establish his life back here? To fasten the ties with his old friends again, for there probably were no obstacles – and to rely on the help of friends? [Jesenská 1996, my translation].

The next section lies in a fulcrum, syntactically, to this first section (moving from the opening "What" – "What could you say to a man like that" – to a kind of answer "That" – "That was tantamount to telling him" – Jesenská translates this fulcrum: "Co" and "To"). Jesenská's more urgent questions fold into a long sentence that replicates the length of Kafka's German and repeats the conjunction "že"/"daß"/"that," linking the clauses and conveying the sense of Georg trying to rationalize an answer. Jesenská, in effect, spools up the beginning of the paragraph in the four tight questions and then, in the second section, lets the syntax loose. It is more urgent and dramatic than Kafka's German and indicates a decision about the character Georg, by suggesting some nervousness, some instability before we get to the father's room, where the seemingly straightforward, stable life that Georg attempts to write down is thrown into question. It is possible to read Jesenská's own anxieties here about being the recipient of such letters from friends in Prague, from Kafka himself, and the fear of her own return to a perhaps changed homeland as a certainly changed self. It is an interesting aesthetic decision on her part, reflecting her own experiences, rather than an attempt to domesticate the text or reflecting a misunderstanding of the German:

Das bedeutete aber nicht anderes, als **daß** man ihm gleichzeitig, je schonender, desto kränkender, sagte, **daß** seine bisherigen Versuche mißlungen seien, **daß** er endlich von ihnen ablassen solle, **daß** der zurückkehren und sich als ein für immer Zurückgekehrter von allen mit großen Augen anstaunen lassen müsse, **daß** nur seine Freunde etwas verstünden und **daß** er ein altes Kind sei, das den erfolgreichen, zu Hause gebliebenen Freunden einfach zu folgen habe. (Kafka 1946: 54)

To by však neznamenalo nic jiného, než mu současně okázati, čím šetrněji, tím bolestněji – **že** jeho dosavadní pokusy se nepodařily a **že** by konečně měl od nich upustiti, **že** je nutno, aby se vrátil a aby se nechal ode všech udiveně okukovati jako někdo, kdo se vrátil pro vždy, **že** jen jeho přátelé něčemu rozumí a on **že** je staré děcko, které by mělo své přátele, úspěchy bohatší, prostě poslechnout (Kafka 1923: 369).

The repetition of "that" is harder to replicate in English without awkwardness, and neither the Muirs nor Hofmann translate all of the several iterations of "daß" but replace it with other conjunctions: "and"; "because"; "while." Both make interesting decisions about translating Georg's characterization of the friend in Petersburg as "Zurückgekehrter" and "ein altes Kind"/"the returnee" and "the old child" (translated quite straightforwardly by Jesenská as "někdo, kdo se vrátil" and "staré děcko"). The Muirs invoke the biblical notion of the "prodigal" and thus underscore the jealousy on Georg's part (his father will later claim to have been in touch with the friend behind Georg's back; the friend may also be an imaginary *alter ego* of his) and give a more normative translation with "a big child." Hofmann, in the latter case, places more emphasis on the aging but immature child in "overgrown schoolboy" (Stanley Corngold translates this as "overgrown baby" (Kafka 2007: 4)). Both of these formulations serve to emphasize Georg's attempted dismissal of his friend and his actions.

Hofmann also attempts to think about the euphony in the passage, since there is poetry in the sound of it, especially the consonance of the "f" in the German as the section closes (which helps to convey Georg's attitude): "daß nur seine **F**reunde etwas verstünden und daß er ein altes Kind sei, das den er**f**olgreichen, zu Hause gebliebenen **F**reunden ein**f**ach zu **f**olgen habe" (Kafka 1946: 54) (which itself speaks to the repetition of "Freund" and "Fremde" in the passage). Hofmann employs consonance through the section of the "f" as well as sibilance to convey this: "thus far … failure … thenceforth suffer himself to be stared"; "schoolboy … stick"; "flourishing," as well as a rather po-faced assonance right at the end of the sentence: "quite properly flourishing at home, now told him to do" (Kafka 2008b: 38). Jesenská also displays a talent for hearing the language and thinking about euphony – she employs consonance at the end of this sentence (not the German "f" but a Czech "p"): "své **p**řátele, ús**p**ěchy bohatší, **p**rostě **p**oslechnout" (Kafka 1923: 369):

But **that** was as good as telling him, and *[that]* the more kindly, the more offensively, **that** all his efforts hitherto had miscarried, **that** he should finally give up, *[that he should]* come back home, and be gaped at by everyone as a returned prodigal, **that** only his friends knew what was what and **that** he himself was just a big child who should do what his successful and home-keeping friends prescribed (Kafka 1971: 77–8).

That was tantamount to telling him (and *[that]* the more carefully one did it, the more wounding it was) **that** his endeavours thus far had been a failure, **that** he should call a halt and *[that he should]* come home – and thenceforth suffer himself to be stared at by everyone as a returnee – because *[that]* it was only his friends who had known what to do with their lives, while *[that]* he was an overgrown schoolboy, who would have done better to stick to what they, quite properly flourishing at home, now told him to do (Kafka 2008b: 38).

The idea of exile as a finality, and its contrast with home, homeland and friends, becomes heightened in the next section of the paragraph, where Kafka switches from notions of coming or being brought home – "nach Hause zu kommen"/"nach Hause zu bringen" – to notions of the homeland, "Heimat" and "Fremde"/abroad:

Vielleicht gelang es nicht einmal, ihn überhaupt nach **Hause** zu bringen – er sagte ja selbst, daß er die Verhältnisse in der **Heimat** nicht mehr verstünde –, und so bliebe er dann trotz allem in seiner **Fremde**, verbittert durch die Ratschläge und den *Freunden* noch ein Stück mehr ent**fremd**et […] hätte jetzt wirklich keine **Heimat** und keine *Freunde* mehr, war es da nicht viel besser für ihn, er blieb in der **Fremde**, so wie er war? (Kafka 1946: 54).

Snad by ani nepodařilo přivésti ho **domů** – říkal sám, že by poměrům své **otčiny** více nerozuměl – a tak by přese všecko zůstal ve své **cizině**, radami jen zhořklý a *přátelům* jen více od**cizen** ... a neměl pak doopravdy ani **domova** ani *přátel*, nebylo by pro něj mnohem lépe, aby zůstal v **cizině**, kde byl? (Kafka 1923: 369).

Jesenská translates "Hause" as "doma"/"home" and "Heimat" in two different ways: "otčina" and "domov" both resonant of "native country," but the first also of "fatherland," which is a very telling choice given the father–son relationship in the story and the breakup of the "father-land" in the Bendemann home ("otčina" is connected with a poetic voice and the German "Vaterland" in Czech). The centrality of the notion of "Heimat" in German culture, its full cultural connotation, is impossible to translate, but the break from that "Heimat" that the friend in Petersburg "no longer understands" and "who does not really have" any more (either "native country or friends") is connotative of a real existential break from any concept of "home." He is made foreign "estranged"/"entfremdet"/"odcizen" from both homeland and friends, so he has to stay in "*his* foreign place/abroad"; "*seiner* Fremde"/"*své* cizině." Would it not be better, the section concludes, if he "stayed abroad where he was?"

The difficulty in translating "Heimat" may be seen in the various English translations of the passage: the Muirs translated it as "native country" and "a country of his own"; Stanley Corngold in both cases as "home"; and Hofmann as "here" and "depatriated." These are all translatorial decisions: the Muirs wanting to convey the sense of country; Corngold clearly wanting to keep the repetition through the paragraph of "home"; Hofmann's "people here" feeds into the connection between the "Heimat"/"Fremde" opposition and "Freund" – "alienated from his friends"; and "depatriated and friendless." Each also makes a decision about how to translate "er sagte ja selbst, daß er die Verhältnisse in der **Heimat** nicht mehr verstünde" (translated very deftly by Jesenská as "říkal sám, že by poměrům své **otčiny** více nerozuměl"). The Muirs seem to make a mistake in translating "die Verhältnisse" as "commerce," but, in fact, it is a deliberate framing of the friend in Petersburg as a failed businessman (in contrast to Georg's pride in his own business success). Corngold's "how things worked at home" could refer to the public and private sphere (and reflect Georg's own misunderstading of the same), and Hofmann's "how people ticked here" connecting the notion of people and place or home.

> Perhaps it would not be possible to get him to come **home** at all – he said himself that he was now out of touch with commerce in his **native country** – and then he would still be left an **alien** in **a foreign land** embittered by his *friends*' advice and more than ever estranged from them … couldn't be said to have either *friends* or **a country of his own** any longer, wouldn't it have been better for him to stay **abroad** just as he was? (Kafka 1971: 78).

> Perhaps it would not even succeed in bringing him back [] – after all, he himself had said that he no longer understood how things worked **at home** – and so, despite everything, he would remain **abroad**, embittered by the suggestions and **alienated** even further from his *friends* … and now no longer had either **a real home** or *friends*, would it not be much better for him to have stayed **abroad**, just where he was? (Kafka 2007: 4).

> Perhaps Bendemann wouldn't even be able to secure his return **home** – the man even admitted he know longer understood how people ticked **here** – and he would therefore be consigned to remaining **abroad**, only further **alienated** from his *friends* and offended by their well-meaning advice … now genuinely **depatriated** and *friend*less; would it not be better for him simply to remain **abroad**? (Kafka 2008b: 38).

To dismiss Jesenská's translations – either by not talking in detail about them or by only mentioning one "mistake" (i.e., the translation of "Das Urteil" as "Soud") as a metonymic representation of all her translation work – is clearly a disservice to her abilities as a translator. She shows a remarkable sensitivity to Kafka's aesthetic style, his use of language, the sounds of his language, and shows herself as a thinking translator (as most are) – that is, someone who is thinking through the implications of the story for the story itself and for her own experiential lens.

As the only – and very minimal – debate about her Kafka translations has centered on whether her German was good enough, doubts are handily sown about whether the translations have any worth at all without even reading them. Marta Marková-Kotyková goes so far as to suggest that Jesenská used her lovers – she would "give literary form to the rough translations by her lovers" with all of whom she "lived briefly and translated" (Marková-Kotyková 1993: 51). Marková-Kotyková cites the plethora of languages from which she translated as the reason to suspect that this happened. She translated from "English, French, Russian, Hungarian, German when the only language that she perfectly mastered was her admirably smooth and exceedingly modern and clean Czech" (51). Alena Wagnerová suggests, in a similar vein, that Pollak perhaps helped Jesenská with her German translations, as "his mastery of German was equal to that of his Czech" (Wagnerová 1996: 100), but Wagnerová questions the contemporary accounts of Jesenská's "bad" German (from her lover Count Schaffgotsch and also Gina Kaus), arguing that it was the Viennese "tone" – cynical, ironic – of Pollak's circle that she could participate in, rather than a linguistic inability (75). The worrying implicit sexism – that Jesenská had to rely on men to translate – is both unproven and damaging even before readers might come to the translations. It also re-imprisons her identity into that of a consummate lover rather than a translator and intellectual.

But even if she did get help from others, which is a tendentious assumption, the final products show (as Kafka acknowledged) a profound understanding of his aesthetic intent and how he articulated it via his use of language. Wagnerová writes that Jesenská "applie[d] her beautiful, rich Czech" to the Kafka translations but also "her empathy" (101), and we see, in the case of "The Stoker" and "The Judgment," that her personal experience of exile and estrangement from language and home seemed to inform how and why she translated the stories.

"Little words"

For Jesenská too, the experience of exile, as well as a multilingual homeland, meant that the question of language and incommunicability laced her work. In an article "Little Words"/"Slovíčka" written for *Narodni listy* in July 1926, after her return to Prague, and a couple of years after Kafka's death, Jesenská asks her readers if they have ever fallen in love with certain words and whether or not they think that these words somehow express things in a more profound way than one might expect. She offers four of her own words, two Czech and two German ones: "kouzelný," "děvče," "heimatlos," and "heiter" – "magical," "girl," "homeless," and (roughly) "funny/bright." She explores what these words evoke; the joy from adding the adjective "magical" to a noun, the physical feelings evoked from the word "girl" that is "a crisp word like fruit, at once simple and still unexpected" (Jesenská 1996: 5, my translation), the untranslatability of "heiter" which means "neither merry, nor joyful. Heiter is something, for which there is no Czech expression. It's a summer Sunday afternoon in the sun, or a town after a storm when the flagstones are wet, there is an aroma from the gardens, and a small yellow sun shines from beneath the clouds" (5–6, my translation). Applied to a person, it is "those affable, kind, unflappable people, sweet and gentle, never bothering another with their own fate, and people with a clear and tough life philosophy" (6, my translation). Such a multivalent and paradoxical sense of a word occurs also with "děvče / girl": "if you are a girl, you are immediately someone firm and healthy and plucky and you smile, perhaps through tears" (5, my translation).

There is a sense of nostalgia behind these definitions; a sense of how personal any understanding of language can be, and the difficulty, without explication, of conveying these subjective associations to others. Translation reveals the complexity of representing what we really mean and the accretions of associations of personal and cultural meaning to language. Jesenská considers the foreignness of language at the heart of the article, in choosing "Heimatlos," or "homeless," as one of the words she is "in love with" (5). "Sad and terribly wistful," she writes. "It's impossible to translate well," and she tries to convey what the word evokes in her in two long sentences, the commas conveying the passing of time, as it is stretched out by isolation and loneliness:

> It means a person who inside is unsettled, wandering, restless, think of a large city park with a bench and on it a grown-up, who is foreign to the city, great woe in his heart and hopeless emptiness in his eyes, it's a hot afternoon, the air trembles above the asphalt, everyone who's walking about knows where they are going, only he doesn't know, as if time just started and moves terribly slowly like honey. Through day and night there are only difficulties and then he perhaps sits in some station on some train, leaves from this city to another, and when he alights, he will have a heart heavy with loneliness, a neck blocked with repugnance at drawn-out time, he will sit somewhere in a cafe and order a brown, lukewarm coffee, a clock with a gold border will be opposite him, and in front of the window will walk unknown, foreign people (5, my translation).

Remember, though, that this is one of her favorite words, ensconced between "magical," "girl," and "bright." Jesenská wrote this after having returned to Prague, after the experience of being in exile and isolated – emotionally and linguistically – in Vienna. Contemporaries of the Viennese café scene dismissed her as Ernst Pollak's "young wife" who was "lost," "foreign," "on the periphery" of the literary and philosophical discussions at the Café Herrenhof; "[h]er incomplete knowledge of German (she and Pollak spoke Czech together) meant that she was condemned to silence" (Wagnerová 1996: 74–5).

But only among a certain Viennese café literary circle; within a year or two of leaving Prague, Jesenská began writing for Czech newspapers, from and about Vienna, and began translating from German into Czech. Jesenská's physical isolation away from home brought her to a textual and linguistic home; one, however, changed by her experiences of isolation – practical and linguistic. Alena Wagnerová argues that her German was clearly good enough for her to be able to represent everyday Viennese life and to translate; complaints about her German had more to do with her inability to capture the ironic, disillusioned, pessimistic Viennese "tone" (75); in other words, her open, wry, optimistic style suited the more hopeful atmosphere in a newly independent Czechoslovakia and could be expressed in her maternal tongue. Her love of the word "Heimatlos" is articulated in this Czech context: both incredibly sad but also somehow lovely, perhaps even redemptive. Her admittance that "you" can "love" even "foreign words" (Jesenská 1996: 5), and her insistence in leaving that foreign word in the Czech text, gives it a new home, but one that is perhaps always estranged. "[D]o you also enjoy foreignness for its own sake?" Kafka asks Jesenská in his first letter to her, and there is an element here of unearthing the benefits of exile, of living and working in a different language and the estrangement of one's mother tongue. Even if Jesenská was not absolutely fluent in German, she brings her experience of being on the periphery of language back to her own: that is where Kafka recognizes her.

The Milena myth – Jesenská translated

Jacqueline Raoul-David recently fictionalized Kafka and Jesenská's relationship in a novelized biography of Kafka's love life, *Kafka l'éternel fiancé/Kafka in Love*. The "imperious and demanding Milena" (Raoul-David 2012: 162) sends Kafka "goading messages (as she most often does), which are as inimical to him as holy water to the devil" (150). Raoul-David surmises that in her letters, Jesenská must have articulated "venom ... resentment, remorse" (165) that exhausted and wore down Kafka. Her ultimate crime, though? "Does it not seem strange," Raoul-David asks her readers, "that in all the letters Kafka writes to Milena (some 150) there is no echo of any admiration on her part for his work? Whereas he heaps praise on the most trivial of her newspaper articles" (177).

She had so much reason and opportunity to praise him! Her translations of Kafka's work "like Ariadne's thread, led her to Kafka and bound her to him ... she sought the most faithful Czech equivalent for the words he had written. ... No one, consequently had read the texts more attentively than she" (177), but Jesenská does not – Raoul-David guesses (since we do not have Jesenská's letters) – praise the stories or indicate their special worth. Even worse, her translations are substandard: "He hardly dares to bring up a few egregious mistranslations" (177). Raoul-David refers here to Kafka's comments on "The Stoker" (discussed above) which focus on his awareness of the untranslatability of certain phrases and his wish to edit his own work. Raoul-David does not speak Czech, she has not actually read Jesenská's Czech translations, and yet she asserts that Jesenská is a bad translator (as well as a writer of "trivial" articles), who makes "egregious mistranslations," and whose work Kafka only admires because he is in love with her.

All the above is based on Jesenská's silence – the lack of textual evidence from her letters and the silencing of her surviving texts (both the translations and her articles) – to turn her into a phantasmal "Milena." Raoul-David mentions Jesenská's surname only once, in the first page of her chapter on her; after that she is always Milena (Milena and Kafka), a construct of Raoul-David's imagination. The goading messages, the imperiousness, her absolute disregard for Kafka's work, the egregious mistranslations, have no basis in evidential material, but they do feed the "Milena" myth that, ultimately, posit her only worth in terms of Kafka's love for her. "In the European and world context," Alena Wagnerová writes, "she has to date mainly been known only by her Christian name as 'Kafka's girlfriend Milena,' as the addressee of his *Letters to Milena*, even though her relationship with him was only one, if important, episode in her rich life" (Wagnerová 1996: 12).

For a translator, Jesenská is an incredibly visible presence – there are numerous biographies of her, novels written about her, songs written about her, and, of course, the *Letters to Milena* – but it is predicated on her love relationship to Kafka (rather than her translatorial relationship and its impact on that love relationship, or her own writing). František Kautman sees this as the ultimate "degradation" for her; "if a 'great man' had not chanced to get to know her and fall in love with her, then not even a dog would bark at her" (Marková-Kotyková 1993: 163). Czech critics tend to feel that this "Milena" is a Western construct that began with Willy Haas's publication of the *Letters*, which resulted in "a perfect mass psychosis" and "a marketing opportunity for publishers, authors, directors" (37), and Margarete Buber-Neumann's memoir of her time in Ravensbrück concentration camp with Jesenská, *Kafkas Freundin Milena* (1963), initially published in English in 1966 as *Mistress to Kafka* and again as *Milena* in the 1970s.

While "Milena" was becoming famous in the West, she was *persona non grata* in communist Czechoslovakia, owing to her rejection of communism in the 1930s and criticism of Czech communists in Ravensbrück. The first public mention of her name in Czechoslovakia after 1948 was in a book on Ravensbrück in 1960 which mentioned the presence of "some Trotskyists" (i.e. in the Stalinist worldview, heretics) among the prisoners: "The Czech Milena Jesenská also belonged to this circle," the book noted, adding, "There was a very strong battle against the incorrect views of these trotskyists" (Jirásková 1996: 101). When it was republished in 1963, Jesenská's name was removed because it was too controversial (102). However, that same year her name was brought up at the famous Liblická conference, where Kafka was rehabilitated (having being banned by the communist regime after 1948) and she was acknowledged as "one of the first translators of Kafka's work into Czech" (102). Yet, "the struggles and attacks were not over" (102) and there was a public back and forth about her in the widely read literary papers during the Prague spring. In 1968, *Letters to Milena/Dopisy Mileně* (translated by Hana Žantovská) was published for the first time in Czech and Jesenská's daughter, Jana Černá, rushed her memoir, *Adresát Milena Jesenská*, to the printers. Following the Soviet invasion in August 1968, "it was too late to escape the clamp-down; the book never reached the Prague shops and only the odd copy was smuggled out of the country" (Černá 1988: 33). Any mention of Jesenská was banned once again in her homeland until the Velvet Revolution in 1989. Černá's memoir, *Adresát Milena Jesenská/Addressee Milena Jesenská* was published in English translation in 1988 as *Kafka's Milena*.

The enforced postwar silence about Jesenská in Czechoslovakia skewed Jesenská's legacy; in the West she became famous as "Kafka's Milena" without much awareness of her writerly and translatorial legacy in her homeland. At the outbreak of World War II, Jesenská, in fact, was far more famous than Kafka in Czechoslovakia, and famous in her own right. In 1920 alone – the year her first translation of Kafka's work appeared and in the midst of a flurry of letters to him – she wrote thirty-one feuilletons for the newspaper *Tribuna* and published translations of works by Franz Werfel, Alfred Döblin, Leo Tolstoy, Upton Sinclair, Rosa Luxemburg, Charles Peguyu, Charles-Louis Phillipe, Gustav Schulz, Gustav Landauer, and Gina Kaus (Wagnerová 1996: 100).

She had returned to Prague in the mid-1920s (after divorcing Pollak) and become a household name as a journalist, writing initially for the women's pages of the relatively conservative *Národní Listy*, where she and her female colleagues "define[d] the sensibilities of a new female generation" (115). Writing about the perceived and defined female arena – children, fashion, the kitchen, and the home – she "hid" in these themes her philosophy, the "clear concept of modern life culture and the modern person" (115). When she was writing about hats or shoes, in fact "she [was] writing about the person who wears them" (115). Certain words are repeated in her articles of the late 1920s and early 1930s that underline a sense of new freedom for her and for women in general: "Sun, air, space, movement, they were her magic words, which described the basic needs of the modern person" (115). In the vibrant inter-war years in the newly independent Czechoslovakia (as opposed to the bleakness and depression of Vienna after the fall of the Austro-Hungarian empire), women were becoming part of the elite and able, for the first time, although in an incremental manner, to define the culture in which they lived (114).

"They were fairly average articles," Jesenská wrote modestly to Jílovská's lover, Adolf Hoffmeister in 1929, "the sort that are in newspapers a lot. I'm not proud of them, I'm not embarrassed by them. If I hadn't needed money, I wouldn't have written a word. But maybe I'll write one book, just one book, and that book will be decidedly not bad" (118). But the articles were important to the women reading them: "How her articles were awaited in Prague, Jaroměř, Jindřichův Hradec, Klatovy and elsewhere!" Jaroslava Vondráčková wrote about her female readers waiting to hear Jesenská's opinions: "What does Milena say!" (116). Her articles may have seemed superficial and borne of necessity to her, but as Wagnerová argues "we, seventy years later, can clearly see more in her articles than she could" (118), partly because we are more used to thinking about high culture through the media of so-called low culture.

Jesenská never got the chance to write that one book, but ten years later she would become even more famous for her political articles, especially those written following the Nazi invasion, in the political weekly *Přítomnost*. When the editor of *Přítomnost*, Ferdinand Peroutka, was arrested by the Nazis in 1939, "she immediately stepped into his place, editing the weekly until it ceased publication" (Demetz 2008: 131); it was an immensely courageous and suicidal move, one that was likely to end only in imprisonment and death (as it did). She felt it her duty: "Her self-possessed voice, her self-possessed and at the same time passionate articles, during those days of horror," Stanislav Budin remembers, "became the one foothold," a means by which her Czech readership could hang on to a sense of "dignity and pride" (Jirásková 1996: 26). In her articles written directly after the Nazi invasion, Jesenská considers the Czech response of silence, resignation, and lack of action which might be regarded as a weak response and forcefully argues it as an articulation of dignity, of a deep humanism, of a nation standing together. The morning after, she writes,

> The trams were full, as usual. Only the people were different. They stood and kept silent. I had never heard so many people keep silent before [...] I do not know where this unified and consistent behaviour of thousands came from, where this

consonant rhythm of many souls, strangers to one another, sprang from all of a sudden

(Jesenská 2003: 206).

There is no shouting or screaming or fighting; instead, "Prague residents" start laying snowdrops by the Tomb of the Unknown Soldier in the Old Town Square, a "remarkable power mysteriously" seems to guide them there: "People stand around and tears run down their cheeks. Not only women and children, but men too, who are not used to crying. Somehow," Jesenská writes, "it is all distinctly *Czech*: it is not a lament; it is not even fear; it is not despair; it is not a convulsion of emotion at all. It is only sadness" (208). Jesenská sees a German soldier walk by and stop. He looks at the "eyes red with crying, at the teardrops, at the snow-covered mountain of snowdrops; he saw people who were crying because *he* was there. And he saluted" (209).

Jesenská uses that human gesture by the German soldier to salute her readers for their human, communal gestures of silence and snowdrops. In another article two weeks later, Jesenská evokes the dignity of "standing still" instead of rushing into battle or retreating. She recounts the story of being at the opera during World War I, when the Czechs were still part of the Austro-Hungarian empire, and the aria "Kde domov můj" was sung. This aria ("Where is my home?") would become the national anthem for the independent republic in 1918, but then it "was only a Czech song" (213). A man in the audience, in front of her, stood up "quiet and calm, with his hands at his sides," then another person stood up, then another, and sang along as "a kind of tribute to the Czech song" (213). "It was not a song *against* anyone," Jesenská writes, "but rather *for* something. It did not wish anyone's ruin, but rather our survival. It was not a militant song, but the song of our Czech homeland" (213). "I realised then," she adds, "that to know how to stand is dignified, honorable and forthright [...] The past year [1938–9] has taught us one thing: one must know how to stand still. To stand by everything that is Czech, with head bared and an ardent love in one's heart, with profound dignity, openness and integrity" (213).

Jesenská did not appeal to a blind patriotism and anger, but instead to Czech decency, a dignified antidote to martial Nazism. The stirring subtext of her portrayal of "standing still" under the Austro-Hungarians was not, however, particularly subtle. Jesenská was continually interrogated in the months following the invasion by the German censor at Gestapo headquarters, until she was banned from writing and *Přítomnost* was forcibly shut down in August 1939 (Hockaday 1997: 194–9). The Gestapo arrested Jesenská three months later; her last letter to her young daughter, written in early 1940, indicates that she was clear about her likely fate: "picture us being together again sometime, in some little room. If we won't have our own room anymore, don't cry, we'll have another room, we'll always find some beautiful room somewhere together [...] I look forward to the day when I can go where you are, my dearest friend" (Černá 1988: 204–5). She was sent to Ravensbrück with the note "Return undesirable" on her file and died there in 1944.

Directly after the war, Czech writers and intellectuals began writing about Jesenská as an important Czech intellectual in her own right: Stanislav Budin wrote about his attempts to persuade her to emigrate; Anička Kvapilová wrote about her time in Ravensbrück; Jiří Weil considered writing a novel about her and started a play; Marie Pujmanová wrote a poem that would later be excised from anthologies (Jirásková 1996: 98–100). After these attempts, and the communist coup, "there was a long silence" (100), a silence that would basically last for forty years (apart from a brief respite in the Prague spring).

In this immediate postwar period, Kafka was barely remembered by Czech readers. When Jesenská's first husband, Ernst Pollak, wrote to her friend Staša Jílovská in 1947 to inquire about Kafka's letters to Jesenská, Jílovská assured him that "you can safely trust me if there is concrete word about sending the letters. I would send them discreetly and safely" but seemed bemused as to why there might be interest in them abroad. "Czech circles are not very interested in Kafka," she writes, "indeed almost no one knows him, and only *The Castle* is translated." She mentions that one Czech publisher "has just said they will publish all of his work, but I don't believe in its success." She promises not to talk about "that Kafka" and feels that little will be said about the Kafka–Jesenská relationship because "our old friends from his circle no longer exist" (Wagnerová 1996: 185); that is, they had been gassed, shot, or forced into exile.

By that same year, 1947, scholarly works on Kafka were already being published in the West and by the 1950s he was world-famous. The letters, which Wagnerová suggests were sent over to England by Jílovská via diplomatic mail, were published in 1952. In 1963, Margerete Buber-Neumann published a memoir of Jesenská, their time in Ravensbrück concentration camp and Jesenská's life before the camp, *Kafkas Freundin Milena/Kafka's Girlfriend Milena*. Yet only one chapter is devoted to the relationship and is almost wholly reconstructed from the *Letters to Milena*, i.e., from Kafka's letters: "It was a passionate, tragic love," Buber-Neumann writes, "as can be seen from Kafka's surviving letters to Milena. When I read them, I was overwhelmed by memories of her" (Buber-Neumann 1977: 59). Buber-Neumann indicates that Jesenská talked about Kafka with her during their time in the camp, but does not report anything that Jesenská might have said. She opens the chapter remembering, instead, what Jesenská told her about Kafka's work. "Even before Milena began to talk about her relationship with Franz Kafka," Buber-Neumann writes, "she told me one evening, as we were walking back and forth between the barracks in the pale evening light, the story of the commercial traveler Gregor Samsa in Kafka's *Metamorphosis*" (56). It is the first time that Buber-Neumann has heard the story and she realizes after the war that:

> what she told me then was her own private version of Kafka's novella. *She* was the commercial traveler, the helpless, misunderstood Samsa, metamorphosed into an enormous beetle and hidden by his family because they were ashamed of him. She went into special detail about the beetle's illness and how, afflicted with a wound in his back, in which dirt and mites have become encrusted, he is left alone to die (56).

It is hard not to be moved by this image of the two women eeking out a moment of mental and physical freedom in the concentration camp and Jesenská, who translated the story (but never published the translation), applying it to her own life, her own expulsion from her family, going "into special detail" about the "wound in his back" and being "left alone to die." But what is also striking is that this is the only actual memory Buber-Neumann relates about Jesenská referring to Kafka; the rest of the chapter could have been written by any reader of the *Letters*. By the time the memoir was written, Jesenská was already famous as "Milena"; Buber-Neumann importantly gives some sense of her life and an account, otherwise missing, of her last years in the concentration camp, but she reinforces the Milena myth when it comes to Kafka, making their affair central to Jesenská's life, despite no indication of actual memories of Jesenská talking about her relationship with Kafka. At the time of her friendship with Jesenská, Kafka was unknown to Buber-Neumann and to many; his status had completely changed by the time she wrote her memoir.

George Gibian, noting biographical inconsistencies in the memoir (while supporting Jana Černá's also notably inconsistent memoir), also makes the point that Buber-Neumann "underestimates the achievements of Milena as a writer" (Buber-Neumann 1977: 3). Jesenská's life is set up as a tragedy, at the center of which (indicated by the title of the book) was her "passionate, tragic" love affair with Kafka. Jesenská's work, when mentioned, is related to that tragic arc. It was "her own unhappiness [that] gave her a special feeling for his works, and that, no doubt, is what made her decide to translate them, though her knowledge of German was still less than perfect," Buber-Neumann writes of Jesenská's work (56–7) – though noting how "perfect" Jesenská's German was by the time she met her (2). It was Kafka's criticisms of the translations, she adds, that led to them meeting (57) – Buber-Neumann basing this, like others, on Kafka's three comments discussed above and not mentioning his effusive praise for the translations.

In 1968, the *Letters to Milena* were finally published in Czechoslovakia with a fine introduction by the literary critic František Kautman: "Kafka held Milena's translations, which are of a really good standard, in high esteem," Kautman wrote, "and was happy that Milena was translating his work" (Kafka 1968: 23). Kafka was drawn to her strengths as a "translator of the best works of modern literature and a wonderful feuilletonist" (23–4). He elucidates her translations (underlining that they were the first of Kafka's work), the importance of her journalism for Czech inter-war culture, and argues that "Milena connected Kafka to the Czech nation, to its language and culture" (32). His letters to her were "a part of our cultural heritage" (34), a work of art in themselves. He also connects Jesenská to *The Castle*, making an informed reading of two of Kafka's characters, Frieda and Amalia, as variations of Jesenská (28–33), as Kafka's fictionalization not only of his lover but also of the intellectual artist. Kautman's introduction was in fact a re-introduction of Jesenská to her homeland, after twenty years of being erased as a non-person by the communist regime, and it is important to note that he presents her as a translator and writer above all. After the Soviet invasion that same year, though, Jesenská (and Kautman) were banned.

The dearth of Jesenská's own work outside of the Czechoslovak borders (and banned within them) allowed for a romanticizaton of "Milena" as a figure. Two novels, based on a "Milena" figure, both full of breathy exclamation points, were published: Maggie Ross's *Milena* (1983) and Alina Reyes's *Nus devant les fantômes* (2000). In Reyes's novel, Jesenská reminisces about her grand love, Kafka, as she dies in Ravensbrück: "Franz Kafka, stop looking at me with those big grey eyes!" (Reyes 2000: 129); "Franz. Franz, how hesitant we were that first day! And it wasn't the other's body that we had to get used to, but our own bodies which became so new, so intimidating, so unrecognizable!" (146). To be fair, Reyes's dying "Milena" also manages to remind dead Franz with the big grey eyes about her work; she relates how she becomes a true journalist when she begins to work for *Přítomnost*:

> I did not deal with fashion any more; I was not satisfied any more with evoking small scenes of daily life; my country was living through difficult times; it was time for me to get involved with political news. I was liberated from Communist ideology. After ten years of dependence, I was also liberated from morphine (177).

Following complications during her labor with her daughter, Jesenská became a morphine user, and there were rumors – but only rumors – that she had been a cocaine user in Vienna. Reyes's Milena begins writing "little articles" in 1919 to escape her addiction to cocaine (121). She also begins translating. "Of everything that I had read recent to that," Milena says (of "The Stoker" although she speaks in the plural of "texts"):

> your texts were the ones that left a deep mark. Not only did I understand that this was a work of genius, but I felt close to what it was saying, this exiled soul, this stranger to the world around him and who still works without pause to find his place. ... Soon after your death, I left Ernst. Why did I not have the strength to do it before? When you asked me to do it and live with you? (121–2).

Reyes actually attempts some (albeit brief) analysis of why Jesenská may have wanted to translate Kafka's work, specifically "The Stoker," when she herself was alone and in exile – which is more than many literary critics have done. Yet it is couched in scandal (the cocaine! The divorce!) and delivered in the breathy language of romance cliché. The tone is not only kitsch but also off; Jesenská's letters to Max Brod that he quotes in his biography are passionate and panicked, but they were written when she was in her twenties after the relationship broke up. She was in her late forties when she died (and when this narrative is set), an experienced journalist and translator, having had numerous serious love affairs after Kafka. The voice in her writing, even in her "little articles," is far more original and insightful.

The feminist impulse to ressurect Jesenská from her silence as a missing recipient in the *Letters* is admirable, but with both Reyes's and Ross's novels it is a resurrection of an already iconized lover figure. In Ross's novel *Milena*, an artist and translator, Amy, spends the novel trying to draw a collage that represents Milena and her life: "There would have to be a window" in the picture, Amy thinks to herself, "She thought it might adequately represent the Czech nation's history of defenestration [...] from her window she could see nothing but tracks forming a great Star of David around Milena" (Ross 1983: 25). Amy is doing exactly what her author is – painting a kitsch portrait of this woman she admires. It was "turning into an obsession with the woman who was the first to translate Kafka's works from German into Czech," Amy thinks (8). Her husband Ernest snorts, "'Translators are second-class citizens,' he would say, ignoring the fact that his wife's days were frequently spent giving substance to other people's words" (8). Amy is in fact translating the work of "Frank," a writer who has written about a stoker, into pictures – she is an illustrator. "It is gloomy here," she writes to Frank (who is "[t]hin, emaciated … with strange, winged" (27) ears):

> Never mind! All I have to do is go on board ship again, and all is well. My worries at the moment consist of translating this magnificent stoker of yours into the stubborn personfication of frail family you see so clearly. But should I draw him with the face of someone rejected? I think he shall stay in shadow (26).

Amy is so ensconsced with "Milena" that she does not seem to realize that the love triangle she falls into with Frank and Ernest of course replicates Jesenská's and ends the same way, but instead, to give her hope, she still has Milena and her painting of her. "It was a strong face," the novel ends, "and a real one; the face of a woman who was courageous enough to stand up on her own" (280). Amy's and Ross's translation of Jesenská into a feminist icon is worthy but ultimately lifeless, and still predicated on Jesenská's love affair rather than her work and cultural import.

Blank spaces

Jesenská's life is a "biography full of blank spaces," one of her biographers writes, "in which reality is quite indistinguishably intertwined with speculation and gossip resulting in the creation of myths" (Wagnerová 1996: 188). Between the "myth" of Milena and her "aura" even biographers attempting to "de-mythologize" her can fall into mystification (188). "Milena lived several lives," another biographer writes, "there is practically no one who knew her in the full spectrum of her character. The people who knew her in Vienna, did not know her in Dresden, in Prague, in Ravensbrück" (Marková-Kotyková 1993: 12). If her biography is "full of uncertainties and legends," created by "friends and enemies," these legends were also, Kautman argues, perhaps added to by Jesenská herself (Kautman in Marková-Kotyková 1993: 163). "No human life yields up its secrets readily," Jesenská's daughter wrote in her memoir, "Even the ordinary lives of ordinary people are in fact inscrutable" (Černá 1988: 39). Even our own biographies are impossible legends. Černá, though, was keen to challenge the perception of Jesenská as just "the angelic companion of a genius" (40) and, in this notoriously unreliable (but fascinating) memoir, she demands the right to forget; it is an "inalienable right … one of the few freedoms each of us has which can neither be curtailed nor taken away" (38). Her demand is in contra-distinction to her mother who carried "the burden … of total recall," who refused to forget anything (39). Černá, thus, defends her right to lose the tooth the camp inmate kept for her, the last physical remnant of Jesenská, the "part of a mouth that once talked to me."

Beyond the myth, beyond the physical body, though, is what is left behind: her translations, her writing, her words. Jesenská's Kafka should be considered; her translations were the first-ever translations of Kafka's work; they were part of a sustained translation effort in the inter-war years in Czechoslovkia that helped create a modern canon of Czech literature. They brought Kafka into the Czech sphere of his native country. They have been overlooked because translation is regarded as a secondary literary activity (an unvalued copy of the original text) and because Jesenská's worth, as a woman, has been defined as, and limited to, a love interest for Kafka – in effect, a double marginalization. The love affair was clearly important to both Jesenská and Kafka, but it was predicated on literature and, specifically, on her translation of his work. Translation is a place through which their relationship was explored, as is clear even from the one-sided remnant of the correspondence, but it can also be a place of exploration for the reader; a place where questions of cultural, linguistic and sexual identity are mediated.

In translation, as in Kafka's work itself, misunderstanding is at the very heart of the enterprise; "every great artistic act is in itself incomprehensible" (Jesenská 2003: 68), Jesenská wrote in her article "The Letters of Eminent People," because of its "ability to see the world anew" (68). Kafka recognized that this is what Jesenská's translations did; they renewed his stories, they brought a sense of newness to the voice "from the old grave." Kafka has brought her through the subterranean passages of his prose; it is time to see Jesenská through "the daylight at the exit."

Willa Muir

In a masculine civilization the creative work of women may be belittled, misinterpreted, or denied: but if it is a reality, its existence will be proved at least by the emotional colour of the denial.

Willa Muir, *Woman: An Inquiry*, 1925

Broke, and living in Weimar Germany, the Scots couple Willa and Edwin Muir were offered translation work. Willa Muir was delighted; a trained Classics scholar (among the first generation of women to be awarded a degree), she could not believe she would be paid for something she enjoyed and was good at. The Muirs only had enough money to send a two-word telegram: "Yes. Muir" (Muir 1968: 106). That the couple could only afford to sign in the singular became prophetic of how their translatorial relationship would be perceived. When they returned to Britain, "Edwin was hailed everywhere as the translator," Willa Muir writes in her 1968 memoir *Belonging*, "which amused me but irritated him" (Muir 1968: 126). In private she was less forgiving: "everyone assumes that Edwin did them. He is referred to as 'THE' translator. By this time he may even believe that he was." She adds: "Most of the translation, especially Kafka was done by ME" (St. Andrews MS 38466/5/5: August 20, 1953).

Born into a poor family on Shetland, Muir grew up initially speaking Scots, then mainland Scots, then English – the latter always an official, public language. She graduated from St. Andrew's University in 1910, having excelled in Classics and co-founded their Women Students' Suffrage Society; she wrote a feminist tract for the Woolfs' Hogarth Press in 1925 called *Woman: An Inquiry*. She published two "groundbreaking" (Allen 1996: v) modernist novels in the 1930s, *Mrs. Ritchie* and *Imagined Corners*, and a moving memoir about her marriage to Edwin and their literary life, *Belonging*.

She wrote a further two novels, both autobiographical and both unpublished: *The Usurpers*, a fictional account of the Muirs's experiences in Czechoslovakia in 1948, and *Mrs. Muttoe and the Top Storey*. *Mrs Muttoe*, set in London in the 1930s, is about a harried female translator, Alison Muttoe, who has to translate German writers (including a fictionalized Kafka) in order to keep her family afloat: specifically, her writer husband Dick, who spends most of the novel isolated in the top storey of their house, writing things few people read or buy. Theoretically, he helps with the translation work, but only once in the novel does he offer, quite unconvincingly, to help. Critics suggest the novel failed because it was too autobiographical, too mundane.

Kafka, banned by the Nazis, became famous posthumously in English and in the English translations by the Muirs. Between 1930 and 1948, Willa and Edwin Muir translated Kafka's unfinished novels *The Castle* (1930), *The Trial* (1937), and *America* (1938); as well as his *Aphorisms* (1932), *The Great Wall of China and Other Pieces* (1946), and *In the Penal Colony* (1948). Since Malcolm Pasley re-edited the Kafka manuscripts in the early 1980s, adding and rearranging material edited by Max Brod, the Muirs's first translations seem outdated, based on Brod's "deeply flawed" editions. A surprising amount has been written on the Muirs's translations, elucidating various criticisms of their work beyond this: they made simple mistakes because they were not fluent German speakers; they did not understand Kafka's aesthetics because they were anti-modernists; they over-domesticated the texts accordingly; and they read Kafka through a theologically simplistic lens (Coetzee 2001; Crick 1981; Damrosch 2003; Gray 1977; Harman 1996; Mellown 1964). The criticism is largely based on Edwin Muir's forewords to the translations, paratextual writing that made him the more visible translator of the two, and these forewords do posit Kafka as an allegorical writer, his characters as pilgrims moving toward grace, and thus, in Edwin Muir's schema, making Kafka an anti-modernist. Common to all the criticism on the Muirs's translations is an assumption that Edwin was the real translator with no proof other than stating that he was the writer of the two, and thus the "primary stylist." Willa Muir is consistently quoted from her memoir *Belonging*, in which she asserts that their translation relationship, like their marriage, was absolutely egalitarian.

But her claims are as consistently dismissed; the most that scholars imply is that she "supplied the basic version" (Gray 1977: 242) for Edwin Muir to "remodel" because Muir was "the gifted poet" whose "mastery of English shows at every turn" (Gray 1977: 242); he was "the poet and man of letters" who "was most adept at polishing the English, while Willa, with her training as a classical philologist, ensured a degree of accuracy in the rendering of the German" (Harman 1996: 298). In other words, Edwin Muir, as the creative writer, is judged to have more influence over the translations than Willa Muir, who is a mere interlingual translator. So, while critics have not necessarily discriminated against Muir because she was a woman, they have resigned her to a marginalized and feminized role because they implicitly present the translation process as a marginalized and feminized art; Edwin, the writer-translator, produces a text that is "original and 'masculine,'" Willa produces a text that is "derivative and 'feminine'" (Chamberlain 1992: 57). They implicitly deny Willa Muir's possible influence on the translations by first relegating her to being only responsible for supplying the "basic version" but also in assuming that interlingual transfer is a non-interpretive and non-creative act, denying the agency or "active presence of the translator" (Cronin 2003: 64) and the "creative nature of the process itself" (Cronin 2003: 127).

Even if Willa Muir was "only" the interlingual translator of Kafka's work, in other words, her interpretations of the texts may have influenced the translations. Unlike her husband she was a modernist novelist; she was anti-Church (seeing it as a patriarchal institution); she was a trained linguist and perhaps more open to her Scots-speaking background than he; and she was a strident feminist believing that she had to live and promulgate a sense of equality between genders. Her "translator-effect" (Von Flotow 1997: 35), the influence of her own strongly felt ideas as an "early feminist" (Simon 1996: 77) on Kafka has never been studied, and yet seems important to acknowledge at the point at which the Muirs's translations are being superseded and on the cusp of being forgotten.

As she grew older, Muir panicked in private about her legacy being elided in literary history. In a 1953 journal entry, she wrote:

> even the translations I had done were no longer my own territory, for everyone assumes that Edwin did them. He is referred to as "THE" translator. By this time he may even believe that he was. He has let my reputation sink, by default; as now I fear that if the Feuchtwanger publishers are told that I am prepared to do his beastly novel, they will refuse unless Edwin engages to do it, or to put his name to it.
>
> And the fact remains; I am a better translator than he is. The whole current of patriarchal society is set against this fact, however, and sweeps it into oblivion, simply because I did not insist on shouting aloud: "Most of this translation, especially Kafka, has been done by ME. Edwin only helped." And every time Edwin was referred to as THE translator, I was too proud to say anything; and Edwin himself felt it would be undignified to speak up, I suppose. So that now, especially since my break-down in the middle of the war, I am left without a shred of literary reputation. And I am ashamed of the fact that I feel it as a grievance. It shouldn't bother me. Reputation is a passing value, after all. Yet it is now that I feel it, now when I am trying to build up my life again and overcome my disabilities: my dicky back-bone, for instance. Because I seem to have nothing to build on, except that I am Edwin's wife and he still loves me. That is much. It is almost all, in a sense, that I could need. It is more than I deserve. And I know, too, how destructive ambition is, and how it deforms what one might create. And yet, and yet, I want to be acknowledged. That is why I say: I am a mess. (St. Andrews MS 38466/5/5: August 20, 1953).

Muir identifies the problems she faced with the "whole current of patriarchal society" set against her dominant skills, but also her complicity in the occlusion of her contribution, that she "did not insist on shouting aloud" that she was the main Kafka translator because she "was too proud to say anything" and also Edwin's complicity "it would be undignified to speak up." Aileen Christianson dismisses her claim because it contradicts Willa Muir's public assertions about the equal distribution of translation work (Christianson 2007: 130); Christianson puts it down to "resentment at the assumption that Edwin was the main translator" and dismisses it as "her own feminist interpretation that she is a woman writer whose work has been subsumed into the male's area of credit" (128).

Fifteen years later, in her memoir, *Belonging* – which begins with her marriage to Edwin and ends in his death – Willa Muir is absolutely programmatic at asserting that they had an equal input into the translations and that they would literally tear the books in half to achieve this. But if even her public statements about this equality of labor have been ignored, or at the very best sidelined, does the private Willa Muir (it was "done by ME") have a point that "the whole current of patriarchal society is set against" the possibility that she "was the better translator" and did the majority of the work, "especially Kafka"? Can we reread the translations through Willa, rather than Edwin, Muir?

A book torn in half

In 1960, after Edwin Muir's death, Robert M. Macgregor at New Directions wrote asking Willa Muir to translate additional "fragments" of Kafka's *Amerika*, the only translation solely published under Edwin Muir's name. "You will remember that your husband, you and I had conversations several years ago when you were in Cambridge about translating the fragments of AMERIKA by Kafka for a new edition by us," Macgregor writes, and adds: "as I understand that *you were largely responsible for the original translation*, it would seem most appropriate and right to have the new part also done by you" (St. Andrews MS 38466 N/1; June 22, 1960, emphasis added). The letter and her journals are in her archive; publicly no such claims that Willa Muir was "largely responsible for the original translation" were ever made, partly because she did not believe that anyone would believe her. Her husband, known for years as "THE" translator, had "let my reputation sink by default" and she was worried that publishers would not employ her as a translator "unless Edwin engages to do it, or to put his name to it." Why did Willa Muir – never mind her publishers – "not insist on shouting aloud" that she had done much of the work (St. Andrews MS 38466/5/5: August 20, 1953)?

Muir deeply loved her husband and committed herself, even sacrificed herself, to support his literary career as a poet and critic. The translations helped buy him time to write and helped cement his literary reputation; Muir had suggested the unknown Kafka to his publisher and wrote eloquent prefaces to the translations introducing the writer. Muir was born into poverty on Orkney and, like his wife, grew up speaking

Scots; he was forced out to work at the age of 14 and was essentially self-taught. Willa Muir may have "voluntarily sacrificed her own identity to that of 'the poet's wife'" (Allen 1996: v), but part of the impetus for that sacrifice was a recognition of another outsider who would have to struggle to become accepted in the mainstream literary world (one defined at the time by London). Shouting aloud about her own work might have betrayed that, however paradoxical her silence may seem in relation to her ardent feminist beliefs.

While clearly in love, their concept of marriage had its political aims. Willa Muir felt consistently boxed in by patriarchal attitudes and institutions. She came of age just before the outbreak of World War I – "the great shock of my adult life ... which knocked me to pieces for a time" (Muir 1968: 20) – and saw her son grow up in the shadow of World War II; Muir explicitly connected male dominance in the home and public life with the pursuance of warfare. Men, she believed, were trained into aggression and dominance and women into subservience. She believed that if equality reigned at home, then the pugilistic tone and terrible after-effects of the political scene would be tempered. She and Edwin could start with their own marriage: "I did not assume that Edwin and I had invented marriage based on True Love," Muir wrote in *Belonging*: "or even marriage comprising intimate partnership, but I did think we were in the front line of advance for such marriages, and therefore very much in the front line of advance for the making of a new unwarlike society" (140).

The Muirs married in June 1919, only months after the end of World War I. Edwin "refused to boost himself up the ladder to becoming a dominant male" because:

> it led to violence, fighting and warfare [...] even those who were alarmed by industrial violence and had had enough of warfare between nations, where the lust was, as it were, written large [...] did not see that the desire for dominance could also be overbearing and destructive when written small in civilian life. (138–9)

Willa herself "refused to be pushed down into subservience" so that she was "sometimes decried as a virago" and "Edwin decried as a weakling" (138). She was not wrong. Wyndham Lewis's satire of the 1920s London literary scene, *The Apes of God* (1930), in which he honed in on Willa and Edwin Muir, gives a sense of the contemporary reaction to the Muirs's marriage of equals. Horace Zagreus points out the "Keiths," as they are called in the novel, to his acolyte, Daniel Boleyn:

> He is as you see, a very earnest, rather melancholy freckled little being – whose dossier is that, come into civilization from amid the gillies and haggises of Goy or Arran, living in poverty, he fell in love with that massive, elderly Scottish lady next to him – that is his wife. She opened her jaws and swallowed him comfortably. There he was once more inside a woman, as it were – tucked up in her old tummy. In no way embarrassed with this slight additional burden (the object of all her wishes, of masculine gender – but otherwise little more than a sexless foetus) she started off upon the *grand tour*. And there in the remoter capitals of Europe the happy pair remained for some time, in erotic-maternal trance no doubt – the speckled foetus acquiring the german alphabet (Lewis 1965: 315).

Lewis attacked the whole London literary scene in the novel, but the cruel misogynistic wit showcases why the struggle for equality was so central to Willa Muir's life. Equality was connected not only to sex, but also to class, nationality and profession. "Com[ing] into civilization" (i.e. into the dominant London literary scene) meant putting behind them a Scots life associated with "poverty" and the working class. Lewis sniggers about Willa putting her "speckled foetus" in her "pouch" and going off on the "grand tour" of "the remoter capitals of Europe" because of course the grand tour was the province of the wealthy male; going to places like Prague and Dresden, as the Muirs did in the early 1920s, made a sham of the tour, a pretension to "com[ing] into civilization." But it is only the "speckled foetus" who acquires "the german alphabet" – Lewis's snide reference to their translation of German literature, the means by which they survived abroad. The "massive, elderly Scottish lady" (Muir was 40) is not even allowed to have acquired the alphabet. That they had to work to earn money on their "grand tour" is bad enough; translation is not even worthy of its name (just rote learning of an alphabet). The Muirs's very personal struggle for sexual equality was connected to the minoritizing, by a British colonial and patriarchal culture, of other aspects of their identities: their working-class roots, their Scots backgrounds, and their professional literary work in what was regarded as jobbing translation (rather than writing).

Willa Muir's public descriptions of the translation process with Kafka manifests their commitment to equality. She is quite clear in her memoir and in interviews about the equal division of labor. "People have often asked me what was our technique in our joint Kafka translations?" Muir writes, in her 1968 memoir *Belonging*:

> It was simple enough. We divided the book in two, Edwin translated one half and I the other, then we went over each other's translation as with a fine-tooth comb. By the time we had finished the going-over and put the two halves together the translation was like a seamless garment, for we both loved the sinuous flexibility of Kafka's style – very unlike classical German – and dealt with it in the self-same way (Muir 1968: 150).

To a friend in an interview, she conveyed a similar "rigorously egalitarian" (Simon 1996: 77) notion of the process:

> When [the Muirs] decided to translate *The Castle* and *The Trial*, they tore the book in two (though [Willa] assured me they didn't normally do this to books). They then tossed a coin to see which half each of them would take. After translating their own part, they exchanged halves, and went through them carefully, correcting each other's mistakes. After the mistakes had been put right, then the real work began (Soukup, quoted in Christianson 2007: 127).

In her excellent book on Willa Muir, Aileen Christianson concludes that, because Muir repeated this in interviews and in her memoir, "the weight of the evidence seems to be that they did divide the translating although [Willa] Muir may have done most of the preliminary work" (Christianson 2007: 130). Christianson believes that Muir's comment in her journal about doing most of the translation work was a result of her being upset about Edwin not reading her novel *The Usurpers* and about his decision to go public in his *Autobiography* about a brief affair he had had, thus breaking the public mask of their marriage (in her own memoir Willa mentions the affair, writing that it "was important in our marriage, helping it to become a more conscious partnership" (Muir 1968: 93), shaping it as a consolidation of their equal union).

Yet Willa Muir's public comments about their absolutely equal input to the Kafka translations are so insistent of the fact of that equality that one wonders whether her comments fit too perfectly into the mythos and political aim of the Muirs's marriage of equality. The language she uses in both of the above descriptions creates a rhetoric of this notion of equality: "our joint Kafka translations"; "We divided the book in two"; "Edwin translated one half and I the other"; we "put the two halves together"; "like a seamless garment"; "we dealt with it in the self-same way" (Muir 1968: 150); "tore the book in two"; "which half"; "exchanged halves"; "each other's mistakes" (Christianson 2007: 127). Is it too perfect, his division?

Willa Muir wrote her memoir after Edwin's death, and, even posthumously, he was far more well known in the literary world. Although Willa had published two novels they were largely forgotten by this time, and she "had no real public existence other than as co-translator" (130). Willa Muir was staking her legacy as far as she could without damaging her husband's legacy; if she could not insist on her worth as a writer, she could to some extent as a translator. Nearly twenty years earlier, as she was writing *The Usurpers*, she had written in her journal: "Why are we alive at all? ... Edwin's poems will live. But of himself only a legend. Of me, only a very distorted legend" (St. Andrews MS 38466/5/5 January 13, 1951).

Even in her memoir, as she consolidates this rhetoric of equality, Willa Muir at times falters, "moving between 'I' and 'we' in many of the passages dealing with translation" (Christianson 2007: 125). In many of the passages, too, Willa Muir writes about herself as the main translator, who thus financially enabled Edwin Muir to write. Thus, from 1928 onward:

> it can be taken for granted that I was always translating something and any other work I did was sandwiched between translations ... If there was a troublesome deadline for a translation, and if he had time, he helped with it (Muir 1968, 114–15).

When the Muirs are contracted to translate Lion Feuchtwanger's *Jud Süss*, Edwin Muir is busy with his critical work and "I was getting on as fast as I could with this translation, which was wanted by the month of May" (122) and while he was writing *The Structure of the Novel*, "I had already done a little light translation of two plays by Feuchtwanger" (146) and then when he is contracted to write a: "Life of John Knox. We were going to be up to our ears in work, if we were to earn ourselves the needful leisure for our own writing. So I began, little by little, to do translation again" (146). In terms of her own writing – barely mentioned in the memoir – "any other work I did was sandwiched between translations," it is always put in tertiary position to Edwin's work and her translation which allows him to work: "Edwin's novel was finished, though mine was not, since I was translating" (151). She writes of staying up through the night to finish translations, and adds: "I cannot now tell how I managed to finish a second novel, but it does not surprise me that I lost control of it" (163). She felt her own writing was affected because of financial necessity and the subsequent pressure on her to translate.

On the other hand, she felt that she was successful as a translator and trained for the job. After being approached to translate three Hauptmann plays at a time when they needed the money, Willa Muir writes:

> I was pleased because this was something I felt I could do; I did not know why I had not thought of it before as a possible means of earning money. The many years I had spent translating Greek and Latin into English had given me a sense of competence; I was well trained in accuracy, at least, and that was all to the good, for Edwin's interpretations tended to be wild and gay. We hammered out our blank verse and it was rhythmical enough, but I should not care today to be faced with those translations. When we had finished all three plays and got three hundred dollars we were Rich, with a capital R" (106).

Scheiss and the bowels of translation

Muir conveys a conflicted sense about translation; that it was something she could do and was competent at, but it is also something that has to be "hammered out" for money even if it made them "Rich with a capital R." The "I" changes to "we" and she slips in a little criticism of Edwin's skills as a translator; she has to take control of the translation because his interpretations are "wild and gay." She slips between confidence in her competence and insecurity about the result: "I should not care today to be faced with those translations." But translation was an outlet for Muir's talent for and interest in languages; in 1910 St. Andrew's asked her back to teach Classics, as she had excelled there in Greek and Latin. When the Muirs went to Prague in 1921, Edwin Muir wrote that he "never got very far" in Czech, but that Willa "made enough progress to read one of [Karel] Čapek's plays in the original, as a reward for which he presented her with another play that he had just written" (187). In a charming radio interview (filled with laughter) about their time in Prague, recorded after Edwin's death in 1963, Willa Muir said:

> Edwin took one look at the Czech language and decided he didn't believe it. He couldn't believe it (LAUGH). However, I have a – our other interest in languages, because (NOISES). Classics was my particular line. I had a Classics degree and been doing Latin and Greek for years, and I liked languages anyhow and I couldn't live in a place without learning the language, so I wanted to learn Czech, and I did (St. Andrews MS 38466/2/5).

Her cheeky comment about Edwin refusing to believe a language is followed by an interesting slip, again from the "I" to "we," where she begins to talk about her interest in languages but makes it "our." Then the end of her sentence is lost, before she works back to *her* skills and interest in language. The Muirs moved to Dresden after Prague and then taught at a progressive high school in Hellerau, where they began to learn

German which, "compared with Czech, was generous with clues to its meaning" (Muir 1968: 66). In the radio interview, Willa Muir said that "German was the main common language" between all the international students:

> And that's how I learnt German, that's how Edwin learned German. When you were sitting at meals and you have to ask for a thing in German or not get it, you asked for it in German. And I was teaching in German [...] so German it was, anyhow, everywhere. And we went down at night to the local "pub" and sang popular songs and danced [...] we were all very happy there, and actually one learned a great deal of German. That wasn't the reason for going there, it was one of the by-products. We knew a lot of German (St. Andrews MS 38466/2/5).

The German they picked up as a "by-product" would enable them to live off translation from the end of the 1920s until World War II. But Edwin Muir would write negatively of the experience: "too much of our lives was wasted in the following years turning German into English. It began as a resource and hardened into a necessity" (Muir 1990: 227), he wrote in his *Autobiography*, "we turned ourselves into a sort of translation factory" (222). For him, translation was "a secondary art" (Muirs 1966: 93) in which, inevitably, one would cause "unavoidable injury" to the original text (93). At the outbreak of war, however, their professional translation life was decided for them: "We discovered what we might have foreseen but did not," Willa Muir wrote, "publishers no longer wanted translations from German" (Muir 1968: 205). The patriotic mood against German writing meant serious financial hardship for the couple; but, by the end of the war, Willa Muir said that "the last war prejudiced me, I think, against the German language" (Muirs 1966: 95). Apart from the Kafka fragments, the Muirs did not translate anything after World War II.

Willa Muir wrote in her journal that "the structure of the language we use shapes our attitudes" (St. Andrews MS 38466/6/9) and, at a postwar conference on translation, posed the question: "Could one then deduce Hitler's Reich from the less ruthless shape of the German sentence? I think one could, and I think that is why I have come to dislike [the German language]" (95). She wrote specifically:

> I find myself disliking the purposive control, the will power dominating the German sentence. I dislike its subordination of everything to these hammer-blow verbs; I dislike its weight and its clotted abstractions. I have the feeling that the shape of the German language affects the thought of those who use it and disposes them to overvalue authoritative statement, will power and purposive drive (95).

Muir's linguistic PTSD – the fallout from two wars – goes into more "surreal" territory (Von Flotow 2012: 3), when she adds that "the right image for the German sentence, I suggest, is that of a great gut, a bowel, which deposits at the end of it a sediment of verbs" having noted that "we [should not] forget that the favorite German word of abuse is *Scheiss* [shit]" (Muirs 1966: 96).

Muir's comments do seem surreal, bizarre and prejudiced but they are connected to her thinking about language, power and the patriarchy. She delivered the comments at a translation seminar at Harvard (Edwin was invited to spend a year there in 1955/6), "which was not so enjoyable," she writes, "I remember being bored by the abstract analytical quibbling" (Muir 1968: 300). The papers from the seminar were published, and Muir is the only woman in the collection; the idea that a woman in her mid-sixties in the Harvard of the 1950s was throwing "Scheiss" around gives us a sense of her provocative and rebellious streak.

More importantly, though, was the basis of these arguments in Muir's feelings about how language could be used as an instrument of power. In her talk, Muir questioned whether you could turn "classical German into sound democratic English" (Muirs 1966: 96), suggesting, of course, that the English language was somehow at the basis of British soundness and democracy, proven in the face of fascist Germany. But elsewhere Muir, the native Scot, had her doubts about English too, and its connection to colonialism, war and the patriarchy.

The old wife's grumble

"I'm an old wife, and I want to grumble to you about some voices I hear on the Scottish BBC," Willa Muir wrote in one of her journals – a draft of a letter never sent to the BBC. "It's no' the things that are said that I want to grumble about, but the *way* some of them are spoken" (St. Andrews MS 38466/6/9). Muir was listening to two men speaking in received-pronunciation English and pondering the effect it had on the Scottish female listener (this, after all, was a local BBC station aimed at a Scottish audience). "I aye thought that a talk was a kind of comfortable crack between friends – friends, mind you; and that means no' tryin to bring somebody else down, or to hammer, hammer, hammer something into another person's lug, the way Jael did to Sisera in the Bible," she added, "The tone o' voice is the thing in a crack between friends; it should be a kindly tone, do you no think?, and it shouldna sound like preaching or lecturing" (St. Andrews MS 38466/6/9).

It was not simply the idea that the BBC was imposing a specifically English standard of speech on Scottish listeners, but the violence that lay behind it: "[they] lay *violent e'mphasis on e'very o'ther sy'llable*," she complained:

> And, mind you, it's no an emphasis that makes the meaning clearer, it's just a *mechánical émphasis of évery sécond or third sýllable*, that hurts my ear and makes a hash o' the meaning… I grant you, if you want to frighten anybody, or master anybody the short emphatic syllable is all you need; you can just say Fée, Fí, Fó, Fúm, or 'Shún!, but that kind o barking is surely far removed from the flow of friendly talk. … For if they're unaware o the mechanical violence in their treatment o words, it means that they're used to a world of mechanical violence (St. Andrews MS 38466/6/9).

And that "world of mechanical violence" she understands is one of war. "They've got the habit of it, poor laddies; that's why they dinna notice it," she writes. "Two wars, ay, two wars; and these BBC laddies have grown up among wars. Maybe they dinna notice the machine-gun rattle o their voices because they've been used to the rattle o machine guns" (St. Andrews MS 38466/6/9).

Muir makes an astute connection between the standard, normalized, postwar English and the effect of horrendous violence underneath its rhythms. She answers it in the actual language she grew up in: Scots. Her act of protest is written in that Scots dialect, of which, she adds in her letter of complaint, there are many versions from her own Shetlandic:

> it's very different frae the East coast tune – say, the lilt followed in Aberdeen, where folk begin low down an go up before they come down again, or in Fife, where all the sentences end up high in the air; and naebody could enjoy these differences more than I do. I like to hear them, they're a kind of speech music (St. Andrews MS 38466/6/9).

"Now, you needna think that I'm asking the laddies to croon to me on the wireless," she adds, nor should they "use the kind o creamy gurgling voice that's breathing wi pumped up emotion. Feech, na! I'm just asking for ordinary, kindly, considerate speech, following the lie o the meaning. I'm just saying that words are no wee hard facts like bullets to be shot into folks' lugs."

Willa Muir never sent her complaint to the BBC about the martial, mechanical language that was shot like bullets into folks' lugs. Right underneath her pages-long Scots outburst she rearranged herself in language, by ending in the final sextet of a mock-Shakespearean sonnet in mock-literary English:

> And so, and so, let the loud tongue fall dumb.
> Cease to mock Time with forced, unseemly jests;
> Compose the aching limbs, protuberant bum,
> still more protuberant belly and slack breasts,
> Lay them all down, relax the vertebrae,
> and sleep, old wife, after your too long day (St. Andrews MS 38466/6/9).

Muir metamorphizes from her spirited, highly ironic Scots self into a wry, classicly formed but still very subversive self, not only in the bathetic language of the "bum" and "belly" but also in the form: the use of trochees ("Cease to"; "Compose"; "Lay them") and spondees ("mock Time"; "slack breasts; "old wife") which forcefully challenge the iambic meter. Her "old wife's" body – bum, belly and breasts flop out of the pentameter with an extra syllable, their alliterative unity demanding attention. Seemingly about resignation to invisibility – the pointlessness of old wives' past sexual and reproductive use (bum, belly, breasts) – the form and humor point to rebellion, a chafing against imposed identities – linguistic and sexual.

Letting the loud tongue fall dumb

"My people spoke Shetland at home," Muir writes in her memoir, "so my first words were in the Norse dialect of Shetland, which was not valid outside of our front door" (Muir 1968: 19). As a result the "question of 'belonging' had preoccupied me nearly as far back as I could remember" (19). One of Muir's first memories is being excluded because she speaks a language "*which was not valid outside of our front door*"; an early sense that some languages were associated with the dominant culture and with power, but also an early sense that language was associated with identity, and for both Muirs (Edwin grew up speaking Orcadian), their Scots dialects were connected with each other, with their private identities. "I became 'peerie Willa,'" Muir writes, "and Edwin reverted to his mother's name for him, 'peerie Breeks'. As time went on we shortened these pet names into P. W. and P. B., in the private Orkney language we spoke to each other for the rest of our married lives" (34). English became constitutive of their public selves.

In her memoir, Muir considers Edwin's choice to write in English rather than Scots and how this led to a falling-out with major figures of the Scots Renaissance because of his "flat denial of the gospel according to Hugh MacDiarmid" (195). Edwin "had already adopted English as his language and preferred to graft his poetry on to the great tree of English literature" (115–16), she writes, and he deliberately chose sides, arguing that "After the Reformation, English became the Sunday language for serious thought and reflection while Scots was the language of everyday domestic sentiment, not a whole language but only part of one" (195). From her memoir, it becomes clear that the Muirs, both from modest island backgrounds, acutely felt that they had to adopt English to be accepted into the literary mainstream; Willa tells a story of training Edwin to drop his Orkney 'o' in his speech so that he will be taken seriously as a lecturer (49). "Yet I grieved," she writes, at the "uncharacteristic acerbity of Edwin's remarks about Scotland" (195).

Their Scots backgrounds sometimes did break through to their public lives. *The Scotsman* newspaper, reporting on Edwin Muir's honorary doctorate from Charles University in Prague in May 1947, noted that "It was something of a shock […] to hear a Czech choir singing *Ho Ro, mo Nighean Donn Bhoidheach* – to say nothing of 'Ca' the Yowes tae the Knowes' and other Scots songs" at the British Council. "Dr and Mrs Muir joined in the choruses of the songs," *The Scotsman* reported, "which the Czechs rendered with characteristic verve and almost perfect accent, catching the mischievous spirit of 'Green Grow the Rashes O' and 'Comin' through the Rye,' as well as the gentler rhythm of 'O Can ye Sew Cushions.'" The Czech choir had a good teacher: "Mrs Muir confessed to having coached them in the Gaelic. … It was a very merry evening" (St. Andrews MS 38466/5/9).

The Muirs spent three years in Prague when Edwin Muir worked for the British Council, a time Willa fictionalized in *The Usurpers*. The novel is wrought with the snobberies, put-downs and infighting of the institution (metaphysically akin to the growing political tumult in the country around them, ending with the communist coup). The Muirs, both very popular among the students, never quite fitted in. Willa Muir, who was translating Kafka's stories at the time ("*I finished Kafka*" – St. Andrews MS 38466/5/4: April 28, 1948, her underline, italics added), wrote a poem in her journal – obviously influenced by Kafka – in February 1947 about the "metamorphosis" Edwin had to undergo to work there:

Metamorphosis
My only love, daily I see you change,

donning hard rows of buttons, buckled, braced,
brushed smooth and shaven till you are bare-faced,
and then disguised with large and horn-rimmed glasses,

shod, scarved and spatted,
gloved and behatted,
lined with edged note-books for your students' classes, –
should I not find this frightening and strange?
(St. Andrews MS 38466/5/2).

Muir again (like her semi-sonnet) writes in literary English to describe this English transformation, change, metamorphosis. The abundance of plosives in the poem gives it the "hard rows" of sound, which makes this dressing seem like an encasing that is "frightening and strange" – bringing to mind Kafka's insect shell – but it is an encasing that Muir is encountering in her own use of the language.

Muir's connection of literary English and the English language with formality, disguise and distance appears in a stark comment on her reaction to hearing about Edwin's brief infidelity with a student in Hellerau in the 1920s: "In as level a voice as I could command, speaking in English, not in Orkney, I told him that we had not made our marriage to be a cage for either of us" (Muir 1968: 83). Her reversion to English at the moment when she thought her marriage might be over underlines the meaning of Scots as an articulation of their identities in that marriage. It also shows her putting on the tough shell it offered.

Englished

If the Muirs chose English as their public and literary language, they realized that their publishers in London would also expect a certain form of English in any translations they published. Their break-out translation – a bestselling success – was with Leon Feuchtwanger's *Jud Süss*. "I cannot say that we translated *Jud Süss*," Willa Muir writes, "what we produced was a polished rendering" (125). The Muirs realized that any authors, especially unknown ones like Kafka, might have to be domesticated to find an English publisher and audience. Dependent on translation income, they had to be judicious in pleasing the tastes of the publisher. But after their "wildly successful" (Simon 1996: 77) translation of *Jud Süss*, Willa Muir wrote that they did try to be more faithful to Feuchwanger's style when they translated another of his novels. It was a financial flop. "In one sense it was a good translation," Muir writes, "but it was not destined to be a popular success. The British public, presented with authentic Feuchtwanger, did not take to him" (Muir 1968: 134).

It is important to note Muir's self-awareness about the need to domesticate the German-language writers they were translating for the "British public" and to note that it was not necessarily the way they might wish to translate, had they not been dependent on translation for money to live. Always pragmatic, Willa Muir accepted this, in the same way that she accepted having to write in English – with some conflict and a sense of paradox. She knows the second translation is "a good translation" and "authentic" but she also knows what is expected in terms of British "good style." In addition, her husband's reputation was growing as a reviewer and a poet; the perceived literary quality of the translations would reflect on his writing skills, since everyone assumed he was the translator.

"They opted for the natural surface rather than for the unnatural undercurrent," Joyce Crick writes about the Muirs's Kafka translations (Crick 1981: 167). This "naturalness," she argues, is actually related to Edwin's literary endeavors because he wanted to produce a "literary language" (164) "which reads not as English translation but as *translatable* English" (163). Edwin Muir's self-consciousness about language from his Orkney background, she argues, found affinities in Kafka's own "problematic linguistic and cultural situation" (164) and that both Kafka and Edwin Muir "search[ed] for a literary language [...] they both developed, Kafka supremely, towards a sobriety and clarity which strike one as interchangeable; hence what emerges from Muir's renderings reads 'naturally' as 'literature' and not as 'translation'" (164-5).

The "naturalness" of Edwin's translations is only upset by "the lively Willa's contribution" (166); whereas Edwin's diction – in affinity to Kafka's – is "restrained and general," Willa "turns a dusty 'Rumpelkammer' into a glorious Scottish 'glory-hole'" (166). When Edwin uses the word "shilly-shallying" in a translation from "The Great Wall of China" Crick writes, "I would like to think that that was slipped in by a brilliant lady with a penchant for music-hall songs, who had no fundamental doubts" (166) – the brilliant lady being, of course, Willa Muir. Although "[t]here is no proving it" Crick implies that "the Muirs' vocabulary is more vivid than Kafka's neutral speech" when Willa gets her hands on the translation. Crick mentions in passing Willa Muir's own experience with "language as problematic" because of her "domestic Shetlandic vernacular [...] mocked on the mainland" but dismisses it because of Willa Muir's pragmatism: "her [Willa's] response was one of confident adaptability" (as opposed to Edwin's artistic struggle to "acquire a new language so readily") (164). Willa Muir's glory-hole and shilly-shallying are mistakes, in Crick's eyes, that Edwin would not make as he strove for a smooth, natural literary language pared down and neutral like Kafka's.

But how much of this "naturalness," "natural surface" and new "literary language" is natural? Why is "literature" and not "translation" "natural" when it is clearly as much an artifice? In essence, the Muirs had to produce a "natural" Kafka for the "British public" even though their own relationship to the norms of English literary language was problematic and part of a colonial discourse. Willa Muir acquired new languages "readily" because she was trained to, even forced to, from elementary school onward. She understood from an early age that language was associated with power and with what was "valid outside the front door." There was nothing "natural" about the Muirs's decision to translate a smooth, domesticated English Kafka by a poor, Scots couple, "neither of [whom were] likely to be conformists in Britain" (136).

Crick, like every other critic writing about the Muirs's translations, assumes that Edwin was "THE translator" because, Crick argues, of his "restrained and general" diction in his poetry that is reflected in the translations (166). The only "contributions" "the lively Willa" makes are judged to be mistakes, examples of overtranslating, even though Crick quotes Willa Muir from her memoir insisting on the egalitarian translation relationship. But what about these two examples that Crick cites to back up her suspicion of Willa's negative and misleading influence – the "glory-hole" and "shilly-shallying," both of which are connected to a specifically Scottish and Northern English meaning and provenance that seem to irrupt into the "natural" English in the translations?

The first example comes from diary entries by Kafka that Willa Muir published under her name in 1945. Kafka was writing about his desk and the disorder it was in, comparing the letters and postcards, and tie and shaving brush sticking out of the desk to a theater; one pigeonhole on the desk is jammed with

> old papers [...] pencils with broken points, an empty match-box, a paperweight from Karlsbad, a ruler with an edge the unevenness of which would be awful even for a country road, a lot of collar buttons, used razor blades (for these there is no place in the world), tie clips and still another heavy iron paperweight" (Kafka 33).

This pigeonhole:

> already hemmed in by the small closed drawers, is nothing but a lumber-room [Rumpelkammer], as though the first balcony of the auditorium, really the most visible part of the theatre, were reserved for the most vulgar of people, for old men-about-town in whom the dirt gradually moves from the inside to the outside, rude fellows who let their feet hang over the balcony railing (33).

Kafka's description of the detritus of his writing and his working life, sticking out and visible on his desk, is evocative of the process and physical actuality of writing. Both the motif of the desk (especially in *Amerika*) and of the theater run through his writing: here, the comparison of the two belie a humorous anxiety about what should not be seen in a finished text – the reality of the process and struggle of writing, and the impact of the physical and incidental world on that reality. It is also a colorful and expressive description, full of lists and excess, as the subject is itself excess. If it hems around the idea of the writing life it is also suggestive of the translation workshop too, the impossibility of keeping everything in and neatly stored away in the translated text, which always has the "rude fellows who let their feet hang over the balcony railing" bringing attention to misprisions, misunderstandings and untranslatable terms. Willa Muir's use of "glory-hole" dangles its feet over the railing, but it is a valid – if Scottish – description of a "Rumpelkammer" (i.e., a room into which everything gets thrown (in Scotland it denoted a cupboard, usually under the stairs, a wonderful name, tinged with irony)). The term may be outdated; "glory-hole" is now more associated with a form of sexual activity – a hole bored into toilet cubicles for anonymous sex – than with Scottish under-stairs cupboards, but at the time Muir's choice was not necessarily a mistake, but it was culturally specific.

In incisive recent appraisals of Scots translation by scholars such as Bill Findlay (2004), John Corbett (1999) and Martin Bowman (2000), the act of translating into the vernacular is presented as a "political act" (Bowman 2000: 27) that questions the asymmetric division between "standard" and "demotic" languages (26) and tries to escape the colonial bind in which English is the serious and "standard" language. As the Muirs were translating, writers of the Scots Renaissance were deliberately employing translation into Scots as a means of enriching a Scots tradition (Findlay 2004: 2). The Muirs publicly rejected the aims of the Scots Renaissance, but Scots was their private language and the vestiges of that Scots tradition shown in choices like "glory-hole" speak perhaps to an inability to completely repress that tradition in Willa Muir's translation practice.

The choice of "shilly-shallying" perhaps speaks more to an English literary tradition, one with roots in Restoration plays but also in Northern England and Ireland. The OED marks the first appearance of a similar phrase in William Congreve's play *Way of the World* in 1700 and then of the phrase in Richard Steele's play *Tender Husband* in 1703. Both Congreve and Steele grew up in Ireland (Steele was born there, Congreve was born in Yorkshire), although of English and Anglo-Irish stock. Although it seems to be a demotic term when the Muirs use it, it is in fact a term steeped in British literature (used by Thackeray and Frances Burney) introduced into that literature by playwrights with Irish roots. The Muirs used it in translating one of Kafka's aphorisms, which they first published in *The Great Wall of China and Other Pieces* (1946). Crick notes "quite soberly and rightly" (Crick 1981: 166), as "There is a goal, but no way; what we call the way is wavering" but this then changed in Edwin Muir's "Introductory Note" to *America* (1938) to "What we call the way is only shilly-shallying" (166). Although Edwin Muir wrote the introduction and the translation was solely attributed to him, Crick suggests that Willa "slipped in" the "shilly-shallying" because of her colorful and lively nature (166). Of course, as we have seen from *America*'s publisher's letter above, Crick may be right about Willa Muir's influence, since they actually attribute the *America* translation to her, albeit secretly. But the phrase "shilly-shallying" does not necessarily come from her "penchant for music-hall songs," thus denoting a quirky unthinking mistake. Rather it seems connected to a British literary tradition that has its roots in its slightly subversive colonial edges. In this case, the tone may not match Kafka's original stark aphorism, but it is a deliberate and interesting choice – rather than rushed mistake – on Muir's part.

The fact that the Muirs's translations are generally in a standard and domesticated English speaks volumes about the pressures they were under and the choices they had to make to be part of a mainstream literary tradition that paid and enabled them to survive. The "mistakes" also speak volumes as points of contact with a private linguistic world of "peerie Willa" and "peerie Beekes" that strove to keep out the patriarchal, warlike underpinnings of a colonial language.

Auf! Auf!

The only partial MSS of a translation in Willa Muir's archive are three-and-a-half pages of the fragments from *Amerika* that Robert M. Macgregor at New Directions had asked her to do in 1960 after Edwin's death, since he understood "that you were largely responsible for the original translation" (St. Andrews MS 38466 N/1: June 22, 1960). They cover the wonderfully burlesque scene of Brunelda in the bath, and Karl Rossman's initiation into the demands of being her slave. The usually indolent Irishman, Robinson, scurries around trying to show Karl his duties, while the near-naked Delamarche washes Brunelda in her bath behind a screen. It is slapstick and sexual. The few pages give some idea of Willa Muir's process of translation, and perhaps thinking behind a domestication of Kafka's text. It is striking, at first glance, that the first page is heavily edited, gone over, while the next two and a half are not as much, suggesting Muir getting into her stride as she translates.

The question of domestication comes up in the very first paragraph, when Robinson shouts at Karl to get up to witness Robinson's unusual frenzy in doing tasks Karl will have to undertake:

"Get up! get up!" cried Robinson, before Karl's eyes were well open in the morning. The Venetian blind had not been drawn up, but one could tell from the level sunbeams shining between the slats how late the hour was already. Robinson was busy running to and fro with anxious looks, carrying now a towel, now a bucket of water, now items of underwear and clothing, and every time he passed Karl he urged him with a jerk of the head to get up, and displayed whatever he was holding in his hand as a sign that this was the last time he was going to bother showing him the details of his duties he could not be expected to know on this very first morning (St. Andrews MS 38466/6/6).

"Auf! Auf!" rief Robinson, kaum daß Karl früh die Augen öffnete. Der Türvorhang war noch nich weggezogen, aber man merkte an dem durch die Lücken einfallenden gleichmäßigen Sonnenlicht, wie spat am Vormittag es schon war. Robinson life eilfertig mit besorgten Blicken hin und her, bald trug er ein Handtuch, bald einen Wasserkübel, bald Wäsche- und Kleidungsstücke und immer wenn er an Karl vorüberkam, suchte er ihn durch Kopfnicken zum Aufstehn aufzumuntern und zeigte durch Hochheben dessen war er gerade in der Hand hielt, wie er sich heute noch zum letzen mal für Karl plage, der natürlich am ersten Morgen von den Einzelheiten des Dienstes nichts verstehen konnte (Kafka 1994: 274).

What stands out immediately is Muir's translation of "Türvorhang" as "Venetian blind" and, consequently, "die Lücken" as "slats" which seems to particularly date the translation in the new domestic fashion of the Venetian blind in the late 1950s and 1960s, and which is a liberal translation of curtains hanging on a door. But, interestingly, Muir adds "Venetian blind" in as an edit:

The ~~door-curtain~~ Venetian blind had not been drawn ~~aside~~ up, but one could tell from the ~~steadiness of the~~ level ~~sunlight~~beams shining ~~through~~ between the ~~gaps~~ slats how late the hour was already (St. Andrews MS 38466/6/6).

We see Muir second-guessing or "smoothing out" the translation in the edits for her English-language readership – also evident in her change of "Sonnenlicht" from the straightforward "sunlight" to the more lyrical "sunbeams." The use of "Venetian blind" is clearly not a mistake or an odd, colorful phrase randomly thrown in; Muir knows what the literal translation of "Türvorhang" is (and, having lived in Europe, would have encountered them), but we can see her thinking about the readership of the translation here and over-domesticating the translation accordingly. Another example appears in the next paragraph when Karl realizes that "eine große Waschung" is underway, a quite arch and humorous description of Brunelda's bath. Muir initially translates this as "a grand bath" but the use of "bath" is too prosaic: Michael Hofmann translates this as "great ablutions" (Kafka 2002a: 184) and Mark Harman as "a great washing" (Kafka 2008a: 242). Muir changes her initial translation to "a grand tubbing" which seems archaically British (and possibly Scots) but, though it is a domestication, the oddness of the term conveys some sense of Karl's unusual and funny view of the ritual.

At the same time, what is striking about the initial paragraph is Muir's sense of the rhythm of the first paragraph in the initial and edited version of the translation. Karl is woken up abruptly by Robinson; he measures the time by the sunlight; and then Robinson's actions are described in a long, unbroken sentence, the pace of which conveys the speed – wholly out of character – of his acts. The speed and slapstick nature of the scene is also indicated by the "to and fro/hin und her" and the repetition of "now/bald":

> Robinson was busy running to and fro with anxious looks, carrying now a towel, now a bucket of water, now items of underwear and clothing, and every time he passed Karl he urged him with a jerk of the head to get up, and displayed whatever he was holding in his hand as a sign that this was the last time he was going to bother showing him the details of his duties he could not be expected to know on this very first morning (St. Andrews MS 38466/6/6).

It shows that Muir was not deaf to the rhythmic tone or the humor of the passage. Although it is a sentence that could invite domestication in English by being broken up into shorter sentences, Muir understands the impact of it. She also catches a little bit of the exasperated tone (funny because it goes against Robinson's indolent nature) at the end, which she had initially translated as: "this was the last time he was going to bother to show him the details of his duties he could not understand on this very first morning." In changing this to "this was the last time he was going to bother showing him the details of his duties he could not be expected to know on this very first morning" Muir heightens the irony in Robinson's unexpected diligence and his bizarre worship of Brunelda.

Delamarche is bathing Brunelda behind two chests, and the narrator tells us, via Karl, only what we can see and hear of "the great tubbing" from the subsequently limited view:

> Man sah den Kopf Bruneldas, den freien Hals – das Haar war gerade ins Gesicht geschlagen – und den Ansatz inhres Nackens über den Kasten ragen und die hie und da gehobene Hand des Delamarche hielt einen weit herumspritzenden

Badeschwamm, mit dem Brunelda gewaschen und gerieben wurde. Man hörte die kurzen Befehle des Delamarche ... (Kafka 1994: 274).

The limitations of view the narrator marks are set up by the repetition of "Man" – "Man sah" and "Man hörte" – which gives a nicely odd and voyeuristic sense to the passage; Brunelda's gigantic but apparently irresistible body is seen in parts. There is something of a lyrical euphony in the passage (the alliteration of "h" and "g") that adds humor because of the strangeness of the situation. Muir translates it as:

> Brunelda's head – the back of her bare neck – her hair was tumbled right over her face – the beginning of her nape showed over the chests, and every now and then Delamarche's hand rose into view holding a widely-dripping bath sponge with which she was being washed and scrubbed. One could hear the curt orders Delamarche ... (St. Andrews MS 38466/6/6).

Muir conveys the lengthy syntax that takes in the length of Karl's look at the action; he is seeing her bit by bit, along with Delamarche's hand and voice appearing. She had initially translated this as a passive construction: "Over the top of the chests, Brunelda's head was visible" which diluted that action of looking, but her edited translation, though more active, sacrifices the repetition of "Man sah"/"One could see" or "You could see" with "Man hörte" that showcases the acts of seeing and hearing for the sake of domestic style. Muir also changes the second mention of Brunelda by name; in her initial draft she writes: "bath sponge with which Brunelda was being washed and scrubbed," probably to avoid the repetition of the name for the sake of good English style, but the repetition of Brunelda's name is important because of her objectification in the passage.

What is harder to translate is the ironically lyrical tone of the passage. Michael Hofmann does an excellent job here:

> You could see Brunelda's head, her bare throat – the hair had just been pushed into her face – and the nape of her neck, over the chest of drawers, and Delamarche's raised hand waving in and out of view, holding a liberally dripping bath sponge, with which Brunelda was being scrubbed and washed. You could hear the short commands Delamarche ... (Kafka 2002a:184)

Hofmann cannot replicate the exact same alliteration of the German – instead here we see alternative alliteration: "Brunelda's head, her bare ... the hair had ... her ... nape of her neck ... holding a liberally dripping bath sponge." The two six-syllable clauses "and the nape of her neck" and "over the chest of drawers" rhythmically set up Delamarche's hand waving "in and out of view" followed by the plosives in the next clause. It is very intricately constructed and redolent of the tension between lyricism and irony in Kafka's German.

Repetition is important in the passage – not only in the constant repetition of "chests"/"Kasten" – the objects that are hiding Brunelda from complete view – but in the comic repetition of action: "Every requisite for washing and dressing that in Karl's opinion should be needed once only," Muir translates, "was here demanded and provided time after time in every possible sequence"/"Alles was man sonst nach Karls Meinung zum Waschen und Anziehn nur einmal brauchte, wurde hier in jeder möglichen Reihenfolge viele Male verlangt und gebracht" (275). Muir translates "viele Male"/"many times" quite thoughtfully here as "time after time," giving a sense of those nonsensically repeated actions that end in the exasperated Robinson throwing a scrunched-up shirt over the chests.

The objectification of Brunelda is subverted by Brunelda's confusing magnetism, her seeming ability to enslave men despite her non-traditional beauty. The sinister Delamarche is reduced to soaping her in his underpants, and though Brunelda complains of his violent methods of scrubbing, she is clearly in control, teasing him by suggesting either Robinson or "the youngster" could take his place. Brunelda's methods of manipulation come across beautifully in her monologue from the bath:

> "Oh!" she shrieked, and even Karl, who was keeping out of it all, could not help jumping, "How you are hurting me! Go away! I'd rather wash myself than suffer like this! Now I can't lift my arm again. I'm all aching, the way you're punching me. My back must be black and blue all over. Of course, you wouldn't think of telling me. Wait, I'll get Robinson to look at it, or our youngster. No, I won't really do that, but do be a little less rough. Do be careful, Delamarche, though I can keep telling you that every morning and you'll never, never be careful – Robinson!" she cried out suddenly and waved flimsy lace-trimmed drawers over her head. "Come to my rescue, look what I have to suffer, this torture is what he calls washing, this Delamarche! Robinson, Robinson, where are you, are you quite heartless too?" (St. Andrews MS 38466/6/6).

Muir's Brunelda sounds quite stentorian in a formal English style ("How you are hurting me!"; "I'd rather wash myself"; "do be a little less rough"; "do be careful"; "are you quite heartless?") but it echoes the quite clipped nature of Brunelda's speech in German, comic because it comes from "the great tubbing" and is interspersed by Brunelda "wav[ing] flimsy lace-trimmed drawers over her head"/"schwenkte ein Spitzenhöschen über ihrem Kopf" (Kafka 1994: 275). Michael Hofmann, in fact, emphasizes that clipped English tone in his translation, translating "unserem Kleinen" (275) as "the little new chap" (Kafka 2002a: 185) and "ein Spitzenhöschen" as "frilly knickers" (185). Notable about the domestication in this instance is that formal English is being used for comic effect, but it is quite a black and sinister comedy: Brunelda is powerful but also sinister and bullying. Muir emphasizes the power by adding a couple of exclamation points when Brunelda addresses both Robinson and Delamarche, underscoring these clipped, perhaps even arguably colonial, tones. Robinson – the Irishman – refuses to go to Brunelda, although Karl is silently pointing to him to answer her, because, he tells Karl, he fell for it before and Brunelda and Delamarche had tried to drown him.

Though this one brief example of a translation manuscript in Muir's own hand shows no unfettered Scots experimentalism, it does show her professionalism and savvy: she clearly understands what is expected of her and what sort of language is expected of her. It also suggests – beyond the publisher's letter admitting that she was the actual translator of *Amerika* – that she was clearly capable of producing a translation that was not simply a mythically literal translation from the German – to be tidied up by her husband – nor was she the "lively Willa" persuading him to introduce anomalies or mistakes. She clearly understands the importance of Kafka's syntactical rhythm and the importance of repetition in the passage – instances of which she could have further domesticated and did not. She also clearly understands Kafka's humor – something the Muirs have been accused of completely misunderstanding – here conveying the slapstick nature of the passage, and also the sexual humor heightened, and subverted, by Brunelda's clipped colonial commands.

"Brunelda is a monster of sex," Milan Kundera writes, "on the borderline between the repugnant and the exciting, and men's admiring cries are not only comic (they *are* comic, to be sure, sex *is* comic!) but at the same time entirely true" (Kundera 1996: 48). Kundera castigates Brod, "that romantic worshiper of women," for seeing "no truth to Brunelda" (48) because of her baseness, her sexy ugliness, and men's fallibilities. Physical love cannot be funny in Brod's scheme of things, where beauty is sainthood, but it can in Muir's. The translator who wrote a subversive sonnet in her colonial tongue to her "bum" and "breasts" writes movingly in her journal when she is in her late fifties about waking up, after dreaming of trains "with an orgasm." "The morning before," she adds, "I had flutterings inside me, twice, when E. squeezed my hand tenderly, so I was in a receptive state" (MS 38466/5/2: January 14, 1947). In Prague, and translating Kafka's stories, Muir agonized over the anomaly of being ignored and desexualized because of her age and gender while still a sentient sexual and intellectual being – the dark side of the "monster of sex." "Queer that it should be important to wash one's hair and powder face and dress neatly, that one's appearance should be a reality," Muir writes a few months later in her journal:

> For it is. If I neglect my appearance I look ugly, and Edwin sees that I am ugly, and insensibly is affected by the fact. Even queerer that, left to myself, I <u>am</u> ugly; queer, because I don't <u>feel</u> ugly. I feel that I am an attractive interesting well meaning me, so I don't feel ugly. Yet I look ugly without some care. I think probably I always did (MS 38466/5/2: June 13, 1947).

She writes a poem in her journal at this time called "Address to Edwin," turning her sense of physical invisibility into, at first, a lighthearted joke: "I hope that old age makes me merely comic,/a funny, fat old woman with false teeth," but that becomes darker:

> I was not born to be a comic figure,
> but life has changed me into one at last.
> I hope, my love, you will not find one tedious
> although my double chins are doubling fast (MS 38466/5/2: April 10, 1947).

Muir's self-deprecating humor only barely glosses over her acute sense of the cultural invisibility of the older woman, an outsider and a joke, in her mind, because of their lack of usefulness in a male-oriented society (no longer seen as sexual or nubile or fertile). Muir fulminates against the need for older women to button up in public

– unlike the naked, gigantic Brunelda wiggling her "flimsy lace-trimmed drawers" over her head – and the need to be powdered and washed and dressed neatly. Just before mentioning her orgasm, she writes:

> In a society with a stable tradition unthinking people are always maddeningly sure of what to expect from others: behaviour becomes for them simply a cliché. "Spoken like a true gentleman." "No lady would do such a thing." "Most unEnglish!" "Just what you would expect from someone of that class." And dress is proscribed by convention as well as behaviour. Consequently foreigners seem always to be "outsiders" in dress and behaviour. Allowance, of course, is made for them; they are only foreigners. But for thinking individuals born in the country no allowance is made; they find it difficult to behave with natural spontaneity unless they do not mind being classed as eccentric, if not rank outsiders (MS 38466/5/2).

No lady would do such a thing. Most unEnglish! Someone of that class. The working-class Scots feminist is acutely aware of the subterfuge and disguises of belonging to the literary and cultural mainstream circles. Foreigners are only foreigners – Brunelda can be appreciated for her outré behavior, even while speaking her clipped English, because she is a foreign invention – but "thinking individuals born in the country" like, of course, Muir herself, cannot "behave with natural spontaneity unless they do not mind being classed as eccentric, if not rank outsiders." What she does with language is the equivalent, trying to repress the "natural spontaneity" and to fit in to gain respect. But what she discovers is that this metamorphosis into a neat, elderly woman, in effect, makes her invisible.

The Top Storey

There is a note jotted in the corner of one of Muir's notebooks, under the word "translator":

> "intellectual bi-location"
> mentioned with surprise as a feat – being yourself and another
> women do naturally (St. Andrews MS 38466/6/16).

Muir strongly felt that this "being yourself and another" was necessary for women in a patriarchal society and that this experience ("women do naturally") made women more sensitive to being in another's skin, the "intellectual bi-location" necessary for translation. Muir's thoughts about the translator, specifically the female translator, are given more extended consideration in her unpublished novel *Mrs Muttoe and the Top Storey*. The largely autobiographical novel is set in the Muirs's Hampstead years (1932–5) when they were back in London, existing on translation work, and was completed in 1940 when they were living in St. Andrews, and just before Willa Muir had her breakdown and Edwin Muir's subsequent religious conversion.

Although flawed, and unpublished, *Mrs Muttoe*, like other modernist novels, follows a character, Alison Muttoe, via "narrative introversion" (Fletcher and Bradbury

1991: 395) in her mundane life through "the literary construction of the inner self that Modernism offered her, and the psychoanalytical model of identity" (Elphinstone 1997: 406). Valuable in itself as the portrait of a female translator in the modernist period, and insightful of Willa Muir's working practices as a translator, it is also somewhat written against the grain of its superficial realist and linear narrative. While Christianson thinks it "may fail as a novel because its narrative line consists of the fairly uneventful life of Alison and [her husband] Dick over a few months, interspersed with Alison's resentful ruminations on modernity, London, gender, 'meditating on the queerness of being a woman'" (Christianson 2007: 143), the narrative contains a circular motion counterpointing its surface linearity that is more experimental and which centers around Alison Muttoe's search for a cook housekeeper, or, in her words, "a wife" (St. Andrews MS 38466/1/2: 13), to care for domestic issues while she translates so that her husband can write. The narrative of the novel follows a rhythm defined by the hiring and dismissal of these servants. Margaret Elphinstone strongly criticizes Muir for what she sees as a condescending attitude in her portrayal of these servants (Elphinstone 1997: 411) and Christianson for portraying Alison as only able to think in circles (Christianson 2007: 144), both seeing this as indicative of Muir's essentialist feminism. Yet Muir's point is very contemporary, that the rhythms of the professional female are: first, often tied into and defined by "uneventful" domestic rhythms; and second, are often dependent on the labor of other women; the servants in her novel are as they are because they are caught in the trap of modern capitalistic patriarchy, just as Alison Muttoe is. The only time she has to herself is night-time, dream and the unconscious.

Christianson does write that "there are aspects of [the novel] that show an interesting relationship to modernist preoccupations" (144), notably the mix in narrative style "everyday realism interwoven with social satire and indications of nightmare worlds" (145) – it is worth noting that Muir was also translating Hermann Broch at this time, as well as housing him as he fled Nazi Austria – and its "suitably discordant representation of modern life, noisy, dehumanized, and uncontrollable" (145). There are two dream-like sequences in the novel that reflect and refract the realist preoccupation with women's work that are "Kafkaesque" (146). Christianson writes that this is "an interesting footnote to Muir's own feelings about working on Kafka whose *Great Wall of China* they were 'to get out' at this time" (146); yet I would argue that it is more than "a footnote"; rather, an engagement with Kafka's themes and aesthetics.

The novel is particularly influenced by *The Castle*. Mrs Muttoe begins with the arrival of a potential housekeeper who is also something of a con-artist, and somewhat of an unreliable narrator, who views the Scottish couple, Alison and Dick Muttoe, as potential marks. This use of an unreliable narrator, the subsequent cyclical structure surrounding the arrival and departure of female servants, and the final descent into an oneiric narrative suggest a reading of K., the various female servants he encounters, the cyclical nature of story-telling and exegetical narrative in *The Castle*, and the oneiric quality of the novel. Kafka also appears in the novel under the name "Garta." Alison pursues translation work throughout the novel, both of the hated "Rheingold" – a thinly disguised Lion Feuchtwanger – and of her much beloved "Garta" (Garta is the name of Brod's fictionalized Kafka in his novel *The Kingdom of Love*). As opposed to the grunt work of the Rheingold translation, translating Garta makes her "fanciful":

> Garta's work seemed to come straight out of the region which evoked dreams and nightmares. He showed an uncanny skill in describing the twists and turns of frustrated feelings; merely to read him was like having an anxiety dream by proxy. And every incident in his ~~imagery~~ stories, almost every phrase, carried so many implications that the translation had to be done slowly, with extreme care.
>
> Yes, Garta is making me fanciful, decided Alison Muttoe, opening her jotter. I'm turning into a creature like the Princess in the fable, who couldn't sleep because of a single hard pea under a dozen mattresses (St. Andrews MS 38466/1/2: 252–3).

The "single hard pea" of metaphysical discomfort turns Mrs. Muttoe suddenly into a dream narrative in which Alison is catapulted into a bizarre web-like glassy fabric structure called "the Money fabric" (257) where women are defined on different "storeys" of this world, dependent on the earnings of their husbands and who all seem to know the rules, except for Alison who has been thrust into this world of alternate and indecipherable boundaries, much like Josef K. in *The Trial* and K. in *The Castle*, where the women, too, are conduits and messengers.

Muir also plays with the idea of an inscrutable and invisible command structure in the Muttoes's house, not unlike the castle in Kafka's novel. Alison sees her house as divided between the "Top Storey" of the house, where her husband Dick has his office, and "the Centre" where the domestic activities take place. But she also anthropomorphizes the house, in which the "Top Storey" represents the brain, and "the Centre" some kind of mystical soul. For Alison, Dick "lived too much in his top storey" both physically and mentally, isolated in his office and in his own brain and failing to understand where the real power lay: "How easy for the official in the top storey, the head official, to imagine himself and independent autocrat!" Alison thinks, but:

> The routine work of the building was looked after by the Centre, a mysterious, invisible agency housed somewhere in the windowless part of the structure. The Centre, it was understood, had appointed the head official, and he was responsible to it, although it remained for him a capricious, not to say enigmatic authority (99).

The "capricious, not to say enigmatic authority" is associated with the soul and femininity (the women engaged in the "routine work of the building") and, at first, this seems an essentialist reading of gender with the logical, male brain and the soulful place of feelings a female "windowless" place. But it is the "Centre" that "had appointed the head official"; if Dick is the patriarch, he is still there only at the will of the "Centre"; if he chooses to "sit in splendid isolation" away from that "Centre", then "all the chutes would get choked, messengers piling up, head official would have to assert his authority, silence!" (100). "And what then?" Alison asks. "How long could the autocrat in the top storey hold his fort against the Centre?":

Sooner or later, for instance, the Centre might quietly fill the top storey with a drowsy gas, so that the autocrat, hypnotised into non-resistance, would unlock the doors and fall helplessly asleep across his desk. He would waken the next morning to find his papers sifted through and re-arranged, new reports on top of the old, maps re-drawn, conclusions queried, grievances re-stated. ... A text in crude lettering might even had been mounted over his desk, saying:

"Intellectuals of the World, unite; you have nothing to lose but your brains."

Alison chuckled to herself as she considered the scene. The Centre in human beings was well able to remind top-storey autocrats that they were interpreters and not dictators (101).

The subversive gassing of the autocrats in the top storey to remind them that "they were interpreters and not dictators" speaks to the exegetical momentum of *The Castle*, in which K. the putative land-surveyor ("maps re-drawn") is constantly forced into positions of interpretation in a world full of desks, papers, texts, maps. The top storey autocrat might be "equipped, like a detective, with every device that could help him to interpret what was happening outside the building or within in" but he still cannot decipher what is going on in the enigmatic "Centre," and fails to understand that the house, or the house of the body, is being run from there.

"Dick … lived too much in his top storey," Alison says, and throughout the novel Dick Muttoe keeps isolating himself in his office to write, while Alison, who has an office downstairs, is constantly interrupted by her son, her servants, her visitors, the dog. While she has to deal with these domestic interruptions, Dick was "already withdrawing himself in spirit towards his study, a bare room on the top floor, containing little save an electric heater and a view of the sky" (15). She envies him being able to "withdraw himself so effortlessly, so completely, from his surroundings" (15) but she cannot because of her physical space at the Centre:

> Her study was at once more accessible to intrusion and more crowded. It communicated with the living-room by a pair of folding doors, gave on the back garden and besides a desk planted in the middle of the floor harboured a sewing-machine, an odd sofa, a shabby Morris chair, a couple of small book-cases and four deck chairs leaning against a wall" (15).

"The Centre" of the household is the messy heart of the enterprise, and, most definitely, a female domain, where Alison works, mothers their child, and runs the household. It is a center both of strife but also what Alison calls "loving-kindness," a quality that is suppressed outside of the home in the capitalist, patriarchal world but one that can be fostered by women within their four walls: "she looked upon the Home as an oasis in a desert of mercenary values" (31). For Alison, "cherishing" (133) her husband, son, and servants is a job that produces results, but is "unpaid," unlike translating which she does and which keeps the family going in a material sense:

> But the translation!
> Mrs. M began to count pages. No, the translation results were meagre. ~~Utterly inadequate~~. She wasn't even earning her keep.

> Damn money, said Mrs. M to herself, beginning to translate at high speed.
> "Damn money," she repeated later to her husband. "The activities I get paid for don't seem to me nearly so important as those I don't get paid for. This book of Rheingold's I'm translating, for instance, isn't even a good book of its kind. I'm translating it well; I'm putting a polish on it; but that only means putting a gloss on what is essentially cheap wood. It wouldn't be worth doing but for the money."
> "I know, darling. All the same, it will sell a good deal more that my book of essays," commented Dick M ruefully.
> That was the problem. The delicacy and clarity of Dick's literary gifts delighted only a small circle of appreciative readers (133).

At first, Alison's insistence that a female "loving-kindness" could change the world seems reactionary, smacking a little of essentialist presumptions about women's soulful and mystical powers, but Muir's representation has its complexities. Alison is reacting to the world she sees around her, one that values male-defined productivity. Even though Dick's "literary gifts" only delight "a small circle of appreciative readers" his work on the "top storey" is predicated on the work of his wife at "the Centre", and, lower down in the house, on the labor of women in the kitchen and cleaning the house. The women, in Alison's and Willa Muir's eyes, provide the glue to keep the mechanism of the house moving, both practically and spiritually. Translation, in this schema, is the one labor that Alison can get paid for in material terms, and it keeps her husband alive and able to write; in fact, her Rheingold (Feuchtwanger) translation is more materially valuable than Dick's work.

In her memoir, Muir writes about the antipathy to Edwin Muir's poetry in their Hampstead period (the time and setting of the novel); "he was swimming against the currents" and "went on writing his unfashionable poems" (167). His poems were "disparaged" and "sent ... right down the drain" by critics (167), but he carried on: "In his study at the top of the house which contained only a table, a chair, an ink-pot and a fine view over roofs and tree-tops, Edwin now and then produced a poem" (162). Meanwhile, "Translation went on busily [...] but many hours of hard work were needed to earn a sizeable sum" (162). Muir's use of the impersonal ("Translation went on ...") turns into her writing about those hours of hard work: "*I* reverted to a student habit of mine, working at furious speed late at night and into the small hours ... *I* sat up all night ... but *I* did this only when a translation had to be finished in a hurry" (163, italics added). During the day her office was "intruded upon at all hours by household staff, the weekly washerwoman, any casual caller ready for a gossip, and Gavin [their son]" (162). She "envied" Edwin his ability "to concentrate in solitude on what he wanted to do" (163).

The second chapter of *Mrs Muttoe* is taken up with interruptions; each time Alison sits down to work in her cluttered office, someone knocks on the door and wants something from her. In an interesting way, Muir is at once trying to portray the reality of life for a woman (and, more unusually for the 1930s, a professional woman juggling household and career) in all its mundanity while also, in some ways, a reference to the public nature of K.'s life in *The Castle* that is lived constantly under the eyes of others.

Milan Kundera notes that K.'s assistants are harbingers of modernity, "agents of the total destruction of private life" (Kundera 1996: 52), but what Muir conveys in her novel is that women are rarely allowed a private life of the sort required for creative activity.

To get privacy to finish a translation, Alison (like Willa Muir) does it at night finishing at 5 a.m.:

> She collected on a tray all that was needed for making tea, abstracted a few of Peter's biscuits, supplied herself with cigarettes and matches and carried this equipment into her study. It was a familiar routine, for several times already, in an emergency, she had worked all night long, usually correcting proofs. ... She had just broken into the last chapter and she was not going to give up now. Sipping tea, nibbling biscuits, reminding herself that this was the very last lap of Rheingold's silly book, she roused her flagging energies and went on writing. The final two paragraphs of the chapter bothered her extremely; she had to revise them three times before she was satisfied. Her head ached a little, her fingers were cramped, she yearned to stretch her limbs (St. Andrews MS 38466/1/2: 174–5).

The resentful feeling ("Rheingold's silly book") has to be set aside because of necessity. It is a job that has to be done with the necessary equipment (tea, cigarettes) before morning breaks and the household needs to be looked after. Alison indicates that this is "a familiar routine" with her working "all night long" to get this translation job done, so that Dick can get on with his essays in solitude. But it is not entirely a rushed job; "she had to revise [the final two paragraphs] three times before she was satisfied" indicating the work she puts in, and also perhaps her disdain for Rheingold's writing, which prevents her from pursuing her own writing.

Translation is not always portrayed negatively in the novel. Translating the Kafka figure, Garta, is inspirational and creative, because it feels like a dialogue. But, even when it is not an author she loves, the skill itself interests her. She describes it as a "mysterious and interesting" process that "flowed more or less sinuously" but part of the problem is having the physical and mental space to enjoy the skill and maintain creative interest in it. She is constantly being interrupted:

> For about twenty minutes after that she worked steadily, writing in a child's jotter with a book propped open before her. Each foreign sentence on the printed page entered her mind, found a meaning there, flowed more or less sinuously into it and came out again, altered in shape, as an English sentence, a process which seemed always mysterious and interesting to Mrs Muttoe, although sometimes she claimed that it was as exhausting as stone-breaking. When she was in the middle of a sentence, a knock sounded on the door (19).

Translation is a constant stress in the novel because it is associated with keeping the household alive, and because it prevents her from giving full attention to the "lovingkindness" she wants to propagate. Dick is never once shown translating in the novel and only once does he offer to help Alison when a deadline is looming:

> "They want the translation middle of September, didn't you say?"
> Mrs Muttoe's voice sounded woe-begone.
> "Can't you finish it by then? Shall I give you a hand?"
> "Oh no, Dick, you've got to finish your own book. It's up to me. I took it on, and I'll do it."
> "Don't go pottering round the house so much. Leave Alice to herself, and you'll manage" (108).

Alison is upset by Dick's admonishment to her not to go "pottering" around and not to spend time helping their new servant Alice, a young, disadvantaged girl. It implies that she is deliberately not working on the translation and not working full stop; that her cooking and the time spent with their son and Alice, in an attempt to nourish them and her husband, is worthless in the world of work. This comes straight after Alison placing his work first: "you've got to finish your own book"; this is more important than the translation that is actually bringing in money.

Given the novel's proximity to autobiographical events, it is also suggestive of how their translation relationship actually worked. In her memoir, Willa Muir notes that because of all the time spent translating, she hardly had time to write. When she finished this novel she found no publisher and had a breakdown. Writing about this period in her journal later, she said that when she recovered from the breakdown, she "had the conviction that I had come back to life only to devote myself to Edwin, and in a lesser way, to Gavin [their son], and that I must kill my 'vanity', my ambition to write." But from the vantage point of the 1950s, she added: "My intelligent Unconscious now told me that in killing, or trying to kill, my vanity, I had nearly succeeded in killing myself" (St. Andrews MS 38466/5/6; October 1, 1955). She was quite clear, privately, about the impact of playing the "poet's wife."

At one point in the novel, Alison looks back at her house and thinks: "Two people called Dick and Alison Muttoe carried on the work of the firm there, in partnership" (St. Andrews MS 38466/1/2: 247). But Alison is working through her resentment that though they are in love it is not a partnership in terms of public respect and private help. Her power lies in propagating "loving-kindness," even if it is neither understood at home nor outside the home, where the vitriol and violence she associates with the patriarchal system is burgeoning in the geo-political world:

> in Germany National Socialists were openly repudiating loving-kindness and making a creed out of its denial. She went to bed and dreamed that she was an ark tossing on an angry flood of waters, a small and pitifully vulnerable ark, for bombs were hailing from the sky and Peter screamed to her for the shelter she could not provide.
> Homes might be brimful of loving-kindness, yet once outside the home loving-kindness seemed to be dispersed in a void, atomised, powerless.
> "Just where does it get lost?" said Mrs Muttoe aloud, shutting her eyes to the translation of Garta that lay on the desk before her (241–2).

Alison, thinking about the "loving-kindness" she instills in her son Peter and how mothers' love seems to dissipate outside the home, is thinking about it as she translates

Garta/Kafka. When she feels that "it get[s] lost" in the patriarchal, warlike world, she then "shut[s] her eyes to the translation of Garta." Quite unexpectedly the question of how Alison seems to read "loving-kindness" in the fictional Garta arises and whether it indicates that Muir herself read her similar notion of "True Love" in Kafka's work while she was translating it.

God

One of the major criticisms of the Muirs's translations is that they read Kafka via an overly religious lens. Their "simpleminded theological exegesis" (Harman 1996: 301) is a fault of the translation: "one of the problems with the Muirs's *Castle* is that it furthers their theological agenda," Mark Harman writes:

> which was heavily influenced by Brod's. Brod regarded the Castle as the seat of divine grace; Muir stated bluntly that "the theme of the novel is salvation." Moreover, in his introduction to the first English edition (1930) he depicts the novels as the modern equivalent of Bunyan's seventeenth-century prose allegory *The Pilgrim's Progress*. That notion, which was to dominate the critical debate for decades to come, is now widely discredited. Muir himself had forceful views on such matters. He was convinced that literature could not survive the demise of religious belief. [...] These strong convictions leave their mark on the Muirs's translation (Harman 1996: 297).

Just as Willa Muir moved ambiguously between "I" and "we," Harman here writes of the religiosity of "their translation" and "the Muirs's translation" but only of "Muir" [Edwin] stating his religious beliefs and [Edwin] Muir's "forceful views" and his [Edwin's] "strong convictions." Similarly, George Steiner, in his introduction to the Muirs's *The Trial*, writes that Edwin Muir was not only influenced by Brod's religious reading of *The Trial*, but indeed brought his own Calvinist twist to it: "Muir's reading and the translation which it underwrites is distinctly *his*" (Steiner in Kafka 1992: xii, emphasis added). The translations came "armed with forewords," J. M. Coetzee writes, that Edwin Muir felt might help guide "English readers through new and difficult texts" (Coetzee 2001: 75), but the problem is "Inevitably the conception of Kafka as a religious writer influenced the choices the *Muirs* made as they translated his words" (75). Osman Durrani adds that the Muirs simply "went along" with Brod in his religious reading of Kafka's work (Durrani 2002: 214).

Certainly, Edwin Muir argued that the Castle in *The Castle* was "the dwelling-place of divinity" and that when K. gazes on the Castle he looks at "a shape which he has often seen before in his journey, but always far away, and apparently inaccessible; that shape is justice, grace, truth, final reconciliation, father, God" (Muir 1963: 120). Edwin Muir's beliefs seem to manifest themselves in small choices in the translation of the novel that "whittle away at the interpretative choices open to the reader" (Harman 1996: 300). Harman gives an example from the first description of the Castle: the church tower is described as "an earthly building – what else can men build? – but with a loftier goal than the humble dwelling-houses, and a clearer meaning than the humble muddle of everyday life" (12, q. Harman 1996: 299). Harman argues that

> In German a pregnant phrase – "mit klarerem Ausdruck als ihn der trübe Werktag hat" – merely hints at the symbolic implication of the church-tower. I echo Kafka's terseness by rendering the phrase as "a clearer expression than that of the dull workday." That phrase may seem baffling, though no more so than it is in German. The Muirs spell out what is merely implicit in Kafka. … In their translation the church-tower symbolizes all too clearly the superiority of religious truth over the confusion of everyday life. The voice we are hearing here is not Kafka's, but Brod's (300–301).

In another instance – the opening paragraph of the novel – Robert Alter argues that the Muirs, in heavily domesticating the text, describe the Castle hill as "both 'hidden' and 'veiled,' introducing a small but alien effect of dramatic heightening that is like an ominous soundtrack in a suspense film" (47). In addition, they add, "nor was there even a glimmer of light to show that a castle was there," suggesting, he argues, that the Castle is "a realm of illusion" (47), whereas in the German original the Castle just cannot be seen at that moment. These small choices imply a more mystical and possibly religious tone.

Of the two Muirs, Edwin was, of course, the more visible because the translations were "armed with forewords" written by him rather than by Willa. It makes sense that scholars would rely, after all, on Edwin's interpretation of the novels (and of the novel as a genre being predicated on a belief in eternity and God). Yet, Willa Muir's relationship with religion is far more complex than these readings suggest and, since she had a greater influence on the translations than these scholars assume, how can we then read this apparent religious interpretation of the translation? Can we read it through her answer to patriarchal thought, this notion of "loving-kindness" or "True Love"?

"A belief in True Love was my brand of non-conformism," Willa Muir writes, adding, "the patriarchal Law rated us as second-class citizens (we could not vote) and the patriarchal Church assumed that we were second-class souls" (Muir 1968: 140–1). Muir rejected the Church because of its sexism and its role as an institution upholding the patriarchy and the inherent violence such a system perpetuated. "Christ was for government by Love," she wrote in her journal, "But the church governed by fear: the fear of Hell, (devil and witchcraft)" (St. Andrews MS 38466/5/2: June 15, 1947). Willa Muir was especially critical of Calvinism and its effect on Scottish culture: "the exercise of power was of central importance to [the Calvinists]," she wrote,

> A Father seemed more powerful to them than a Son … more jealous and vengeful than the original, dealing out terrible wrath and punishment. As is usual in systems motivated by a desire for power, there was no room for love, compassion or generosity in theirs (Muir 1965: 192).

K.'s search, in Willa Muir's interpretation, may be for Love rather than for God. As such, it is a translation that has at the heart of it an earnest quest for a mystical center, and the same criticisms could be made: that Willa (and not Edwin) Muir does not allow for ambiguity in meaning. But, at the same time there is something quite radical in this notion of a feminine truth rather than an aping of Brod's belief that Kafka's character was in search of religious salvation. In such a schema it is possible to see K. as a character moving from woman to woman in the novel: Olga, Mrs. Brunswick, Frieda, Amalia, Pepi in a search for a meaning that he cannot quite grasp. Alison's musings in *Mrs Muttoe* about the "autocrat" in the top storey being reminded by a mystical "Centre" that "they were interpreters and not dictators" – the brain checked by a soul that is constituted of "loving-kindness" – speaks to K.'s rationality and logic failing. He keeps being reminded that he is an interpreter, an exegete, because he has to keep trying to decipher the narratives of others, but his critical faculties are not enough.

Harman remarks that, in the Muirs's translation, K. is "a pilgrim in search of salvation" (Harman 1996: 301) and that the Muirs miss or elide the ironic humor in the novel, thus also eliding K.'s unreliability and ambiguity; "K. is about as calculating and self-centered in my translation as he is in the original," Harman writes (301). Harman gives the example of a phrase Kafka uses to describe K. thinking "nach seinen Berechnungen": he translates this as "according to his calculations"; the Muirs as "by his reckoning" (301). "Joseph K." in the Muirs's translation, Joyce Crick writes, "is a much more decent fellow than Josef K." (Crick 1981: 166). This includes the Muirs omitting a reference at the beginning of the novel to K.'s wife and child at home. K. is never mentioned again and he has sex with Frieda immediately after meeting her, a moment of intense and quite violent passion. This, too, is much more "decorous" in the Muirs's version (Alter 2005: 47). The implication is that the Muirs shy away from the real K. because of their Calvinist piety and perhaps because of English domestic norms of the time (*The Castle* was published in 1930).

The vein of humor in *The Castle* lies in K.'s lack of real and unselfish interest in others; his self-absorption hobbles his crafty attempts to eke out information from the opaque villagers and castle officials. He is not a compassionate or loving figure; he is as faulty and fallible as we are. The more earnest portrayal of K. by the Muirs as an innocent searcher may, however, have more to do with Willa Muir's interest in a figure seeking "loving-kindness" in something of a matriarchal world in the village, if not the Castle. If *Mrs Muttoe* is a thematic, and to some extent an aesthetic or stylistic response to *The Castle*, then we can see Willa Muir thinking about the Castle as schematic of the patriarchal world (the intellect, the top storey) and the village as the mysterious, matriarchal center. K. is a male figure with potential in Muir's ideal; a man guided by women and a man who listens to them. It is a far too idealistic response to K. but, given Muir's strong resistance to her circumstances as she was translating the novel, it suggests a far less traditional approach to the translation than has been suspected. If K. is a pilgrim, he is a pilgrim in Muir's ideal, anti-war, anti-patriarchal world of True Love. It is not a sophisticated approach, and is one charged perhaps with essentialist readings of gender, but Muir came of age in the very early 1900s, in the vanguard of the twentieth-century feminist movement. Her interpretation of K. and his quest is part of her articulation of this struggle. It is not a conservative or reactionary reading of the character.

Critics' assumptions that the religious reading is caught up in the Muirs' old-fashioned and backward-looking approach to aesthetics also need to be challenged. Edwin Muir did argue that modernism perhaps heralded the decline of the novel because, for him, the novel had historically been tied into a sense of eternity against which "the life of man is a complete story (Muir 1967: 148). The "complete decay of the religious sense would bring with it the atrophy of the creative imagination," he argued and implied that modernist writing might herald such decay and atrophy (148). Edwin Muir's own poetry, Seamus Heaney writes, was "a standoff with modernity" (Heaney 2002: 254), a rejection of the currents of the day.

Edwin Muir's resistance to modernism, Mark Harman argues, leads to misreadings and mis-renderings in the text:

> The Muirs's translations fail to do justice to Kafka's modernity in part *because the literary sensibility of Edwin, the primary stylist*, had been molded by nineteenth-century figures such as Thackeray and Dickens rather than by modernists such as Joyce and Virginia Woolf. [...] For Muir unity is a *sine qua non* of great literature. Is it any wonder then that *he* should seek to impose it on Kafka's *Castle*? (Harman 1996: 297–8, emphasis added).

He argues that because of this they were "not as familiar as we are today with devices such as indirect interior monologue" (Harman 1996: 304). David Damrosch similarly argues that the Muirs's translation was faulty because of resistance to modernism: "the Muirs missed the deceitful truth about K., perhaps *in Edwin Muir's case because he* had little patience for the fragmented narratives and unreliable narrators often favored by modernist writers" (Damrosch 2003: 196, emphasis added). Damrosch notes Edwin Muir's attack on Joyce in 1928 and then goes on to castigate Brod's lack of affinity even though, "*Unlike the Muirs, Brod was a novelist* and an active member of modernist literary circles" (Damrosch 2003: 196, emphasis added). J. M. Coetzee challenges these readings, but only refers to Edwin, who was "a modern master in his own right, certainly no hankerer after a lost nineteenth-century world" (Coetzee 2001: 86). Not one article on the Muirs's translations mentions that Willa Muir was a novelist, and a modernist novelist at that.

It must be remembered that the Muirs brought Kafka to the notice of English publishers and that they advocated for his writing, and translated him, when he was unknown in the English-speaking world and not a major figure in the German-speaking world. If Edwin Muir rejected or misunderstood modernist writing, he would perhaps not have chosen to advocate for Kafka's work, which he clearly admired and which influenced, at least thematically, his own poetry. Muir had his disagreements with modernism but he was steeped in it. The Muirs's library was fully stocked with modernist writers (according to an inventory before Willa Muir's death); Willa Muir's feminist tract, *Woman: An Inquiry*, was published by the Woolf's Hogarth Press in 1925.

The Muirs's smoothing out of Kafka's texts (Harman notes, in particular, their smoothing out of seemingly awkward transitions that are innate to Kafka's writing) appears connected to the demands and norms of the English publishing industry.

Willa Muir clearly knew what was expected and what would get them paid. As someone who was actively writing modernist fiction while translating Kafka's work and who wrote a modernist novel about a female translator translating a fictional Kafka, it seems unfair to argue that the Muirs, and Willa Muir by implication, did not understand Kafka's aesthetics because of perceptions about Edwin Muir's aesthetic preferences, read through the prism of his forewords.

Muir wrote in her memoir that there "was a difference in emphasis between our separate appreciations of *The Castle*"; in other words, that there was a difference in their interpretative acts as translators. She continues:

> As then Edwin was more excited by the "whence" and I by the "how". That is to say, Edwin tried to divine and follow up with the metaphysics of Kafka's universe, while I stayed lost in admiration of the sureness with which he embodied in concrete situations the emotional predicaments he wanted to convey, situations that seemed to me to come clean out of the unconscious, perhaps directly from actual dreams (Muir 1968: 150).

Here she is arguing that her interest lay in those modernist aesthetics, in the "how" – the "concrete situations" from "clean out of the unconscious" – whereas the "why," the "metaphysics," appealed to Edwin. Willa Muir's interest in the unconscious and in Kafka's use of a seemingly oneiric narrative is directly explored as a connection to Kafka in *Mrs Muttoe*, in which Alison Muttoe dreams about the Money Fabric after translating Garta/Kafka. *Mrs Muttoe* fails as a novel mainly because of the mixture of experimental styles: it begins strongly with an unreliable narrator (indirect free-style through a housekeeper who seems to be a con-artist), turns into a more traditional narrative (albeit with free indirect discourse), then into a cyclical narrative following the arrival and departure of female servants and finally into a dream narrative. But it shows aesthetic experimentation, directly influenced by Willa Muir's experience of translating Kafka.

This aesthetic experimentation is deeply connected to Muir's feminism. Alison's dream narrative arises because night-time is the only time she has to herself. As she settles in for the night she asks herself: "where, Alison M asked herself, do females get the assurance that life is worth living? ... what was their function in the day-time world?" (St. Andrews MS 38466/1/2: 97). Sidelined in a patriarchal world, at night they occupy a primal role:

> On a woman's breast children and men lost their day-time selves, descending softly into secure darkness. That might be why women had been associated so often with the idea of night; moon-goddesses shining in crepuscular quietude, lulling the day-time world to sleep. [...] Now she was fully awake again, awake and at leisure. The house, sheltering its sleeping inhabitants like a many-chambered womb, was acting as her deputy; she was free of family responsibilities and isolated in a chilly bed, the vague circumference of her personality shrinking to a focussed point of waking life, somewhere behind her eyes. I'm in my own top storey, said Alison to herself (97–8).

Alison's top storey is connected to the non-material world of dream and the unconscious, a place of compassion, even if her arm, cradling Dick, has gone numb and she has to scramble past him to the other twin bed "where the sheets felt glacial" (98). "Soothing and cherishing other people is apparently a full-time job for a woman," she thinks, even at night, and yet this is the one time women have creative space to think as the house "like a many-chambered womb" takes over as her deputy. Alison's dream, of being caught in the strange, hypertrophied picture of the real world – its materialism and sexism moved into the surreal Money Fabric – uses the dream-like *mise-en-scène* of Kafka's novels: the stranger shored against un-interpretable worlds, but in essence what Muir explores is this estrangement as a constant of the female predicament in a male world. In the real world, Alison thinks, women still have to be a "*femme couverte*," having to dress up and put on a hat to walk out of the door (33). The strange, surreal dream-world, the unconscious, needs no such disguise.

Alison's sense of estrangement in the real world is also connected to nationality and class. Right at the beginning of the novel the putative housekeeper immediately notices that Alison and Dick are Scots; "there was no mistaking those r's," she thinks (4), and the Muttoes' child, Peter, is taunted at school for being a "Scottie" (Alison tells him, when he asks, what a "Scottie" is, that it is a dog). In her memoir, writing about their time in Hampstead, Willa Muir writes:

> Our style and behaviour must have been as un-English as our accents and voices, only we never thought about these at all, until Gavin [the Muirs's son] told us one day that in his school they said he spoke like a little Scotch boy (Muir 1968: 170).

The writing, like the translations, is not "un-English." Alison and Dick might be Scottish but their dialogue and Alison's interior monologues are presented in standard English. Only occasionally does Alison show some critical self-awareness of language; one particular example is when she has to advertise again for a cook-housekeeper:

> Exprd ck-hskpr wntd immdtly. It sounded, she thought, like the ultimatum of some tight-lipped dictator rather than the plea of a housewife in distress. But in London over-crowding was the rule; space was so expensive that even words were bound to suffer. She regarded the bony consonants with distaste; they seemed a horrid symbol of her life for the coming week (St. Andrews MS 38466 /1/2: 32).

The clipped consonants – necessarily so, because language is a product and for sale – mimics an upper-class English accent, "like the ultimatum of some tight-lipped dictator." There is little humanity in these "bony consonants." Alison's resentment at the language is located in the falseness of the address (it's not "the plea of the housewife") but also in the real "Money Fabric." Alison needs help from another woman and that woman has to be found and paid for: "translation was one of the things that was going to be crowded out" (32). Looking for a cook infringes upon Alison's financial worth as a translator and upsets notions of class. The con-artist at the beginning of the novel distrusts the fact that Alison described herself and Dick as a "professional couple" because she is not sure what that means (it being an unusual description for that era).

She hates the fact that Alison is trying to talk to her "woman-to-woman," feeling that "there was an unfairness" in this pretence of equality (8).

Alison's idealism about a relationship with a servant being "like a love-affair" is consistently undermined by the con-artist, by a couple of girls stealing from the household, by a rabidly religious Irishwoman who terrifies Peter with stories of Hell (the latter based on Muir's experience and a reason the Muirs left London – their son Gavin was so terrified, that he ran off and was run over by a petrol tanker). Margaret Elphinstone regards the negative portrayal to be condescending, but in some ways these female servants are at the center of the novel; the cyclical nature of their arrivals and departures gives a suggestive form to the novel, but also they are portrayed as being caught in the same Money Fabric as Alison, debilitated and metaphysically deformed because of the patriarchal society they live in. Alison Light makes the point that many middle-class feminists of the era could be dismissive of their servants and "few were strictly egalitarian" (Light 2008: 186), but the Muttoes – and the Muirs – are not quite part of the English caste system. Alison's discomfort with the servants also underlines her uncertain place in the class to which she appears to belong because she is Scots and "professional." "We never considered ourselves as belonging to any one social class," Willa Muir writes of that period. "We were not Bohemians. ... Yet we did not belong to what is now called The Establishment" (Muir 1968: 170). Female labor is part of the ambiguity: Willa Muir is at the vanguard of the emerging professional female class, but that advancement is predicated on the labor of female servants. She, and they, are all working for the "top storey."

Early on his *Diaries*, Kafka thinks about the "secondary characters" in literature. In one play, he says, "there is mention made of two seamstresses who sew the linen for the play's one bride. What happens to these two girls? Where do they live?" he asks:

> What have they done that they not be part of the play but stand, as it were, outside in front of Noah's ark, drowning in the downpour of rain, and may only press their faces one last time against a cabin window, so that the audience in the stalls see something dark there for a moment? (Kafka 1964: 30).

Kafka goes on to populate his work with these women – bartenders, cooks, maids, washerwomen, landladies – and lets Noah's ark sail. These women are repositories of knowledge, however opaque, and strangely powerful in the worlds they inhabit. They may not run the worlds they live in, but they understand them and find their own nodes of power – Leni in *The Trial*, the Johanna Brummer, the Head Cook and Brunelda in *Amerika*, the landlady Frieda, Olga and Amalia in *The Castle*. "Service," Alison Light writes:

> has always been an emotional as well as an economic territory ... [servants] were witnesses and eavesdroppers, allies and sometimes friends, whose emotional and sexual lives were entangled with those who gave them orders. ... Servants were the body's keepers, protecting its entrances and exits; they were privy to its secrets and its chambers; they knew that their masters and mistresses sweated, leaked and bled. ... Servants have always known that the emperor has no clothes (Light 2008: 4).

This intimacy with human fallibility and the vulnerability of the body – think of Leni with her webbed hands – reveals perhaps a darker but also a more human world, touched and seen by these women in Kafka's texts, all outsider-insiders. Muir is more prosaic and materialist in her representation of the servants, but her novel is an attempt to work out their place in the Money Fabric, the locus of power, while Alison Muttoe is attempting to forge her own place there too.

Mark Harman

My ears grew up in Ireland …

Mark Harman

The highly stylish windowless room at the Austrian Cultural Forum was jam-packed for a 2009 PEN event called "Kafka in America." Two very personable employees of the Forum gave intensely long introductions to themselves and the panel, in the excessively polite and hierarchically aware Austrian style, and the writer and Kafka biographer, Louis Begley, began to speak. The aging audience, clad in New Yorker black, started bouncing in their seats, chirruping, then shouting, "We can't hear you! We can't hear you!" The chirrups, the shouts, meant that, for quite a while, in the tiny acoustically padded room, no one could hear anything.

The slightly claustrophobic and inadvertently funny atmosphere suddenly did turn to humor – the Irish writer Colm Tóibín told a story about his friends dressing up as the Muirs for a fancy-dress party, Tóibín rearranging his eighteenth-century squire's face into appropriate Calvinist piety to convey the effect. Beside him sat one of Kafka's new re-translators, another Irishman, Mark Harman, who read from the opening of his translation of *Der Verschollene/Amerika: The Missing Person*. "Are you a German?" Harman read from the text. "Karl sought to assure himself, for he had heard a great deal about the dangers facing newcomers in America, especially from Irishmen" (Kafka 2008a: 4). Harman threw his head back and laughed heartily; it's "difficult for us not to chuckle," Harman writes in his preface to the translation, despite "our increasing empathy with the hapless young hero" (Harman 2008: xxiii).

Harman, like the hapless young hero Karl Rossman, emigrated to America. Born in Ireland, Harman grew up in Dublin, encountered Kafka during his undergraduate degree at University College Dublin, and moved to America initially to write a PhD dissertation on Kafka (and Kleist) at Yale. He has spent his academic career writing on Kafka and two of the writers who influenced him: Robert Walser and Heinrich von Kleist. Schocken published his translation of *Das Schloß* in 1998 and his translation of *Der Verschollene* in 2008. He is currently translating a selection of Kafka's stories for Harvard University Press.

Listening to Harman talk, and read Kafka aloud, that night at the PEN event made me think about the imprint of the translator on their work, what Luise von Flotow has called the "translator-effect": what effect their background has, their relationship to the

English language as much as to the source language, what draws them to translating certain authors, what it feels like to re-translate a modern classic, their reaction to reviews of their translations, and the relationship between a scholarly interest in an author and an attempt to translate the same author. I was particularly interested in Harman's Irishness; having grown up in Ireland myself, it was hard that evening not to hear an Irish tonality to the translation, a rhythm and phrasing that sounded familiar, as well as the background of an Irish literary tradition attuned to linguistic subversion and with a propensity for dry and absurd humor. Harman has written about Kafka and Joyce, and Beckett and Kafka, and, while translating *The Castle* in the early 1990s, was "immersed more than usual in Beckett's prose," especially Beckett's *Trilogy* (Harman, personal communication).

The notion of what Irishness might be is of course a contested question; when the Irishman, Robinson, scuppers Karl's chances at the Hotel Occidental in *The Missing Person* by turning up drunk, the head waiter is suspicious of Karl's explanation because he "can't even believe" there can be an Irishman called Robinson; "ever since Ireland has existed, there's never been an Irishman of that name" (Kafka 2008a: 165). Robinson is an Irish name, or rather a transplanted name from English settlers, and usually denoting a Protestant heritage. (As I was teaching this passage in 2010, the DUP politician in Northern Ireland, Peter Robinson, was embroiled in scandal, as his wife Iris revealed an affair with a teenager; cue many renditions of the Simon & Garfunkel number.) In a short biographical sketch about his background and its connection to his interest in Kafka, Harman notes how his branch of the family were perceived as outsiders in the Irish countryside because of their name. Traveling back to a great-grandfather's house in Cavan, the relatives refuse to let him and his father through the door, "Oh, the Harmans, they were all Protestants," the relatives reason. They were worried that this Dublin branch might be after their land. But, despite his great-grandfather converting to Catholicism, Harman adds, "There was nothing Gaelic about the name Harman" (Harman 1998a: 375).

Elements of Harman's Irish background do seem important in laying a path for his interest in philology and language; growing up in the 1950s and 1960s in Dublin, Harman was part of a Dublin generation who received mixed signals about the idea of a native language – who spoke English, but learned Irish at school. As Harman points out in his sketch, learning Irish, for a certain class (including his civil servant father), "was primarily a stepping stone for professional advancement" (377). You had to (and still have to) pass Irish-language exams to teach or enter the Civil Service. His father, "who was no [Irish] language revivalist" (377), sent Harman to an Irish-language school, Coláiste Mhuire, "where all subjects – except for English – were taught through Irish" (376-7). The problem was the "wretched" teaching of the language; Harman writes about "a sadistic little Christian Brother, much given to inventive linguistic exercises. At the beginning of class, he would burst in, crying odd sounds such as *beo, ba, meo, ma*" (377). This bizarre, plaintive methodology was "intended to make us purer speakers of the Irish, but actually made us laugh at him" (377). In retaliation, the monk was "a nimble wielder of the leather strap" and Harman gives us the grotesque image of the beating: "he would first straighten out the offender's palm, rise on his tip-toes, put on a Janus-like expression, scowling at his victim and grinning at the class, before bringing the strap down full force" (377).

Irish perhaps seemed not so much a mother tongue as a father tongue; a language connected with patriarchal and reactionary institutions. Harman did not want any school misdeeds to be conveyed back home because his father, "like many Irish fathers of that era, was partial to the strap and cane" – the ridiculous, and funny, overstocking of canes, sabers and umbrellas in the male-dominated opening of *Amerika: The Missing Person* seems almost documentary in this Ireland. The death of Harman's mother when he was a young boy thrusts him into this male environment. The "magical world came crashing down in 1961 when my mother died of a heart attack" (376) but also moved him toward another language from a female carer. His father

> hired an Austrian housekeeper, Fräulein, to take care of us. Fräulein brought us our first words of German, *Schürze* (apron) and *Mahlzeit* (bon appetit) as well as a first visit to Austria. Each year from then on my father would send us to the Continent to learn languages – this was long before such Gabriel Conroy-like enthusiasm became de rigueur among middle-class Dublin parents (376).

Harman invokes the protagonist of James Joyce's story "The Dead," Gabriel Conroy, who looks toward Europe as the future for Ireland; during the story he is reprimanded by Miss Ivors for rejecting the beauty and importance of his own homeland – the real Ireland, represented by the West Coast and the Irish language. For Joyce himself, of course, Europe provided an escape from both colonial and parochial Ireland. For Harman, it seems here that the introduction of "Fräulein" opens up this other world – the trips "to the Continent," but also a renewed and new world of the home. The first words of German he learns are connected to the hearth – "*Schürze* (apron) and *Mahlzeit* (bon appetit)" – to being cared for. In contrast, his father "for days on end … would refuse to speak to us" (378), and Harman would "sit around speculating about the causes" with his siblings (378).

Encountering Kafka's *The Castle* as a student of German and French at UCD – Kafka "was not sufficiently in accord with Catholic values to be on the syllabus" at school (378) – was a moment of revelation for Harman in coming to terms with these silences and his father, whom he had dubbed "H.":

> I myself had spent numerous years speculating about the actions of my own equivalents to Kafka's father and fictional father figures. H. was my Castle, and I myself a real-life Irish K. I spent much of my adolescence speculating about H. and the workings of the command center, which I dubbed the H.Q. Just as Kafka's alter ego in *The Castle* tirelessly interprets each gesture and action of the mysterious Castle officials, so too did I ceaselessly interpret the enigmatic gestures and actions of the parental H.Q. (378).

Harman's excitement at K.'s "prowess as an interpreter, his frenetic hypotheses about the moves of his supposed antagonist" (378) is an excitement of recognition, a validation of how Harman had to approach his own father's silences, his "piggy moods." The minute analyses of how his father functioned, what he meant, however, was ultimately unsatisfactory; in choosing "to admire K.'s inventive hypotheses about surrogate father figures, I was actually clapping myself on the back for my own ingenious explanations for H.'s erratic behavior" (379). But Harman realized there was "really no cause for self-congratulation, for in life – mine as well as Kafka's – such frenzied overinterpretation leads only to indecision and inaction" (379). In the end, after years of refusing to admit a personal connection with Kafka, despite his scholarly attention to his work, it took the act of translation for some form of catharsis:

> For Franz Kafka, writing *The Castle* was a cathartic experience. … As for me, translating *The Castle* was like an axe for the frozen sea within me: in impersonating Kafka in English I drew on my own father-obsessed Irish upbringing and in the process distanced myself from it (379).

Harman's description of his translation process being an "impersonat[ion] of Kafka in English" brings to mind Homi Bhabha's colonial "mimic man" (Bhabha 1994: 87). While the colonial subject appears to have to mimic the colonial power in order to have access to it, s/he is always "*a subject of difference that is almost the same, but not quite*" (86, italics in original). Thus, "the *ambivalence* of mimicry (almost the same, but not quite) does not merely rupture the [colonial] discourse, but becomes transformed into an uncertainty" (86, italics in original). Mimicry's "*double* vision" discloses this ambivalence and "disrupts its authority" (88). Thinking in terms of the translator and their relationship to the authority of the author and the original text, the notion of impersonation is a self-deprecating, humble approximation of the translator's role, as only a mimicking of that authority (and therefore not quite it). At the same time, that mimicry destabilizes the authority of the original, and opens it up to a new text, both Harman's and Kafka's: a double vision, a hybrid possibility. The notion of a "not quite" escape is important. To translate Kafka, Harman "drew on my own father-obsessed Irish upbringing" but, in doing so, "distanced myself from it," a double vision that acknowledges the roots of Harman's language and the shoots of it (via Kafka's German).

Harman did not set out to write an Irish-English version of Kafka's work; if anything, in his translation of *Amerika*, he aimed for a "mid-Atlantic" form of English which he "didn't want to be too American," sensing that it would suit Kafka's own "slippage of details in *Amerika*" (the Statue of Liberty holding a sword, the bridge between New York and Boston) and would provide a complementary "slippage in language" (Harman, personal communication). Though he was "not aiming" to convey an Irish-English tonality, he said that it "comes with the territory" (Harman, personal communication); that there are "probably inevitably" elements of Irish-English in the translation, but that he "doesn't consciously" include them. However, he noted, "my ears grew up in Ireland" (Harman, personal communication).

An example at the beginning of *Amerika*, right before Karl asks the stoker whether he is German (in order to ascertain that he is not Irish because he "had heard about the dangers facing newcomers in America, especially from Irishmen"), which Harman read that night at the PEN event, is as follows:

the man said with a certain pride as he tinkered with the lock on a small suitcase, which he opened and closed continually with both hands, listening for the bolt to snap into place. "But do come in," the man continued, "you're hardly going to stand like that. "Am I not disturbing you?" Karl asked (Kafka 2008a: 4).

sagte der Mann mit einigem Stolz und hörte nicht auf an dem Schloß eines kleinen Koffers zu hantieren, den er mit beiden Händen immer wieder zu drückte, um das Einschnappen des Riegels zu behorchen. "Aber kommen Sie doch herein," sagte der Mann weiter, "Sie werden doch nich draußen stehn." "Störe ich nicht?" fragte Karl (Kafka 1994: 10).

Harman's use of "tinkered with" for "hantieren" and the use of the adverb "hardly" (that equates to the use of "doch") typical of Irish-English speech: "you're hardly going to stand like that" and Karl's very Irish-English usage of "Am I not" rather than the more standard UK English (that Michael Hofmann uses) of "Aren't I" gives some Irish-English tone to the exchange between Karl and the stoker. This is not to argue that these terms are necessarily confined to Irish-English usage – Hofmann, too, translates "hantieren" as "tinkering with":

said the man with some pride, and carried on tinkering with the lock of a small suitcase, repeatedly shutting it with both hands to listen to the sound of the lock as it snapped shut. "Why don't you come in," the man went on, "don't stand around outside." "Aren't I bothering you?" asked Karl (Kafka 2002a: 4).

But Hofmann's exchange sounds more English, especially in the direct speech: "Why don't you come in"; "don't stand around outside"; "Aren't I bothering you?" Hofmann also thinks lyrically – the stoker's double use of "doch" – hard to translate – is euphonically suggested by the repetition of "don't" and Hofmann introduces a repetition of "lock" – an important word for Kafka – which isn't in the original where the stoker tinkers with a "Schloß" and "Riegels" but which speaks both to the importance of the image and Kafka's aesthetic use of repetition (also emphasized by Hofmann's use of sibilance). Both are quite lovely responses to the difficulty of translating what seems on the face of it a straightforward passage; their "ears" are different.

The Muirs's translation is interesting also; they use "fiddling" instead of "tinkering," "sea-chest" instead of "suitcase" – a wonderful image, but it detracts from the connection between Karl's "Koffer," which is one of the founding images of the novel (as it is inspired by David Copperfield's loss of his trunk in Dickens's novel), and the stoker's "Koffer." Interesting, too, is the very technical "wards" instead of "lock" or "bolt" (wards is, according to the OED, used by their fellow Scot, Walter Scott, in a couple of his novels):

the man said with a certain pride, fiddling all the time with a lock of a little sea-chest, which he kept pressing with both hands in the hope of hearing the wards snap home. "But come inside," he went on, "you don't want to stand out there!" – "I'm not disturbing you?" asked Karl (Kafka 1962: 4).

This example from the Muirs – the possible literary influence seen in the word "wards" – also evokes another element of the translator's background language, the language formed from their reading, something Harman himself regards as important; the linguistic influence of "what you read as you grow up" (Harman, personal communication). Harman's turn to Beckett as he was translating *The Castle* perhaps leaves its fingerprints on the translation; one example might be the use of the word "shambles." In a review of Harman's translation, J.M. Coetzee criticizes Harman for the use of this word:

> Harman is not immune from the temptations of overtranslating that so mar the Muir version. To translate *Ihre schmutzige Familienwirtschaft* as "your dirty family shambles" (p. 133) introduces ideas of blood and death not present in the original. "Your sordid family setup" would be better (Coetzee 2001: 85).

Coetzee is quoting from a part of the novel, in which K. is criticized for his makeshift home at the schoolroom, where he, Frieda, and his two assistants are living, and are expected to clean and clear before the teacher and Miss Gisa arrive with the schoolchildren. The teacher dismisses K. because "nobody can expect a young girl like her to impart lessons amidst your filthy family setup [shambles]" (Kafka 2008a: 133). Coetzee references the historical use of the term "shambles" as a place of slaughter or meat-market, rather than the current Irish and English, as well as some US, use of the word as a "mess" (a few weeks ago, for instance, an ESPN headline ran: "Red Sox in Shambles as [Josh] Beckett Stumbles"[3]). At the same time, *Samuel* Beckett does use "shambles" in his *Trilogy*, with some reference to the historical use of the word. Molloy's mother lives by "the shambles" in *Molloy* (Beckett 1994: 22); when he falls into a ditch on his travels to his mother, he wakes to find a shepherd with a dog and sheep looking at him and asks him if he's taking them "to the field, or to the shambles" (28). The inscrutable shepherd doesn't answer, and Molloy realizes that neither direction matters, that "if he was going away from [the town] that meant nothing either, for slaughter-houses are not confined to towns, no, they are everywhere, the country is full of them, every butcher has his slaughter-house and the right to slaughter, according to his lights" (29).

The affinity – though hotly denied by Beckett – between Kafka's and Beckett's prose is clear: the repetition of "slaughter," the many commas in a long sentence, the seemingly oppressive dark vision ("no, they are everywhere") undercut by irony in the rhetorical persistence of the idea. Beckett read *The Castle* in German but complained, "I must say, it was difficult to get to the end" (Shenker 1956) – "a phenomenon," Harman writes, "not entirely unknown among readers of Beckett's own prose" (Harman 1998b: 179). Beckett's assertion, in a 1956 *New York Times* interview, that he did not like Kafka's prose because it "goes on like a steamroller," pinpoints what Harman identifies as one of its most important and original "stylistic trait[s]": "its relentlessness" (179). Not only this, but "the relentless momentum of the language itself which presses on in a manner [...] anticipates Beckett's own steamroller effect" (180). Beckett, Harman argues, was "annoyed at what was characteristic of his own

---

[3] David Shoenfield, May 10, 2012. Available at http://proxy.espn.go.com/blog/sweetspot/post/_/id/24207/red-sox-in-shambles-as-beckett-stumbles

work" (personal communication). It was only by going back to translate *The Castle* that Harman finally understood what Beckett meant by this "urgent forward drive" of the prose (180); something Harman recognized via Beckett's work. He "felt that there was a lot in common" between *The Castle* and *The Trilogy*; that in "trying to get inside the head of K." when translating, "Beckett really helped me" (Harman, personal communication).

So, is " family shambles" an example of "overtranslating" as Coetzee claims? On the face of it, it is not an accurate translation of "Familienwirtschaft"; " family setup" is technically more literal. The final paperback version of Harman's translation, published by Schocken, does not include the "dirty family shambles" but reads "filthy family setup" (Kafka 1998a: 133). But this is not to say that it's wrong or some linguistic deficiency of the translator; it's a deliberate choice, an interpretation consciously or unconsciously connected to an intertextual reading that can open up avenues into understanding both Kafka's and Beckett's formal and thematic qualities.

Gotcha!

Harman's translation of *The Castle* garnered several high-profile reviews; even the reviews noted how his "new version has been greeted with unusual acclaim immediately upon publication" (Ormsby 2001: 136). Part of the surprise is that a translation – and certainly, a retranslation – gets reviewed at all, but the nature of the reviews is very telling about the expectations and assumptions about the skills and intent of the translator. Harman's translation was fairly lauded, but in reviews that often came with a sting in the tail, what Harman calls the "gotcha mentality" of translation reviewing (personal communication). Harman is open about the likely impossibility of total consistency on the part of the translator; no translation is ever going to be perfect. At the same time, reviewers often hone in on perceived "mistakes" in order to justify their own taste preferences and to present their own legitimacy as experts in judging a translation. Rarely glimpsed is a consideration of the translator, or where the translation fits into their career and their background (Venuti 2008: 2), and what the nature of their contribution should be.

Harman was applauded and criticized for the same thing: his lexical and semantic fidelity to Kafka's work. If the Muirs had to "English" Kafka, Harman's translation gave closer cognizance to the idiosyncrasies of Kafka's writing, and the rhythms and word order of the German language he wrote in, resulting in, Robert Alter argued, "a much better sense of Kafka's uncompromising and disturbing originality as a prose master than we have heretofore had in English" (Alter 2005). J. M. Coetzee wrote that Harman had produced "a version of the novel that is semantically accurate to an admirable degree, faithful to Kafka's nuances, responsive to the tempo of his sentences and to the larger music of his paragraph construction" (Coetzee 2001: 84).

Ironically, this stylistic fidelity caused problems for reviewers who argued that, as a result, "Kafka had become so stylistically unappealing (even, it must be said, so *boring*)" (Ormsby 2001: 137). Coetzee argued that since "Kafka slips on occasion into some very tired-sounding prose" in the second half of *The Castle*, Harman's fidelity to Kafka's lexical style "produc[es] sentences as slack as Kafka's own" (Coetzee 2001: 82). Coetzee thought that while this was "in principle ... the right decision" he added that "it is only Kafka's classic status" that allows for such stylistic fidelity to moments of bad writing; "translating a more run-of-the-mill writer, one would be eminently justified in lightly and silently fixing up the original" (82).

Coetzee's rather startling statement, that if Kafka wasn't so famous translators could happily make him a better writer, is followed by an example from the "Hans" chapter of *The Castle*. Hans is the son of Mrs. Brunswick – a woman who caught K.'s eye at the beginning of the novel – and Otto Brunswick who is something of an antagonist of K.'s. Hans, a child, decides to help K. and speaks with "a certain imperiousness in his nature, but mixed with childish innocence so that you were glad to submit to him, half sincerely, half jokingly" (Kafka 1998a: 142). Here Kafka warns his reader about Hans's speeches to come – Hans seems to want K. to help his mother, then doesn't want him near his mother and his intent becomes entirely ambiguous, and all of this is conveyed in a strange mixture of the Austrian bureaucrat channeled by a child, with "a faint smile around his soft mouth [that] seemed to suggest he knew very well that this was merely a game" (142). Coetzee criticizes this part of Hans' plea – and Harman's adhesion to it – as stilted and badly punctuated, "tired-sounding prose":

> Father ... had actually wanted to go and see K. in order to punish him ... only Mother had dissuaded him. But above all Mother herself generally didn't want to speak to anyone and her question about K. was no exception to that rule, on the contrary, in mentioning him she could have said that she wished to see him, but she had not done so, and had thus made her intentions plain (Coetzee 2001: 82, quoting Harman 145).

What Coetzee seems to miss is the humor; Hans has just seemed to ask for K.'s help for his mother (a woman K. is attracted to) and out of the blue K. claims he "had some medical knowledge" and that at home, "on account of his healing powers, they always called him 'the bitter herb'" (Kafka 1998: 145). K's unreliability makes us question this sudden and rare revelation about his status "at home" – in the next sentence he dismisses it, and his real, and sexual, interest appears: "Anyway, he would like to take a look at Hans's mother and talk to her" (145). Just as he reveals his so-called medical and healing expertise, the child backtracks and comes out with what Coetzee criticizes. If we look at the full passage (without ellipses) below, we can see that what Kafka approximates in the light punctuation is this strange – and humorous – mixture of a child's breathless commentary, perhaps skirting round the truth, and the register of the Austro-Hungarian bureaucrat: "dissuaded," "But above all," "no exception to that rule," "on the contrary," "and thus made her intentions plain":

> Father had become very angry at K. and would certainly never allow K. to come and visit Mother, indeed he had actually wanted to go and see K. in order to punish him for his behavior, except Mother had dissuaded him. But above all Mother herself generally didn't want to speak to anyone and her question about

> K. was no exception to that rule, on the contrary, in mentioning him she could have said that she wished to see him, but she had not done so, and had thus made her intentions plain (145).

K. cannot fathom what exactly the child is saying; all that K. "learned" was "that Hans's powers of reasoning had noticeably improved now that he had to shield his mother from K." (145–6). The child has turned into a cunning lawyer! The humor also comes from the rhythm of the passage, moved along as it is from the childish opening "Father had become very angry at K." by the conjunctions, the "and"s, "indeed," "except," "But," "on the contrary," "but," and again "and." These make what the child says quite obfuscatory but also give the passage a forward motion – what Beckett called the "steamroller" effect of Kafka's prose (and what is so emblematic of his own prose).

In his "Translator's Preface" to *The Castle*, Harman underscores his approach to what the prose does (rather than what it is) in the novel. Arguing that the lexical and semantic style perhaps emanates from Kafka's initial version of the novel in which it is told in the first person, Harman writes,

> As in much first-person fiction, the tempo of the prose charts the state of the central character. When K. is agitated, it is choppy. When K. loses himself in the labyrinth of his paranoid logic, it is tortuous and wordy. When the emphasis is on K.'s actions rather than on his thoughts, the prose becomes terse (Harman 1998c: xiv–xv).

In other words, rendering a "polished" or "elegant" version of the novel, and straightening out what seem like stylistic inconsistencies, might threaten the core of *how* the novel means. Harman goes on to talk about the more "opaque" passages such as Hans's above:

> At times, however, the prose slows down and is almost asphyxiated by clotted passages of opaque verbosity. That wordiness may well parody the prolixity of Austro-Hungarian officials, which, incidentally, occasionally amused Kafka, who once embarrassed himself by erupting in uncontrollable laughter during a speech by the president of the Workers Accident Insurance Company in Prague. In the course of one key chapter in *The Castle* an official called Bürgel drones on in almost impenetrable pseudo-officialese, which I have tried to keep as murky in English as it is in German (xv).

Toward the end of the novel (the end as it stands), it seems as if K. might get some real information from the minor official Bürgel; the problem is that Bürgel keeps repeating that he wants to "fall asleep" (Kafka 1998a: 259) and K. can't stay awake as Bürgel drones on: "K. had been half-dozing, but now he was roused again: 'What's the point of all this? What's the point of all this?' he asked himself" (263). The joke is on us; as readers we have been asking the same question, waiting for some answer to the enigma of the Castle and K.'s fate. Bürgel's – like Hans's – "opaque verbosity" stretches us taut in its very style, frustrates us, makes us feel some of both the claustrophobia and humor in K.'s ridiculous situation. Harman is attempting to convey the effect of that prose, even if it seems "murky" in terms of straightforward lexical meaning. For the meaning is not so much in what Bürgel or Hans say, but in how they say it.

Coetzee argues that Harman's "striving toward strangeness and denseness" (Coetzee 2001: 87) in the translation – a foreignizing rather than domesticating style – makes it a text of the literary taste of the moment, so that it is as "pointed toward obsolescence" as the Muirs's translation (87). David Damrosch argues accordingly that Harman gives us a fashionably postmodern Kafka in a more "calculating and self-serving K." (Damrosch 2003: 198), who is "at home in the America of *Gravity's Rainbow* and *Seinfeld*" (199), and also presents a fidelity to Kafka's uncorrected punctuation, a style "we now like […] because we have passed through postmodernism's love of fragments, internal contradiction, and incompletion" (204). Damrosch reignites the debate as to whether or not Kafka would have corrected the seemingly lax punctuation in the novel before publication (the novel was left unfinished and unpublished in his lifetime). He argues that while "Kafka's loose punctuation reflects the way he would read a text aloud, he clearly distinguished print from oral delivery" (202) and that he would have "normaliz[ed] his style" just as Max Brod did in editing *The Castle* before publication (202). Harman's fidelity to the punctuation and paragraph style of the manuscript reflects, for Damrosch, a nod to current literary taste, rather than to Kafka's intent.

Harman sets out his store in the "Translator's Preface," writing that punctuation is "another thorny issue" in the translation of the novel (Harman 1998c: xxi), noting that German critics "objected to Kafka's frugal use of punctuation" in Pasley's critical edition of *Das Schloß* and that Kafka might well have "inserted conventional punctuation had he prepared the text for publication" (xxi). Nevertheless, Kafka wrote with this "frugal use" in the manuscript and mused about the aesthetic possibilities of the "omission of the period" in his *Diaries* (xxi). "Would he have tidied it up?" Harman said in an interview "Maybe so, maybe not"; for Harman it is an "open question" (Harman, personal communication). Kafka was famously a "natty dresser, maybe he would have buttoned up his prose" but he was "writing unbuttoned" and this perhaps allowed him to "do away with [writing's] proper side" (Harman, personal communication).

In his "Translator's Preface" Harman turns back to Beckett to suggest his approach to the punctuation and lack of paragraphs breaks – the "breathless momentum of Kafka's prose" (Harman 1998c: xxi), again quoting Beckett saying in the 1956 interview that "You notice how Kafka's form is classic, it goes on like a steamroller – almost routine" (xxii). Harman's attunement (though not wholesale fidelity) to "Kafka's decision […] to omit most punctuation except for commas and an occasional period" that "lends his prose a breathlessly modern tone" (xxi) is not a blind adherence to Pasley's critical edition, an attempt to create a more correct version of Kafka's intent, but a nuanced understanding of the loosely punctuating Kafka via writers like Beckett. Damrosch and Coetzee are keen to emphasize the new translation as being a product of the literary now, inflected as it is by various forms of postmodernism (and post-postmodernism), but such a reading should be more nuanced and less critical. A translator is a literary being, partially constructed by the history of their reading in the source and target languages; a translator cannot but help be influenced by the literary present and their history of reading. As Jorge-Luis Borges wrote in "Kafka and his Precursors" he set out to find those whose work foretold Kafka's but discovers that having read Kafka now "perceptibly sharpens and deflects our reading" of the earlier work. "[E]very writer creates his own precursors," Borges writes. "His work modifies our conception of the past, as it will modify the future" (Borges 1970). Kafka was a lodestone for modernist and postmodernist writers, one of the most influential writers of the twentieth century; in going back to read Kafka now, we are invariably influenced by our reading of works that are very often inspired by his own. Every translator also creates their own precursors – writers and translators – which are as bound to influence their own reading of the work they translate.

Nevertheless, Harman is not presenting us with a Beckettian Kafka; rather Beckett allows him to see elements of Kafka's text that might have seemed odd, wrong, inconsistent or jarring. He does not magic out of the air a Seinfeldian K.; K. *is* cunning and ambiguous, but, as Damrosch suggests, we are now, post-modernism and after postmodernism, ready to recognize and accept unreliable narrators. Harman knows that he is working with an advantage as a retranslator at the present time; unlike the Muirs who had to translate Kafka as an unknown author and for the tastes of a pre-war English readership, Harman is translating a now modern classic author who influenced many contemporary bestselling authors (Marquez, Kundera, Rushdie, Bolaño, Foer, Franzen, etc.). He felt that he had "more freedom" as the retranslator of an established author; he could "echo the voice, hiccups and all" (Harman, personal communication). The "stylistic offences should be preserved" in a retranslation, and, in fact, often these "deviations from good style" are constituent of the "uniqueness" of a literary text (Harman, personal communication).

In his essay on the French translations of one sentence from *The Castle*, "A Sentence," Milan Kundera argues that translators do not look to the authority of the "*author's personal style*" but rather to "the *conventional version* of 'good French' (or good German, good English, etc.). ... That is the error: every author of some value transgresses against 'good style,' and in that transgression lies the originality (and hence the raison d'être) of his art" (Kundera 1996, 110, italics in original). The issue is more complicated – as Kundera well knows with his own work – because often it is not the translator who wants to "obey" the authority of conventional domestic style, but the publisher. The desire for domestication is "as strong or even stronger" in the publishing industry than in the Muirs's day, Harman argues; publishers want "smooth" translations and reviewers want translations that read "smoothly, fluently" (personal communication). While retranslators of classic literature have an advantage in that they can give "more of a flavor of the original" than the initial translators who are trying to "get a foot in the door" for a foreign author – a process that often means domesticating them to the target audience's tastes – there is still push-back for retranslators (as we have seen) who do not provide "smooth" or "elegant" Englished translations. "The translator's primary effort," Kundera writes, "should be to understand that transgression" (110) and suggests that sometimes they miss the style of those authors (including Kafka and himself) whose transgressions are "subtle, barely visible, hidden, discreet" and thus "not easy to grasp" (111), but often the translators, who have spent months, if not years, with the text, are exactly the readers who do grasp these subtle transgressions: in repetition, punctuation, paragraph length, etc. The question is whether, and when, the publishers, reviewers, and literary culture in general, are ready to accept translations that are faithful to the author's style without, as Coetzee suggests, "lightly and silently fixing up the original" (Coetzee 2001: 82).

Pre(facing) the rivals

There are translator prefaces to both of Harman's translations of *The Castle* and *Amerika: The Missing Person*; Harman explicitly wanted to include prefaces as they are "helpful for the serious reader" and "good for translation" in general, because people tend to think of translation as "easy, an uncreative act" (personal communication). It enables the translator to give a sense of their approach to the translation, and to the difficulties they may have encountered, often difficulties associated with subtle transgressions of style, or untranslatable words or phrases. Harman noted that because he wrote about the problems of punctuation in the "Translator's Preface" to *The Castle*, he felt that he received less reaction to his choices, that the preface "takes the wind out of the sails" of critics who might just suppose it was not an interpretive choice (Harman, personal communication). The prefaces also allow a retranslation to explain how and why their translation differs from previous ones, and in the case of *The Castle* the preface began life as an article, "Digging the Pit of Babel," written to persuade the publisher, Schocken, that a retranslation was needed at all.

Schocken – a publishing house associated in the US with Kafka's work – were bought by Random House in 1987, at which point Pantheon's (an imprint of Random House) managing director, André Schiffrin "said he expected to commission new translations of Kafka" (McDowell 1987). Copyright issues were part of the reason; Schocken, in their new incarnation, "wanted to prolong" copyright via new editions; it "quickened the pulse" in favor of new translations (Harman, personal communication). A colleague of Harman's saw the comment about Schocken thinking about new translations in the *New York Times* and Harman sent a sample of *The Trial* but Schocken chose another translator, Breon Mitchell. Harman then, in the early 1990s, sent a translation sample of *The Castle*, and it was sent out to a number of academics, some of whom thought a new translation was necessary, and some who did not. As a result, for a while, the publishers hesitated. Harman felt that "room had to be made for a new translation of *The Castle* in the US," and wrote his article on the deficiencies of the Muirs's translation, hoping that in some ways it might put some "pressure on the publisher" to finally make a decision (Harman, personal communication).

"I am loath to criticize the Muirs," Harman writes in "Digging the Pit of Babel," "whose smooth translation I read with relief, alongside the more puzzling original, while still an undergraduate in Dublin" (Harman 1996: 294). But he has to, in order to persuade the publisher that a new translation is needed; he situates this need in a recent history of scholarly criticism of the Muirs's translation: "critics and scholars have been faulting the Muirs," he writes, "for taking excessive liberties with Kafka's texts, for failing to capture the stylistic tone of the original, for misleading readers about its texture, and even for distorting its intellectual substance" (294). In addition, "the Muirs had to depend on Max Brod's deeply flawed editions" (294). Harman is especially critical of two elements of the initial translation: the Muirs's "theological agenda," which, he writes, left "their mark on the Muirs's translation" (297) in their deliberate use or suggestion of a mystical lexicon; and their lack of understanding or sympathy for modernism (Harman predicates this criticism on the widespread assumption that Edwin was the "primary stylist").

Harman places his retranslation within a contemporary wave of retranslations of the modernists – Thomas Mann, Robert Musil, and Marcel Proust – "a great era of retranslation" because of "the widespread dissatisfaction in literary circles with the first translators of the great modernists, whose sense of style had been formed by nineteenth-century literature and who therefore often failed to capture the modernist idiom" (292). Harman suggests that the literary hindsight of the translator after modernism allows a more holistic view and understanding of modernist writing. In addition, he argues that translators "have a different conception of the art [of translation] than that which held sway in the early decades of the century" (292), when smoothness, domestication and fluency were celebrated (although adding that translation reviews have not caught up).

Harman's article, and subsequent preface, were seen in the reviews of his translation as a "trenchant attack" on the Muirs, "his rivals" (Coetzee 2001: 86) and a deliberate whitewashing of "his rival" whom he does not mention, J. A. Underwood, who translated *The Castle* for Penguin in the UK (Ormsby 2001: 137). (Harman, in fact, was unaware of Underwood's translation until after his own had gone to press.) It is "of course to be expected that Harman should be hostile to his rivals," Coetzee writes, for a justification of his own translation (Coetzee 2001: 86); Eric Ormsby also sniffed at "the crowing self-praise in which both Harman and his publisher Schocken engage" (Ormsby 2001: 137). The language of rivalry, hostility, attack and self-praise postulates a kind of Oedipal envy among translators and retranslators, and that a retranslator's worth can only be judged by other translators. They also indicate that there is some hostility toward hearing the voice of the translator at all.

It is important to note that Harman's audience was not the Muirs (or, rather, their legacy) but the publishers and the reviewers. Harman is obliged to "make room" for his translation, to justify it; in a literary culture that has long devalued translation and accepted a certain form of translation – smooth, fluent, Englished – Harman has to begin in an embattled position. In an interview, Harman stressed that he did not intend for the article to be "small-minded" about the Muirs and that he felt that they had done a "brilliant job as first time translators" (personal communication). The "ripple effect of their translations has been really important" as they established Kafka not only as an important writer in English, but also worldwide (as he came into fame in English). In his preface to *The Castle*, Harman describes their translation as "elegant" (xiii); in his preface to *Amerika* as "beautiful" (Harman 2008: xvi).

Coetzee sees these compliments as "backhanded" (Coetzee 2001: 87), regarding words like "elegant" and "smooth" as indictments of the Muirs's old-fashioned methodology of Englishing or polishing their translations (in opposition to what he sees as Harman's foreignizing and estranging translation that is "as of its time" as the Muirs were of theirs). But Harman is not being "patroniz[ing]" (Ormsby 2001: 136) to the Muirs by using these terms; rather, he is implicitly challenging the expectations of publishers and reviewers who want exactly this smoothness and elegance despite the form and style of the original.

In his article "Digging the Pit of Babel," Harman is cognizant of the potential criticisms of his own work not being "smooth" or "elegant":

> many reviewers especially those writing for newspapers, continue to assess a translation exclusively on the basis of whether the English is "smooth" and "natural." This insistence on conventional aesthetic qualities often precludes any consideration of the specific texture of the original (Harman 1996: 292, ft 2).

Sure enough, Robert Alter, in his review, tells his readers that Harman's translation of *The Castle* is "less elegant" than the Muirs's translation for two reasons: first, "because Harman wishes to convey the abruptness and the idiosyncrasies of Kafka's style without 'improving' it" which is exactly what Harman was trying to achieve; but also, secondly, "because Harman does not have so firm a sense of English style as the Muirs" (Alter 2005). What is this sense of English style? A sense of "proper literary prose in English" (Alter 2005), or, as Kundera put it, the "conventional version" of "good English" – there is no indication here, or elsewhere, of the cost of this to the Muirs themselves, or the necessity of that choice for them (economically reliant on translation, they had to translate in "proper" English literary prose). Alter admits that this changes the style of Kafka's original: it "soften[s] the starkness" of the prose; adds "dramatic heightening"; gives "a kind of prefabricated interpretation of the narrative"; makes the prose "more decorous" thereby "obscuring the vein of violence in his writing" (Alter 2005). Harman's translation, he adds, "gives us a sounder English equivalent of the original. […] It gives us a much better sense of Kafka's uncompromising and disturbing originality as a prose master than we have heretofore had in English" (Alter 2005).

Yet there are still problems of English fluency for Alter and for others; "Harman's ear for English idiom occasionally fails him" Alter writes, and wishes that "his publisher had subjected the translation itself to more stringent editing" (Alter 2005). Eric Ormsby complains that the "problem lies, it must be said, not in Harman's grasp of German but in his English" (Ormsby 2001: 138–9). For Ormsby, not only does Harman include too colloquial language, but he is not even

> consistent in this "Americanization" of *The Castle* […] incongruously, Harman will avail himself of a term with British rather than American overtones such as "cheeky" for the German keck (instead of, say, "impudent" or even "smart-alecky"). Now "cheeky" and "cheekiness" are perfectly correct as translations of keck and Keckheit, but in an American context they have an unavoidably arch overtone. To such overtones – and there are, alas, many – Harman remains deaf (Ormsby 2001: 137–8).

Both critics assume that alongside a "proper" English literary style is a "proper" form of English into which Kafka should be translated. The fairly contemporary internationalization of English (influenced by old and new media) has not resulted in a standardized English-language literary language or style; in fact, it has perhaps resulted in an acceptance of variances. To expect it in translation seems to be placing unattainable demands on translators who come from different linguistic and cultural backgrounds. Robert Alter – long-time California resident, Eric Ormsby – long-time Montreal, and now London resident, J. M. Coetzee – South African and long-time Australian resident, and Mark Harman – Dublin raised and long-time US resident will all have different "ears" for English idiom and a variant literary lexicon. Harman said, if he was trying for anything, it was a "mid-Atlantic" form of English, which makes sense given his background, between Ireland and America. That there are Americanisms and "British" usage is unsurprising, and reflective of Harman's "ear." What it is not, is a mistake.

The reviews (apart from Ormsby's) are, in fact, positive reviews of the translation, but their divisive nature – what's expected of translation reviewing: having to point out inconsistencies, creating rivalries, and making assumptions about Harman's work in the language of mistakes and "inattention" (rather than interpretive choices) – leads to a less than holistic consideration of the translator's job and their role as an interpreter of the text. Not one of the reviews mentions either Harman's Irish background, his translation expertise, or his background as a Kafka scholar. None treat Harman as a literary figure, but rather as an intruder placing his linguistic paws on Kafka, and, in the old language of translation criticism, as a betrayer.

Slow reading Kafka

"Philology is the slowest form of reading," Harman says, "and translation even slower" (Harman, personal communication). In translating *The Castle*, Harman became "much more aware of Kafka's style" and his use of repetition, because of this slow, close reading. The translation took him over two years to complete; he had a "sense of obligation to do the best possible job and to make it work better for a contemporary audience" (Harman, personal communication). During the translation process, he read at different stages the entire translation aloud to various audiences, some of whom would be reading the German original as he spoke, which was "useful" with "others listening in English"; "in the beginning [of the process, I] was too much the scholar," Harman said, and "it ended up being too stiff" (Harman, personal communication). Reading Kafka aloud, engaging with the audiences and their reactions and comments, enabled him to revise the translation. When Harman finished the written version of his translation, he requested an editor from Schocken "to go over" the translation "line by line." Schocken hired a translator, Melanie Richter-Bernburg, to give this "different perspective" and "reams were faxed" between Harman and Richter-Bernburg over Harman's decisions.

The "deliberate quality of reading the translator has to do," the slow reading, is a skill much undervalued in weighing up the worth of translators, who are often just seen as "hobbyists" (Ormsby 2001) with some foreign language skills, rather than textual interpreters, experts and writers. Harman – a Kafka scholar for nearly forty years – is excited about how much he is still learning about Kafka's work in rereading it for translation with "new things popping out all the time" and "revising some of the things you thought" previously about the work, while trying to bring "knowledge" and "insights" to the translation from his scholarship and teaching on Kafka (Harman, personal communication), although the translations were not "directed by a hermeneutic reading" of the novels.

Working from the critical edition and a facsimile edition of *The Castle*, Harman would "stick at it" trying to get long periods of time (and time off teaching) to get into the "stream" of it and keep the "connective tissue" of the rhythm and tone of the text. While for Harman, a translator's attitude to translation "undoubtedly affected the translation" there was no hard and fast methodology; his attitude "changes and evolves in the course of a project" and there had to be "pragmatic decisions for local examples" (Harman, personal communication). Harman's style of translation changed also; whereas initially he would "translate quickly and revise and revise," he now "slows down and does it as it might remain"; with experience came "a certain amount of confidence, more intuition and less second-guessing" but "the intuitive was based on thousands of tries and amassed from an awareness of hundreds of details" (Harman, personal communication). The "deliberate quality of reading" based on this experience going through the translations led to "a total experience of the text" in which sometimes he was "not thinking about questions of reading but sometimes felt 'that's right!'" (Harman, personal communication). But he was "very particular about Kafka," more so perhaps than a less well-known writer. For first-time translated authors, Harman felt that "you had to be a bit of an editor" in order "to gain an audience in an English-language environment" because of demands for domesticated translations, whereas, as a retranslator, he felt he had an "escape-clause" and could translate the experimental style of Kafka's work because of Kafka's eminence; that the point was "not to fix up" Kafka's work but to translate what he felt could be translated that hadn't been, to "focus on what can be carried across" (Harman, personal communication).

Two important elements of this were the tonal rhythm and the humor of Kafka's prose. In translating, Harman became aware of the amount of word repetitions in the text. An example is the one Kundera elicits in "A Sentence" – the scene in which K. makes love to Frieda in a beer puddle:

> Hours passed there, hours breathing together with a single heartbeat, hours in which K. constantly felt he was lost or had wandered farther into foreign lands than any human being before him, so foreign that even the air hadn't a single component of the air in his homeland and where one would inevitably suffocate from the foreignness but where the meaningless enticements were such that one had no alternative but to go on and get even more lost (Kafka 1998a: 41).

K. is a foreigner, from elsewhere; the notion of foreignness with Frieda and the nostalgia but also break from home is caught in the repetition of "foreign"/"die Fremde" around "homeland/Heimat[luft]" and this is consolidated by surrounding repetitions: "hours," "lost," "air." Coetzee thinks Harman "copes well" (Coetzee 2001: 83) translating this passage but frets about the impossibility of translating a word like "die Fremde" and is unhappy with Harman's translation of "Heimat," another culturally loaded word, as "homeland" (84–5). The point is that these words are impossible to translate with all their connotations; Harman said he "could write paragraphs" about the difficulty of translating "die Fremde" but that what was perhaps more important was the translation of the repetition which carries with it its own tonal meaning: the repetition of "foreign" itself is foreign or strange, especially surrounded as it is by the other repetitions.

The light punctuation throws these repetitions into an interesting melody – the repetition of "hours" in the opening of the passage, "Hours passed there, hours breathing together with a single heartbeat, hours in which K. constantly felt he was lost" is contradicted by the pace of the syntax giving a sense of the "hours" speeding by in the language and style of a romance novel (and with a sexual rhythm); the repetition of "foreign" and mention of "homeland" seems to turn it into the epic which is undercut by the odd officious turn, "inevitably suffocate" and "meaningless enticements" and then turns back to the wistful in the "go on and get even more lost" (Kafka 1998a: 41). Coetzee sees this as "K. wandering into disturbing spiritual territory in the sudden act of sex" (Coetzee 2001: 83), but this effaces the fact that it is also funny, "comic poetry" (Kundera 1996: 52). The repetitions are beautiful, mesmeric, but also deliberately odd and slightly ridiculous, *too much.*

"*Post coitum omne animal triste*," Kundera writes, "Kafka was the first to describe the comic side of that sadness. The comic side of sex" (47). Frieda chooses K. over Klamm, disappointing K., who sees her as a means to getting to Klamm; he realizes that "he had rolled about all night in the beer puddles, which now gave off an overpowering smell" and that "Sitting on the counter were his two assistants, they were somewhat tired from a lack of sleep, but cheerful" (Kafka 1998a: 42); the two assistants were laughing after a night spent watching those hours pass and K. and Frieda's single heartbeat, these "lecherous voyeurs whose presence imbues the whole novel with the sexual scent of a smutty, Kafkaesquely comic promiscuity" (Kundera 1996: 52).

Harman describes reading a section of his translation of *The Castle* aloud at the Czech Center in Vienna and having a woman approach him afterwards saying that she had read previously the first sixty pages of *Das Schloß* and "hadn't laughed, hadn't even smiled" but "she was laughing at it in English" (Harman, personal communication). For Harman, reading Kafka aloud brings out "the humor and irony" of his prose, something that is "absolutely misunderstood" partly because of Kafka's "reputation for being grim" (Harman, personal communication). Harman also makes the point that reading Kafka on your own, with these preconceptions, often your "first impression is of disorientation and angst created by the text, so you're not noticing other things," i.e., the subtle and wry humor underpinning it. Hearing the breath and melody of the sentences – with their light punctuation – adds to the humor; what seems to be a dark sentence on the page can give a different impression on an "auditory level" (Harman, personal communication). "Kafka's loose punctuation," David Damrosch writes, "reflects the way he would read a text aloud" (Damrosch 2003: 202) – these readings that Max Brod tells us would have his audience in fits of laughter – but Damrosch (as a criticism of Harman's translation) adds that Kafka "clearly distinguished print from oral delivery, and the several stories he published during his lifetime all appeared in standard High German" (202). Did Kafka's ideas about this change as his writing developed? Did he approach his novels differently? Did he feel he had to alter punctuation for prevailing literary expectations? It's unclear, but humor is innately tied into the length and melody of the syntax.

The question of "High German" is also a very contested one, and connected also to humor in the prose. Deleuze and Guattari influenced a reading of Kafka as someone who wrote, subversively, in a Prague German dialect; Damrosch follows this reading and feels that Harman should have emphasized the "regional dialect" in *The Castle*, perhaps by including "Black English" as a means of doing so (203). Coetzee disagrees and makes the point that the villagers, "as much as the Castle officials, seem able to produce exegetical monologues at the drop of a hat" (Coetzee 2001: 82); he adds: "the temptation to be resisted is to introduce a linguistic variousness that is absent in the original" (82). Corngold dismisses the idea of Kafka writing in a dialect at all; "the so-called 'Prague German' that Kafka allegedly spoke was only a faintly dialectical coloration of High German" (Corngold 2004: 273). Harman notes that there are some "Austrianisms" in Kafka's German, but that what is interesting is how Kafka uses High German; he writes in "eerie High German," "surreal High German" influenced by the "19th century narrative style" and language of Stifter and Kleist but with a "live colloquial" tone and Kafka's idiosyncratic use of repetition and punctuation. Kafka pushes the High German of the Austro-Hungarian bureaucracy to its limits; the humor is not in "parody but in the reality" of the pervasiveness and insinuation of bureaucracy into everyday life, or "High German out in the countryside" (Harman, personal communication). The change in tone even within sentences (as the "Hours passed" sentence shows above) from the intimate or colloquial to the officious lends a strange and funny aspect to the prose.

The magpyre's babble towers

In a couple of his academic articles, Harman tells the story of Beckett's conversation with Joyce about Kafka: "Beckett himself sadly informed Joyce the intellectuals [in Dublin] were not interested in reading *Ulysses*, because they were too busy reading Kafka" (Harman 1998b: 179). Joyce was horrified, thinking Beckett meant Irene Kafka, a translator who had misattributed a Michael Joyce story for one of his (Harman 1993: 66). Joyce includes a reference, Harman argues, to one or the other Kafkas in *Finnegans Wake* and their "magpyre's babble towers," probably Irene Kafka "getting her comeuppance for mixing up the two Joyces" (70).

Harman wrote three academic articles about Beckett, Joyce and their relationship to Kafka in the 1990s when, or just after, he was translating *The Castle*: "Joyce and Kafka" (1993); "Terminal Fantasies: Beckett and Kafka" (1998b) and "'At Least He Could Garden': Beckett and Kafka" (1999). The latter title refers to Kafka's diary entry:

"Gardening. No hope for the future" and Beckett's famous comment on it: "At least he could garden" (Harman 1998b). Beckett's determination to distance himself from Kafka just heightens the obvious affinity between the two in their mordant humor. But Harman argues for serious affinities: their "fantasies [...] written on the edge of silence and of death" (Harman 1998b), the fear of disappearing into nothing on the page and in life. Harman gives the textual example of the end of *Malone Dies* which "tapers off" with "fragmentary phrases" and the end of his new translation of *The Castle* which does the same (ending in mid-sentence) (Harman 1998b: 183):

> or with his pencil or with his stick or
> or light light I mean
> never there he will never
> never anything
> there
> any more (Beckett 1994: 289).

> She held out her trembling hand to K. and had him sit down beside her, she spoke with great difficulty, it was difficult to understand her, but what she said (Kafka 1998a: 316).

Although Beckett claimed that "it was difficult to get to the end" of *The Castle* which he read in German and found "serious reading," he, as Harman writes, "captures a key feature of Kafka's prose – its relentlessness." (Harman 1999: 574). It "goes on like a steamroller," Beckett said, "almost serene. It seems to be threatened the whole time – but the consternation is in the form. In my work there is consternation behind the form, not in the form" (574). The relentlessness of the form is, Harman argues:

> a stylistic trait that had passed unremarked in voluminous discussions of *The Castle* by German-language writers and critics. Beckett was the first to note the odd discrepancy in Kafka's third and final novel between the lack of action ... and the relentless momentum of the language itself which presses on and on in a manner that anticipates Beckett's own version of the steamroller effect in his Molloy trilogy. Sometimes it takes an outsider with the linguistic discernment of a Beckett to spot essential characteristics of foreign masterworks (574).

Harman's point is astute; Kafka's unobtrusive stretching of the norms of German syntax might not have been as immediately perceptible to German speakers, but Beckett as a linguistic "outsider" seems to show an interest here in the tension between physical stasis (Malone dying in his bed, obsessively circling around ideas) and movement (in the use of syntax and repetition) in language that becomes so evident in his own work. While Beckett thinks that the consternation in his own work lies behind the language and not, like Kafka, in it, the consternation is effected by his use of language, as with Kafka. "On first reading Beckett's comment on the steamroller-like quality of Kafka's prose," Harman writes, "I couldn't quite see what Beckett meant" (Harman 1998: 180). Only in translating *The Castle* did he come to see that quality in Kafka's prose and its refraction onto his reading of Beckett's prose: "While Beckett's prose is more colloquial than Kafka's, it too has an urgent forward drive" (180).

Harman quotes a remarkably similar passage in *The Castle* and *Malone Dies*: the sentence examined above in which Frieda and K. have sex, and one of Malone's cogitations on sex:

> Hours passed there, hours breathing together with a single hearbeat, hours in which K. constantly felt he was lost or had wandered further into foreign lands than any human being before him, so foreign (Kafka 1998a: 41; Harman 1999: 576).

> Let us think of the hours when, spent, we lie twined together in the dark, our hearts labouring as one, and listen to the wind saying what it is to be abroad, at night, in winter, and what it is to have been what we have been, and sink together, in an unhappiness that has no name (Beckett 1994: 263; Harman 1999: 576).

Harman suggests that the affinity here is in a similar view of sex as "suffocating" rather than "replenishing" (Harman 1999: 575), nothing "more than a gateway to a nameless unhappiness" (576). But what is striking also is the similar method and the mechanics of the sentences: the beauty of Kafka's sentence is achieved through repetition (which accentuates the temporal length and rhythm of their love-making) and we see a similar effect in Beckett: "what it is to be … what it is to have been what we have been"; "together," "at night, in winter" and the constant assertion of togetherness: "Let us," "we lie twined together," "as one," "what we have been," "sink together." It is alienating and hopeless but at the same time strangely affirming because of the insistance of language.

The Beckett sentence is actually from an "inflammatory" letter by Moll, the nurse who keeps bringing letters to Macmann in St. John of Gods psychiatric hospital, "that enchanted world of reading," to incite love and sex (Beckett 1994: 261). After he reads it, "she put[s] it under her pillow with the other there already, arranged in chronological order and tied together with a favour" (263). The letter is humorous and sad, from "Sucky Moll" to "sweet old hairy Mac" (263) and is the only way they can communicate: "Moll, despairing no doubt of giving vent to her feelings by the normal channels, addressed three or four times a week to Macmann, who never answered, I mean, in writing" (263). The reliance on text, and the materiality of text, reflects Malone's writing (his exercise book and pencil) and is, of course, central to the workings of *The Castle*. "'A lot of writing goes on here,' said K., looking from a distance at the files. 'Yes, a bad habit,' said the gentleman, laughing again" (Kafka 1998a: 110).

The steamroller nature of both writers' prose creates the mechanics for, Harman argues, "their characters' obsessive cogitations [that] are merely a distraction … from the death that awaits them"; the characters' "preoccupation with death is often displaced into febrile reasoning about inconsequential activities," that contains these repetitions, long sentences and unfinished sentences (Harman 1998: 177). Harman points out that the first three chapters of *The Castle* were written initially in first-person narration, "a mode more characteristic of Beckett than Kafka" (Harman 1999: 575). While writing the third chapter, Harman writes, "Kafka went back and replaced all the Is with K.s. The traces left by these first-person origins accentuate the sensation that we are stuck inside K.'s head, eavesdropping on his obsessive thoughts" (575).

Yet, in rendering the obsessiveness, Kafka and the elusive narrator of *The Castle* create an ironic distance between K.'s obsessiveness (and that of most of the villagers) and what the reader understands: if a character "is trapped in the joke of his own life like a fish in a bowl; he doesn't find it funny," Milan Kundera writes. "Indeed, a joke is a joke only outside the bowl; by contrast, the *Kafkan* takes us inside, into the guts of a joke, into the *horror of the comic*" (Kundera 1993: 104, italics in original). The comedy is horrific, Kundera argues, because there is no hope in Kafka's world (and in Beckett's) of majestic tragedy: the characters are not heroes in a classical world doomed to, but elevated by, tragedy, they are fallible people in a fallible world.

The Castle, like *Molloy*, references *The Odyssey*, and in doing so subverts the idea of the heroic while referencing elements of style in *The Odyssey* (certainly in its obsessive story-telling – much of the action is decribed through stories within the text; and in its circular geotextuality: I consider this further in Chapter 2). James Joyce began writing his subversion of *The Odyssey*, *Ulysses*, of course, in Central Europe, in the dying days of the Austro-Hungarian Empire. "Like Joyce," Harman writes, "Kafka enjoys playing around with Homer," Harman specifically drawing paralles between Kafka's short prose piece "The Silence of the Sirens" and Bloom avoiding "becoming trapped by the sirens" in the "Sirens" chapter in *Ulysses* (Harman 1993: 79). Harman makes some interesting parallels between Joyce and Kafka in their biographies: their relationship to Judaism; Joyce's reactions to notions of authentic Irishness (as purveyed by the Irish Revival) – specifically the enshrining of the Irish-speaking West Coast as the authentic identity – and Kafka's relationship to Eastern Jewishness; the importance of the notion of exile to both; and he provides sensitive readings of paralles between Joyce's "The Dead," and Kafka's "The Judgment" (thinking of this East/West divide) and of "Josefine, the Singer" and *Finnegans Wake* (in the move beyond language). Given the amount of critical writing on both Kafka and Joyce separately, Harman notes that it is surprising that "critics have largely ignored" this "intriguing relationship between Joyce and Kafka" (66). Joyce was certainly not affected by Kafka's writing – there is no indication at all that he read any of it – and although Joyce was translated remarkably quickly into Czech – *Ulysses, Portrait of the Artist as a Young Man* and "Anna Livia Plurabelle" had been translated into Czech by 1931 – it was after Kafka's death (Woods 2012: 7). However, there are some clear affinities: as Joyce remarked in a letter to his brother in 1920, "Odyssey is very much in the air here," here meaning Paris, but Kafka would soon be writing a novel that would also have clear allusions to *The Odyssey* (Butler 2004: 75). Kundera, too, reminds his readers that Kafka was embedded in a "generation of great innovators – Stravinsky, Webern, Bartók, Apollinaire, Musil, Joyce, Picasso, Braque – all born, like him, between 1880 and 1883" (Kundera 1996: 44). Kundera argues that these modernist affinities have been ignored by "Kafkologists" in order to preserve a sense of Kafka's exceptionalism and *sui generis* genius, whereas reading him within this context could open up fertile readings of his – and their – work (44).

Waiting for Klamm

At around the same time that Harman was translating Kafka's *The Castle* (1998), he published his two articles on Beckett and Kafka (1998b and 1999) and also the personal essay, quoted above, on his upbringing in Ireland, his relationship with his father, and the importance of *The Castle* in decoding that relationship (the essay was also published in 1998). Harman's "slow reading" of *The Castle* while translating it leads him to remark that "Kafka's depiction of the elusive Castle official Klamm clearly inspired Beckett's remarkably comparable rendering of Mr. Knott, who is of course the forefather of Youdi in *Molloy* and of Godot in *Waiting for Godot*" (Harman 1998c: 181). He then adds:

> By a piquant coincidence, one of Kafka's original chapter headings, not included by Max Brod in his editions but restored by Malcolm Pasley in the 1982 German critical edition, was "'Das Warten auf Klamm,' or 'Waiting for Klamm'" (181).

It would be impossible for someone seeing that chapter title not to think about Beckett; it, in some ways, comes into meaning after Kafka's death, because we are reading Kafka – post 1982 (and in English, post–1998) – after Beckett.

In the chapter "Waiting for Klamm," K. goes to the Gentlemen's Inn to find Klamm; Pepi – who has taken Frieda's job in the taproom – tells him that Klamm's sleigh is waiting outside in the courtyard, and K. goes to wait outside. The coachman – Gerstäcker – tells him there is cognac inside the sleigh and K. climbs in, wrapping himself in the furs and blankets inside and pouring himself cognac from one of the bottles there. Momus comes out to ask K. to enter the Inn for his interrogation:

> "Come," the gentleman repeated, not in the least deterred, as if he had wanted to show that he had never doubted that K. was waiting for somebody. "But then I'll miss the person I'm waiting for," said K., flinching. ... "You'll miss him whether you wait or go," said the gentleman, whose opinion certainly was dismissive but also showed remarkable indulgence for K.'s train of thought: "Then I would rather miss him as I wait," said K. defiantly, it would take more than mere words from this young gentleman to drive him away (Kafka 1998a: 105).

The repetition of "waiting/wait"; "warten/warte" and "miss"/"verfehle[n]" humorously shows K.'s stubbornness and the futility of it – he is determined to catch and speak with K., but Momus (who some think is Klamm) is sure that Klamm will never appear if K. is there. He orders Gerstäcker to unhitch the horse; once K. goes into the inn, suddenly the landlady spots Klamm, through a peephole, entering the sleigh. The elusiveness of Klamm and K.'s stubborn waiting elucidated through the repetitions of the verb "wait" certainly suggest a fraternal text to *Waiting for Godot* and Estragon and Vladimir's rhythmic consideration of waiting for the elusive Godot: "Let's go" "We can't" "Why not" "We're waiting for Godot" (Beckett 1990: 66). We can hear Vladimír in the "Then I would rather miss him as I wait."

There is also a hint of this scene in *Malone Dies*, when Macmann is unraveling and he gets into a coach:

you see the cabman too, all alone on his box ten feet from the ground, his feet covered at all seasons and in all weathers with a kind of rug. ... But the passenger, having named the place that he wants to go and knowing himself as helpless to act on the course of events as the dark box that encloses him, abandons himself to the pleasant feeling of being freed from responsibility, or he ponders on what lies before him, or on what lies behind him, saying, Twill not be ever thus and then in the same breath, But twas ever thus, for there are not five hundred different kinds of passengers. And so they hasten, the horse, the driver and the passenger towards the appointed place, by the shortest route or deviously, through the press of other misplaced persons. And each one has his reasons, while wondering from time to time what they are worth, and if they are the true ones, for going where he is going rather than somewhere else (Beckett 1994: 231–2).

The coach Macmann enters actually moves because, Malone thinks, "in order not to die you must come and go, come and go" (232), but "he is going where he is going rather than somewhere else"; there is no import to his destination and he is "as helpless to act on the course of events as the dark box that encloses him." This helplessness lets him abandon "himself to the pleasant feeling of being freed from responsibility." K., too, abandons himself in the much less coffin-like interior of the static sleigh:

How extraordinarily warm it was in the sleigh ... there were so many blankets, cushions, and furs; on each side one could turn in every direction and always sink down soft and warm. With his arms extended, his head supported by the abundant supply of cushions, K. gazed from the sleigh into the dark house. ... His forgetfulness was reinforced by the conduct of the coachman, who must have known he was in the sleigh, but left him there without even asking for the cognac (Kafka 1998a: 103).

The interior of Klamm's sleigh is the equivalent of the many beds that K. sits beside and on when listening to the Castle stories of various officials and villagers: the Council Chairman, the landlady, Bürgel, places of forgetfulness, little Ogygian islands of Calypso, consistently detaining K. K. comes and goes and comes and goes in the novel, but is always held up: the sleigh that is supposed to move does not. The very things in this passage that hold K. up – the sleigh, cognac, doors, Klamm, the lights – are words, however, that are repeated through the passage, giving the prose momentum and the passage movement. Beckett's prose works with a similar tension – there is movement here – the passengers moving in the coach but the constant sibilance in the passage (and the repetition of "passengers") lulls the reader slowly. The idea of the passenger – so redolent of travel – is also presented as someone who is carried along regardless. "What questions! What answers!" K. exclaims in a Vladimirian manner when Momus asks what he is doing in the sleigh. "Perhaps he should assure the gentleman that the path on which he had set out with such hope had led nowhere" (104).

We can see Kafka in Beckett and, thanks to Harman, Beckett in Kafka, and we can see the particular influence in certain passages, particularly in the last one. The chapter ends with a very long sentence:

> Und als nun nach Beendigung der Arbeit im Stall der Kutscher quer über den Hof gieng in seinem langsamen schaukelnden Gang, das große Tor zumachte, dan zurückkam, alles langsam und förmlich nur in Betrachtung seiner eigenen Spur im Schnee, dann sich im Stall einschloß und nun auch alles elektrische Licht verlöschte – wem hätte es leuchten sollen? – und nur noch oben der Spalt in der Holzgallerie hell blieb und den irrenden Blick ein wenig festhielt, da schien es K. als habe man nun alle Verbindung mit ihm abgebrochen und als sei er nun freilich freier als jemals und könne hier auf dem ihm sonst verbotenen Ort warten solange er wolle und habe sich diese Freiheit erkämpft wie kaum ein anderer es könnte und niemand dürfe ihn anrühren oder vertreiben, ja kaum ansprechen, aber – diese Überzeugung war zumindest ebenso stark – als gäbe es gleichzeitig nichts Sinnloseres, nichts Verzweifelteres als diese Freiheit, dieses Warten, diese Unverletzlichkeit (Kafka 2002b: 168–9).

Gerstäcker, the coachman, has dismantled the harnesses, put the horse in the stable, and is now shutting the gate and the lights are being switched off. K. thinks that the Castle and its officials have cut off "contact"/"Verbindung" with him – connections or contact that he has been searching for since he arrived in the village (the word is repeated through the novel); it makes him feel free, but that freedom has a bite to it:

> And now when after finishing his work in the stable the coachman walked straight across the courtyard with his slow swaying gait, closed the large gate, then came back, all this slowly and meticulously, focusing only on his own tracks in the snow, then locked the stable behind him, all the electric lights went out – for whom should they have shone? – and only the opening above in the wooden gallery remained bright and briefly arrested one's wandering gaze, it seemed to K. as if they had broken off all contact with him, but as if he were freer than ever and could wait as long as he wanted here in this place where he was generally not allowed, and as if he had fought for this freedom for himself in a manner nobody else could have done and as if nobody could touch him or drive him away, or even speak to him, yet – and this conviction was at least equally strong – as if there was nothing more senseless, nothing more deperate, than this freedom, this waiting, this invulnerability (Kafka 1998a: 106).

Harman's translation is lovely, and its length and paradoxes (waiting and freedom) are enunciated in rhythmic clauses that convey the coachman's movements and K.'s thought pattern, but also seem to bear witness to Beckett (especially the second half of the sentence): "nothing more senseless, nothing more deperate, than this freedom, this waiting, this invulnerability." The push and pull between enervating isolation and the need for contact – the bridge between which is language, desperate and freeing in its textuality – is also echoed in Harman's translation of "wem hätte es leuchten sollen?" as "for whom should they have shone?," a seeming allusion to John Donne's famous meditation that "no man is an island": "never send to know for whom the bell tolls; it tolls for thee." K., as Kundera points out, is not suffering from isolation, but from a *"violation of solitude"* (in Beckett, the violation of solitude is often imaginary, the intrusion of memory); his time in the sleigh is one of the few private moments he has in the novel, hence a sense of freedom but also – since he wants to be connected – a sense of desperation (Kundera 1993: 111, italics in original). Later in the novel, of course, the officials in the Gentlemen's Inn will set off their electric bells warning the landlord of K.'s unacceptable presence that rang initially "out of necessity" then ring out "as a game and in an excess of joy" as K. is being led off, but not banished, they were then, "repeatedly rung as if in celebration" (281).

As discussed above, Harman explicitly decided to keep Kafka's "frugal punctuation" and the "extraordinarily long" paragraphs, long "even by the standards of literary German" as he felt "Kafka's decision to embed the dialogue in the narrative and to omit most punctuation except for commas and an occasional period lends his prose a breathlessly modern tone" and immediately connects this to Beckett (Harman 1998c: xxi). Although the narrative can be confusing, he argues that it is Kafka's use of language that keeps the "relentless momentum" going (xxi): "Kafka holds us in thrall through a startling combination of breathless intensity and ironic – and at times even drily humorous – detachment" (xxii).

We can see a slightly different approach in Anthea Bell's recent translation of *Das Schloß* (2009) in which she divides the last sentence of "Waiting for Klamm" into three sentences. Bell says in her introduction that she "would have liked to have set out this translation in the modern English manner, with new dialogue beginning on a new line" to show how "useful [it is] to remember how much of *The Castle* is told through the mouths of the characters" but that this would not "have been in accord with the usual tradition of Kafka translation" or with the aims of the new Oxford Classics retranslations "which is to follow the layout of Kafka's manuscripts" (xxx–xxxi). Notable in her remarks is the apparent pressure to not produce a domesticated version "in the English manner" of the novel and her valid point that in fact it may be revelatory to do so (in terms, at least, of dialogue). There is a case to be made to have a translation "in the English manner" *alongside* a translation like Harman's not simply in order to make Kafka more accessible to English-language readers but to think about what difference it makes to read the long paragraphs and long syntax, what it might mean. Bell does decide to slightly domesticate this last sentence in dividing it up. We still have the long opening scene with the "driver" fulfilling his tasks, locking up, but then there is a very decisive end to the first sentence – K. feels "all contact with him had been cut, and he was more of a free agent than ever." Between that realization and the next sentence is a decision marked by the period: "He could wait here …" and be free: "why, they hardly had a right even to address him." Another pause and then his rational thought: "But at the same time … he felt …":

> And when, having finished his work in the stables, the driver crossed the yard with his slow, swaying gait, opened the big gate, then came back, all the time moving with slow formality and keeping his eyes bent on his own tracks in the snow, shut himself into the stable, and put out all the electric lights – why would they be left on for anyone now? – and the only remaining light came through the gap in the wooden gallery above, catching the wandering eye for a moment, it seemed to K.

as if all contact with him had been cut, and he was more of a free agent than ever. He could wait here, in a place usually forbidden to him, as long as he liked, and he also felt as if he had won that freedom with more effort than most people could manage to make, and no one could touch him or drive him away, why, they hardly had a right even to address him. But at the same time – and this feeling was at least as strong – he felt as if there were nothing more meaningless and more desperate than this freedom, this waiting, this invulnerability (Kafka 2009: 95).

Bell's K. is a much more actively rational creature than Harman's; decisive and clear-thinking – a change in characteristics put into effect by small changes in punctuation. It is also a less humorous portrait, a more tragic portrait of K.'s grandiloquence, perhaps arrogance, and knowing hopelessness.

What Beckett has opened up for Harman, it seems, is the humor in the relentlessness, bleak but funny (in the obsessive back and forth, the paradoxical, cyclical clauses) and it is something that was opened up for Beckett perhaps in his reading and apparently negative reaction to Kafka. There is a dialogue going on here between writers and translators.

Michael Hofmann

In reviewing a book on the state of translation, Michael Hofmann suggests that the author should have done so "more in the manner of Dean Swift":

> and modestly proposed the elimination of translation: who would miss it? Who needs these traitorous (non-)writers of English and talentless parasites on our domestic English literature, these enablers of writers with unspellable names ending in vowels; down with these purveyors of accents and tildes and diacritics and umlauts; literature should stick to the familiar; we want honest single-authorship, not the spectral, pseudo-duo with the translator; we want one name only on our book jackets and on our title pages; the Nobel is an obscure foreign plot to make us feel inferior at least once a year, and should of course be ignored, or as the Berliners say, "not even ignored" (Hofmann 2010).

The idea of translators *not even being* ignored (after, perhaps, being fricasseed) deftly underlines the unease with which most translators are regarded in the "generally apathetic, complacent and mistrustful English-speaking world" (Hofmann 2002a: xvi). After translating Kafka's "Metamorphosis" Michael Hofmann notes (below in the printed interview) that he "kept seeing darting black shapes out of the corner of my eye" and it is perhaps an apt metaphor for the reader's relationship with the translator, trying and failing to not even ignore them.

Hofmann, though, is one of the more visible literary translators into English: "What I dream of," he said, "is acquiring a kind of *imprimatur*, so that readers and publishers might trust me enough to think that a book I've done is going to be worth getting" (Brearton 1999), and, to the extent it is possible in a parochial literary culture,

Hofmann has succeeded, translating modern German-language literature (mostly novels) and producing an underestimated canon of inventive, darkly funny, history-wrestling literature. "It's probably the zaniest, gloomiest, and funniest thing you've read in a long time," Hofmann warns the readers of his father's novel (in his translation) *Lichtenberg and the Little Flower Girl*, "if not ever" (Hofmann 2004: 245).

Given the lack of enthusiasm about translated literature and the lack of sustained work for literary translation, it is hard, in general, to discern a translator's sensibility. Hofmann presents a real opportunity to think about what – in an ideal world – might be achieved literarily if translators had more scope and more avenues through which to publish translations they choose and to make some sort of living. Hofmann's sensibility does not announce itself in any overly intrusive presence, but rather in his choice of translations and in his framing of them through prefaces or afterwords. Hofmann's talent and reputation have afforded him this opportunity; he shows how important an intimate reading and knowledge of a text can be for an uninitiated and adventurous reader; and how important a translator can be as a cultural mediator, opening up another world for what tends to be (in the English-language sphere) an insular readership.

The obviousness of the benefits sometimes becomes apparent: Hofmann's 2009 translation of Hans Fallada's *Alone in Berlin* became a word-of-mouth bestseller. The *Guardian*'s reviewer sniped at the publisher (Penguin) for claiming that this was a "'rediscovered' masterpiece" (Buchan 2009) when it had been perfectly well known in its native Germany for 60 years; "I suppose by 'rediscovered,' Penguin means 'translated into English'" (Buchan 2009), he adds, commending Hofmann's work ("although he may prefer Kafka or Josef Roth or Wolfgang Köppen, he gives this tough and shady author his all"). But Hofmann has been instrumental in translating and introducing a series of small masterpieces (thanks to relationships with editors and publishers) – the kinds of books that "travel by word of mouth among readers" (Hofmann 2002a: xvi), including those by Roth, Koeppen, Thomas Bernhard, and his own father, Gert Hofmann.

Hofmann translated *Amerika: The Man Who Disappeared* in the early 1990s (it was published in 1996 by Penguin in the UK and in 2002 by New Directions in the US) and a collection of Kafka's stories (those stories published in Kafka's lifetime) in 2007 (in the UK, 2008 in the US) under the title *Metamorphosis and Other Stories* and, finally, Kafka's *Zürau Aphorisms* (2006, Schocken). During that time, he also translated books by Wim Wenders, Joseph Roth, Peter Stamm, Ernst Jünger, Patrick Süskind, Herta Müller, Wolfgang Koeppen, Peter Stephan Jungk, Gert Hofmann, Fred Wander, Gert Ledig and Thomas Bernhard. Some of these works are stylistically diverse (Müller – who went on to win the Nobel Prize in 2009 – being very different to someone like Bernhard), in most of the work (here, Hofmann speaks about his and his father's writing) "bleakness swings into a kind of exhilaration" (Brearton 1999). Borges who first thought Kafka "to be as singular as the phoenix" discovers "after frequenting his pages a bit" that he could suddenly "recognize his voice, or his practices, in texts from diverse literatures and periods" (Borges 1970: 234) and thus Kafka had created "his own precursors. His work modifies our conception of the past as it will modify the future" (236). The same, I think, may be said for Kafka in this translator's œuvre, where that sensibility of bleakness swinging into exhilaration is refracted.

Hofmann's prefaces to *Amerika* and *Metamorphosis* underline where the mechanism for the comic sadness lies: in Kafka's use of language and, specifically, in his use of the German language (not what German language he uses, but how he uses it). For Hofmann,

> Kafka comes out of the genius of his language. It is German that made possible his effects and set his limits. It allowed him the disciplined, linear persistence of his explorations, the wit of his changes of direction, the dim susurration of life in his speakers (Hofmann 2008: xiv).

Kafka "specialize[s] in chords, in exquisitely geared sentences in which complex events are shown to be made up of divers things happening at different speeds" (x), what Hofmann calls "Kafka-time" that allows not only for a comedy of situation but also of pacing (xi). He cites the example of the chief clerk trying to leave the Samsas promptly but being held up by Kafka's sentences, "a comedy of the conflicting imperatives of celerity and unobtrusive slowness" (xi). In this sense, Kafka's prose is "grammar-driven" (see below) rather than presenting an obvious literary and modernist "high style" (xiii).

Even when Kafka's prose is unedited – in the case of *Amerika* – "a rough, unedited and error-strewn manuscript of a book" (Hofmann 2002b: ix) that seems "fanciful and airy" (x), Hofmann notes that it "is actually extremely tightly and purposefully composed, full of careful echoes ... objects and relationships are not haphazard, but more like deformed replicas of each other" (x). Hofmann gives the example of the various meals in the book and the various "washings" and the repeated motifs of "tickets, passports and visiting cards, music, drink and beards" (xi). As a result the novel's "plunging onward movement breeds hope, its cyclical organization guarantees doom" (x). The sense of expansiveness, of adventure is juxtaposed with the architecture of the book and its language; Hofmann points out the deliberately artificial, static nature of some of the set scenes, "an emphasis on blocking, grouping, distance, movement, positioning" which makes it almost like a "director's notes" (xii). There is a precision in the large number of sentences "that do nothing but advance the action" right beside the "fluid, bewildering and hilariously destabilizing description" (xii). Hofmann connects the filmic or theatrical elements of the narrative and its language with his approach to translating it, with its "speed and unevenness" allowing a "compatibility" and "parity" between the "rough old one" and the "rough new text" (ix), as if it were a kind of script being interpreted: "Theatre people in particular," he writes, "will understand the importance of freshness of language" (ix), but it is also a freshness of use of language: the fluidity and stasis, the cyclical and the forward-moving motifs that lead to a movement between hope and doom.

Hofmann situates that odd mixture of precision and make-believe within his own translatorial œuvre. The mythical "Amerika" as seen through a European lens appears, Hofmann tells us, in Joseph Roth's *Hotel Savoy*:

He loved America. When a billet was good he said "America." When a position had been well fortified he said "America." Of a "fine" lieutenant he would say "America," and because I was a good shot he would say "America" when I scored bullseyes (xiii).

The repetition of the word "America" is pure Kafkan, letting the language in its kinesis spin a myth and comically destroy it too. Hofmann mentions Karl May's Westerns "peopled by Indians and Saxons" as being "oddly like Kafka's *Amerika*" (xiii), "bizarre – mad German Westerns" that Hofmann said in an interview introduced him to reading in German as a teenager (Brearton 1999). Brecht's "frontier ballads" too remind him of this mythical, skewed America.

It is not just the writers whom Hofmann has translated that relate to the language and mystifications of Kafka's *Amerika*, but also, interestingly, two Irish poets quoted by Hofmann in the preface: W. B. Yeats and Seamus Heaney. Hofmann notes that "Kafka's characters like to talk, in Seamus Heaney's line 'like a book of manners in the wilderness'" (Hofmann 2002b: xii), a beautiful simile from Heaney's poem, "A Dream of Jealousy" in which the poet, his wife and his muse walk in "wooded parkland"; their "conversation a loose single gown/Or a white picnic tablecloth spread out/Like a book of manners in the wilderness" (Heaney 1990: 123). The poet asks the muse to see what he has "much coveted, your breast's mauve star./And she consented. O neither these verses/Nor my prudence, love, can heal your wounded stare" (123). The wife's jealousy of the poet's muse, and the oneiric drift of the poem, leads to the "loose single gown" of conversation "Like a book of manners in the wilderness." It is a lovely image for Kafka's dialogue, just slightly and oddly skewed, connected, stitched into "and half-concealed in endless paragraphs" (Hofmann 2002b: xii). Hofmann notes that an element of Brod's editing was to "break up those prose blocks," adding "exactly as a British editor would have done" (xii), speaking to norms and expectations of what dialogue should look like, and what is important and integral to Kafka's presentation of the dialogue as "a loose single gown/Or a white picnic tablecloth spread out/Like a book of manners in the wilderness" (Heaney 1990: 123).

A dream-like accord and discord in dream and marriage connects Heaney's poem with Yeats's. Hofmann notes that Brod edited out the last two paragraphs from the "Nature Theatre of Oklahoma" chapter, thereby ending the novel on a positive note, "Such a carefree journey in America they had never known" (Hofmann 2002b: viii); "a falsely and quite preposterously un-Kafkaesquely ringing summary, instead of where Kafka actually broke off, 'so close that the chill breath of them made their faces shudder'" (viii–ix). The tone of the actual end of the manuscript is "characteristically menacing, peculiar, physical, ambivalent, something visual becoming palpable, words growing teeth" (ix). For Hofmann, these "words growing teeth" bear "an odd resemblance too to Yeats's poem of disenchantment, 'Towards Break of Day,'" four lines of which he quotes: "Nothing that we love over-much/Is ponderable to our touch./I dreamed towards break of day,/The cold blown spray in my nostril" (ix). Yeats lies next to his new wife (Georgie Yeats – not quite the love of his life, Maud Gonne) and they both dream "under the first cold gleam of day"; he of the waterfall by Ben Bulben from his childhood that he can no longer touch as it is just a memory; she of Arthur's stag which takes her attention from her husband. If I "could but have touched/Cold stone and water" Yeats writes (Yeats 1983: 185). The impalpability of language, its inability to recapture the physical, the past, the dream, has to become as physical as it can get, "words growing teeth."

As a poet, Hofmann said in an interview that "because they're not English, I always felt drawn to the Irish" poets, "I had a green passport too, before they made them all maroon" (i.e., he held a German passport). The affinity is in an inside–outside relationship with the English language. Hofmann, who was 4 years old when his family moved to England from Germany, mentions in a couple of interviews how untraumatic the move to another language was: "No trauma at all, no memory of learning English, not memory of not knowing, or being scared or other" (Brearton 1999); "I have no memory of learning it; it was as painless as these things can be" (Licari n.d.). "Strange," he says, Karl-like, "I must have been a good little immigrant" (Brearton 1999), and notes that his first English "school report said 'keen as mustard'" (Licari n.d.). At the same time, however, he spoke German at home; his father, the novelist Gert Hofmann, would read out loud to his children in German – including Kafka – and Hofmann was acutely aware of his un-Englishness because of attitudes toward the Germans in 1960s and 1970s England when the "atmosphere and feelings were basically post-war; I don't think England had moved on at all" (Licari n.d.). He acquired an "almost parodic Englishness" at boarding-school (Brearton 1999). As one interviewer notes, he is "Not quite English, and not quite German," though his father referred to him as his "English son" (Knight 2008). Through most of his teenage years, Hofmann said that he "was very loath to tell anyone that I was German" but "Sooner or later, when I seventeen or eighteen, I turned and embraced it, and said, actually I'm German" (Licari n.d.). At home, this hybrid identity was celebrated "as an emblem of distinction; it was a sort of a mixture of necessity and distinction, a kind of preferment. ... It was somehow more exciting" (Licari n.d.).

Asked whether he had a "feeling of stylistic freedom which comes from writing in a language made your own rather than 'inherited,'" Hofmann answered,

"For sure ... I could imagine that it would take a 'native speaker' a while to shake apart 'inherited' connections and registers and expectations – if he wanted to do such a thing – rather than use an intact and organic language, a language that was *echt*, as he would put it" (Brearton 1999).

The notion of any Englishman using the word "echt" to describe his relationship to English is a lovely, if perhaps unconscious, twist here, both summing up a relationship to a native language and a slight twist away from one. In using English to translate, Hofmann notes (below in the interview) his preference for smooth translations, something he connects with "passing" for English, "becoming English"; at the same time, finds in his choices "an orientation towards a slightly fancy, comedic language" that delights in a slightly formal register of the language, "the French-Latin parts of English, that half of the language that is basically doomed because so few people get it any more."

This kind of incursion into English opens up (similarly to Heaney) the language's hybrid roots and the capaciousness and protean nature of languages. Hofmann does this explicitly in his poetry, in which he might,

> Dip into German, dip into American, use asides – "ask Steiner"! – bits of French, lots of London landmarks, lots of abroad, one poem from Ovid that has Kafka in it, another that condenses one of the most famous speeches in Latin – Lowell has an essay about it – into a single filthy line of English. The American "whatever" (Brearton 1999).

Hofmann's statement is itself quite Kafkan in style – his repetition of "dip," and "lots," their resonance with "bits"; the fulcrum use of "one" and "another"; his use of the em dashes to lengthen out the sentence and then the one short, sharp sentence about American English (so resonant of its brevity): "The American 'whatever.'" In thinking and talking about language, Hofmann displays his own intricate sensitivity to how it works and what it does.

Machine reading

Hofmann's ear for the rhythm and sound of language gets him into trouble with reviewers. Hofmann "has won prizes for his translations," J.M. Coetzee writes, a tepid, vague assurance, before adding that what Hofmann does in a translation (of Joseph Roth's stories) "is cause for concern" (Coetzee 2007: 91). Coetzee's problem with the translation is that he feels he hears the translator in it, specifically at times when he thinks Hofmann makes the language of the stories better than the original. Coetzee wants literal translations of Roth's prose and gives a few examples: when Roth writes, a "long nightshirt, sprinkled with a number of irregular black spots, evidence of fleas," Hofmann translates this as "long, flea-spotted nightgown" (91). A character in Roth's text met "with embraces and kisses, laughing and crying, as if in him they were recovering a friend decades-long not seen, and long missed" is translated as being met "with embraces and kisses, like a long-lost friend" (91). "Hofmann seems to have decided that he can better render Roth's meaning by recasting or condensing the text than by translating every word," Coetzee tells his readers, implying that they are not getting an unmediated and unchanged text, not the real Roth (91–2). "But," he snarls, "is it part of a translator's job to give his author lessons on economy?" (92).

This charge, that Hofmann is improving on Roth, excites Coetzee further; in fact he feels that Hofmann improves on Roth so much that he is at "the point of rewriting him" (92). He gives the example of Roth writing that the sun reflected in the samovars is translated as the copper samovars being "burnished by the setting sun" (92). The "trouble is that none of this verbal ingenuity is to be found in Roth" (92). Further, Hofmann "is British, and now and again uses British locutions whose meaning may escape the American reader" (92). There is a case, Coetzee argues in conclusion, "for using a linguistically neutral, as mid-Atlantic, a dialect as possible" (93).

What Coetzee cannot accept is that translation is inevitably a rewriting, that a translator does make choices; these choices may not be to Coetzee's liking but he fails to recognize that translations fundamentally cannot be literal (or that trying to be literal – *pace* Nabokov – is a choice in itself). He reinforces the idea that the translator is inferior to the author (upset about the idea that the translator "give[s] his author lessons") and implicitly that translators should neither be seen nor heard; they should simply present through blank transparency the literal spirit of the original. It seems surprising that a bilingual writer thinks that a translation should be – or could be – "linguistically neutral" and "mid-Atlantic," namely in the kind of impossibly hidden-in-plain-sight commercial publishing dialect that would please all (i.e. that regards "mid-Atlantic" as being a neutral choice). Coetzee is, of course, a beneficiary, even a representative, of that culture. The problem does not lie in Coetzee's opinion – each to his own – but to the assumptions underlying that opinion.

Look back at the examples he cites: "with embraces and kisses, like a long-lost friend" he argues is simply economy, the translator teaching the author a lesson about a too-lengthy formulation. Coetzee's "literal" translation of Roth shows Roth using clauses to lengthen out the scene (more awkwardly than Kafka would do this), thus giving a sense of its drawn-outness. Hofmann takes a different path in approaching that sense by using alliteration: "like a long-lost friend." Similarly, when Hofmann decides to translate the sun being reflected in the samovars as "burnished by the setting sun" also, he uses consonance that provides a sense of the effect (perhaps conveying how Hofmann viscerally sees the image): the plosive "b"s "burnished by" gives a metallic sense of that sun touching the copper; the slowness of the sibilance conveys a sense of that sun going down.

Coetzee's puzzling attribution of "British locutions" that "may escape the American reader" to a laziness or sense of superiority about British English and to the fact that "Hofmann is British" (something that is and is not true – and something that Coetzee is surely aware of) assumes that the translator is either not thinking consciously about that language or thinking too consciously about it (trying to turn Roth British). Coetzee zeroes in on three examples, "see off," "been poorly," and "havers" [sic: hovers] (92), but does not consider them in any wider context or with any background information on Hofmann or interest, perhaps, in his relationship to or thoughts about language, specifically British English (and the possibility of a subversive enjoyment of it). As Hofmann writes in his preface to *Amerika*: "I may have meant 'elevator,' but I enjoyed writing 'lift'" (Hofmann 2002b: ix).

But, fundamentally, Coetzee is not interested in Hofmann's opinion or thinking: *he* is the expert here on translation, not Hofmann. Coetzee's almost unimpeachable cultural authority – certainly compared to any translator according to literary norms – surrounds the book which enables his opinions to elide the actuality of the translator. "Coetzee is the ideal reviewer," Derek Attridge writes in his introduction to Coetzee's reviews (in which this review of the Roth translation appears): "He seems to have read everything relevant to his subject. ... We have little sense of a moonlighting novelist" (Coetzee 2007: xiii). The book cover of these reviews leads with "Winner of the Nobel Prize" (Coetzee won the prize in 2003, a writer who, the Swedish Academy announced, "in innumerable guises portrays the surprising involvement of the outsider").[4]

---

[4] Press release (http://www.nobelprize.org/nobel_prizes/literature/laureates/2003/press.html).

What Coetzee writes has an impact; as I have been writing about this, the English novelist A. S. Byatt published a review of Hofmann's recent translation of another Joseph Roth book, *The Emperor's Tomb*. "Hofmann's translation is tough and readable," she writes, but

> I began collecting colloquialisms that felt out of place and brought me up against the fact that this book was not written in English or American. JM Coetzee once complained that another Hofmann translation used English colloquialisms for an American market, and this is always a problem. "A ways," "gussied up," "sprog," "sharp cookie," "gobsmacked," "pinkie" – these words were just not at home in the discourse they were in (Byatt 2013).

What upsets Byatt is that these words – a mixture of British (northern British), Irish English and American demotic – "brought me up against the fact that this book was not written in English or American" and that "these words were just not at home in the discourse they were in." It is an odd statement, since the book was not written in English or American but in Roth's German; the words Hofmann uses are fundamentally not at home, they are in a different language – and, importantly, not only a different language (English) but a language of differences (different Englishes). Byatt is upset that she is not allowed to forget that this is a translation or that there is a translator involved.

She invokes the authority of J. M. Coetzee to back up her claim that Hofmann is wrong to use these "Englishisms for an American market" even though she is vague about which translation Coetzee speaks of – "another Hofmann translation" – the work is not even acknowledged (another throwaway remark about a throwaway art). Worse, she implies that Hofmann deliberately does this for commercial reasons: "for an American market" in some kind of saccharine attempt at quaintness to lure the American reader. Yet, her examples of "Englishisms" include American demotic: "gussied up" and "pinkie" and "sharp cookie."

There is a real paradox in both Coetzee's and Byatt's reviews in that they both clearly use (and reference) Hofmann's prefaces to both books for insight into Roth's background and aesthetics – they accept his authority here – but both refuse to accept much authority (however subjective that might be) from him as a translator. Byatt does not think of finding out what Hofmann may have written or said about translation (and there are numerous interviews); instead she turns to Coetzee. The one heartening part about this assertion of writerly and institutional authority over the translator is the challenge made by the readers of Byatt's review.

Thanks to new technology (here, comments on uploaded reviews), we now have some sense of how readers respond to comments such as the ones Byatt makes. There is a small but passionate discussion in the "Comments" section about Byatt's review, Hofmann's translation, Roth, Coetzee and translation. Having read Roth's "work in both German and English," one commenter writes, "Hoffman's [sic] translations cannot be improved upon," adding that s/he felt it was an "appalling review" (Byatt 2013). "It is terrible," another commenter adds, "that Hofmann, such an excellent translator and devotee of Roth's work, can be slandered in this way – and erroneously"

(Byatt 2013). "Along with others here (also speaking German and English and other languages!)" another commenter writes:

> I found this review harsh and not at all representative of Roth's novels or, indeed, Hofmann's (in my mind) brilliant translations. The man has spent most of his working life bringing Roth to an English-reading audience, and his outstanding work is undermined by a moment's misreading from a big name writer. Is that fair? (Byatt 2013).

When another commenter (kayfilex) remarks that Hofmann has made a mistake in the title, translating *Die Kapuzinergruft* as *The Emperor's Tomb* instead of the "Capuchin Crypt," Kuba points out that "Hofmann spells out why he has translated Die Kapuzinergruft/The Crypt of the Capuchins as 'The Emperor's Tomb'" in "the very first line of his introduction," thereby indicating to kayfilex that this was not an oversight or mistake but a decision, explained by the translator in a platform open to him (Byatt 2013).

A separate commenter is quizzical about Byatt's reference to "Americanisms" in the translation: "I did not recall" them, stefkl writes, but thinks that "Byatt raises an interesting issue about translation here: if an idiom is used that is alien to one's own usage – an Americanism, for instance – then it is going to jar, and affect one's response, if it feels out of place" (Byatt 2013). Stefkl adds: "publishers aren't going to commission two translations, British English and American English" which means that "the USA is always going to win, through economies of scale" (Byatt 2013). Bluemoonmajestic corrects stefkl, reminding him/her that "Byatt harks back to an ancient gripe by Coetzee about ENGLISH colloquialisms being used for a US edition" which "is in no ways relevant to this review, which is an ENGLISH edition, and brilliantly, poetically nay masterfully translated by Hofmann" (Byatt 2013).

Apart from the readers' defense of Hofmann and appreciation of his abilities as a translator and as a cultural mediator – his dedication to translating a body of Roth's work and the worth of his prefaces – the comments are important in showing that a traditional form of translation reviewing is being questioned (and perhaps always was, but only previously in private). The commenters form a brief community to think about questions of the authority of the reviewer (does the reviewer speak the source language of the text? Does it matter whether or not they do? Do they know anything about the translator and writer?) and the target language (What type of English is the text being translated into? Are there market reasons for this, determined by the publishers (not the translators)?). The commenters do not all agree on whether the review was particularly harsh, but they are actively questioning its validity and its effect on the translator.

"Translators ask for terribly little," Michael Hofmann writes,

> just to be read, just to be included, just to be understood – and don't get it … nobody much cares for or about translators – not authors, not publishers, not reviewers, not readers. I don't know what can be done to remedy this. They are very much alone with their secret pride and their public humiliation, their mean

"labour for hire" contracts and their skimpy never-never royalties, their perpetual useless agitation for pennies and credits (Hofmann 2010).

Hofmann's evident frustration at "the public humiliation" and the "useless agitation for pennies and credits" and the basic underpinning of this, that "nobody much cares for or about translators" (they are "not even ignored"), seems counterintuitive in "a global age" in which we "eat in Ethiopian restaurants and cook Thai recipes ourselves, we listen to Senegalese music, we go on holiday to Peru or the Barrier Reef, we are truly exercised about Haiti and the Uighurs and Kyrgyzstan. And yet we can't find it in us to make a few harmless drudges (*pace* Dr Johnson) feel valued" (2011). "I don't think anyone reading a foreign book in English has ever been able to supply the name of the person who translated it," he adds, in a particularly (and, fortunately, as evidenced above, not entirely true) pessimistic moment. Part of what motivates him to translate is that he worries that we are "in the twilight of translation – every time I take one on, part of me thinks it might be the last time I get asked" (2011).

Some of the disregard for translation lies in a misconception of what it actually involves: "Translation, for all that it seems a technical matter, is actually anything but," he writes. "It's a mode of reading so sympathetic and transitive that the outcome is a wholly new work, it's hunch and nerve and (my own muse) impatience. It's approaching the avowed-impossible, and shrugging your shoulders and just getting on with it" (2011). The general misunderstanding (or anxiety about understanding) that a translator is engaged in a "mode of reading so sympathetic and transitive that the outcome is a wholly new work" rather than just being a technical transfer from one language to another (as if that did not involve an interpretive reading) leads to a devaluation of what the translator does and expressions of anxiety when their presence is felt. Coetzee and Byatt unconsciously accept Hofmann's readings of Roth in his prefaces, for example, but do not connect these incisive readings with the act and process of translation, that intimate and "sensitive" reading.

Hofmann has been quite outspoken about this form of translation reviewing or reception which regards the process as simply a technical one that is either right or wrong and therefore the reviewer can quote a few examples of incorrectly translated words or phrases (i.e., their preference or their sense of what is a literal translation). "There is no more dismal – or, frankly, stupid – way of reading a translation than to pick on single words," Hofmann writes, "(as though the first duty of a translation were that it should be reversible – it's not – and as though words were tokens of unchanging value, the way money used to be, in its dreams – they're not either)" (Hofmann 2010). In response to a letter writer's comment, regarding Hofmann's translations of Benn's poetry, that "Hofmann's word choices strike me as not quite the best available" (Lutz 2009), Hofmann writes: "My 'choices' (detestable word) are absolutely 'the best available' (certainly to me), and if they can be improved, then at least it won't be by any obvious so-called 'literal' so-called 'dictionary equivalents'. (I'm curious: does Lutz think I don't *know* these words; or that I'm just avoiding them for fun?)" (2009). Hofmann's frustration is palpable, but his last point is important: his choices (even if it is a detestable word!) are not incorrect, they are his own choices based on his reading of the poems in their entirety; it is not a matter of a technical transcription of one word for another (Lutz's reading of the poem may be completely different, and therefore so might his putative translation). "'Machine translation never happened,' Les Murray writes in a poem that remembers his time when he was 'a translator at the Institute,'" Hofmann writes. "Maybe not, but machine reading is alive and well, and standing there with its Taylorean stopwatch in its hand – the 'translation police,' as exasperated acquaintances have called it" (2010). Hofmann's point about "machine reading" by the "translation police" should be taken seriously, underlining as it does what gets mistaken for authoritative readings of translations, i.e., identification of "mistakes" as a way of proving your own authority and as a way of saying anything at all about the translation if you are determined to elide the translator and their literary world and background.

Asked whether he sees translation as his "dayjob" and as a creative act, with the implicit understanding that his real métier is as a poet, Hofmann answers that translation:

> takes every last word out of me, that's for sure, and I do have the highest hopes and ambitions for it. I don't fool myself that the translations are "by" me, but they are "my books", and carry my imprimatur. I like to think there is something in them that sets them apart, that they wouldn't have been exactly the same if someone else had done them. Or a machine (Thwaite 2005).

From *The Emperors Tomb* to the emperor's deathbed

Hofmann's translation of Kafka's published stories, *Metamorphosis and Other Stories* (2008), includes a short, short story entitled "A Message from the Emperor" (published in 1920 in the collection *A Country Doctor*). This short prose piece is also part of the unpublished story, "The Great Wall of China," which describes the never-ending building of the wall, and which may have been, at least according to one scholar in the story, built on the foundations of the Tower of Babel. In "A Message from the Emperor" a dying Emperor whispers a message into the ear of a messenger for an unnamed "you"; the problem is that the messenger cannot find his way out of the palace – he is met with endless stairs and courtyards and further palaces, leaving the "you" to sit by the window to dream and wait for a message that never arrives. The story seems to be "apparently self-cancelling," a deconstruction of words and meaning with the endlessly deferred message happening but never arriving (Corngold 2002: 106). Yet, the kinesis of the recursive language and syntax (that viscerally shows the movement of the messenger), as Corngold argues, points to meaning in itself: "What happens is this movement, which appears at first to be a play of language and logic finishing in the absence of an end. And yet this movement – chiastic and apparently self-cancelling – is ... an event ... something has taken hold" (106).

The story may also be read as an analogy of the translation process: the dead or dying author passing on their message (that has to be whispered back) to a translator. The crowd watching the deathbed scene who the messenger/translator has to push past are the crowd of choices open to that translator who attempts to move past the palace or text and ends up in further palaces and stairs and courtyards. The "you" waiting and dreaming might be the reader. Kafka certainly uses this figure of the messenger (as we shall see) in *The Castle* as a means of thinking about (mis)interpretation and translation, and in this story, too, there seems to be some affinity with this translator figure.

The kinetic nature of the story is not only thematic (the messenger/translator trying to get out of the palace/text) but is also based on the stylistics of the text, specifically the axis of the repeated key terms: Emperor, message, messenger, sun, ear, crowd, stairs, courtyard, palace, through/Kaiser, Botschaft, Bote, Sonne, Ohr, Menge, treppen, Höfe, Palast, durch – evident in the opening two sentences of the piece:

> Der **Kaiser** – so heißt es – hat dir, **dem** Einzelnen, **dem** jämmerlichen Untertanen, **dem** winzig vor der **kaiser**lichen **Sonne** in die *fernste Ferne geflüchteten* Schatten, gerade dir hat der **Kaiser** von *seinem Sterbebett aus seine* **Botschaft** *gesendet*. Den **Boten** hat er beim *B*ett niederknien lassen und ihm die **Botschaft** ins **Ohr** geflüstert; so sehr war ihm an ihr gelegen, daß er sich sie noch ins **Ohr** wiedersagen ließ (Kafka 1946: 169).

> The **Emperor** has – it is claimed – sent you a **message** on his deathbed, to **you, you** alone, **you** miserable subject, the tiny shadow fleeing as far as it can from the **imperial sun**. He asked the **messenger** to kneel down at his bedside, and whispered the **message** in his ear; and it mattered to him so much that he had the man say it back to him (Kafka 2008b: 209).

What is so funny about the first sentence is that this apparently straightforward event – the Emperor has a message for you – is constantly delayed by language itself: the repetitions of Kaiser, dem, Botschaft; and the use of consonance and sibilance – "*fernste Ferne geflüchteten,*" "*seinem Sterbebett aus seine Botschaft gesendet.*" As a result of the syntactical structure of the German sentence, Kafka can wait for the "Botschaft" to be "gesendet" only right at the end of that sentence.

If we look at the Muirs's translation, they translate the sentence quite directly and get it across – the one seemingly odd choice might be the translation of "– so heißt es –" as "so it runs" which is not particularly accurate (and it removes the lengthening em dashes) but it is an interesting choice given the running messenger and the movement throughout the piece (rather than being a translatorial mistake):

> The Emperor, so it runs, has sent a message to you, the humble subject, the insignificant shadow cowering in the remotest distance before the imperial sun; the Emperor from his deathbed has sent a message to you alone (Kafka 1971: 244).

Hofmann, as a translator, is thinking more about the sound and breath of the sentence; the repetition of "you, you alone, you" gives some sense of the repetition of "dem"; there is some light sibalance "sent you a message … miserable subject" and also some inflection of the consonance "fleeing as far as it can from." What begins as a more direct (and syntactically English) conveyance of the message "The Emperor – it is claimed – sent you a message on his deathbed" slightly subverted by the "– it is claimed –" is then delayed by the commas, the repetition and the consonance. It is a very sensitive reading of the rhythm of the sentence, the form of which is central to the meaning (and humor) of the passage.

Other recent translators also show a sensitivity to the sound and rhythm of the sentence; Stanley Corngold, for instance, emphasizes the sibilance all through the sentence and introduces a different consonance "distant of distances" to lengthen out the sentence (and connect into the final word of his translation of the sentence: "deathbed"). He introduces some text – the Emperor, in fact, here sends the message twice "sent a message to you"; "sent a message from his deathbed" which allows for it not to sound odd syntactically to an English-language ear, and to correlate to its placement in the German sentence, thus placing emphasis on that act (in contrast to Hofmann's choice of emphasizing the recipient in the repetition of the "you" at the beginning):

> The Emperor, so it goes, has sent a message to you, one individual, a puny subject, a tiny shadow who has fled from the imperial sun into the most distant of distances, to you alone the Emperor has sent a message from his deathbed (Kafka 2007: 120).

Joyce Crick, too, places the sent message at the end of the sentence, here in a deliberately foreignizing way, through inversion (it sounds more unusual and slightly awkward – but deliberately so). Crick is having fun here; she goes to town with the sibilance and the "f" consonance until it almost strains credulity, thus emphasizing her humorous take on the sentence:

> The Emperor – so it is said – has sent to you, the solitary, the miserable subject, the infinitesimal shadow who fled the imperial sun to far and furthest parts, to you, and none other, the Emperor from his deathbed has sent a message (Kafka 2012: 108).

None of the four translations is wrong (though I think the Muirs miss the importance of the euphony); looking at the four we can see the translators making choices, determining what they want to emphasize and where. Looking at those choices enables us to look back at the story and consider how much the form affects the kinesis and, ultimately, the meaning of this story about failed communication and, perhaps, translation. Each provides its own way to read the story. What is interesting in terms of the Muirs's and Hofmann's translation is the final emphasis in that first sentence on the recipient of the message, explicitly in the Muirs's case "you alone" which connects the first sentence with the last – the only times the "you" is mentioned: "But you sit at your window when evening falls and dream it to yourself" (Kafka 1971: 144). Hofmann, on the other hand, does so implicitly, ending the first sentence with the "you" fleeing from the "imperial sun," thus tying into the image of light in the last sentence: "– But you, you will sit at your window and dream of it as evening falls" (Kafka 2008b: 210). This placement emphasizes a circularity to the story but also emphasizes the agency of the "you," the recipient of the message, the reader.

Most of the page-long passage is taken up with the messenger trying to get out past the crowd and through the palace (and not succeeding); the arc of the attempt is desperate and funny:

> **Aber** statt dessen, wie nutzlos müht er sich ab; immer noch zwängt er sich durch die Gemächer des innersten **Palastes**; **niemals** wird er sie überwinden; und gelänge ihm dies, nichts ware gewonnen; die **Höfe** wären zu **durch**messen; und nach den **Höfen** der zweite umschließ*ende* **Palast**; **und wieder Treppen und Höfe**; **und wieder** ein **Palast**; und so weiter **durch** Jahrtaus*ende*; und stürzte er *end*lich aus dem außersten Tor – **aber niemals, niemals** kann es geschehen –, liegt erst die Residenzstadt vor ihm, die Mitte der Welt, hochgeschüttet voll ihres Bodensatzes. Niemand dringt hier **durch** und gar mit der **Botschaft** eines Toten.

> But instead, how futile are his efforts; still he is forcing his way through the apartments of the inner palace; never will he have put them behind him; and if he succeeded there, still nothing would be won; he would have to battle his way down the stairs; and if he had succeeded there, still nothing would be won; he would have to cross the courtyards; and after the courtyards, the second, outer palace; further staircases and courtyards; another palace; and so on for thousands of years; and once he finally plunged through the outermost gate – but this can never, never be – then the imperial city will still lie ahead of him, the middle of the world, piled high with its sediment. No one can make his way through there, much less with a message from a dead man.

Reading the opening and closing of these two sentences – the idea of futility and the message from a dead man – it seems at first a negative comment on the possibility of communication with the endless journey of the first sentence here showing the endless deferment of meaning. The profusion of semicolons works almost viscerally as barriers, conveying the sense of the messenger fighting past the staircases and courtyards and palaces. On closer view, however, there is hope within the desperation: the semicolons also show the back and forth between the two states: "futile efforts"; "still he is forcing"; "never will he"; "and if he succeeded"; "still nothing"; "he would have to battle"; "and if he had succeeded"; "still nothing"; "he would have to cross"; "and after", "further", "another", "and so on"; "and once he finally plunged" – "but this can never, never be." The beautiful use of the semicolon (and comma) as a fulcrum between hope and hopelessness works to move the prose along but also ties the two states together (the affinities with Beckett here are evident). This is – as Hofmann shows beautifully – a translatable element of the passage that is as vital to the meaning of it as the words themselves. Although the messenger does not get out, he is in "the middle of the world," and though he cannot – and "No one can make his way out of there" – escape, "much less with a message from a dead man," this is followed by a dash and then the last sentence focuses on the "you" dreaming that message. The messenger/translator, stopped at the limits of the text, allows the reader to do so.

The status of the messenger in Hofmann's translation changes once he bends his knee and whispers the message back into the ear of the Emperor; he becomes an "envoy." The Emperor "dispatched his envoy. The envoy set off straightaway" (Kafka 2008b: 209). Kafka uses the same word for "messenger" throughout, "der Bote," but here we see Hofmann deciding to convey a shift in identity as the messenger becomes the envoy of the message, and also the envoy of the Emperor – in the sense of the concluding word. It is a grander title and a grander job; the envoy now has the right to push through the crowd:

> The envoy set off straightaway; a strong man, tireless; now putting out one arm, now the other, he clears a way through the crowd; if he encounters any resistance, he points to the emblem of the sun displayed on his chest; he gets ahead easily, better than anyone else. But the crowds are so great; their abodes are never-ending. If a path opened before him, how he would fly, and ere long you would hear the majestic pounding of his fists on your door.

> Der **Bote** hat sich gleich auf den Weg gemacht; *ein* kräftiger, *ein* unermüdlicher Mann; *einmal* diesen, *einmal* den andern Arm vorstreckend schafft er sich Bahn **durch** die **Menge**; findet er Widerstand, zeigt er auf die Brust, wo das Zeichen der **Sonne** ist; er kommt auch leicht vorwärts, wie kein anderer. **Aber** die **Menge** ist so groß; ihre Wohnstätten nehmen kein **Ende**. Öffnete sich freies Feld, wie würde er fliegen und bald wohl hörtest du das herrliche Schlagen seiner Fäuste an deiner Tur.

Hofmann conveys the new purpose of this "envoy" through the language and punctuation suggested by the German text (again, the use of the semicolons as barriers being pushed through) and the consonance (the repeated "g" sound: gleich auf den Weg gemacht; ein kräftiger) and the repeated "ein" and "einmal." Hofmann uses sibilance: "set off straightaway; a strong man, tireless" and consonance: "clears a way through the crowd; if he encounters" for that strength and urgency, as well as the repetition of "now" for "einmal." He has the seal of the Emperor, the sun on his chest, but he cannot get past the crowds and has to dream: "If a path opened before him, how he would fly, and ere long you would hear the majestic pounding of his fists on your door." We are in the envoy's head here; he is imagining how wonderful it will be to pound on "your door" and Hofmann invokes the kind of lyrical register of our delusional dreams (sad and funny at the same time) as the envoy thinks "ere long" that the "majestic pounding of his fists" will be heard: he adds emphasis to the "bald wohl" with the archaic "ere long" but the register is suggested in Kafka's text with the "herrliche Schlagen."

If we think of the envoy as a translator figure, the translation becomes poignant: the sense of pride and accomplishment at being the envoy of the dying/dead author, the constant movement, pushing through the crowds (of text, choices, decisions), the dream pushing you on to connect with the reader, to produce the perfect text, and the inherent irony of it never being possible, still hoping, still failing, never exiting a final battlement, or final text – and yet, the reader connected to that message in dreaming of the communication and thus making it perhaps possible: to paraphrase Roland Barthes, making it a translatorly text.

An interview with Michael Hofmann

You said in an interview (Licari) that your father read Kafka aloud to you when you were a child. What was your initial impression of him? Did you hear Kafka in German before reading him in German?

Yes, by quite a few years. I think I was 10 or 12 at the most when my father first read him to us – Metamorphosis, *or* The Stoker, *or* The Judgment. *(I mean, in German, of course.) Other scenes from the novels. (He read us things he particularly liked, Thomas Mann, Gogol, Hofmannsthal's* Andreas, Büchner. *The fist-fight in* Vanity Fair. *It always felt like a great and slightly parlous distinction to us.* Ex aequo *and dramatic readings, not condescending to us, not "bedtime readings" – if anything rather the opposite!) I wouldn't have read Kafka myself till I was in my upper teens, 16-plus, once I was finally reading German (because I did resist it for a long time). One of the things that stuck with me is the terrible fight with the father, when the father throws these small dessert apples at Gregor, and a few of them get wedged into the platelets of his armour, and later start to rot. That made me squirm with awfulness. I think I've known those apples for almost my entire life.*

Do you associate hearing Kafka read with becoming aware of the humor in his work? Or did that become more apparent when translating his work?

Yes, I do, with hearing it read. Not that the story of the apples is remotely funny. But I suppose there was enough else that was. There are things that are obviously funny, mostly from Amerika, *Brunelda's bath, Karl being chased by the police, and so on, but I don't really have those in mind. I think what I'm getting at is actually a feeling of forlornness, indomitableness, dauntlessness. Those places where Kafka meets Bernhard. Things look so bad, but you have to go on. You step out into the corridor and your candle blows out. You get up at four o'clock to go riding, and your riding is and always remains hopeless. Your shower is a sort of crying-machine. Your admired friend's sister starts rough-housing with you, and you fear for your friendship. Your other, Irish friends break open your suitcase, and help themselves to its contents. When you try and evoke them separately, these things mostly seem just desolating, and it seems rather tasteless to find them amusing. It's the humor of being in a hole and going on digging. In the teeth of the conventional advice.*

Kundera talks about "a poetics of surprise; or beauty as perpetual astonishment" in Kafka's work (as opposed to a flamboyant modernist style) (Kundera 1996: 50). You wrote that you didn't want to introduce any strangeness into Kafka's prose, because you wanted the reader "to have a sense of his writing as something perfectly ordinary" (Hofmann 2008: xiv–xv) – how important was it for you to convey the ordinariness of the tone in order for the understated – but funny – poetics to come through in English?

I don't know about beauty. I think beauty (in the eye of the beholder, and so on) is a rather surprising category to come upon. I'm not sure how much Kafka thought about beauty. I might almost as well have said that I didn't want to introduce any beauty into Kafka's prose. A word like efficiency or functionality would make more sense to me. That said, there are these sort of "pedal moments" – the things I quote in my introduction, about the tram-driver and the conductor sitting together on the steps of the immobilized tram after the demonstration has passed; or the glimmering of bunches of bananas way down in the lift-shaft; or Karl's belated bite into the aromatic apple he's been carrying around with him all evening. Those resonate and vibrate. They're not middle any more, they're permitted to echo away (hence pedal). They're strangely pacific. They almost have a quality of silence about them. It's the moment the needle is taken off the record. The rest, though, you might say, is like a mechanical piano. Something composed on wax cylinders, with those dense, almost unnatural intervals and clusterings and a mechanical jauntiness.

Writing of Elizabeth Bishop, you compared her to Kafka, in that she "arranges impressions into complicated chords, full of revised, contradictory, accumulated notions. Elements of 'design' or 'meaning' seem almost frivolous, compared to these precisely chaotic chords" (Hofmann 2001: 45). To what extent do you think translating Kafka has to do with conveying such "chords" in his work?

I've got out of phase, and refer you to my previous answer, as they say in Parliament! I suppose I see it as that – or: ich hab's mir so zurechtgelegt – but that's descriptive or analytical, and comes after. It's not the part of me that does the translating, in other words. I think it's true to say I always translate naively and if you will, idealistically. I don't make up my mind about something, and translate it accordingly. But because I am of an analytical cast, I will then ponder, reading something back, 'what is this like? What have I done? How does this work?' The dish comes first; I only stumble upon the recipe afterwards!

You wrote about the "over-plus of meaning" in his work that makes it so tempting to interpret Kafka, to look for codes – how hard is it as a translator to avoid doing so? (Hofmann 2008: x). And should a translator do so (my guess is that translators often interpret the work; you wrote about Felstiner's book on Celan that "a translation should sound as though it understood, even in some sense compassed an original; it is 'catching' something and throwing it on to the reader" (Hofmann 2001: 115) – can this be a positive thing)?

Again, the interpreting isn't my job, or not with Kafka. I translate the surface, and have to hope I haven't wrecked the "unknown depths" below. In fact, the thought of Kafka being read by exegetes made me miserable while doing it. I kept reminding myself that I was translating for normal readers; hermeneuts, pass by! That said, I don't think it would be sensible to look for "codes" in a translation: it's not what translating is for. I'm not responsible for their well-being. You cup your hands for water, you don't try to shift the entire well!

Celan would be a completely different case, though. He wrote between words, in a highly personal, traumatized German. All surfaces are deliberately broken. Kafka is described as having an "ironically conservative" style (I love that – too rarely are those two ever paired), Celan by contrast would have a lyrically broken one. Just translating those mostly meaningless surfaces – as Michael Hamburger did – accomplishes nothing. That's not catching, that's shipping on something basically unknown, from author to reader. It seems supine to me. You can't translate Celan with a dictionary, you have to get behind the words and inside the words, as Felstiner did, listening to his voice when reading, reconstructing his whole experience while writing something. The Celan translator has to do so much more. In Rilke's poem about Death and the cup on the back of the hand, it's similar. The broken script, Hoff-nung, most translations go Ho-pe, but that's so feeble, that's really not possible. It's not the word qua word that matters (any more than in Celan), it's having a word that's big enough to break. I would say Endea-vour, *one of those other ships' names.*

You seemed taken by John Felstiner's peek into the workshop of translating Celan (Hofmann 2001: 105–15) and I wondered if you would be tempted to do so, to show the interpretive choices being made as translations happen – of Kafka's work, you said it is perhaps more *der Prozess* than *das Urteil*, and it struck me that this is perhaps true of translation too?

I think again Celan is different – hard cases make bad law – there are no equivalents, there is no adequate rendering. What stunned me about Felstiner was that he managed to work his way around the original. He successfully presented a foreign author you could read with just English. You have your floor plan, and you explain where the doors and windows would have been, and the furniture, and you put your reader in this alien world of which very little exists. And yet the whole thing is just air; hence the biography-with-translations-and-commentary is much more impressive than just the book of translations. You miss the commentary, the guide. As translations, they don't work very well.

I think maybe translations have two alternative, mutually incompatible aspirations. In the one – yes – everything you do is noticed, yes, process, the reader is at your elbow, everything is explained, justified, found good. He goes aha, aha, the whole time. There's a kind of detailed approval, Oskar Krause OK's every sentence. But in the second one, nothing much is noticed, the thing is waved through, the reader reads the whole thing asleep, in a dream. It reads perfectly naturally, as if it'd been written in English, give or take. That's disappointing in terms of a reaction, but a relief in that no one picks you up on something, says what is this fraud, pass me the original, what does it really say. I think in terms of my own history – arriving in England, 'becoming English,' 'passing' – and in terms of the novels I mostly ended up translating, my aspiration is the second kind. Alternatively, I very quickly became resigned to never finding the first type of attention – either that, or else there really aren't that many choices, and it really isn't that interesting...!

I've often wished I kept a record while I was translating something by, say, Kafka. I never have. All those insights end up disappearing by the wayside. There is only the outcome.

I was struck, too, by a letter you wrote defending your translatorial decisions with Benn's poetry (Hofmann 2009) – I thought it was a very fair and articulate defense against the norms of translation reviewing by the "translation police" that tends to pick on certain words, "machine reading," assuming that the translator just got it wrong rather than thinking that they're making interpretive choices. Do you think that translation reviewing ought to be more aware of what translators do, and do you think translators themselves should have a hand in showing what they do (through prefaces, articles, etc.)?

I thought I was rather fierce myself. I feel these things too much, I don't like it when someone looks at my fingers, as you say in German. It wasn't an aggressive letter that I got, but my heart still sank. There is, or there can be, such a disproportion between the amount of thinking that you do, and the mechanical eye of the suspicious and ungrateful reader – really the accountancy movements – going from one column to the next. Where's this word? Where's that word? What have you done with the semicolon? I tend a priori to favor the opposite anyway: if you avoid the "obvious" word, you're almost already ahead of the game. Those fifty-year-old translations of Benn by Middleton and Hamburger are so awful, so wooden. I thought I had made him readable for the first time in English, and felt so crestfallen to have someone like that take me up on what I'd done.

In answer to your question, I do. All my Roths have introductions, I think I must have written thirty or forty introductions. It is one of the things that set me apart as a translator. That said, if you look them up, you'll see I write about the authors and their books, I have hardly anything to say about the translations! It's the disappearing subject, isn't it?!

It seems that you fell into translation and that often projects come up because you've been asked to do something by publishers. Did Penguin approach you to translate *Amerika* and the stories?

I suppose that's broadly true. I never studied German or comp. lit. or translation at university. I started off as a poet. My father gave me something of his to do – or I helped myself to it (his Lenz*) in the early 1980s – then I translated a Tucholsky, a Süskind, Beat Sterchi's* Blösch *(though that was my idea). I saw translation as something I could offer, perhaps a book a year, a bit of a substantial change from the poems and freelance book reviews I was otherwise doing. After a while I was able to "place" authors and books myself from time to time, like Koeppen, or my father or Peter Jungk.* Amerika *was offered me by Paul Keegan, then at Penguin. I remember thinking at the time that this Kafka title that no one read was probably the only one I could do – when I was feeling so oppressed by the thought of the expert Kafka readership. But even so, it was the one time I experienced a crash. I panicked, and couldn't go on. I felt so devoid of authority, so fallible. I put it aside for months, or even years. Maybe as much as three years. I know I was doing it in 1990 – I think it wasn't published until 1995 or 1996. Then one day I could pick it up again, and finished it. Now I wouldn't even be able to tell you where the joins were.*

I was very interested in your comments in the preface to *Amerika* that you were moved by the "rough, unedited" text that gave you a freedom in translation – itself a "rough new text" (Hofmann 2002b: ix). There is a real freshness to the translation – was that a result of this sense of freedom?

No, that's Kafka. I hear him as fresh. A mixture of breathless and correct. The "rough, unedited text" gave me the confidence to go back to the book. I thought, he wrote this at night in a few weeks, while doing a job in the daytime, he didn't have ideal circumstances to work in either, so it's all right if I have a pad on my knees, look up at the text (it's terrifyingly easy to miss a line, or a sentence, or even a paragraph), and scribble down whatever comes into my mind. It's not a book that ought to require library or laboratory conditions (and of course I don't like libraries or laboratories).

You described yourself, cheekily, as "a good little immigrant" because of your easy childhood assimilation into speaking English (Brearton 1999); was there any attraction to translating Amerika because of Karl who is, or performs as, "a good little immigrant"?

I didn't think of that, though I should have done! Or maybe I did. It's a book of tunneling into a country. Perhaps symbolically or in terms of sacrifice, someone in my position would be more drawn to narratives of failure – Ovid in exile, or Dino Buzzatti's Tartar Steppe, *or* The Sheltering Sky. *I think in particular, Karl's experience at his uncle's in the second chapter would have been far too close to my own in England or America – a tacit competitiveness, being always "under the gun," having so much ground to make up – for me to feel remotely calm about translating it!*

Referring to your poetry, you said that a certain distance from English, a "parodic Englishness" (Brearton 1999) informs your language – to what extent is that true of your translations?

I think that was once largely true, but, like many things, has become complicated over time. There was an orientation towards a slightly fancy, comedic language – which to me is still one of the great strengths – glories! – of English. When I was translating The Good Person of Sichuan, *I had Wodehouse in mind. The waterseller, the gods in mufti, their slightly spifflicated language. If you're close to one of the great strengths of a language, that's helpful to your translation. And Brecht – I saw it in his house – had a copy of a Wodehouse novel. They're both dandies, I'm convinced of that. It felt a little absurd, and I worried about telling people, but I think there was something there. Perhaps it's similar with Kafka and Dickens –* Amerika *is his Dickens novel, after all. That slightly elaborate, heavily circumstantial, benign teetering on the brink.*

I think that'll always be in me. Another way of measuring it, or putting it consciously and externally, is with reference to the French-Latin parts of English, that half of the language that is basically doomed because so few people get it any more, but I adore it!

But then there are other reaches, other levels, other tones. I try to keep learning. I don't want to be circumscribed, or to repeat myself. There's a great strength in plainness. Or I love tinkering with word order in English – there's so little you can do, it's so unrewarding and basically inflexible, I'm always trying to turn things round for a sort of neglected effect.

And then of course there's American. I was here for two years as a boy, and now I've been coming to Florida for twenty years, one semester in two, and I think the greater part of my translations now are American commissions. But I'm getting ahead of us!

Coetzee – and I completely disagree with him – argued that your translation of Joseph Roth's stories were too English (of a certain, but undetermined by Coetzee, dialect) and that you should have aimed for a mid-Atlantic dialect (Coetzee 2007: 93). It seems to me that in neutering your own language, you'll end up neutering the language of the original – and it seemed that some of your "Anglicisms" were deliberate – you said that you enjoyed using lift instead of elevator. How aware are you of your "accent" when you're translating?

You mention in the preface, too, that it seemed right to be translating while in America, and you have a lovely rundown of some of the Fellini-esque color of American life (Hofmann 2002b: xiii–xiv) – did being in the States make you more aware of the differences in English (including different rhythms of speech) as you were translating?

I can do much more with English, and it feels more echt. *Especially spoken language, though dialect is always a problem for me. I will try American – or mid-Atlantic, more like – but that almost involves a further process of translation. I'm actually getting to a stage where I no longer know the difference, and almost invariably get things wrong – "till" and "until"! I wish I could imagine Coetzee praising me for making the effort when I try the mid-Atlantic thing, but I can't – he remains a criticaster, I'm afraid.*

Everything I do is done on a case-by-case basis. The degree to which a book is left in German or all goes into English – I call it the schnapps *or* wurst *(or brandy or sausage) question. Whereabouts on the Anglo–American continuum it goes. There are some books that I set in American, my own choice. Zoe Jenny, for instance – where I think it was unhappy families and the proximity to the* Bell Jar.

I translate mainly early or mid-twentieth-century books. For a long time, I thought it was because I detest contemporary German slang (as I do), but it strikes me as at least as likely that I do it because it will allow me to write more English than American. English is the older, the more conservative, the less changeable, the more hierarchic. If you're translating a book set in Vienna in the 1920s (Roth), or Berlin being bombed in the 1940s (Fallada), or the Bernese Oberland in the 1960s (Sterchi), then English strikes me as positively a godsend – still more for the American reader. What an ideal way of getting a sense of reality being other, being starchier, of the class system, of manners, of an unparadisal life unsaturated in sex and money and publicity. If I was an American reader of old European books I would read only English translations, and I would pray for them to be allowed to persist and not be interfered with. The Anglo–American continuum as I termed it can be an expressive resource. Coetzee's prescription is the worse for being procrustean, for being applied (as surely he would) to everything. Then what happens to English? It's just used by a handful of British novelists, most of whom would rather be American anyway. I think it's really uncouth, really barbarous. A preposterous thing to say, really. I – qua translator, as well as qua poet – have at least as much entitlement to English as anyone else.

I think with Amerika *– especially this newly 'wrong' text, with "Mak" and the New York Boston Bridge and everything, it's essential to get things "wrong" and have "lift" for "elevator," etc. etc. It's not verisimilitude, it's myth and cluelessness, and "exploded Bohemia." That said, what is amazing is how far America has followed Kafka's prescription, those planes circling the stadium in the middle of nowhere, those dismal elections and volatile crowds and packed buffets. But those elements of American reality are readily available to the American or European reader and TV viewer anyway.*

One other thing, to do with English and American. With Kafka, latterly with the stories, the sentences are grammar-driven (not vocabulary or tone). But the correct, complex, even ornate grammar has certain implications for vocabulary. It will perforce bring in a Latinate diction, a larger vocabulary. It will sound more English than American, from the grammar. You can't people those sentences with monosyllabic verbs and nouns, it won't go. And that reminds me that when I was translating the stories, what it reminded me of was translating from Latin at school. True.

I was struck by your comment in the preface to the stories that the big words in Kafka are not the nouns and verbs but the particles – almost impossible to translate into English (Hofmann 2008: xiii). I noticed that you write of your own poetry that sometimes you avoid verbs (Brearton 1999) – I wondered if there's a stylistic connection there (partly due, perhaps, to the influence of German?) and to what extent has Kafka been an influence on your poetry?

I think they are separate phenomena, except inasmuch as they depend on a language being uncommonly adaptable or so to speak deplete-able by someone with unorthodox designs on it. The particles, those flows of logic in Kafka – like the arrows in Paul Klee paintings – but I say that I think it's a mistake to put them into English. English is more "understood," more gestural (though without gestures!). In my own poems, the lack of verbs, especially early on, is something I attribute to a kind of timorousness or nervousness. The writer is un-enfranchised, he has no right to verbs. That's my half-serious interpretation anyway. And far from being influenced by German, my translator Marcel Beyer said he had no end of trouble with those verbs that weren't really there, or that anyway weren't governed by personal pronouns!

I noticed in interviews, interviewers have tended to wonder whether translation is your "day job" (Knight 2008), but it seems to me that you don't see it that way at all, and although you "fell" into it, you've introduced or established some great writers into the English language and sphere. You wrote that you would love for people to pick up books based on seeing your name as a translator (Thwaite 2005) – it seems to me that this is really the case now. Do you feel that you have been influential and do you think this is unusual for a translator?

I would really love that to be the case. I certainly try to avoid giving disappointment by steering clear of bad or indifferent books. There too is a reason to go back in the century for works of literature – most new books are not literature, or not yet. It seems to me we're only here for a few decades, and four or five skinny books of poems are not a lot to show for it. The translations are to help me with Saint Peter. I know I'm not the first to say it, but I certainly feel it – that I'm constituted of literature!

You wonder at a certain point whether you're hiding in translation or whether you do it from a "fealty" to German (Thwaite 2005), but there seems to be a link between a lot of the writers you have translated – the sly humor, the discomfort with national identity, exile, and war. A lot of this has to do with twentieth-century German and Austrian history, but I think there is a certain tone or approach in the writers. Does what you've translated in some ways complement your poetry (where you don't directly deal with war and history, but it's there, and certainly the humor and displacement is evident)?

You're perhaps right, though one can only speculate. On the one hand, there's a bizarre breadth as maybe Germans feel especially strongly – Kafka, Jünger, my father, Irmgard Keun, whatever next! – on the other hand, maybe there are certain common themes. There was a time – when I translated Storm of Steel *– that I did five 'war books' in a row, never having had the least interest in war, in fact, having only horror, disgust and contempt for it! Discomfort with national identity may account for quite a bit of it. There is a way in which for things to interest me, they have to be "German stories" of one kind or another.*

You said, too, that you translate because you're worried that it might be the last time you'll be asked (because of a lack of interest in translation) (Hofmann 2010). Have you noticed any changes in attitudes towards translations? Is there more, or less, interest in foreign-language authors?

I have felt privileged sometimes, noticed where we're supposed to be so many "planes of glass," appreciated, lifted out of the ruck – but then I think, and why the hell not?! I think to begin with it's the unusual profile – even if reviewers haven't read my poems or reviews, they know I'm a poet and a critic, so maybe a different depth of responsibility or authentication or finish may be expected. Which I hope I deliver too.

Then again, I've done books on spec, even fairly recently, and it's taken me five or ten years to persuade someone to publish a translation I've done. I still can't write my own contracts.

You've said that you "dislike the process and the work, but I love the results, the finished books" (Thwaite 2005). How do you approach translating on a practical level – especially Kafka, who comes with so much cultural expectations and baggage?

Well, I've talked about Kafka. It was really my one traumatic, deflating experience. (The results are fine, though, I think I can say.) I had to remind myself that I was translating for readers, and not for scholars. But I think that's true of Kafka anyway, and it's as well to remember it. Another time, I was supposed to translate one of the Freuds in Adam Phillips's edition. The other translators were all exchanging emails, harmonizing their terms, etc. etc., I couldn't stand it – Wild Analysis, *it sounds great, but in fact it's opposed to "wild analysis," which is what non-regulation shrinks do, a really petty and unworthy work, like a trade union or health-and-safety demarcation dispute. Awful. I was so happy and relieved when I finally gave that back! I'm sure he's not all like that, but I can't say I'm much interested in finding out!*

You wrote that translation is "a mode of reading so sympathetic and transitive that the outcome is a wholly new work, it's hunch and nerve and (my own muse) impatience. It's approaching the avowed-impossible, and shrugging your shoulders and just getting on with it" (Hofmann 2010). I thought that was a great description of the translator as a reader; did your translation of Kafka's work change how you interpreted it?

Probably not, but that's because I was so close to it at all times. For that to work, you have to be encountering something new. But I could offer you something like Joseph Roth (whom I was thinking of with "impatience" anyway), that extraordinary combination of speed and – uniquely in The Radetzky March *– glory. I had a much simpler, and wrong idea of him before I translated him. He's a very witty writer, who almost reflexively turns things round before he says them. "What is old, what is young, what is ugly, what is beautiful, what is noise, and what is music? If a day consists of many nights of love, and a night of love is a matter of moments? When the commodity is the woman selling it, and love is worth a dime, and a dime buys love? If night is a hardworking day, and sleep is a business?" ("Marseilles Revisited")*

Do you respond differently to the Kafka work you've translated than to the work in the German language? Do you see yourself in there?

Well, it's a fact that I haven't read the other two novels for a long time. (And I am a chronic rereader of my translations: a mixture of anxiety and a hope to be able to approve of what I find there. I don't think I read the originals of things I've translated, except very rarely, and purely circumstantially. Translations efface originals.) But I can remember when I was writing about Kafka as an undergraduate, reading some of the parables and short prose, and actually thinking, I would hate to have to translate this! So he divides into things the mere prospect of which would frighten me, and some others that I have done already (albeit these too, not without fear). To tackle this fear, and for the sake of completism, I think I probably ought to translate his unpublished short prose, The Great Wall of China, *or* The Burrow.

And the being-there and not-being-there, that's one of those things. *I think it depends on who's saying it: if it was Coetzee saying I was there, then I would of course want not to be. (It sounds like I think about him all the time – he's an idiot, and I really don't.)*

This will sound absurd, but while I was translating Metamorphosis, *I kept seeing darting black shapes out of the corner of my eye. I don't think they were there before. So one pays for what one does.*

You wrote about "the depleting, desiccating activity of translating, which leaves me without words – speechless, as often as not" (Brearton 1999), but is there something exhilarating about this – about speechlessness rather than silence?

It's a kind thought, but I would still rather have words.

2

Kafka Translating

> *Ultimately what Kafka so vividly portrays is the wager of multilingualism.*
> (Kramsch 2008: 331)

In *The Trial*, Josef K. suspects that he is being sent out of the office on random errands so that his colleagues can steal his clients from him. His boss at the bank asks him to show an Italian client around Prague, because K. has some knowledge of the language. K. stays up half of the night reading his Italian grammar and stuffs a dictionary in his pocket for the meeting. But when it comes to it, he "realized with discomfort that he understood only bits and pieces of what the Italian was saying" and only when the man spoke "slowly" could he "understand almost everything, but those were rare exceptions" (Kafka 1998b: 202). The problem was that the Italian's "moustache hid the movement of his lips, the sight of which might otherwise have helped him out," a moustache, so bushy and perfumed that "one was almost tempted to draw near and sniff it" (202).

Kafka's wry representation of Josef K. as a hapless interpreter, failing at the job because of his over-confidence in his language skills and the Italian's moustache, shows a self-awareness of the perils and possibilities of translation. Kafka's work is studded with exegetes and hermeneutical interpreters caught in worlds in which both they and the language they use are not quite up to the job. This is perhaps an understandable motif, since Kafka himself lived between languages and learned several. The concern in his work for the failure of language and communication is often ascribed to his own alienation to or crisis in language, as he was caught between high German, Prague German, Czech, Yiddish. What is often overlooked is the rich vein of humor beneath the anxiety often contained in these translator/interpreter figures. While the theme seems desperate – Kafka's characters fail to come to a final understanding of their worlds and of others, or if they do so, they come to it too late – Kafka's mode of investigation, his constant return to non-communication and mis-communication, seems to delight in our wrong-headed search for ultimate meaning. He teases us as we try to decipher what the characters cannot – they lose concentration, fall asleep, get waylaid by moustaches just at the point when the reader is ready to surrender, to give up.

Josef K. could ask the Italian what he means, to repeat what he has said, but he doesn't; instead K. wants to sniff his moustache, a physical intimacy and proximity which might preclude the need for language. It is enticing but also dangerous. Beards, those animal-like foliages, sprout on the chins of the judges and audience at the court, which they "claw"; K's struggle to understand them and the court is aided by Leni with her "webbed fingers." The human animal body distracts and gives succor, promises a possibility of understanding beyond language while destabilizing the idea of human superiority predicated on having language. Kafka's animals speak German after all and even if the other characters cannot understand them, we can. Kafka's enigmatic and almost invisible narrators translate for them, but turn out to be as slippery as K. at interpreting for us.

As readers, we have to re-enact the inevitably doomed exegetical, hermeneutical acts being described by the interpreters, the exegetes, the narrators, the animals, the immigrants in Kafka's prose, all of whom perform acts of translation. In doing so, in being frustrated and confronting our expectations of understanding, Kafka perhaps posits a humane "way out" toward mutuality in a world where language, both spoken and written, is humorously condemned to over- and misinterpretation. Misinterpretation is not necessarily meaningless, but in fact innate to how we function in life, a recognition of the fallible human condition. What we come to understand is that we understand very little at all, and that is all right and even a release. "Kafka's comedy is always also tragedy," David Foster Wallace wrote, "and this tragedy always also an immense and reverent joy" (Wallace 2006: 63).

The fictional translator

Probably the most famous moment of ambiguous exegesis in Kafka's work is the *Vor dem Gesetz* or "Before the Law" parable, initially published as a free-standing story by Kafka in 1915 and then included in *The Trial*. A priest recounts a parable to K. about a man from the country arriving at a door to the law, and being prevented from going through by a guard though told ingress may be possible. The man waits so long to get through that he dies. Just before he does so, he asks the guard why no one else has tried the door and the guard tells him that this door was meant only for him and that it would now be closed. Read by Derrida as a deconstruction of the parable form, and a consideration of the act of reading and interpretation, the parable itself is an enigma, pregnant for interpretation. Kafka himself deconstructs the form in his short story, "On Parables": "All these parables," he writes, "really set out to say merely that the incomprehensible is incomprehensible, and we know that already" (Kafka 1971: 457).

Critical attention to the *Vor dem Gesetz* parable tends to overlook why K. is having a disquisition with the priest and the very funny pages-long debate between K. and the priest about what the parable may mean. Kafka is not just ready to present us with an enigma, he teases us with a performance (in the form of K.) of our own inadequacy to work it out and our enthusiasm for other people's answers. K. is in the cathedral listening to the priest because he is waiting for the Italian to turn up, so that he can show him the artworks of the church. He is there as an interpreter both of language and art, an embodiment of the twin aspects of translation: linguistic transference and hermeneutical understanding. The fictional translator is often read as a stand-in for the writer with an "affinity" drawn between the writer and translator as the task of both is "to find a way to incorporate, in a new language and for a new audience, the glory or horror that she or he has witnessed" (Maier 2006: 171). The fictional translator is often a figure of unease, playing out anxieties of authenticity on the part of the writer (Theim 1995: 214). But in Kafka's work, the affinity is drawn between the translator figure and the reader and it is a visceral, active affinity. As we follow the translator figure, so the promise follows that they and we will be able "to interpret, to translate the unfamiliar into terms familiar" (Heller 1977: 386), but just at the point that a light of illumination appears, it turns on us, so that we feel that we cannot see anything at all.

In turning Josef K. into a translator, Kafka gives a visible agency to our own anxieties about reading, but in exposing our fallibilities as readers and the limitations of our ability to neatly package texts into a given meaning, makes us enact our own agency and responsibility as readers. We often focus on the product of translation and translators as writers or speakers, and less on the process: the translator as the first reader, the first interpreter of a text. The elision of the translator as a reader allows us to pretend that a text is translated without being touched, without being read beforehand, analyzed, interpreted. We like to see their touch as seamless, transparent. In foregrounding K.'s laughable inadequacy as an interpreter and reader, the joke is also on us.

In the scene, the President of the bank assigns K. to show an "Italian business associate of major importance" around the city and "a few of its artistic treasures" (Kafka 1998b: 199). This request would usually be an "honor" except for the fact of his inexplicable trial but he accedes to the request to help maintain his "prestige" at the bank (199). Although translation is a secondary activity to his role as a CFO at the bank, it is seen as prestigious and a role demanding certain skills – K. speaks "adequate" Italian but it is the office perception of his "knowledge of art history" that qualifies him for the task, even though this knowledge had been "blown far out of proportion" (201) and K. had only belonged to "the Society for the Preservation of Municipal Works of Art" to enhance his career (201).

K.'s slightly fraudulent credentials perhaps speak to the fact that though it is an "honor" to translate, the act is regarded in the office as perfunctory – an "adequate" sense of the language and a brief stint preserving domestic art is seen as sufficient to make one a translator. But, for the first time in the novel, we see K. actually working hard to interpret something. He spends "half the night preparing himself somewhat by poring over an Italian grammar" (201) in preparation for the job, and then, after meeting the Italian businessman and realizing he cannot understand him, goes back to his office and "spent his remaining free time copying down various special terms he would need for the tour of the cathedral from the dictionary. It was a terribly tedious task" (204). While his clients and colleagues revolve "around K. as if he were an axis

[...] he himself listed the words he would need, looked them up in the dictionary, copied them down, practiced pronouncing them, and finally tried to learn them by heart" (204).

For K. the act of translation is one of memorization and a simple interlingual transfer – listing the words he needs, checking their dictionary equivalents and memorizing them. The "terribly tedious task" of learning these Italian words infuriates him and he buries the dictionary under his papers, but takes it out again, realizing that "he couldn't just parade past the artworks in the cathedral in total silence with the Italian" so he "pull[s] the dictionary out again in even greater rage" (205). K.'s surprising assiduity is funny because he has been so easily distracted from gaining knowledge about his trial and from working at the office. But it is one of the last apertures in the novel when K. is offered or allowed to seek out knowledge, and the intent is to use the language to interpret art.

In fact, when K. gets to the cathedral and the Italian businessman fails to turn up, the building is so dark that K. thinks he was right not to come: "there would have been nothing to see, and they would have had to rest content with examining a few paintings inch by inch with K.'s pocket flashlight" (207). The lack of illuminating illumination in the cathedral means that for K. to see, and understand, the art he can only do so "inch by inch" – he cannot see the full picture at once and when he tries this form of appraisal gets excited by the sight of a "tall knight in armor," but is disappointed as he moves his flashlight about to find that "it was a conventional depiction of the entombment of Christ, and moreover a fairly recent one. He put his flashlight away and returned to his seat" (207).

If we read this as analogy of the translator's work, moving from the seemingly straightforward, if tedious, memorization of foreign words, to the act of trying to analyze and understand the art (or text) itself, K.'s putative interpretation of the art shows the difficulties of the process. Using ultra-modern technology (the flashlight was invented in 1898, 16 years before Kafka wrote the novel), K. still cannot perceive the meaning of the art in a transparent and holistically illuminative way; the "inch-by-inch" reading moving from the exciting possibility of epic – the tall knight – to the religious teleology and closure of interpretation – the entombment of Christ.

In fact, despite his relatively intensive preparation for the translation work, K. finds that when he comes into contact with the person he is translating for, the proximity and immediacy of the experience reveals the complexities of the process. When K. meets the Italian, he uses a "few smooth sentences" which the Italian "responded to with another laugh, nervously stroking his bushy, gray-blue moustache several times" (202). But after this, "K. realized with discomfort that he understood only bits and pieces of what the Italian was saying. When he spoke slowly, he could understand almost everything, but those were rare exceptions; for the most part the words literally poured from his lips, and he shook his head in seeming pleasure as he did so" (202). K. has to focus on the physical elements of the Italian because, not only does he speak too quickly but also in "some dialect or other that didn't really sound like Italian to K." (202) and his "French was hard to follow too," so K. ends up instead "observing peevishly the way he sat so deeply yet lightly in the armchair, how he tugged repeatedly at his short, sharply tailored jacket, and how once, lifting his arms and fluttering his hands, he tried to describe something K. couldn't quite follow, even though he leaned forward and stared at his hands" (202–3). When K. "realized he would have little chance of understanding the Italian" he tries to follow the businessman's lips but "his moustache hid the movement of his lips, the sight of which might otherwise have helped him out" (202).

K., unable to understand the language of the foreigner, concentrates on his body, on the physical, and a strange proximity evolves out of it; K's desire to go up and sniff the bushy moustache, and the Italian "press[ing] up so near to K. that K. had to shove his armchair back in order to move at all" (202). The oddness of this physicality raises the question of what the body and the physical represent or do in the translation process, given that most theorizing reflects concerns – perhaps obviously – on language and cognition, though the bodily apparatus is becoming more central to questions of translation in translation theory, whether via neuroscience, eye-tracking (Shreve and Angelone 2010) or the bodily safety of translators in conflict zones (Baker 2006; Inghilleri and Harding 2010). The body is part of the translation process, whether via reading and writing – the eyes and the hand – or physical gesture in the interpreting process (beyond deaf interpreting) – the ears, the hands, the lips. If we think about translator agency, the disembodiment of the translator was symptomatic of the traditional invisibility of the translator and new interests in translator histories, sociology (Tymoczko 2007; Wolf and Fukari 2007) and so on, constitute a re-embodiment of the translator.

Certainly, Kafka's own intercourse with the first translator of his work, Milena Jesenská, who translated "The Stoker," "The Judgment" and selections from *Contemplation* into Czech in the teens and 1920s, was both physical but also concerned with physicality in their textual relationship. "Please send me the translation," Kafka wrote to her, "I can't get my hands on enough of you" (Kafka 1990: 108); "Won't you reach across these stories to me, and leave your hand with me for a long, long time" (116). Thinking about her at work on the translation, he writes: "I see you bent over your work, your neck bared, I'm standing behind you, but you don't know it – please don't be frightened if you feel my lips on the back of your neck" (123).

Hands and lips are central motifs in the novel – Henry Sussman writes that "hands … are often the organs of intercourse in Kafka's fiction, interpersonal as well as sexual" (Sussman 1977: 44) and, in some ways, the hands K. reaches out for in the novel carry multivalent meanings, but in all cases they represent a form of communication and understanding that is extralingual. At the end of the novel, in the execution scene, K. sees a figure in the window who "stretched both arms out" (Kafka 1998b: 230) toward him and K. before he dies, "raised his hands and spread out all his fingers" (231) in what might be a possible epiphany in his final affinity with a character who might be "A friend? A good person? Someone who cared? Someone who wanted help?" (230). Lips are constantly hidden behind beards – beards that are "clawed" by the crowd in the trial scene – but Josef K's lips are visible and noted as the markers of his guilt: "many people believe they can predict the outcome of the trial from the face of the defendant, and in particular from the lines of his lips. Now these people claimed that according to your lips, you were certain to be convicted soon. [...] 'My lips?' asked K., taking out a pocket mirror and regarding his face. 'I can't see anything unusual about my lips. Can you?'" (175). The physical – these hands and lips – are markers of what's missing in the text, a text that can only be mimetic or a form of ekphrasis, and that excludes the physical presence and ultimate authority (in terms of meaning) of the writer, and, by extension, the translator. But at the same time, the constant and repeated motifs of the body also physicalize the language.

K. is left in the dark in the cathedral; he grabs the album of city sights he was going to use as a translation aide but a priest calls him as he makes his escape: "Josef K.!" (211). K. "was still free" and hesitates about whether he should pretend "he hadn't understood" (211); he knows that if he turns around "he would have confessed that he understood quite well, that he really was the person named, and that he was prepared to obey" (211). K. can't resist turning "a bit" to see what the priest is doing and has to go back, whereupon the priest tells him that he is in fact the "prison chaplain" (212); "I had you brought here," he says, "so I could speak with you" (212). K. is completely sanguine about that; so, the translation gig was a ruse. The prison chaplain mistakes the album of city sights in his hands for a "prayer-book" and K. flings it to the floor "so violently that it flew open and skidded some distance across the floor, its pages crushed" (212). K. has renounced his translation job, and the priest – a seeming arbiter of the Word – tells him that the court "think[s] you're guilty" (212).

The priest stands above K. in an "auxiliary pulpit" with narrow steps "not meant for human use" (209); lit up by a lamp while K. stands in the darkness. "I had to speak to you first from a distance," he tells K. "Otherwise I'm too easily influenced and forget my position" (213). But he descends and gives K. the lamp; "You're very friendly toward me," K. remarks and the priest tells him not to deceive himself, beginning the "Before the Law" parable about deception. As mentioned above, Kafka slyly warns his readers about parables in a short story, "On Parables," that "[a]ll these parables really set out to say merely that the incomprehensible is incomprehensible, and we know that already" (Kafka 1971: 457). The gnomic "Before the Law" parable, in which a man arrives at the guarded door of the Law to try and gain admittance, but is prevented by the guard until he dies after years of waiting, has been interpreted and reinterpreted by critics. But perhaps more importantly, the priest and K. spend three times the amount of time the parable takes to tell, dissecting it, trying to work out what it means.

K. comes to the cathedral as an interpreter – a translator for the Italian – who will literally and figuratively interpret the works of art for his guest. The minute he throws his translation aide away, the priest presents him with this oral text to interpret. Whereas K. had stayed up with his dictionary to function as a translator for the Italian, he intends to do no such hard work for this because "he was strongly attracted to the story" (Kafka 1998b: 217). Perhaps because he feels like the man in the parable trying to understand the guard – who, like the Italian is bearded and inscrutable, so much so that the man leans in to ask questions of the fleas in the guard's collar, as K. had wanted to lean in to the Italian and sniff his beard. K. is perfectly ready to accept the priest's interpretation of the parable being about deception: "But it's clear," said K., "and your initial interpretation was quite correct" (217). This, even after the priest admonishes him for being "too hasty [...] don't accept another person's opinion unthinkingly. I've told you the story word for word according to the text. It says nothing about deception" (217). K. thinks that it is about deception because the guard could have let the man through the door, but his opinion frustrates the priest who berates him for not having "sufficient respect for the text and ... changing the story" (217). K. has not read the text; he has just heard the priest's "word for word" version of it, but his reading of it necessarily changes it, because he is interpreting it. In a rather Talmudic move for a priest, the priest tells K. about unnamed commentators who have given various, and contradictory, opinions about the parable but who agree that "the correct understanding of a matter and misunderstanding the matter are not mutually exclusive" (219). K. once again accepts the priest's opinion, leveraged as it is on inscrutable experts, quite blithely or just politely acceding that the priest knows the story better and has known it longer than K., but the priest berates him for paying "too much attention to opinions. The text is immutable and the opinions are often only an expression of despair over it" (220).

On its own (as it was initially published), the "Before the Law" parable seems unsettling because of its incomprehensibility, but in the context of the novel, in which Kafka has a Christian priest perform Midrash on a biblical form of rhetoric – the parable – and deliberately be unable to explain the analogy the parable makes, our relationship to the parable changes. Its unknowability and inscrutability becomes funny; as readers, we, like K., hear the parable from the priest, and expect to be able to uncode it. Our frustration is played out in the following conversation about its meaning; like K. we want the answer and are prepared to accept what the priest gives us (even if we, given the gothic coloring of the cathedral scene, may not trust him). The priest's insistence that the parable, the text, is immutable is both right and wrong: the words don't change but his, K.'s, the commentators, and our reading of them does. By the end of his explanation, the priest proves a contrary stance; that the guard is unluckier than the man he has prevented from going through the door, who seems, finally, to have more knowledge, since he has seen "the radiance which streams forth from the entrance" (222), while the guard has his back to it. K. thinks this argument is "well reasoned" and repeats "various parts of the priest's explanation to himself under his breath" (222). K. performs a mimetic interpretation of the priest's words, repeating them and going over them, but in the end not reinterpreting them. He, like the reader at this point, wants the confusing, ridiculous, seemingly endless explanations to end because he is "too tired to take in all of the consequences of the story" (223). These "unaccustomed areas of thought, toward abstract notions" are meant for the court, not for him; he wants to "shake off the thought of it" (223). He gives up.

In contrast to the intangibility of the parable and the priest's oddly unilluminating exegesis, Kafka's presents an overly unsubtle gothic scene (very reminiscent of Pernath's hallucinatory episode in the cathedral in Gustav Meyrink's earlier expressionist gothic novel, *The Golem*). The cathedral is plunged into darkness, with only the feeble light of the lamp the priest has given K., a lamp that at the end of the exegesis "had long gone out" (223). Because of the lack of light, K. has to shuffle physically even closer to the priest, "not knowing in the darkness where he was" (223). That darkness had come on suddenly when K. meets the priest before the parable, and just after the priest accuses K. of relying too much on the help of women. "What sort of storm could there be outside?" K. thinks to himself:

> It was no longer a dull day, it was already deep night. No pane of stained glass within the great window emitted even a shimmer of light to interrupt the wall's darkness. And this was the moment the sexton chose to start extinguishing the candles on the main altar one by one. "Are you angry with me?" K. asked the priest (213–14).

The cathedral in chiaroscuro underlies the question of exegetical illumination, with K. plunged into an epistemological darkness and the hoped-for light the priest might shed on his fate with the court. But its overdramatic metaphoric simplicity suggests some cheekiness on Kafka's part too, as we can see from the quote above – the dramatic suddenness of darkness, the dramatic lack of illumination from the windows that display iconic religious scenes, the dramatic act of the sexton of the church putting out the lights on the locus of devotion, the altar, followed by a comic beat and the dropping of the penny, the "D'oh!" moment: "Are you angry with me?"

The "In the Cathedral" chapter immediately precedes the short final chapter, "The End," in which K. is executed without being cognizant of his crime. There seems to be nothing funny about it; as Breon Mitchell, the recent translator of *The Trial* notes, the novel "begins as farce and ends in tragedy" (Mitchell 1998: xxi). "Josef K.'s life experience," J. Hillis Miller writes, is "of a horribly unjust social structure. … What happens to Josef K. is entirely irregular and horrifyingly unjust" (Miller 2011: 69). For Miller, the "breakdown in community" that the novel "dramatizes" (72) is a telepathic forecasting of the Shoah and the fact that Josef K. never comprehends the court, his guilt or the verdict but ends up in "uncertainty" (68) is darkly emblematic of the hermeneutical ambiguity of modernity.

This standard view presumes that Josef K. is only a victim, but is he? Is he entirely innocent? When the painter Titorelli asks him whether he is innocent, Josef K. emphatically says yes, which was a "positive pleasure" not because it was the truth, but because "he was making the statement to a private citizen, and thus bore no true responsibility" (Kafka 1998b: 148). The word "innocent" is then repeated continuously in their conversation about the workings of the court until "This repeated reference to his innocence was beginning to annoy K." (152). K.'s contempt, vanity, and sense of superiority over the court and its world makes him sometimes oblivious to the interpretation and explanations of its intermediaries. "Are you angry with me?" he asks the priest and then prods him passive-aggressively, "Perhaps you don't know the sort of court you serve," until the priest screams at him in frustration: "'Can't you see two steps in front you?' It was a cry of rage, but at the same time it was the cry of someone who, seeing a man falling, shouts out in shock" (214).

We don't identify with K. because he is a victim, but because of his human fallibilities, because we too see him walking backwards of his own volition toward the cliff ledge. When he should be listening, he wants to sniff beards, fall asleep, have sex with women, go for a beer. His night of preparation to translate for the Italian is an anomaly; while he is proactive in seeking out the court, the lawyer, the painter and so on, he cannot keep his attention focused long enough to work out the court. The world he discovers might be senseless, incomprehensible, nightmarish in its lack of visible authority, but the question has to be raised as to whether Josef K. is a good reader of this world, and, consequently, since the narrator shadows him, whether we are.

The narrator translator

If Josef K. was trying to pursue his role as the Italian's interpreter with the aid of a pocket flashlight in the dark cathedral, then what does the narrator use? Kafka's narrators are notoriously enigmatic, even seemingly absent. The reader gets a narrow view from the protagonists' perspective but little direct illumination about the thoughts of others; the narrators mostly refuse to interpret the intent and thoughts of other characters. The three novels are told in third person, a "'somebody' doing the telling" (Lothe, Sandberg and Speirs, 2), who "never speaks for itself, but just imperturbably follows K's actions, speech, thoughts, and experience of the behavior and speech of others, repeating them or expressing them in past-tense third-person language." (Miller 2011: 99–100). But the "hovering presence can still be detected" (Lothe et al. 2011: 13) in the ironic tone of a narrator, who, Mark Harman argues, "occasionally winks to the reader over the hero's head" (Harman 2008: xxviii).

The little flashlight of irony, a gentle and wry illumination around the characters, allows the characters to become "vicarious narrators" (Neumann 2011: 88), who tell and retell their own and others' stories, interpret and dissect them, stories that are "transmitted, translated, transnarrated" (88). The almost invisible presence of the narrator, its apparent (but not wholly real) willingness to take a back seat and let the characters reveal themselves, its transposition of a strange world through the stories told by the characters, suggests something of a translatorial presence. The narrator-translator presents us with the language and semiotics of these slightly alien worlds and slightly alien modes of language and linguistic interaction as if it is an "auctor absconditus" (Lothe et al. 2011: 13), with no apparent exegetical or judgmental interpretation of events.

But the more the narrator-translator slips into the background, the more emphatic become acts of interpretation and narration. Indeed the characters even attempt to usurp the narratorial role: when the two men in tourist outfits come into Josef K's lodgings at the beginning of *The Trial*, he asks them if he is under arrest and one of them, Franz, stares at him "with a long and no doubt meaningful, but incomprehensible look" (Kafka 1998b: 8). Josef K. "wanted to slip into his guards' thoughts somehow and turn them to his own advantage or accustom himself to them" (9), but he can't, just as we cannot enter anyone else's head (thus questioning the authority of a fictional entity to do so). "[H]e can't seem to understand anything," one of the guards grumbles and K. "said nothing more; why should I let the idle talk of these lowly agents – they admit themselves that's what they are – confuse me even further? he thought. After all, they're discussing things they don't understand" (9). Josef K. decides that only a talk with "someone of my own sort will make everything incomparably clearer" (9). Josef K. is in a nightmarish situation – a sudden arrest for an unspecified crime – but the farcical nature of the arrest (the men in tourist suits, Josef K. presenting his bicycle license as i.d., worried about his underpants, the interrogation in a lady's boudoir) is presented alongside Josef K.'s supercilious attitude toward the guards. The enigmatic nature of the court is a large obstacle to illumination, but even larger, perhaps, is Josef K.'s own vanity. He is "at once a sympathetic and unjustly persecuted Everyman and a self-pitying and guilt-denying criminal," one of many of Kafka's characters who "are at once sympathetic subjects and dubious objects" (Franzen 2012: 122).

The humor and irony lie in the narrator-translator making Josef K. put the flashlight back in his pocket. Josef K. is capable and, to some extent, proactive in defending his innocence to the amorphous courts, but he cannot – like all of us – see his limitations. He cannot fully understand the world or people around him, even if they are persistent in trying to communicate *at* him, because of the limits of narrative (how can we fully understand another human's intent and motives?) and because of our refusal sometimes (through disinterest, boredom, fear) to push those limits. Josef K. is, at some points to his benefit, perfectly willing to accept the limits of comprehensibility. Whereas another defendant, Bloch, has become a Kleistian obsessive, staying in a maid's room off the lawyer's kitchen poring over legal books, "spending the whole day reading the same page" (Kafka 1998b: 195) without understanding them, Josef K. regards him – again superciliously, but perhaps quite rightly – as no longer "a client, he was the lawyer's dog" (195).

This analogy foreshadows his own end when he is knifed by the men from the courts and he issues his own verdict on his death; he has died "Like a dog!" The narrator ends the novel with the comment: "it seemed as though the shame was to outlive him" (231); "the narrator," J. Hillis Miller points out, "survives K.'s execution" (Miller 2011: 100). Josef K.'s afterlife is in the mouth and "testimony" (100) of the narrator, the "someone or something that never says 'I,' but who (or which) is the issuing place for the language that brings it about that K.'s shame outlives him" (100). The shame is that of becoming the deluded hermeneutic dog, being caught into the court's narratives, being enslaved by the need to find meaning. There is humor here too, tied into Josef K.'s abhorrence of inferiors. But the equivocal nature of the statement that seems to be a judgment (the assassins lean in to read "the verdict"/"Entsheidung" on K.'s face): "it *seemed as though* the shame was to outlive him"/"als sollte die Scham ihm überleben" eschews a final judgment, above all by the narrator. The narrator provides an afterlife for Josef K.'s story and the narratives he encounters.

The importance of narration and interpretation in the novel is the narrator's presence. While Gerhard Neumann points to the empty desk that Karl Rossman passes in the hold of the ship at the beginning of *Amerika* as emblematic of the narrator's "very weak presence" because he "has surrendered virtually all of his authority to the characters who tell and retell the story" (Neumann 2011: 87), Karl is in fact given another mechanized and dynamic desk once he reaches American shores. A quite marvelous contraption, "it had a hundred different compartments of all sizes" and "by turning a handle one could rearrange and adjust the compartments in whatever way one wanted or needed" (Kafka 2002a: 29). Karl imagines that even the President wouldn't have enough files to fill it. If the empty desk on the ship is emblematic of the absent narrator, this desk full of moving drawers may seem suggestive of the mode of narration of the novel: the plethora of stories and narratives, and the different perspectives from which to view them. Uncle Jakob urges Karl not to use the "adjuster" to move these compartments because of its delicacy, but the narrator may do so "either slowly or at incredible speed" (30).

Karl's excitement about the desk is conveyed by the narrator not simply through description but in the very mode of narration itself. In one paragraph, describing the desk, he keeps repeating the words "desk," "compartments," "adjuster" and "handle" ("Schreibtisch," "Fächer," "Regulator," "Kurbel"), finally whipping himself up into a frenzy toward the end of the paragraph when the narrator recounts the uncle's lack of pleasure about the desk: "Unlike Karl, the uncle was not at all pleased with the desk, but he had wanted to buy Karl a proper desk, and all desks were now fitted with the contraption" (30). He is in a frenzy because the desk reminds him of a mechanized nativity scene he saw as a child, when he kept shouting out descriptions of the moving three kings and sheep "until his mother put her hand over his mouth" (30). The mother shutting up her irritating child, who obsessively describes the religious (but mimetic) and epiphanic scene, won't happen in Amerika, where Karl gabbles on obsessively about the desk without the narrator putting a hand over his mouth. We see Karl's childishness in his own repeated words, both endearing and, because of the narrator's seemingly unadulterated transliteration, finely ironic.

Gilles Deleuze and Félix Guattari famously argued that the oddness and newness of Kafka's language, his "deterritorialization" of German, arose out of his cultural alienation to the language as a Jewish speaker of Prague German. He created "his own *patois*, his own third world, his own desert" (Deleuze and Guattari 1986: 18). Stanley Corngold challenged this notion of Kafka writing subversively in a Prague German dialect, arguing that he spoke and wrote in fairly normative High German (Corngold 2004: 273). Milan Kundera, too, discounts Deleuze and Guattari's contention that Kafka's "bareness of vocabulary" was "the cost exacted by Prague German"; instead he argues that this was a deliberate expression of Kafka's style; it "expressed Kafka's *aesthetic intention*, that it was one of the distinctive marks of the *beauty* of his prose" (Kundera 1996: 110, italics in original). Kundera emphasizes an element he feels is lost in translation because it is seen as a transgression against "good style": the repetition of words. For Kundera, this repetition has a semantic and melodic purpose, in both the repetition of concepts and in the euphonic and stylistic effect. Karl Rossman's wonder at the "very modern invention" – the mechanized compartments of his desk – is itself expressed in the very modern invention of Kafka's style. The narrator seems to be interpreting Karl's language and thought without interpretation – here the rush of excitement of a child – but there is a quiet strangeness to the narrator's mode of speech in the melodic repetition, a heightening into a poetic intensity. It manages to convey both a primal desire for patterns, while at the same time pushing that desire to the point of slapstick.

The animal translator

Kafka's "zoopoetics" (Derrida 2002: 374), his interest in the animal, highlights language at the border of the animal and the human; he destabilizes what it is to be human by placing human language and thought processes in the animal body. The question of translation is central to his animals: Gregor is shunned by his family and his boss because they cannot understand his language and he therefore becomes an animal: "Did you understand a single word of that" the chief clerk cries, "That was the voice of an animal" (Kafka 2008b: 98). "Meanwhile," the narrator says, "Gregor had become much calmer. It appeared his words were no longer comprehensible, though to his own hearing they seemed clear enough, clearer than before, perhaps because his ear had become attuned to the sound" (98). The suggestion that his animal body is better at listening – his words are "clearer than before" – is taken up by the narrator who is our translator. While the humans in the story cannot understand him – and his father and his sister, Grete, effectively condemn him to die because they think he cannot understand them and is therefore an animal and not Gregor (139) – we human readers can. Gerhard Neumann argues that the narrator in Kafka's *Amerika* is an "auctor absconditus" (Lothe et al. 2011: 13) who sheds "responsibility almost entirely for relating events by having him act simply as the unseen recorder of a whole series of stories being told and retold" (13). The "unseenness" or invisibility is partly due to the incorporeality of the narrators in his work in contradistinction to the grotesque and/or animal corporeality of the protagonists, but in fact the narrator is more than a "recorder" – there is ironic distance and bathos between what the narrator says and what is happening; often this is based on what David Foster Wallace calls "exformation" in Kafka's work (Wallace 2006: 61), or the deliberate withholding of information that he sees as the fundament of Kafkaesque humor, and in the constant undertow of "deficiency of communication apparent in the internal acts of communication" (Lothe et al. 2011: 12), that "non-communication is the rule rather than the exception in human interaction" (13). We come to understand that the joke is that Gregor was misunderstood by his family and colleagues when he could speak their language.

Stanley Corngold suggests astutely that Gregor embodies language and the untranslatable. The German term to describe him, "Ungeziefer," is notoriously – and deliberately – difficult to pin down in the original. Gregor literally becomes a sign of linguistic difference. "Kafka metamorphoses a figure of speech embedded in ordinary language," he writes. "Gregor harks back to, yet defiantly resists, integration into the 'ordinary language' of the family … Is it too odd an idea to see this family drama as the conflict between ordinary language and a being having the character of an indecipherable word?" (Corngold 1996: 88). Corngold suggests that, with this "mutilated metaphor" (89), Kafka is interested in exploring the strangeness of metaphor and of figurative language that underpins "ordinary language" (93), and suggests that its certainties can be challenged: "his body is the speech in which the impossibility of ordinary language expresses its despair" (89).

The indecipherable body, a "mutilated" sign itself with its altered jaws, speaks to his parents and does so with the sudden awareness of what it might be like to speak a foreign language, or a language with an accent:

> Gregor was dismayed when he heard his own [voice] in response. It was still without doubt his own voice from before, but with a little admixture of an irrepressible squeaking that left the words only briefly recognizable at the first instant of their sounding only to set about them afterwards so destructively that one couldn't be at all sure what one had heard (Kafka 2008b: 90).

This hybrid voice, "his own voice from before" mixed in with "an irrepressible squeaking," is in a passage full of sound: the clock striking; his mother knocking with "a cautious knock"; his father "knocking on the door at the side of the room, feebly, but with his fist. 'Gregor. Gregor?'" and then again "in a lower octave: 'Gregor! Gregor!'" From a door on the other side of the room "he heard his sister lamenting softly: 'Oh, Gregor?'" (90). Here is a vocal quartet: Gregor speaking a hybrid language that defines his new identity (as his family will no longer understand him linguistically); and his family knocking on three doors around him speaking the marker of his identity – his name – with question marks and exclamations. The paragraph is punctuated with repetitions of the word "voice"/"Stimme": the "sanfte Stimme!" of his mother (Kafka 1946: 74); "Gregors Stimme" (74); "seiner Stimme" (75); "seine antwortende Stimme" (74); and the "tieferer Stimme" of his father (75). As Gregor loses speech – he tries to speak slowly as if speaking a foreign language, "by careful enunciation and long pauses between the words to take any unusual quality from his voice" (Kafka 2008b: 90) – speech and the physical voice come to the fore.

The doors of the room prevent his family from understanding that his speech has changed – "the wooden door must have muted the change" (90) – and Gregor is thankful that he thought "of locking every door at night, even at home" (91) so they cannot see or hear him properly. His mouth and jaws, however, change from physical mechanisms of speech to physical tools with which to unlock those doors (99). He puts his new mouth around the lock and, in trying to turn it, at times "he was holding himself upright with just his mouth" (99–100). He had "felt himself back within the human ambit" when his father had shouted for a locksmith (99); using his physical mouth – albeit altered – he feels he can communicate even though "his words were no longer comprehensible" (98).

When he shows himself for the first time, to the horror of the chief clerk and his family, he launches into a reasonable speech to the chief clerk, emphasizing his loyalty to work (repeating the word "work" several times) feeling that "he was the only one present to have maintained his equanimity" (101). The reaction to his long, quite bureaucratic speech is non-linguistic – the chief clerk stares at him "mouth agape" (102) and his father, grabbing the chief clerk's cane and a newspaper, starts beating him back to the room "emitting hissing sounds like a savage" (104), "unbearable hissing sounds" (105); Gregor is "distracted by this hissing" as "he drove Gregor forward with even greater din; the sounds to Gregor's ears was not that of one father alone" (105). The others lose their human speech when they see him and Gregor's father's speech becomes expressly animalistic as he hisses at Gregor. Corngold's notion that

Gregor embodies a threatening form of language (or a mirror that subverts "ordinary language") seems relevant to his body – as the untranslatable Ungeziefer – but also to his actual language that, to us readers, is normal.

After Gregor has interacted through the doors with his family – but before they see him – he lies back on his bed feeling the need for "clarity and calm" and lies there "perhaps expecting that silence would restore the natural order of things" (92). The silence does not even miss a beat; Kafka moves straight on to the next paragraph: "But then he said to himself: 'By quarter past seven, I must certainly have got out of bed completely'" (92). Gregor cannot keep silent even for a moment; we hear him "speaking" through the whole story, the narrator translating his language throughout.

There are also animal translators in Kafka's work: Rotpeter, the ape in "A Report to an Academy," is listened to because he can speak human language, and is translating, for the academicians, his hybrid experience as a humanized ape. His acquisition of language is the key to some form of acceptance in the human world, but he realizes, in a central trope in the story, that language is "no freedom." Human language is not sufficient to describe his ape world; human language is only capable of describing the human world he has entered and therefore becomes a cage in itself. His human rhetoric reflects, in its very rhythm and punctuation, this cage. Look at Kafka's use of semicolons, periods, commas and exclamation marks in the following:

> No, it wasn't freedom I was after. Just a way out; to the right, to the left, wherever it might be; I put no further demands; even if the way out proved illusory; my demand was modest, the disappointment could be no greater. To progress, to progress! Anything but stopping still with raised arms, pressed against a crate wall (Kafka 2008b: 229).
>
> Nein, Freiheit wollte ich nicht. Nur einen Ausweg; rechts, links, wohin immer; ich stellte keine anderen Forderungen; sollte der Ausweg auch nur eine Täuschung sein; die Forderung war klein, die Täuschung würde nicht größer sein. Weiterkommen, weiterkommen! Nur nicht mit aufgehobenen Armen stillestehn, angedrückt an eine Kistenwand (Kafka 1946: 189).

To "progress" along the evolutionary ladder the ape has to translate himself into human language but in doing so, from a "creatural consciousness" (Norris 2010: 30) transforms language and rationality "into a site of perversity" (19). The humans are animals in this story, drinking, whoring and shooting: of his capture, Rotpeter says:

> Shots were fired; I was the only one hit; and was hit twice.
> Once in the cheek; a scratch; but it left a left a bald red scar that got me the disgusting, and wholly unsuitable sobriquet – really, it might have been invented by an ape – Red Peter" (Kafka 2008b: 226).
>
> Man schoß; ich war der einzige, der getroffen wurde; ich bekam zwei Schüsse.
> Einen in die Wange; der war leicht; hinterließ aber eine große ausrasierte rote Narbe, die mir den widerlichen, ganz und gar unzutreffenden, förmlich von einem Affen erfundenen Namen Rotpeter (Kafka 1946: 185–6).

Rotpeter physicalizes human language – look again at Kafka's use of the semicolon to replicate the shots and injury, the "bald red scar" or physical damage at the root of his human name, one, he says – and in doing so, sticks himself in a borderland between man (who he sees as ape-like) and ape (who he sees as less than man in this human language) – that "might have been invented by an ape."

Language allows him to escape the crate where he would "stop still with raised arms" but provides another prison. The image of the raised hands, of course, reminds us of K. at the end of *The Trial* who "raised his hands and spread out all his fingers" (Kafka 1998b: 231) before he died in a last-minute effort to connect physically with another person; both ape and human are stuck at the limits of language, in works which consistently enact a hermeneutic modality of interpretation to bare those limits. As Rosemary Arrojo argues, Kafka's texts and characters, specifically the animal in "The Burrow," "reflect the pathos of every author and of every interpreter, inevitably torn between the desire to control and to forever imprison meaning, and the human condition, which subjects both writers and interpreters to an endless exercise of meaning production" (Arrojo 2002: 69). The human condition, centered on language, is a mediation in Kafka's work of meaning and interpretation; the seams of language are constantly stretched to clothe the human in the human, baring in short glimpses the human animal. Yet language puts off a recognition of animality: "there exists in one and all an essential animality," Clare Callahan writes, "a homecoming that is linguistically deferred" (Callahan 2009: 85). Rotpeter tells his human audience:

> To speak plainly – much as I like florid language – to speak plainly: your apehood, gentlemen, inasmuch you have something of the sort behind you, cannot be any remoter from you than mine is from me. Yet everyone who walks the earth feels this little tickle at his heel: from the little chimpanzee to the great Achilles (Kafka 2008b: 226).

> Offen gesprochen, so gerne ich auch Bilder wähle für diese Dinge, offen gesprochen: Ihr Affentum, meine Herren, soferne Sie etwas Derartiges hinter sich haben, kann Ihnen nicht ferner sein als mir das meine. An der Ferse aber kitzelt es jeden, der hier auf Erden geht: den kleinen Schimpansen wie den großen Achilles (Kafka 1946: 185).

In reminding the "gentlemen" of their "apehood," the "little tickle" at the heel of the little chimpanzee and the "great Achilles," Rotpeter linguistically performs the human deferral of apedom through language, with the punctuation (the commas and colons), multiple clauses, repetition ("Offen gesprochen"), sibilance and consonance ("soferne Sie etwas Derartiges hinter sich haben"). Hofmann in some ways heightens this effect, evident in his translation of "so gerne ich auch Bilder wähle für diese Dinge," as " – much as I like florid language – " in his use of more emphatic dashes and in a quite loose translation; his Red Peter does not like choosing pictures for these things (Corngold translates this as "as much as I like to employ figurative images for these things" (Kafka 2007: 77), the Muirs as "much as I like expressing myself in images" (Kafka 1971: 250)) but, instead, likes "florid language." Yet what Hofmann subtly understands here is the effect of euphony; the beautiful consonance of the original that slows the pace down: "*Offen gesprochen, so gerne ich auch Bilder wähle für diese Dinge, offen gesprochen*" is approximated in his translation: "To *speak plainly* – much as I *like* florid *language* – to *speak plainly*."

Anniken Greve argues that Gregor cannot communicate with his family not just because of his loss of language but his loss of "a human body,"

> the field of expression of his soul ... contrary to the assumptions behind the dualistic conception, human understanding seems to depend on the live expressive human body. The meeting of minds is not so much hindered by the body as the dualist induces us to believe, but rather is made possible by or conditioned by the human body (Greve 2011: 50–1)

But Gregor is a human animal, as is Rotpeter; the stretched arms of the ape are similar to the stretched arms of K. the bank official, both attempting to communicate in the cage of language. Kafka's physicalization of language, his odd, uncanny reminders or remainders of the physical in the texts suggest a notion of a bodily or embodied embedded translator/interpreter already in the texts, reminding us of the need of our own bodily presence to interpret for ourselves. As Claire Kramsch notes, Kafka became attracted to Yiddish when seeing it embodied and performed: "Yiddish theatre opened his eyes to the relation between the language and the dancing, singing bodies of its actors and musicians" (Kramsch 2008: 325) and through a sense of his own multilingualism "carved out for himself a third language of his own poetic creation" (327).

Kafka, of course, addressed the notion of writing and the body in his story, "In the Penal Colony" where the punishment is the incision of the defendant's sentence on their body. Translation, again, is central: the "condemned man" (Kafka 2008b: 149) cannot speak the colonial language, French: "This made it all the more surprising that the condemned man was trying hard to follow the officer's explanations" (152). He "tensed his hearing up ... in the hope of gathering some scrap of information. But the movement of his blubbery pressed lips" shows that he cannot translate what is going on (154). "It will be put to him physically," the officer says (155); "the actual text is traced around the body like a narrow belt; the rest of the body is set aside for decoration ... how quiet the man comes to be in the sixth hour! The very dimmest of them begins to understand ... the man begins to decipher the script, he purses his lips as if he were listening. As you've seen, it's not easy to decipher the script with one's eyes; our man deciphers it with his wounds" (159–60). The officer has shown the traveler the blueprints for the machine, which he could not decipher: "all he saw were labyrinthine criss-crossing lines that covered the paper" (159). "It does take a long time to read," the officer counters, "I'm sure you would eventually be able to decipher it. Of course, the writing mustn't be too straightforward; it's not supposed to be fatal straight away" (159). But the officer also adds that the machine "speaks for itself" (166). It directly translates the sentence onto and into the body.

The machine translates the "labyrinthine criss-crossing lines" onto the body with its glass teeth – the judgments of a dead "Old Commandant" that no one, but the officer, can decipher on paper. The machine promises modernity and objectivity – it just carries out the pre-ordained sentence (one of fidelity) – but the authority behind it – the Old Commandant is bodily dead, and, when the officer realizes the traveler will not defend the machine against the incursion of the New Commandant, he puts himself to death in the machine under the sentence "Be Just." The machine falls apart – cogs from the engraver "came up, fell down, rolled in the sand, and toppled over and lay still" (177). Instead of engraving the sentence on the martyred officer, "The harrow was not writing, it was merely stabbing" (178) and when they get to the body "there was no trace of the promised transfiguration … his lips were pressed together, his eyes were open, their expression was of the living man, their look was firm and assured, and the point of the great iron spike had passed through the forehead" (178–9). The idea of the "promised transfiguration" or bodily translation fails, the spike not going through the heart, but through the brain. The defeat of the body of authority questions even the possibility of authoritative mechanical transposition, even if it ends up attached to the human brain.

The "doggishly submissive" (149) condemned man, meanwhile, is the character who connects to another character – his guard, via "hand signals." The slapstick comic duo act like animals; when the condemned man is tied into the machine he "put out his tongue and began to lap at" the porridge that is supposed to sustain him later as the machine does its work (165). The guard initially tries to stop him but "then reached in with his dirty hands in front of the hungry condemned man, to help himself" (165). The doggishness speaks to the colonial vision of the condemned man who cannot speak French. Even when the officer decides to put himself in the machine, having lost hope in the grace of the traveler, and speaks to the condemned man "in his language," telling him he is "at liberty," the man does not speak back "in his language" (172). Instead, he communicates his surprise in his face: "Had the foreign traveller secured forgiveness for him? What had happened? His face seemed to inquire" (172). As the officer's tragedy unfolds, as he places himself in the machine, the man and his guard squabble over the handkerchiefs, laugh at the condemned man's clothes, "they weren't even watching" (175) – they have found each other. When the condemned man realizes the "reversal" in his and the officer's situation, an "expression of broad silent mirth appeared on his face, and did not leave it" (176).

The traveler is as uninterested in speaking to the condemned man "in his language" as the officer, he only speaks at him and the guard; they point to the Old Commandant's grave "with their hands" (179) and, when they try to follow the traveler onto his boat, "they raced down the steps, silently, because they didn't dare raise their voices" (180). The doggish condemned man is still not allowed to speak, but he manages the only human contact in the story, played out in the body language of silent cinema, the slapstick duo acting in stark relief to the tragedy of the officer and his machine.

The immigrant translator

Taken in by his rich and powerful Uncle Jakob, "naturally" Karl Rossman's "first and most important task" is to learn English, specifically business English taught by a "young teacher from a trade school" (Kafka 2002a: 31). Karl, throughout *Amerika*, is assiduous in learning his business English even after his Uncle throws him out to fend for himself, but, while at his Uncle's apartment, he is already at his "notebooks" or is "walking up and down the room, committing something to memory" even before the teacher arrives. "Karl understood that he couldn't learn English quickly enough, and that his rapid progress at it was also his best way of pleasing his uncle" (31–2). When Karl first recites an American poem, "the subject of it was a conflagration," it pleases his Uncle who "looked out at the darkened sky, and in sympathy with the verse ... slowly and rhythmically clapped his hands, while Karl stood beside him with expressionless eyes and struggled with the difficult poem" (32).

The rhythmic clapping of hands reflects the modern, mechanized world that Karl has entered. Although the view from the balcony in his Uncle's apartment seems to be a "swirling kaleidoscope" (28), the world inside the apartment moves like clockwork, reflected in the narrative style of the chapter, in which the word "balcony" is repeated (this liminal space neither inside nor outside and marked as dangerous and alluring by his Uncle), followed by the insistent repetition of "desk" (in describing its marvelous mechanical nature), and then followed by the repetition of the word "piano," an instrument that mechanically makes sound, and "lift":

> The piano had arrived ... the building had its own service lift, in which a whole removal van might have fitted with ease, and this lift carried the piano up to Karl's room. Karl could have gone on the same lift as the piano and the removal men, but since there was an ordinary lift ... (31).

The acoustics are good; it helps his unease at "living in an iron house ... though the building might look very iron from outside, inside it one had not the slightest sense of iron construction" (31). He plays away at "an old ballad from his homeland" but his Uncle buys him martial and mechanical "American marches" and the "national anthem" and then, obviously fed up, suggests Karl might want to take up the violin or the French horn (31). Karl's learning of English is part of the regimen, like the "whip crack[ing] ... percussively" through his riding arena where he learns "English lamentations" because of his bad riding skills, overheard by his English teacher who has to go to the arena with him but is left "always leaning on the same doorpost, generally dog-tired" (33).

The mechanical nature of communication in this hi-tech New York becomes apparent when his Uncle brings him to the telegraph office of his enterprise, a room that was "actually larger than the telegraph office of his home town" (34). "No one offered a greeting," Karl discovers, "greetings had been abolished" (34). His Uncle shows him into a booth where they watch an operator whose "fingers holding a pencil moved with inhuman speed and fluency" and who mostly listens because it "wasn't his job to talk" (34). The Uncle explains to Karl that the exact same information was "simultaneously being taken down by two other employees and then collated, so that errors were as far as possible eliminated" (34). Just after this visit to the futuristic communication hub, the Uncle comes into Karl's room, "sat down at his desk and looked through an English exercise Karl had just completed, slammed his hand down on the desk and called out, 'Really excellent!'" (35). For the first time, Karl is invited to dinner with his Uncle's business associates Pollunder and Green because "it was a good opportunity to master some business expressions" (35).

Karl is sent to the new world, not by his own choice, and it is a world he has to translate. Part of this relates to the native language in the new world – Karl's Uncle's insistence that he speak English to get on in the world is part of the real immigrant experience of the time, but the emphasis is on "the workings of business" (54) also points to another language that needs to be learned, one almost as opaque for the immigrant: the language of how things actually function in the new culture and the instrumental, even inhuman, language of business.

Arriving in New York, Karl has a stroke of luck; being plucked from steerage by the wealthy Uncle Jakob – the rags-to-riches American dream occurring within a ridiculously compressed time-frame. Karl has already told the stoker (whom he has just met and in whose bed he is lying) that he doesn't have the "stamina" to go to university to better himself, that he was "never especially good at school," "hardly know[s] any English," and figures anyway that "there's a lot of bias against foreigners here" (6). The joke is, of course, that Karl himself has shown that bias: he asks if the stoker is German before he accepts the stoker's invite to go into his room, "as he'd heard a lot about the dangers for new arrivals in America, especially coming from Irishmen" (4).

On the opening page of the novel, Karl gives his suitcase to a complete stranger, so that he can go back down into steerage to try and find his umbrella, despite spending the entirety of the voyage jealously guarding his suitcase for fear of his Slovak cabin mate "who had just been waiting for Karl, finally sapped by exhaustion, to drop off for one instant, so that he could pull the suitcase over to himself by means of a long rod which he spent his day endlessly playing or practising with" (8). By day, the Slovak "looked innocent enough," but by night he "cast sad looks" at the suitcase, something Karl could see because he had, against the ship's regulations, lit a lamp, by the light of which he spent entire nights scrutinizing "the incomprehensible pamphlets of the emigration agencies" (8). Kafka's funny exposé (the Slovak's deliberately ridiculous long rod) of the anxieties of the immigrant anticipating a new world and flung into proximity with other nationalities gives us real sympathy for Karl (the experience of obsessively watching our bags and more alert suspicions as we travel) and, at the same time, shows him exhibiting the prejudices he will himself encounter. Karl is perfectly willing to hand over his suitcase to the German stranger, "Franz Butterbaum" (4), but the Slovak is innately suspicious.

For the stoker, too, nationality promises either friends or enemies; his nemesis on board ship is the Rumanian senior engineer Schubal, "that bastard bossing Germans on a German ship" (6). Karl takes up the stoker's case with brio on the bridge of the ship in front of the captain and port officials – presumably German and American – as well as the man who turns out to be his Uncle Jakob. Karl is skeptical about his Uncle's identity – he points out that Jakob was his Uncle's Christian name, not his surname (which was Bendelmayer) as the Councillor Jakob's is. Karl's assertion makes everyone laugh: "But what I said wasn't so foolish, thought Karl" and he decides he "really must pay attention to every word" (19). Almost immediately after this, the self-proclaimed

Uncle Jakob insults Karl's parents and Karl avers: "He really is my uncle, no question" (19).

The slight ambiguity about Jakob's real identity is moot for Karl (but perhaps not for us readers) because this Jakob has a letter from the maid, Johanna Brummer, and berates his parents for having "got rid" of him like a cat (19), something he won't gloss over because "glossing over isn't the American way" (19). But also perhaps because Jakob is German and powerful; something is being glossed over in this meeting on the ship's bridge, and this is the working of a native semiotics – the semiotics of power – beyond language. This is an Amerika where the Statue of Liberty holds a sword aloft, and where the men on the bridge wear sabers and Uncle Jakob himself wields a bamboo cane.

Quickly, though, learning English gets Karl into trouble. Uncle Jakob allows him to go and spend the night upstate at one of his business associate's country house, with the proviso that Karl return home in time for his English lesson. Karl gets waylaid inside the house, first by the athletic Klara, who wrestles Karl in her room, and then by "the big house" itself, "the endless corridors, the chapel, the empty rooms, the darkness everywhere" (53). "Couldn't you feel a little more at home?" Klara asks (44). At the stroke of midnight, the sinister Mr. Green hands Karl a letter in which his uncle disavows him for his disobedience. Karl, a German speaker, hadn't learned English back in Europe, even though his father was "keen" for him to learn. His reasons? He "had no way of knowing what catastrophe would befall me, and with what urgency I would need English" (54) (i.e. his seduction by, and impregnation of, the family maid and subsequent expulsion by his family); and second, since he was busy already at school, he didn't have "much time for other pursuits" (54). Thus, he tells Mr. Pollunder and Green that he is "utterly dependent on the kindness of my uncle" until his "English studies are complete, and I have something of the workings of business" (54). Because he doesn't escape from Pollunder's house in time for his English lesson, Karl is ejected from his Uncle's instrumental sphere and ends up on the road with the shady Irishman, Robinson, and the even shadier Frenchman, Delamarche.

But he doesn't give up on his English, realizing the power of business English. "Whenever I'm not asleep," he tells the Head Porter and Head Waiter at the Hotel Occidental, "I'm studying business correspondence" (120). The happy times he spends with Therese (in contradistinction to her Dickensian story of what happened to her immigrant mother) lead to him borrowing "a manual of business correspondence"; "Now Karl would spend whole nights with cotton wool in his ears, downstairs on his bed in the dormitory, in all possible positions for variety, reading the book, and scribbling out exercises" (105). When he is interrupted by the other lift boys, he uses it to help his studies "by asking them for little English tips" (105). He thinks they are "reconciled" to their position, and should see him as an "example" of how to get ahead (105). Therese "with excessive pedantry" goes through his exercises and Karl at time disagrees with her using "in evidence his great New York professor" – the young man from the trade school – to cite his prowess. If she "crossed out the passage" he would "usually put a line through her crossings-out to record his disagreement" (105). The Head Cook would be asked for her opinion and always sided with Therese, then talking to Karl about Europe, "which made Karl aware of how much had changed there, quite fundamentally, in a relatively short space of time, and how much must have changed already in his own absence, and was changing all the time" (105). Karl, committed to getting ahead, will be thrown out because no one believes any of the lift boys would be so committed. His naive belief that he can change his position, class and fate through business English is connected to his belief that everything will stay static at home. Here, he realizes as they move from the manual of business correspondence to the Head Cook reminiscing about Europe that he would never be able to go back to the same home, the same Europe. He has already been translated.

Kafka, literary reinterpreter

"We walked about on the cliff after that," David Copperfield remembers, "and sat on the grass, and looked at things through a telescope – I could make out nothing myself when it was put to my eye, but I pretended I could – and then we came back to the hotel to an early dinner" (Dickens 2012: 25). In this, the second chapter entitled "I Observe" of Dickens's novel, Copperfield's future malevolent stepfather Mr. Murdstone brings him to a hotel in Lowestoft; David, still a small child, watches Murdstone intently as he interacts with business acquaintances who are delighted to find out that David is the son of the "pretty widow" and guess Murdstone's intent to woo her (24). Murdstone does not want them to talk of these adult machinations in front of David: "'take care, if you please,' he says, 'somebody's sharp'":

> "Who is?" asked the gentleman, laughing.
> I looked up, quickly; being curious to know.
> "Only Brooks of Sheffield," said Mr. Murdstone.
> I was quite relieved to find that it was only Brooks of Sheffield; for, at first, I really thought it was I (24).

Dickens mines the humor of this "child of close observation" being unable to fully comprehend the adult world around him and what he sees thus ironically destabilizes the rules and exposes the absurdities of that world. Among his first memories are in church, where he does not know where to look: at Peggoty who keeps glancing at their house to make sure it isn't being robbed, at the priest wearing "that white thing" (16) and not his normal clothes, at the sheep that has just roamed in, or at the pulpit that would make a fine castle. David can "make nothing out myself" when the telescope is "put" to his eye, because he has a child's, an outsider's, vision. "Young innocence," as Mrs. Mowcher puts it, versus Steerforth's "Old Guilt" (455).

This motif – of technology helping the vision of an outsider – is picked up by Kafka (who expressly wrote about the influence of Dickens's novel on his own) in *Amerika*. Brunelda watches electioneering for judicial elections from her balcony with a pair of opera glasses, squeezing Karl against the railing as Delamarche and Robinson talk about him. She tells Karl he'll have a "better view" with the glasses and tells him to "try it" but he responds that his "eyesight is very good" and he can see as it is:

> He didn't find it a kindness, more a nuisance when she put the glasses up to his eyes and said just the one word "You!" melodiously, but also with menace. And then Karl had the glasses in front of him, and could see nothing at all.
>
> "I can't see a thing," he said, and tried to remove the glasses, but she held them in place, while his head, was so cushioned on her breast he could move it neither sideways nor back (Kafka 2002a: 169–70).

She keeps insisting and "Karl now had his whole face in her heavy breathing" and he keeps denying it; when she turns to Delamarche, she loosens her grip on the glasses "and Karl could, without her particularly minding it, look out from under her glasses down on to the street" (170). Karl's sight has made her uncomfortable previously: "why is he staring at me like that?" she asks when she first meets him (151), calling him "that stranger boy, who looked at me with wild eyes" (152). Karl had tried to move out of the way on the balcony when she came out to look at the electioneering because "After all, she didn't like him, she was frightened of his eyes" (166).

As Murdstone tries to make David Copperfield see through the telescope from the cliff, so Brunelda tries to get Karl to see America in action from the balcony using the opera glasses, but he has to look underneath them to try to make sense of this new, and unknown, world. The dramatic, and cinematic, scene unfolding underneath – of placards, and car headlights panning the high-rises and the candidate, of people on either side chanting and counter-chanting at each other from balconies – is odd to an immigrant unused to the idea of judges being elected and campaigning for election. It struck Kafka as a notable fact after attending a lecture by a Czech socialist politician on America: "Yesterday lecture on America by Dr. Soukup." Kafka writes in his diary at the beginning of June 1912, "The Czechs in Nebraska, all officials in America are elected" (Kafka 1964: 203). As German critics have noted (Binder 1976; Wirkner 1976), Kafka seems to have read František Soukup's 1912 travelogue in which he marvels not only at the fact of judicial elections, but at the theater of them:[1]

> Here in America judges not only vote but are voted in and the elections of judges of all categories are clamorous, like our elections for the imperial council. They call meetings where the judicial candidate present themselves, distribute leaflets and proclamations, stick up enormous posters with pictures of the candidates – each party wants to see their people in the judge's chamber (Soukup 1912: 91).

Soukup smilingly imagines the "long, horror-filled faces of our bureaucrats" if they were told they had to fight for popular election (91). The right to vote – a right extended in some parts of America by 1912 to women – gives Soukup hope in America, even if the "political life of the US" is

---

[1] Both Hartmut Binder and Alfred Wirkner use private translations of Soukup's book into German. Soukup's book, however, has not been published in German, nor has it been translated into English. As Mark Anderson notes, "Kafka apparently drew heavily from Soukup's *Amerika*" but it "is unfortunately unavailable in English or German translation" (Anderson 1992: 113). All translations from Soukup's book, here, are mine.

rapaciously, barbarously brutal and corrupt to its core, like all of this crazy American capitalism. In America persuasion, programs, policies don't decide it – the dollar does! Politics, like religion, is nothing more that an object of trade, business. Whoever has the most money, wins [...] The Republican party represents capital the most, the Democrats represent capital a little less" (99–100).

He visits the White House and is surprised to find that he and his friend can just walk right in because "there weren't any soldiers or guards anywhere" (99) and it is only until they reach the second floor that they are faced with a door that says "Private" on it. Being polite, Soukup writes, we didn't want to disturb the President, but he was told that to talk to the President, all he would have to do would be to leave his business card. Soukup is impressed that here, in this republic, you don't have "to bend your knee" or "change your clothes" for any person of power (98).

Soukup's book *Amerika*, a "row of pictures of American life," is one of several literary sources for Kafka's novel, including Dickens's *David Copperfield*, Arthur Holitscher's *Amerika Heute und Morgen* and Benjamin Franklin's *Autobiography*. That Kafka had clearly used several sources for his first novel made certain critics see *Amerika* as an aesthetic failure, as not wholly original, because of this "secondhand material" (Politzer 1966: 120): "Kafka was unable to come to grips with it. It crumbled under the touch that was eager to penetrate and transform it" (120). The novel was at its most successful when it contained, for Heinz Politzer, "visions which are completely Kafka's own" (120–1). Ritchie Robertson rejects Poltzer's view but also thinks the novel not wholly successful because Kafka was unable to knit the strands of "the portrayal of the technological and urban world of America" (from Holitscher, but also Soukup) with a theme of "inevitable guilt" that simply "repeats itself mechanically" (using an episodic structure from Dickens), leading to a lack of "narrative dynamism" and "a static portrayal" of America (Roberston 1987: 73).

More recently, however, that very question of stasis and movement in the narrative has become central to an understanding of the newness of Kafka's form in the novel, a newness connected to his re-envisioning or re-viewing of the sources for the novel. "Kafka's idiosyncratic adaptation of actual photographs," Carolin Duttlinger argues, is tied to "his turn towards photography as an underlying narrative principle" so that the "overall narrative strategy" repeatedly showed "the textual flow as disrupted by photographically detailed static tableaux which are thrown into sharp relief [...] such scenes are frequently based on extra-textual sources" (Duttlinger 2007: 67). The narrative style – of cinematic movement disrupted by these "static tableaux" – "takes on a psychological dimension: vision in Kafka's first novel does not demarcate a clear contrast between subject and object, but rather signifies the collapse of the boundaries between subjective perception and objective reality" (67). Duttlinger gives the example here of Karl's first sight of the Statue of Liberty; his observation of it "is supplanted by a sudden heightening of his visual capacities which mirrors his growing excitement"; an intense sunlight that "highlight[s] the statue resembles a photographic flash disrupting Karl's and the reader's mode of perception" (67). The statue is the first photograph in Holitscher's book and the exact same photograph is one of the first in

Soukup's book; they show an unclear, hazy torch that Karl sees as a sword; thus Kafka "subjects his photographic material to a complex process of adaptation and transformation [...] characterized by a mixture of realism and distortion [that ...] disrupts not only the protagonist's but also the reader's acquired cultural knowledge" (67–8).

For Mark Anderson, this disrupted vision is articulated also by movement in the novel, the "destabilizing, anti-mimetic effects" (Anderson 1992: 116) that make "each individual scene, image, and detail part of a phenomenological description of the act of seeing, or rather, the ultimately impossible act of viewing a world caught in a self-cancelling motion that is 'forever newly improvised'" (121). The "socio-political rootlessness" of immigration and poverty – images Kafka gleaned from Holitscher's and Soukup's books – merge with the metaphysical "groundlessness of Karl's existence in a world of changing appearances, unstable impressions, accident, and death: a world of 'traffic'" (113). The anxiety in Soukup's and Holitscher's books about the reality of American progress and the use of this new mechanized world is transformed by Karl's vision into a sense of metaphysical rootlessness in a world in which technology has changed how we see; the odd, distorted moments of movement in the narrative enunciate this tension. Kafka may also have been influenced by his reaction to film, which he allegedly (in the dubiously reported conversations with Gustav Janouch) felt "disturbs one's vision. The speed of the movements and the rapid change of images force men to look continually from one to another. Sight does not master the images, it is the pictures which master one's sight. They flood one's consciousness. The cinema involves putting the eye into uniform, when before it was naked. [...] Films are iron shutters (Janouch 1985: 160). He was apparently delighted when Janouch told him there was a cinema in Prague called "Bio Slepců" [Cinema of the Blind]: "Bio Slepcu! Every cinema should be called that. Their flickering images blind people to reality" (147). The flickering movement of Kafka's own narrative between motion and these "static tableaux" *thinks* about vision, and makes the reader think about vision, about looking at the world anew.

Kafka's transformation or translation of his source texts for Amerika is an abusive one; Lawrence Venuti, writing about film adaptation as translation, uses Philip Lewis's notion of "abusive fidelity" to argue that an abusive adaptation "demands an aggressive interpretation of the signifier" and "will also abuse or deviate from the source text, exposing linguistic and cultural conditions that remain implicit or unstated in it" (Venuti 2007: 39). Venuti argues that it is a mutually "aggressive" intertextual relationship in which "the source text can be seen as equally abusive of the translation" as a "comparison between them will always uncover shifts or deviations that indicate the limitations of the translation, not merely of its mimetic aim, but of the interpretation that it inscribes during the recontextualizing process" (39). For Venuti, more revelatory in this process than any ideological interpretations made by the translator, are "the formal and thematic principles" in the source text that stand out as complex and difficult to translate into the new medium (40). We see Kafka translating both textual and pictorial images interrogatively – thinking about their function and how that function connects form with meaning; thus opening up readings of the source and Kafka's target texts.

There are three pertinent examples of this: Kafka's use of the image of David Copperfield's stolen "box," an image with which he begins *Amerika* and which travels through the novel as a motif; and two pictorial images from Soukup's book – the first, a cross-section line-drawing of an ultra-modern ocean-liner, and, the second, a photograph of the choir of the Christian-Catholic Apostolic evangelical community from Zion City, Illinois. These two last images, as Hartmut Binder very briefly suggests, seem to be at least partial inspiration for the first and final chapters of the novel "The Stoker," and "The Nature Theatre of Oklahoma" (Binder 1976: 90, 155). Both images are placed somewhat ironically in Soukup's travelogue as pictorial evidence of oppression, whether through capitalism and the class system or via a new and American form of commercialized religion; Kafka transforms the images into *mise-en-scène* in the two chapters of his novel, both of which metaphysically question the stasis of power and a static representation of objective reality.

"Wot box?"

After David Copperfield's mother, Clara Trotwood, dies, the evil Mr. Murdstone takes the 10-year-old David out of school and puts him to work in a bottling warehouse and houses him with the incessantly impecunious Mr. Micawber. Copperfield, though always diligent, decides to run away to his aunt Miss Betsey Trotwood. Being "a very honest little creature" (Dickens 2012: 176), he employs a "long-legged young man, with a very little empty donkey-cart" after "staring at him" to bring the box to the Dover coach-office (176). The young man not only takes David's money, but gallops away with the box. David chases after him unsuccessfully, described with a slapstick, but poignant, humor: "Now I lost him," David says, "now I saw him, now I lost him, now I was cut at with a whip, now shouted at, now down in the mud, now up again, now running into somebody's arms, now running headlong at a post" (177–8). The box that he took with him to Mr. Peggoty's house (the ship on the beach) and back home again is lost forever and he walks toward Dover, "taking very little more out of the world" (178). As he walks toward Dover, bereft of his box, he is scared by the "trampers" on the road, some of whom were the "most ferocious-looking ruffians" and one "tinker" who snatches his handkerchief and beats up the woman with him (185–6) that scares him enough to find "a hiding-place" (186) whenever he sees these "trampers." What sustains him on his journey – now that he is traveling without his box and belongings from his past – is his "fanciful picture of my mother in her youth, before I came into the world. It kept me company" (186).

Five years after writing the opening to *Amerika*, Kafka wrote in his *Diaries*:

> Dickens's *Copperfield*. "The Stoker" a sheer imitation of Dickens, the projected novel even more so. The story of the trunk, the boy who delights and charms everyone, the menial labour, his sweetheart in the country house, the dirty houses, et al., but above all the method (Kafka 1964: 388).

The "trunk"/"Koffer" is one of the motifs Kafka picks up and carries out of *David Copperfield*. Like David, Karl Rossman entrusts his "Koffer" to a stranger in the opening page of *Amerika*, for it to be seemingly lost, only to turn up again when he is turned out by his Uncle. He has to defend it and its content then against the "trampers" whom he meets: Robinson and Delamarche, who rifle through it, eating the salami within and destroying the photograph he has of his parents. Karl takes no luggage with him from the Hotel Occidental, and when he boards the train, right at the end of the novel, to go to the Theatre of Oklahoma, he carries nothing and notes the odd and conspicuous lack of luggage among his fellow passengers. It is difficult as post-Holocaust readers not to feel the "chill" and "shudder" from the final lines of the book at that image of people being unloaded of their luggage and placed on trains to an unknown destination, but the passage (written in 1914) does not necessarily place this unburdening in a negative light. The suitcase – associated with his immigrant past (and particularly his father whose "old army suitcase" (Kafka 2002a: 63) it was) – and its loss can also be a symbolic severance with Karl's European identity. In Dickens's novel, those who hold tightly onto their boxes are flawed: Miss Murdstone and her "two uncompromising hard black boxes, with her initials on the lids in hard brass nails" (Dickens 2012: 48) and Barkis who carried his "box, on all his journeys, every day" and so that "it might the better escape notice, he had invented a fiction that it belonged to 'Mr. Blackboy,' and was 'to be left with Barkis till called for'; a fable he had elaborately written on the lid, in characters now scarcely legible" (438–9). On his deathbed, Barkis lies with his head and shoulders out of bed "half resting on the box which had cost him so much pain and trouble"; unable to keep "assuring himself of its safety by means of the divining rod I had seen him use, he had required to have it placed on a chair at the bedside, where he had every since embraced it, night and day. […] Time and the world were slipping from beneath him, but the box was there" (436–7).

Kafka incorporates elements of Barkis's box into *Amerika*: the idea that the box belongs to a fictional "Mr. Blackboy" is suggestive of Karl's fictionalization of himself into "Negro" and the tragic-comical image of Barkis feeling for his box with a "divining rod" is translated into the figure of the Slovak, with whom Karl shares a cabin on the journey across the Atlantic and whom he suspects, comically, and rather sexually, "of having intentions on his suitcase":

> That Slovak had been waiting for Karl, finally, sapped by exhaustion, to drop off for one instant, so that he could pull the suitcase over to himself by means of a long rod which he spent his days endlessly playing or practising with (Kafka 2002a: 8).

Both Murdstone and Barkis *inscribe* their boxes with approximations of their identities, Murdstone with her initials "in hard brass nails" and Barkis with both a fictional and, as a messenger, a real name. In naming their boxes, they appear to take possession of the contents, but Barkis who has been saving his pennies to good effect, also misunderstands some contents of the box, keeping a "much polished" oyster-shell thinking it a pearl: "I conclude," Copperfield says, "that Mr. Barkis had some general ideas about pearls, which never resolved themselves into anything definite" (Dickens 2012: 438). The box seems to be a concrete articulation of identity and material possession, but has a rummage-sale of contents that shift in their signification. It is also inherently movable.

Kafka qualifies his statement that his work is a "sheer imitation" of Dickens; while attracted to "Dickens's opulence and great, careless prodigality" that might lend itself to a picture of teeming modern America, he senses that there "is a heartlessness behind his sentimentally overflowing style" which gives "one a barbaric impression because the whole does not make sense" (Kafka 1964: 388). Although Kafka's "intention" was to write a Dickens novel, he cannot because of "the sharper lights I should have taken from the times and the duller ones I should have got from myself"; he is "wiser for his epigonism" (388). Coming after Dickens, Kafka learns how to transform and translate "above all the method" (388) Dickens uses, especially the return in the text of motifs: while the image of the box returns through *David Copperfield*, Kafka deliberates on the meaning of that return and formally connects the recursiveness of the image to a disquisition of its meaning, using it as a means to forward momentum in the text, and connecting different episodes in the novel. It is a much tighter, more focused approach to an image generated by Dickens's novel; interrogating the image as a sign each time it returns in the text.

While Copperfield loses his box once to a thief, Karl's "suitcase" survives the Slovak, Franz Butterbaum, Schubal, even – though relieved of some of its contents – Robinson and Delamarche. Each time Karl "opens" the box – whether in memory or actuality – the contents or its form change: lying on the stoker's bed, Karl remembers that there is a clean shirt, a sort of "emergency suit" and a "piece of Verona salami" in the "expensive suitcase" (Kafka 2002a: 7). When Mr. Green gives him back his suitcase, it is now his "old suitcase [...] a suitcase that soldiers in my home country enlist with [...] it's my father's old army suitcase" (63). After renting a room at the inn, he opens the suitcase "to take a look at his belongings, of which he only had a vague memory"; he finds the suit and shirt he had worn on the voyage, the salami which "lamentabl[y]" had "imparted its smell to everything in the suitcase," including a "pocket Bible, letter paper and photographs of his parents" (67). As he checks on the contents, the cap he is wearing slips off his head into the suitcase. Mr. Green had given him the cap at Pollunder's country house, because Karl had mislaid his hat, and Karl had been astonished at how perfectly it had fitted him; looking at the cap in the suitcase, he now recognizes it in "its old setting [...] it was his cap, the cap his mother had given him as a travelling cap" (67–8). Karl is angry, feeling he was set up by Green and his Uncle, and he shuts the suitcase in an "unintentionally furious movement," waking up Robinson and Delamarche (68).

The unrecognized cap that has no meaning for Karl – other than as a seemingly kind gesture by Green – only garners signification for him once it slips into the suitcase and "its old setting": a parting gift from his mother to be used for travel and to be used also to enable him to fit into the new world because "in America caps are generally worn in place of hats" (68). But he "had been careful not to wear it on board ship" because he "hadn't wanted to wear his out before he even got there" (68).

Connected with his old identity (his mother and Europe) it is also connected with the new American one; also, in swapping his hat for the cap, a new class one. Yet, though it fits him perfectly, it slips off his head, bringing up but also bringing into question the notion of clothes as indicators of identity; instead of a "legible" societal signifier, the cap becomes "an impenetrable, opaque, 'unreadable' surface," overdetermined in its meaning (Anderson 1992: 32).

Karl is concerned about order in his suitcase, but it gets lost, things keep being taken out and being put in, it gets opened and fiercely shut: it does not remain static and legible. When he opens it in the inn, he panics because everything seems "crammed in in such a higgedly-piggedly fashion that the lid flew up when he opened the catch" (Kafka 2002a: 67); the disorder of the contents, in other words, threatens to break through their encasement. But he realizes that the "sole cause of this disorder" was the suit he had worn on the voyage "for which of course the suitcase had not allowed" and, so, it "had been crammed in afterwards" (67). Packed tight already, the suitcase cannot comfortably contain his suit that traveled on his back on his movement from Europe to America, an added signification to the contents.

Karl takes everything out and lays the contents on a table; "if [Robinson and Delamarche] were thieves they needed only to make their way to it and help themselves" (68) and, in a way, Karl's anxieties are founded. Karl's travel suit had been swapped, when living with his uncle, for a "good suit" (68), and Robinson and Delamarche persuade him to sell that good suit to the cleaner at the inn; Karl suspects that they take a cut from the sale while he changes back into his "old suit" (71). The cleaner runs in and "gathered up his things in both hands and slung them into the suitcase with such force, as if they were wild animals being brought to heel," not giving Karl any time "to put his suitcase in order" (71). Karl, trying to understand his present state, has spent the night examining a photograph of his parents, but he has arrived and departed from the inn in a state of disordered meaning and signification; the contents of the case being compared to "wild animals being brought to heel" at least temporarily, but once again by someone else.

Robinson agrees to carry the suitcase as they go on their travels but complains "incessantly about its weight" until Karl realizes that he is doing so because he wants to "lighten it of the Verona salami" which he had noticed at the inn (73). Forced to unpack his case, Delamarche takes the salami and "set about it with a sabre-like knife, and ate almost the whole thing" (73). Robinson gets a few slices, Karl nothing, and he is forced to carry his case "if it wasn't to be abandoned on the highway" (73). When he goes to the Hotel Occidental to try to get some food and is generously given some by the Head Cook, the food packed in a "light straw basket" (81), he returns to discover that "his suitcase, which he had left behind locked, and the key to which he had in his pocket, was wide open, with half its contents scattered about on the grass" (83). He shouts at Robinson and Delamarche to "Get up!" because he thinks they have left the "suitcase standing unprotected" (83). In fact, they are the thieves: "we thought there might be something to eat in your suitcase," Delamarche says, "so we tickled the lock until it opened" (83).

Karl starts repacking the suitcase, accusing them of being "envious of my few possessions" because they "have nothing," they have "broken open my suitcase" and then insult Germans because he is naturally upset; "he's a vicious German," Delamarche says, "he can't leave without offending our honor and calling us thieves, just because we had a little laugh with his suitcase" (84). The Frenchman and Irishman are looking for money, but what goes missing is Karl's photograph of his parents, his last personal link with home: "It mattered more to me than everything else in that suitcase," he says. "It's irreplaceable, you see, I'll never get another one" (86). He offers the men the "entire suitcase plus contents" if they give him back the photograph (86). Delamarche and Robinson deny seeing any photograph in the case: "But that's not possible," Karl says. "It was right at the top, and now it isn't there any more. If only you hadn't played your joke with the suitcase" (86). "An error is out of the question," Delamarche answers, "there was no picture in the suitcase" (86).

While Delamarche and Robinson are clearly untrustworthy, is there a possibility here that they are telling the truth? Karl had taken the photograph out and examined it thoroughly at the inn, disappointed that this realistic picture of his parents failed as a representation of them, that it did not automatically show anything, but, instead, needed to be interpreted. He sees his mother's forced smile in the photograph and feels it is obvious that the photograph betrays her feelings as she tries to hide them; it gives "an irresistible sense of the concealed feelings of the subject" (69). But his father's "heavy horizontal moustache didn't look anything like the real thing" and Karl moves his candle about to try and make his father come alive (69). Karl falls asleep while looking at the photograph; it "slipped from his hands" (70), just as his cap had slipped from his head. Whether or not the photograph was repacked (hastily by the cleaner) is left unanswered. The anxiety about representation and meaning is manifest. The final end of the photograph, suggested by the waiter from the Hotel Occidental, is that the two men have "probably torn up the photograph and thrown away the pieces" (87), figuratively dismembering the sign. But it could equally have simply "slipped from his hands," having become insignificant in its new context.

The notion that it is all a joke, a laugh, a tickle of the lock, carries sinister overtones, but also the destabilizing element of humor when it comes to signification. Karl's past, his sense of an ordered world and of an ordered language, is articulated by his suitcase that is the given emblem of emigration and what we carry across with us. But Karl is not only careless about his suitcase from the start; even before his voyage his father had predicted "in jest" that he would lose the case: "I wonder how long you'll manage to hang on to it for?" (7). "It's very practical," Karl will later tell Mr. Green "smiling" when he gets the suitcase back, "If you remember not to leave it somewhere" (63). That – unlike David Copperfield's box – it keeps getting left "somewhere" and others rummage through it, changing its contents, as Karl's slippages also change the contents and disorder the world within the case – questions the idea of possession, of possessive signification (sometimes trans-linguistically: the Frenchman and the Irishman trying to own the contents of the German's case but leaving them "scattered') as a quixotic struggle. "'What kind of strange suitcase is that?'" Mr. Green asks Karl as he hands it back to him (63); and it is a strange suitcase, a seemingly obvious, stereotypical emblem of the emigrant life that, instead in Kafka's novel, keeps changing, disappearing, reappearing in different guises and with different content.

Kafka was interested in Dickens's "method" and we see him mining Dickens's sense of euphonic comedy, but also heightening and intensifying it. As we have seen, Copperfield chases after the thief and his box, and we get a sense of slapstick chase through Dickens's repetition of "now": "Now I lost him," David says, "now I saw him, now I lost him, now I was cut at with a whip, now shouted at, now down in the mud, now up again, now running into somebody's arms, now running headlong at a post" (177–8). The repetition of the temporal adverb makes the text and the language dynamic; it introduces a rhythm and pace that mimics Copperfield's physical chase. The deictic frame is at the same time undercut by the movement being interrupted: Copperfield falling in the mud, running into people and running into a post.

When the suitcase turns up in Karl's thoughts or in his vicinity, it, too, is repeated and becomes a lexical presence. In the opening pages of the novel, the stoker invites Karl into his cabin and persuades him, oddly, to lie down on his bed. Karl suddenly remembers he has left his suitcase up on deck with a stranger: "Oh God," he exclaims, "I've quite forgotten all about my suitcase!" and as he debates the consequences with the stoker, the repetition of the word "suitcase" (and "umbrella") heightens the tension while containing, in the incessant repetition, also the faint whiff of absurdity and ridicule:

> "Is the suitcase important to you?" "Of course." "Well then, so why did you give it to a stranger?" "I forgot my umbrella down below and went to get it, but I didn't want to lug my suitcase down with me." [...] "And now you've lost your suitcase. Not to mention the umbrella," and the man sat down on the chair, as though Karl's predicament was beginning to interest him. "I don't think the suitcase is lost yet." "Think all you like," said the man. [...] "In Hamburg your man Butterbaum might have minded your suitcase for you, but over here, there's probably no trace of either of them any more" (4–5).

Karl tries to get up from the bed but the stoker pushes him back down and they suddenly get into a conversation about the trade of stoking, Karl's plans, and the injustices that the stoker feels he has suffered on board. The noun "suitcase" disappears, as does Karl's anxiety about it. Karl tells the stoker that he should go to the captain and complain but the stoker rebuffs him and Karl is petulantly annoyed: "it seemed to him that he would have done better to fetch his suitcase, instead of offering advice which was only ignored anyway" (7). As his mind turns back to the suitcase, it again becomes a lexical presence:

> When his father had given the suitcase into his possession, he had mused in jest: I wonder how long you'll manage to hang on to it for? And now that expensive suitcase might already be lost in earnest. [...] But Karl felt sad that there were things in the suitcase that he had hardly used. [...] Apart from that, the loss of his suitcase wasn't so serious, because the suit he was wearing was better than the one in the suitcase. [...] Then he remembered there was a piece of Verona salami in the suitcase as well. [...] Now the only thing Karl had left to give was his money, and if had indeed already lost his suitcase, he wanted to leave that untouched for

the moment. His thoughts returned to the suitcase, and now he really couldn't understand why, having watched it so carefully for the whole crossing that his watchfulness had almost cost him his sleep, he had now permitted that same suitcase to be taken from him so simply [...] he had incessantly suspected the Slovak [...] of having intentions on his suitcase [...] he could pull the suitcase over to himself by means of a long rod [...] he cast sad looks across at Karl's suitcase (7–8).

The repetition gives voice to Karl's anxiety, as the image of the suitcase returns again and again, but the passage becomes increasingly humorous: first, we as readers recognize the obsessive incantatory nature of panic; but, second, realize that the suitcase and its loss may not be as important to Karl as the language of panic might suggest. The rhythm of the passage seems to be gearing toward high levels of panic, but Karl keeps getting sidetracked in his thoughts (by the lucky fact of his father not being here, of the contents of his suitcase and why they might not be important, of the Verona salami and how it might appease the stoker, just as his father might pass out cigars, and of the loss of sleep on the crossing because he was worrying about the Slovak stealing his case). "That Butterbaum had better look out, if he should ever run into him somewhere," the passage ends, in a final note of Karl's defiance, a defiance ironically undercut by the fact that he is still supine on the stoker's bed, not quite sure if the loss of his suitcase is that important.

Kafka stretches Dickens's "method" to the point of aural absurdity, having the "suitcase" return again and again, but each time it returns in this passage it means something different for Karl: a present and warning from his father, a sense of relief that his father is not there, something that is not that important, something that might be useful (the Verona salami), something that kept him awake needlessly, something that invoked a fear of others. In *David Copperfield*, the "box" is a concrete thing that might travel back and forth to Lowestoft and, putatively, Dover, but it is never opened, it remains semiotically closed and concrete: we have no idea what is inside it but we see it as a symbol of Copperfield's past, of his belonging as well as of his belongings. In carrying off this box from Dickens's text, Kafka opens it up and rummages around in it; the contents are disturbed when it travels.

The social pyramid

When Kafka received a copy of "The Stoker" from his publisher, Kurt Wolff, he was "alarmed" (Kafka 1978: 98) at the picture Wolff had chosen to put on the frontispiece. It was an engraving by G. K. Richardson called "View of the Ferry at Brooklyn, New York" that had been published in 1838 (443). It is a pastoral engraving, showing a small, low, disc-shaped wooden boat with a handful of people on it, and a couple of horses pulling a hay-cart. Behind it, Manhattan is a stony outcrop with a couple of church steeples. "When I saw the picture in my book," Kafka wrote to his publisher in May 1913, "I was at first alarmed":

For in the first place it refuted me, since I had after all presented the most up-to-date New York; in the second place, the picture had an advantage over my story since it produced its effect before my story did, and a picture is naturally more concentrated than prose; and, thirdly, it was too pretty (98).

A large part of Kafka's anxiety was that the image would make readers pre-interpret the world his story described, giving them this "pretty" sense of a pastoral scene. He wants the image left open for the reader to create. But, in addition the ship Karl is on is a world away from the small, flat wooden boats of the mid-nineteenth century: he crosses on an ocean liner in steerage, the very year that the Titanic sank. Kafka likely saw a "most up-to-date" version of an ocean liner in František Soukup's book, which carries a stylized cross-section of an ocean liner divided into ten decks: right at the bottom, ten stokers stoke twelve ovens in four large circular funnels; right at the top, the captain steers the ship, while two other men in uniform are bent over a table. In between, in ascending order, are: a deck of provisions and kitchens; steerage packed with racks of beds; second class and the luggage hold; the first-class ballroom, its dome breaking into the deck above; a first-class dining-room and cabins; first-class promenades and dining-rooms; the large first-class dining-room and promenades; and finally, beneath the captain's cabin, first-class lounges and promenades. Light fills those upper decks; the stokers at the bottom, undersea, feed the fires.

For Soukup, the ocean liner is a "social pyramid" (Soukup 1912: 16), a microcosm of the class stratification not only of Europe but also of the America that the emigrants are traveling to. Because the Hamburg port is too small for the ship, travelers are rowed out to the ship on small boats with flags that indicate what class the travelers belong to (10), and they are placed accordingly on the ship – the poorest at the bottom and the richest on top (In *Amerika*, Karl sees boats being rowed ashore, "full of passengers who obediently kept their places" (Kafka 2002a: 13)). Soukup travels in second class, and marvels over the first-class menu for lunch: three soups, eggs, salmon, corned beef hash, lamb, roast veal, potatoes, fruit compote, different puddings, fruit, salad, chicken, ham, a selection of fish, cheeses, conserves, coffee and tea – all for one table. In steerage, they have "potatoes and grits, cabbage and and fetid scraps of meat" (14). He travels down to steerage and is horrified by conditions there, with 900 people packed in together and "dirt, filth, putrid rotten air, a real racket, deafening shrieks and bustle" (16). "Up above," he writes, "the parasites of human culture and underneath their creators – the unknown and uncounted children of the proletariat, to whom society on the boat only gives dirty water, rotten potatoes and the rotting leftovers of meat" (16). He watches the funeral of a 4-year-old boy from steerage, whose corpse is lowered down into the ocean in a bucket, where the "sharks finish off the funeral" (16). Those in steerage pray to reach the "land of Carnegie and Rockerfeller" alive, but when they get there, they and those in third class have to pass through Ellis island, that today is "an island of horror and barbarity" (29), nicknamed "the island of tears" (29). Those in first and second class pass through customs quickly; for the others it can be a matter of days (29).

"'You mustn't stand for that,' Karl said in agitation," Kafka writes, as Karl decides that the stoker has to face the captain of the ship to be fairly treated. "He had almost forgotten he was in the uncertain hold of a ship moored to the coast of an unknown continent, that's how much he felt at home on the stoker's bed" (Kafka 2002a: 6–7). They move upward through the ship, detouring through the kitchens, and then

> reached a door that had a little pediment above it, supported on little gilded caryatids. For something on a ship, it looked distinctly lavish. Karl realized he had never been to this part of the ship, which had probably been reserved for the first and second class passengers during the crossing, but now the separating doors had been thrown open prior to the great ship's cleaning (9).

Everyone and everything is movement: the ship's band, the "few girls in dirty aprons – they were spattering them on purpose" in the kitchen (9) and the "few men carrying brooms over their shoulders" by the captain's cabin. Karl "was amazed at all the bustle, between decks where he had been he had had no sense of it all" (9). It is not only people moving but also technology: he notices for the first time the "electrical wires" along all the passages and the continual "ringing of a little bell" (9). Although movement is indicated in Soukup's illustration of the stratified class levels of the ship – we see the stokers stoking, the rich dancing, etc. – in Kafka's interpretation the mobility shifts through the levels of the ship with Karl running down to the very bottom of the ship and then right to the very top (he breaks through the strata); the workers are still workers but they are moving through the ship where "the separating doors had been thrown open." Kafka, in effect, makes Soukup's picture, and its stratified levels, move, something that is echoed in Karl's later profession of a lift-boy.

His one attempt to live the American Dream for himself is when the Head Cook of the Hotel Occidental saves him from Robinson and Delamarche's clutches and gets him a job as an elevator boy:

> "he was starting as a lift-boy at an age in which the more advanced boys at any rate where almost ready to move on to better jobs. It was perfectly right and proper that he should be starting off as lift-boy, but by the same token he was in a hurry. […] By the end of the first week Karl could see that he was well up on the job. The brass trim on his lift was the most highly polished of all, none of the other thirty lifts could compare with it, and it might have gleamed still more if the boy who worked on the same lift as him had been anything like as conscientious, instead of taking Karl's diligence as an excuse for his own sloppiness" (95–6).

Karl masters "the quick, deep bows that the lift-boys were expected to perform, and he could catch tips in mid-air. ... He would be ruthless, and pull strongly on the wire, hand over hand, like a sailor" to bring the elevator down to collect customers (97). The up-and-down mobility of the lift-boys expresses the democratic hope of a better future, the possible constant social motion that Soukup had admired with awe in his descriptions of the elevators in the Met Life building and Marshall Fields, the "railroads" of the skyscrapers in which anyone could ride. But the constant motion in the skyscrapers – the harbinger of technology and the future – is ironically and wryly exaggerated – it's ridiculous! – in this hotel with only five floors that somehow has thirty lifts and a thousand employees (Kafka 2002a: 107). The elevators hold a promise of wealth, as Soukup writes, "Surrounded by grand luxury on plush velvet seats you fly up in the lift" but they are driven by workers, and contain within them an unenunciated unfairness, specifically "an elegant black man, who operates the lift, stops at every floor, calling out the number" (Soukup 1912: 34). Karl's assiduous, if slightly slapstick – in the constant motion – attempt to work hard and move up in the world presupposes a level playing field, a clean, fair start, but he is finally unfairly fired, partly because he is mistaken for another lift-boy. Karl is in a traditionally "black" job – promise of crossing class boundaries but stuck in the uniform of other's sweat. When he gets to the Theatre of Oklahoma – a surrealistic giant job fair – he "was reluctant to give his real name" (Kafka 2002a: 210) and instead "gave what had been his nickname on his last jobs: 'Negro'" (210). There is a strong irony here in Karl being cunning but at the same time choosing a name of the oppressed – a name that automatically puts him at the bottom – but at the same time he is honest about how he is seen.

Reaching Zion

At the end of the novel, Karl sees a poster for the Theatre of Oklahoma that promises "a place for everyone"; "All welcome" the poster said, "even Karl." He travels to Clayton by subway to a giant racetrack where the theater is recruiting for unspecified jobs and when he gets out of the train, "the sound of many trumpets greeted his ears" (203). There is a stage outside the entrance of the racetrack, "on which a hundred women dressed as angels in white cloths, with great wings on their backs were blowing into golden trumpets" (203). They each stand on a pedestal that cannot be seen,

> because the long billowing robes of the angel costumes completely covered them. As the pedestals were very high, as much as six feet, the figures of the women looked gigantic, only their little heads looked somewhat out of scale, and their hair, which they wore loose, looked too short and almost laughable, hanging between the big wings and down the side of them. To avoid uniformity, pedestals of all different sizes had been used, there were some quite low women, not much above life size, but others next to them seemed to scale such heights that they were surely in danger from every breath of wind. And now all these women were blowing trumpets. There weren't many listeners (203).

Those waiting for jobs are completely intimidated by this apparently religious welcome; they persuade Karl to go up to the stage to ask what is going on; as he climbs up, one of the angels, Fanny, recognizes him: "she parted her robes, revealing her pedestal and a narrow flight of steps leading up to it" (204) and Karl runs up the stairs to shake her hand. She gives him her trumpet and he "played a tune he had heard once in a bar somewhere at the top of his lungs" (205), delighting all the giggling angels. Fanny tells Karl he's an artist and when he asks if he can get a job playing the trumpet, she tells him he can; "we are relieved by the men," she says, "who are dressed as devils. Half of them are trumpeters, the other half are drummers. It's very nice" (205).

Karl is surprised, given the promise of jobs, how few people are waiting to get into the racecourse for their interviews: "Could it be," he says to Fanny, "that the lavish displays with angels and devils put off more people than they attract?" "Hard to say," said Fanny, "but it's a possibility" (206). Karl leads the jobseekers into the racecourse, where offices for different professions are set up in the betting booths; the names of the newly employed are displayed on the mechanical winner's scoreboard. Karl, in an attempt to reinvent himself, tries to pass himself off as an engineer, pretends to have identification, thinks he agrees to be an "actor" and is finally led to the most modest betting booth where he becomes "Negro, Technical Worker" but no one is quite sure what the theater is and what exactly their jobs will be. Fed at a feast with other employees, he is finally put on a train that seems to be going West; everyone is put on the train without their luggage; "they plunged under the bridges over which the train passed," the book ends, "so close that the chill breath of them made their faces shudder" (218).

The Theater of Oklahoma has been read as an innocent "vision of Heaven," (Hofmann 2002b: x), a place where Karl would "find his old home and his parents" again at the end of the novel through some "celestial witchery" (Kafka 1962: 300). More recently, commentators have pointed to the uneasiness under the imagery, the sense that this may be a sinister "sort of afterlife" through which a dead Karl walks (Hofmann 2002b: xi), connected as it is to the image of the lynching in Arthur Holitscher's book. But I think it is also a comic distortion of a photograph from Soukup's book; a photograph from a putative utopia, Zion City, Illinois. "Until I die," Soukup wrote, "I'll never forget Zion City" (Soukup 1912: 130). And not in a good way. The photograph is from the church, seemingly showing the choir, though the caption reads, "Residents of Zion City."

Founded in 1901 by a Scots immigrant and founder of the Christian-Catholic Church, an evangelical sect, John Alexander Dowie, as Zion on earth, Zion City was in receivership by his death in 1907 amidst murky rumours about sexual and financial shenanigans. Dowie was internationally famous for his odd evangelism; he even permeates the consciousness of Leopold Bloom in James Joyce's *Ulysses* – "Elijah is coming," he thinks,

> Dr. John Alexander Dowie, restorer of the church in Zion, is coming.
> Is coming! Is coming ! ! Is coming ! ! !
> All heartily welcome (Joyce 2000: 190).

Maybe not all were heartily welcome; on arriving in Zion City, Soukup sees a sign: "Foreigners are welcome. But tobacco, beer, gambling, pork, medicine, doctors and other vices are banned under pain of punishment" (Soukup 1912: 130). Zion City's fortunes had been somewhat restored by Wilbur Glenn Voliva, and Soukup, astonished by the ban on doctors, goes into "the Zion church which they said was the most miraculous healing place in the world" – illnesses were caused by the devil and cured by prayer. The church was:

> A huge covered wooden shed, in which carpenters had made six thousand seats. At the back of the hall a huge white banner, with black letters: "Christ is all and in

all." On Sundays, a choir of 600 sings, dressed in white tunics, the representative of the church, some [Wilbur Glenn] Voliva thunders various "human vices" and based on that – the kingdom of God on earth! I've never seen a sadder and deader place on earth than that one (131).

There is a double-page photograph in Soukup's book of the choir underneath the "Christ is all and in all banner"; it is a staged, formal photograph with the small orchestra holding their instruments but not playing and the choir are holding their hymn-books stiffly and not singing. There is no sense in the photograph of the fiery passion of evangelism, no sense of movement at all; the women in the choir are arranged in nine rows; the men arranged on either side of them. All, including the orchestra except for the two pianists and the conductor, wear white surplices. The two pianists are a very glum-looking young woman, her hands on her knees, and the only black man in the photograph staring gamely at the photographer. The nine rows of women, robed in white, are suggestive of the nine choirs of angels – from seraphim to archangels – and they stare silently and unmoving at the camera, as if articulating the firm order of heaven.

Soukup is amazed by the prevalence of various religious sects in America, wondering why immigrants still hew to religion when, here in America, they have to pay for everything associated with it: "Whoever wants to meditate with their God," he writes, "has to pay. You have to pay for christenings, for weddings, for burials, for confession, for communion, and for your last rites – everything the priest has a hand in" (133). He finds churches that offer free lunches and beer to attract a congregation, priests realizing that "Commerce is commerce. They know their people and they understand their business" (135). He is distraught at how religion – which he associates with oppression in Europe – is not only intimately connected with capitalism in America, but actively – certainly in the Czech immigrant community – anti-socialist.

He quotes articles from two American Czech-language Catholic periodicals that attack socialism – the first, a Catholic daily called "Hlas," condemns socialists for calling "for the destruction of everything central to Christianity" and suggests it does so because the Czech socialists are "commanded mainly by Jews" – the "Jew Adler" and those who befriend Jews, his "friend Dr. Soukup" (139). The second, a Catholic magazine "Katolik," argues that socialism is "the biggest danger and misfortune for America" (141) because it goes against the natural order of Heaven which is hierarchical and akin to the capitalist system:

> We know that even amongst angels in heaven there are levels of difference. Angelic power is based on nine different choirs (!). The angel spirits stand in rows, one over the other. The saints and angels do not shine with the same light and none among the chosen show hate or unhappiness. Order is the first law of Heaven ... as long as this world lasts, some will be rich and others will be poor ... God gives you wealth so that you can use it to buy a house in His eternal home (141–2).

Soukup writes that he felt "physically sick" reading this, worried that uneducated immigrants would accept their position in life because of the Church's teachings: nine choirs of angels and that grand claim that with money a person can obtain the grace of heaven, no, even "buy their own eternal home" (142). "I'd had this 'kingdom of God on earth' up to my eyeballs," he writes of Zion City. "Novak and I hightailed it out of there, so that we could shake the dust of that miraculous Zion off our feet as quickly as we could" (132).

Soukup's palpable anger at what he sees as the dangerous absurdity of these religious claims, which serve to construct the very kinds of oppressive hierarchies in the New World from which people were escaping Europe in search of democratic opportunity, is transformed by Kafka into absurdity (full stop). Rather than Soukup's eyewitness account, Kafka turns this dour, stiff, silent choir into a hundred women in white cloths with wings playing trumpets loudly and badly and with Karl naughtily and suggestively opening up Fanny's white cloth to go up the narrow stairs of her pedestal. These angels are on different-sized pedestals – a nod to Catholic hierarchies – and once Karl gets up onto Fanny's pedestal – though somewhat afraid he'll topple it – he stretches out his hand to measure those different heights. The exposed pedestals lay bare the constructed nature of these angels' heights and their hierarchy, which is quickly and continually replaced (every two hours) by the male devils. The devils not only have trumpets; they have drums too.

Karl understands that the rampant theatricality of the angel/devil show may put people off from entering the racecourse but in mounting the pedestal under Fanny's skirts and blowing her trumpet he demystifies the hierarchy. Approached and greeted by the "head of personnel" of the Theater of Oklahoma, Karl "wondered if this might be the moment to let the man know that the inducements of the publicity team [the angels and devils], by their very magnificence, might be counter-productive" but decides not to, thinking it won't make "a good impression" if he starts trying to suggest "improvements" even before he is hired (Kafka 2002a: 206–7). The theater itself seems to espouse democracy: "All welcome!" the poster reads: "We are the theatre that has a place for everyone," it continues, but with a qualifying clause: "everyone in his place" (202). Karl cannot just reinvent himself here – he tries to pass himself off as an engineer – but ends up being sent to a betting "booth on the very periphery, not merely smaller than all the others, but lower too" (209). The idea of the lottery, betting on one's future, is directed at the theater and controlled.

There is a possible reference here to another part of Soukup's book where he writes about homesteading in Oklahoma. It is a warning to potential Czech immigrants that the US government is no longer offering free land (as it had with the Homestead Act in 1862) but he wrote that even "fifteen years ago" (in the 1890s), the government had been giving out homestead "lots in the state of Oklahoma" (Soukup 1912: 121). They had a particular mode of doing so, which I think connects to the racecourse setting of the Theater of Oklahoma in *Amerika*. "[A]t given hour on a given day," Soukup writes:

> they opened the borders of the territory that was being allocated. A huge amount of people were waiting there on that day, all on horses, and when a gun went off as a signal, they whipped their horses and flew like madmen to the land. Whoever arrived first at a homestead, seized it. Whoever had the fastest horse and the most accurate knowledge of the area, they of course got the best homestead (121).

The seemingly democratic method of getting land, which, when worked on, would be deeded over to the lucky winners, depends in fact upon who has the fastest horses and the most local knowledge; it is not quite a fair lottery. Once inside the Theater of Oklahoma, Karl actually "felt like seeing a horse race" because he had never seen one in America, and had only been to one once in Europe where in "effect, he had never really seen a proper race" because he was a child and no one at the racecourse would "let him through" (Kafka 2002a: 211). The aura of meritocracy and democracy is somewhat destabilized by the notions of luck, betting, winning in arenas – the racetrack, the Theater of Oklahoma, Europe, America – which may not be innately fair.

Karl and the other new theater employees are raced to the train and Karl notices that "no-one had any luggage"; stripped of their past and their property, they venture into the unknown, the novel ending with the "chill breath" of the bridges making them "shudder" (218). It is hard to read this passage, as Michael Hofmann points out, for us as post-Holocaust readers without thinking of the "Judentransporte" (Hofmann 2002b: xi). But Soukup notes the difference in American trains, where "there is no space for bigger luggage" in carriages so this luggage is, instead, brought to "a designated carriage" before departure and is given back to you at the end of the journey (Soukup 1912: 73). What also surprises him is the silence on American trains: "no one looks at another's face," he writes, "As opposed to the constant hubbub, clamor and talking on our trains, here it is quiet and calm" (70); a correlative to the uneasy silence ending Kafka's novel, even though other boys are pinching Karl's leg. Luggage is a central motif in the book – Karl's suitcase that gets lost and reappears through the novel, flickering in and out of the narrative: it is a motif inspired by one of Kafka's favorite books, Charles Dickens's *David Copperfield*, a story about an unmoored boy whose box, his only possession, is at one point stolen, as he tries to escape from industrialized labor.

When Kafka was asked about Karl and the Stoker as characters, he said, "They are images, only images" (Janouch 1985: 31); throughout *Amerika*, Kafka is interested in ways of seeing, of repeated images and motifs, and especially of tableaux that suddenly and unexpectedly move, an element of what Milan Kundera has called "a poetics of surprise" (Kundera 1996: 50). Rather than straightforwardly adapting the images from Soukup's book (or Holitscher's, or Dickens's) which would have resulted in a more overtly ideological novel, Kafka interrogates the way in which the pictures produce meaning. He is interested in the theatrics of power – class and religion – and the pictorial advertising of both, but also in the way modern technology affects the way we see. The novel plays with the tension between stasis and mobility – the elevators in constant motion that keep everyone still in their place; the ocean liner crossing the Atlantic with its immoveable class structure; the angels and devils of fixed religious hierarchies changing places every two hours. "One photographs things in order to get them out of one's mind," Kafka said, holding images in tableaux that still waver and move and haunt and question the status quo. "My stories," he added wryly, "are a kind of closing of one's eyes" (Janouch 1985: 31).

The Castle: gods, messengers and interpreters

Stop interpreting everything! said K.

(Kafka 1998a: 205)

Kafka imagines Poseidon, the god of the seas, as a bureaucrat, stuck "at his desk doing the accounts" (Kafka 2007: 131). Poseidon has "a great many" assistants but does not trust them to do as good a job as he, so "his assistants were of little use to him." He is annoyed at the iconic image of him; that "he continually went dashing over the waves with his trident" when in fact "he was seated at the depths of the world's ocean, continually doing the accounts." Although he complains about the job and "had often applied for what he called more cheerful work […] it turned out that nothing really appealed to him so much as his present office." In addition, "his complaints were not really taken seriously; when a mighty man pesters, one must try to seem to accommodate him, even when his case has absolutely no prospect of success." So, he remains at his desk and "had hardly seen the oceans"; he plans to stay there "waiting until the end of the world" and then in "a quiet moment […] just before the end" he will make "a quick tour" of the oceans (131).

Homer's Poseidon, on the other hand, does what gods do: meddles in a fit of pique and revenge in the affairs of humans and makes sure that Odysseus is sabotaged for ten years in his attempt to sail home (because he tricked Poseidon's son, the Cyclops). As an epic hero, Odysseus is a man of action, but he is also continually subject to digression, delayed from returning home by sirens and seductresses, cannibals and the dead, but also – importantly – by storytelling. In Kafka's *The Castle*, Amalia admonishes K. for being in thrall to the "Castle stories" (Kafka 1998a: 205); from K.'s arrival in the village, his journey in that village has largely been one of words, with K. "the stranger" continually trying to interpret what the locals say, what the Castle writes and what the Castle's telephones murmur and sing into his ear. While Kafka's Poseidon does not make an appearance in *The Castle*, the Castle bureaucrats resemble him. If Homer's Poseidon can move the sea to delay Odysseus, these gods have a sea of words to delay K. When K. receives his first letter from Klamm, the shape-shifting Castle official, he pores over the outwardly straightforward official letter trying to interpret it. He reinterprets it in front of the Chairman and his wife Mizzi (the real power in the house); they then reinterpret it, Mizzi holding and "dreamily playing with Klamm's letter" (74). She physically alters the paper just as the meaning has continually altered; "she had turned [it] into a little boat" (74).

Both the content and style of the novel consist of "acts of interpretation (by K. or by others) that often contradict one another in the midst of a sentence" (Hillis Miller 2011: 113); the novel's momentum is powered by conversations and texts, and K. "becomes a kind of hermeneutic machine, having to interpret every aspect of what he sees, hears and reads" (Bernheimer 1977: 371). K. is from an unspecified elsewhere, but he seems to speak the same language as those in the village and from the Castle. Yet, the novel consists of the locals trying to translate the meaning of their world, with its specific but always unclear referents, for "the stranger." Acts of translation abound:

from Frieda insisting she speak for K. to the copyists at the Castle writing what they think they hear from the Castle officials' whispers, to Barnabas taking that message (perhaps long stored in the copyist's desk) in a roundabout manner to K. In addition, if the Castle is a sea of words, a language in itself, constructed and maintained by language, then K. may be seen as a foreign element that wanders into this textual sea and, in doing so, resists and opens up its hermetic impulse. The novel, too, is a series of partial translations: of subversive allusions to *The Odyssey*, the Bible, to Jonathan Swift's *The Battle of the Books*, and presents a possible double fictionalization of one of Kafka's translators, Milena Jesenská, in the characters of Frieda and Amalia (Kautman 1968).

Translated gods

As K. finally seems to be penetrating the Castle, he starts to doze off on a bed of one of the Castle officials, Bürgel, and dreams about him:

> A secretary, naked, very like the statue of a Greek god, was being hard-pressed by K. in battle. That was quite comical, and in his sleep K. smiled gently at the way the secretary was being constantly startled out of his proud posture by K.'s advances and quickly had to use his raised arm and clenched fist to cover up his exposed parts, but he was not yet quick enough. The battle didn't last long, for step by step, and very big steps they were too, K. advanced. Was this even a battle? There was no real obstacle, only so often a few squeaks from the secretary. This Greek god squeaked like a little girl. And then finally he was gone (Kafka 1998a: 265).

Falling asleep seems to be "a great victory" in itself and he dreams of someone "raising a champagne glass in honor of the victory" (264), but as he wakes up and sees the actual official, Bürgel, and "his bare chest" a "thought from the dream came to him: 'There's your Greek god! Pull him out of the sack!'" (65). The "comical" dream of a Greek god who "squeaked like a girl" and who has to use his "clenched fist" to "cover up his exposed parts" is as comical as K.'s re-envisioning of his circular journey in the village, a journey mainly of words, interspersed by islands of beds, as a battle in which he advanced "step by step, and very big steps they were too." The iconic and epic image of a Greek god is undercut not only by bare-chested Bürgel, but also by K., a hero who does not seem to have progressed very far, who is dealing with bureaucratic, whimsical human gods, and who does not seem to want to return home.

Kafka was writing *The Castle* at around the same time as Joyce published *Ulysses* (1922); like Joyce, Kafka up-ends the epic mode, views it through a modernist lens with humor and subversion, but without being as clearly schematic. Elements of *The Castle* speak to an allusiveness to *The Odyssey*: the Castle disrupting K.'s quest; Klamm as a god-like protector but sometimes Polyphemus-like adversary whose villagers reject hospitality and guests; the Siren song of the telephones in the village, the Calypso- and Circe-like women who keep K. occupied with their words as much as their embraces, the suggestions of Nausicaa and Penelope in Frieda and Amalia, the Hermes-like messenger Barnabas, and K's lotus-eater-like forgetting of his own past (his wife and child, as well as, perhaps, his actual reason for coming). Instead of being thrust from place to place by the seas, and the god of that sea, like Odysseus, K. is moved from bed to bed: the "straw mattress" he begins on, the audience with the landlady, the Chairman, Bürgel, the bed in the maids' room at the inn, in the schoolroom, and Klamm's enveloping furs in his sleigh. Odysseus, after all, does not return to Ithaca victorious with all his men; they are all lost and he is delivered, alone and "sound asleep," "dead to the world" by his gracious hosts, the Phaeacians, much to their relative, Poseidon's, chagrin (Homer 1997: 290).

K's adversary, the god of the bureaucrats, seems to be Klamm, a man whose name is suggestive of the Czech word "klam" which means fraud, fake, illusion. No one is quite sure what Klamm looks like: "They say he looks completely different when he comes to the village and different when he leaves it," Olga tells K., "different before he has had a beer, different afterwards, different awake, different asleep, different alone, different in a conversation, and, quite understandably after all this, almost utterly different up there at the Castle" (Kafka 1998a: 176). Klamm's appearance depends on the "momentary mood" of the observer, she adds. K. sees Klamm once, through a peephole; he seems to be an unprepossessing "medium-sized, fat, ponderous gentleman" on whose nose is a "precariously balanced pince-nez, which reflected the light, concealed his eyes" (36). Frieda sticks "a small wooden stick" in the peephole to cut off sight from him (36). When her brother Barnabas goes up to the Castle, he thinks it is Klamm he sees reading a book or "busy cleaning his pince-nez [...] at such moments Klamm's eyes are almost closed, he seems to be asleep and to be cleaning his pince-nez merely in a dream" (179). But Olga throws doubt onto whether this is Klamm or just a secretary "affecting Klamm's drowsy, dreamlike manner"; "Klamm, who is so often the object of yearning and yet so rarely attained," she says, "easily takes on a variety of shapes in the imaginations of people" (181). At one point, after Momus, one of Klamm's secretaries – "you can find people in the village who would swear that Momus is Klamm," Olga notes (181) – tries to interrogate K., K. imagines Klamm as an eagle because of

> Klamm's remoteness, his impregnable abode, his muteness, broken perhaps only by shouts the likes of which K. had never heard before, his piercing downturned gaze, which could never be proved, never refuted, and his, from K's position below, indestructible circles, which he was describing up there in accordance with incomprehensible laws, visible only for seconds – all this Klamm and the eagle had in common (115–16).

"Who can glimpse a god," Homer asks, "who wants to be invisible gliding here and there?" (Homer 1997: 248). Athena, protecting Telemachus and determined to get his father home, continually shape-shifts in different human forms, but also, after conversing in human form with Nestor, suddenly "winged away/in an eagle's form and flight" leaving Nestor and the Achaeans staring in amazement (119). The funny equation of the black-moustached, fat and sleepy bureaucrat with the gods (especially the grey-eyed Pallas Athena), somehow able to slip here and there, his shape determined by the fears and wishes of the villagers, is underscored by the sinister tone of possible surveillance: the open but sleeping eyes, the obscuring (but perhaps also acutely observing) pince-nez. This emphasis on sight and sleep recalls Polyphemus, the Cyclops and Poseidon's son, who Odysseus blinds with a stake when he is asleep (whose injury leads to Poseidon's anger and sabotaging of Odysseus's return home) – Frieda's "small wooden stick" stops the sight of him (and allows her love-making with K.). Polyphemus goes against the tradition of hospitality toward strangers – to the extent of eating these strangers! – and stands in contrast to the Achaeans, and Menelaus, the Phaeacians and others, who do not want to provoke the ire of the gods and so, not knowing who Telemachus or Odysseus are, provide these "strangers" with food and beds.

In the village, K. is told that "the lack of hospitality may surprise you […] but there is no custom of hospitality here, we do not need guests," something K. reacts to with equanimity. "'Certainly,' said K. 'What would you need guests for?'" (Kafka 1998a: 12). The rightful harmony of the ancient world (disrupted by the inhospitable Cyclops and the overly hospitable Calypso) is turned on its head in this village, where the "stranger" is only grudgingly allowed to stay and only under pain of constant, if odd and unstable, surveillance. This unfriendliness may be due to the difference in the classical and modern hero: Odysseus weeps for seven years for home on Calypso's island, but K. does not seem to want to go home. Later in the novel he blames Schwarzer (who initially reported his presence in the village to the Castle) for making him stay: "he hadn't the slightest intention of staying longer" than a few days initially, and only then as a "journeyman" or "farmhand" who had "found a place to sleep at a local citizen's" (165). Yet, when Frieda urges him to take her away from the village, abroad to France or Spain, K. has no wish to leave.

He only momentarily thinks of his "homeland" at the beginning of the novel; he mentions "his wife and child" once, seems to forget them (if they ever actually existed) and sets up home with Frieda in the village (5). When he sees the Castle, he is disappointed and "fleetingly" recalls "his old hometown" which was "scarcely inferior to this so-called Castle"; if he was just a tourist, he thinks, come to see this Castle, he would have been better instead to go back "to visit his homeland again, where he had not been in such a long time" (8). His most sustained memory of the past and his homeland comes later, when he runs after the messenger Barnabas, and physically hangs on to his arm, hoping that Barnabas is heading toward the Castle; "he could no longer control his thoughts. Rather than remaining fixed on the goal, they became confused. His homeland kept surfacing, filling him with memories" (28). In fact, only one memory, an absurd version of the narratives of Homeric battle: of climbing the cemetery wall, which few boys had managed to conquer. The cemetery no longer held any fascination; the boys had gone in and out of this underworld many times, but once, K. got to the top of the wall and rammed a flag in; he looked down "at the crosses sinking into the earth; there was nobody here, now, bigger than he" (29). This "feeling of victory" he thinks "would sustain him throughout a long life," not a "foolish" thought because now that sense of victory "came to his aid" as he hung "on the arm of Barnabas in this snowy night" (29). Barnabas is in fact bringing K. "home," only "it was not they who were at home, only Barnabas was at home" (30); but it is the only home in the village – a home of outcasts – in which K. is welcome (a welcome he dismisses).

K. sees Barnabas as a Hermes figure sent from the gods of the Castle, a figure who shines in his immanence; "his expression, his smile, his gait, seemed to bear a message, even if he himself was unaware of it" (26). His name also alludes to the biblical apostle Barnabas, a messenger of Christ, who traveled with St. Paul to spread the word, imbued with that word of God. At one point, in Lystra when Paul performed a miracle, the locals declared that Paul was Hermes "because he was the chief speaker" of the two, and they anointed Barnabas as Zeus (Acts 14.12). Paul and Barnabas tore at their clothes to prove that they were no gods, shouting "We, too, are only human like you" (Acts 14.15). Kafka's Barnabas is "only human like you"; though his apparent uniform seems angelic – he "was dressed almost entirely in white, the material could scarcely be silk, it was winter clothing like all the rest, but it had the delicacy and formality of silk" (Kafka 1998a: 22) – and impresses K. with its obvious connection to the power and meaning of the Castle; in fact, when Barnabas takes K. to his home, he undoes the jacket, "revealing underneath a coarse, dirt-gray, often-mended shirt over the powerful square chest of a farmhand" (30). We find out that Amalia has sewn this pretense of a Castle uniform (if such a thing exists), and that she and Olga took in his trousers as part of this pretense. Barnabas presented himself to the Castle as a messenger, in the hope of mitigating Amalia's crime of insulting the messenger who had brought Sortini's lewd letter.

K. wants to believe in Barnabas's immanence because then Barnabas is not only a connection to the Castle but its explainer, its messenger imbued with the truth, its faithful translator. Twice, Barnabas arrives with a letter from Klamm: the first, a letter welcoming K. as the land surveyor (even though he seems to be fibbing about being a land surveyor); and the second, telling K. what a good job he and his assistants are doing (even though they have done nothing). Textually, both letters seem very straightforward, but K. agonizes over their real meaning as the texts don't seem to mean what the letters perhaps signify. "'Service,' 'superior,' 'work,' 'terms of employment,' 'accountable,' 'workers,' the letter was crammed with such terms," he thinks, mulling over the meaning of the letter, "and even if it referred to other, more personal matters, it did so from the same point of view" (24). Barnabas, the messenger, does not "know the contents" of the letter" because "he was only a messenger" (26). His ignorance of the contents finally irritate K. "It's a misunderstanding," K. says about the second letter, and has to repeat himself because "Barnabas did not understand him" (115) and "it weighed upon his heart that Barnabas obviously couldn't understand him, that though his jacket gave off a brilliant sheen in times that were calm, when the situation became serious Barnabas was no help at all, he simply resorted to a kind of silent resistance" (116).

K. himself tries to imbue Barnabas with meaning, giving him oral messages to pass on to Klamm, and, when Barnabas fails to understand Klamm's letter, he attempts to prove his prowess as a messenger by repeating word-for-word the first message K. gave him. The only problem is that he failed to deliver that message, because he had too much work to do as an apprentice cobbler to his father. "Shoemaker – orders – Brunswick," K. cries "bitterly, as if trying to make each word forever unusable. 'And who needs shoes here on these everlastingly empty paths?'" (120). K., trying to control the language of the village, making it "forever unusable," is agitated because the paths – like the language of the village itself – never seem to go where they are supposed to, and certainly not to the Castle. His bitterly funny observation about the uselessness of shoes is perhaps a subversive reference to Hermes's "supple sandals" (Homer 1997: 154) that the gods' messenger slips on to deliver their wishes. Here, these sandals are pointless, since, as Barnabas reassures him, "Klamm doesn't wait for the news, he even gets annoyed when I come" (Kafka 1998a: 120).

The notion of willful non-translation in the village is further substantiated by a description of the messaging process that Olga passes on to K. when she tells him her "Castle stories." She tells him that Barnabas speaks to officials and gets messages in the Castle: "But what kind of officials, what kind of messages are they?" she asks (175). She reports to K. what Barnabas has told her about the oblique origin of the messages:

> there's no loud dictation to be heard, one barely notices that someone is dictating; on the contrary, the official seems to continue reading, only he begins to whisper and the copyist hears it. Often the official dictates so softly that the copyist cannot hear it sitting down, he must constantly jump up, catch the dictation, sit down and make a note of it, jump back up, and so on. It's so strange! It's almost incomprehensible (178).

Barnabas thinks one of the officials may be Klamm, but he cannot be sure and the indeterminacy of the message-giving process in all its sonic and interpretive ambiguity puts in question the origins of the message (the non-presence of a person who is definitely Klamm) and any notion of an original text (written by a copyist who "catches" the dictation from whispers). What the copyist writes down is placed in "many files and correspondences that he keeps under the table" (179) and when he pulls out a letter "From Klamm to K." it is "not a letter he has just written, but more likely by the looks of the envelope a very old letter that was lying there for a long time" (179). If the origin of the message is shrouded in whispers and dust, than the addressee is also uncertain and certainly decided only after the message is created. The decision about who the addresser and the addressee are consequently seems to append an *a posteriori* meaning to the message.

Barnabas "wants to find honor in your eyes by acting like a real messenger, the way he thinks real messengers act" (229), Olga tells K. and, to do so, not only wears the semblance of a messenger's uniform, but attempts to imbue meaning to the letter with his bodily presence; once he receives these old letters from the copyists he runs home "breathless" with the letter "under his shirt on his bare skin" (179). Yet, he feels he should not actually read the letters (unlike Olga) because "as a messenger, he wouldn't allow himself to do so" (230); in other words, he can try to give the letters meaning by placing them on his body, giving the message a bodily presence, but he cannot, ethically, attempt to interpret them.

After hearing Olga's explanation of the process of messaging, however, K. announces that he has been led astray in assuming Barnabas's immanence because he now sees him as an "uninformed youth [...] who has never gone beyond the village surroundings" – not to the Castle, not abroad, and certainly to no Olympus or heaven. As a result, K. concludes, one should not "then expect faithful reports from him and scrutinize his every word as though it were a word from Revelations and make one's own happiness in life depend on the interpretation" (183). The explicit reference here to the New Testament and the Book of Revelations underscores K.'s ridiculous expectations of ultimate revelation from a messenger imbued with religious meaning who might provide "faithful reports" from the gods/God and also the dawning awareness that even if such revelations were made, it might not end in a correct "interpretation" that might make one happy.

Nevertheless, there is not a vacuity of meaning, although it appears as if this is the case. The copyists' desks are packed with files and correspondence, the officials' carriages are "crammed with files" (216), the council chairman's "cabinet was crammed with papers" and, once opened, the "papers already covered half the room" (60). The physical appearance of an abundance of meaning (and manifestation of the textual culture of the Castle) appears to have an emptiness at the heart of it – the file regarding the appointment of a land surveyor is missing "either because the contents of the file never left us, or because the file itself got lost on the way" (62); the "jumble of files" in the chairman's room yield nothing (70); the files in Sordini's office keep "falling down" because "files are constantly being taken from and added to the bundles" and the sound of them falling "those endless thuds in rapid succession" have come to characterize Sordini's study (66); K. challenges the notion that officials' carriages are "crammed with files" because he has been in Klamm's sleigh "and there were no files there" (217); Barnabas, the messenger in white silk, has no idea of the content of his messages.

However, K. has begun to realize that what the letters say may be void of apparent meaning, but first, the letters in themselves – as semiotic objects – signify something. "Barnabas is being offered something," he tells Olga, because:

> we do have the letters in hand, which I certainly don't trust much, though far more so than the words of Barnabas. Even if they are old worthless letters pulled out indiscriminately from a pile of equally worthless letters, indiscriminately, and with no more sense than that employed by canaries at fairs who pick someone's fortune out of a pile, even if that is so, then at least these letters bear some relation to my work, are clearly intended for me, though perhaps not for my use, and, as the council chairman and his wife have testified, were personally signed by Klamm, and have, once again according to the council chairman, a significance that, while merely private and scarcely transparent, is nevertheless quite considerable (184).

Second, though the significance is "scarcely transparent," K.'s cogitation on their meaning displays the effect the letters have had on him; his formal prolixity is Castle-village-like. The syntax and its rhythms are what signify in this world, not the actual meaning of the words, the "worthless letters" that "still bear some relation to my work." Olga agrees; she read the letters before Barnabas gives them to K. and finds their content "unimportant, obsolete" (231); "weighing the letters correctly is impossible," she tells K, "their value keeps changing, the thoughts that they prompt are endless and the point at which one happens to stop is determined only by accident and so the opinion one arrives at is accidental" (231). The accidental stopping at a certain point is evaded in this strange ontological system by not stopping at all.

K. goes to Barnabas's house to look for his messenger who is absent; Amalia walks out without saying goodbye "as though she knew he would stay a long time" (170) and indeed he does, listening to and talking with Olga – their conversation spans five chapters of the book. When Amalia returns unnoticed she repeats what Olga has just said about the "influence of the Castle"; "telling Castle stories?" she asks. "Do you even care about such stories? There are people here who feed on such stories, they sit together as you sit here, regaling one another, but you do not strike me as one of them.' 'Yes I am,' said K. 'I am indeed one of them'" (205). K. is an initiate of the endless talking, the endless interpretation that constitutes this world. He becomes initiated as he finds out about Amalia's ejection from this community, an exile largely based on her stubborn silence, her refusal to abide this performative and endless story-telling: her crime is not so much based on her refusal to sleep with Sortini as in her act of tearing up his letter in front of his messenger, a deliberate refusal to partake in and uphold this linguistic world.

In contrast, K. had physically latched onto his messenger, Barnabas, and in doing so had arrived "home" – both mentally, in his memory of his homeland, and physically in arriving in Barnabas's home. Corngold's argument that Gregor Samsa, defined by his existence as "an indecipherable word," is in conflict with "ordinary" or "characteristic" language (88) can perhaps be extended here to "the stranger" coming into "a purely textual world" (Bernheimer 1977: 368) of the Castle, disrupting its signification practices and its hermetic sense of meaning. Still believing Barnabas to be the Word of the Castle, K. attaches himself in a kind of translation act (bringing memories of the past and arriving in a home that is not his). He arrives in a home of outcasts, the "accursed" Barnabas family that he rejects but then returns to, discovering that his arrival finally effects a connection with the Castle and turns Barnabas into the messenger he was trying to be (to assuage the sins of his sister against Sortini's messenger). Thus, although K. is representative of a foreign signifying system that seems to threaten the status quo of meaning, and to highlight foreignness within this apparently hermetic world, his "quest inscribes him more and more deeply into the very textual freeplay he seeks to ground and delimit" (373), but, also, inscribes or reinscribes others in the process.

K's failure to get to the Castle is often seen as his failure to find meaning (or God) and integration into the community. Yet he does integrate himself into the community via its iterative use of language. When he wanders into the "connecting secretary" (Kafka 1998a: 259) Bürgel's bedroom with its enormous bed (Bürgel deliberately eschewing other furniture to fit in this massive bed), Bürgel launches into a pages-long assessment of K's case, suggesting that in the almost unheard-of night-time intrusion into a secretary's room, K. may have found the chink in the armor of the "seamlessness" of the Castle (265), it may be an "opportunity" (265), and he recursively considers the situation, not necessarily because it is interesting but because "a conversation is the likeliest means of putting me to sleep" (259). K. – who has visited, been in and seen many beds in the course of his few days in the village – desperately wants to sleep; Bürgel's prolixity, "his soft, complacent voice," is putting him to sleep: "Chatter on, chatterbox," K. thinks, "you're chattering away just for me" (267). K. "thought that now he understood everything perfectly, not because it affected him but simply because he was convinced that in a few moments he would fall sound asleep" (267). K. had already nodded off and dreamed of a secretary "like the statue of a Greek god" with "the battle and the victory [that] were being repeated once again, or perhaps they weren't being repeated but were taking place for the first time. [...] Was this even a battle? There was no real obstacle, only every so often a few squeaks from the secretary" (265). K. finally falls asleep at the point at which Bürgel seems to be imparting important information, but, in fact, the information itself is not important, rather it is the method of imparting it in the long, convoluted sentences that lull K. into the fold. The epiphany is in not seeing this prolixity and performance as a battle but as a mode of living, of telling stories.

After a long sleep in the taproom, this time uninterrupted by Schwarzer or Frieda as it had been at the beginning of the novel, K.'s quest in some sense comes full cycle (even though the novel is unfinished). When he wakes up, Pepi launches into a long, alternative and critical version of Frieda's motives for abandoning the inn for K., but K. replies in like and kind; instead of battling Pepi, he presents an alternative version because Pepi is "interpreting everything incorrectly" (309). He recognizes the mistake that he and Frieda made; they "had struggled too hard, too noisily, too childishly, too naively to obtain something that can be easily and imperceptibly gained" (309). Pepi invites him to live with her and the other chambermaids, where "we'll tell you stories about [Frieda] until you have grown tired of them" (310). Even the landlady comes around; "perhaps you are not cheeky," she says, "you are like a child who knows some silly thing and cannot be kept silent" (314). K. is granted leave to stay with the coachman, Gerstäcker, and the novel ends in the middle of a sentence, with Gerstäcker's mother about to launch into another speech; the old woman "deep inside an alcove sat bent under the crooked protruding beams, reading a book" and "had him sit down beside her, she spoke with great difficulty, it was difficult to understand her, but what she said" (316). We never find out what Kafka might have written next, but it is unsurprising that this last figure, partially hidden by light and the alcove, is bent over a text, "difficult to understand" but nevertheless about to perform another story.

Among the "defects" of Kafka prose that Theodor Adorno reluctantly identified was the "monotony"; "The presentation of the ambiguous, uncertain, inaccessible, is repeated endlessly, often at the expense of the vividness that is always sought. The bad infinity of the matter represented spreads to the work of art" (Adorno 1981: 254). Adorno recognizes that this may be deliberate, that like Kierkegaard, Kafka "sought to irritate the reader through his diffuseness and thus startle him out of aesthetic contemplation" (254). Adorno is not convinced: "why the effort?" he asks, figuratively throwing his hands up in the air, "why not restrict oneself to the given minimum?" as the idea of ambiguity could be clearly conveyed and interpreted with a "given minimum" of examples (254).

However, the point of these long disquisitions in the novel is not simply that any act of interpretation is necessarily ambiguous in its result – and that we are constantly looking for others to interpret the world for us – but is rather the texture and rhythm of these acts of interpretation which seem at first to reject the foreignness of K. but at the same time to slowly lull him (and us – reluctantly, and with irritation, perhaps) into that texture and rhythm. This form is in itself an allusion to the form of *The Odyssey*, the momentum of which seems predicated on action and adventure, but is in fact predicated on story-telling about such adventures. Odysseus returns home, of course, but here, in Kafka's novel, the siren song (of the telephones, of Bürgel's sleepy cadences) seems to win, wiping out memory and the past. Such a loss of home is presented as a horror in *The Odyssey* – "the founding epic of nostalgia" (Kundera 2002: 7) – but not so much so in *The Castle*. K. has no intention of returning to his unnamed homeland, and, even when he sets up a home in this foreign village, wanders off again. Pepi points this out as K.'s mistake: "he hardly ever stays at home," she says of him, "wanders about, has discussions here and there, is attentive to everything, only not to Frieda" (Kafka 1998a: 303). K.'s Penelope has left him, not waited patiently, as he "wanders about" and "has discussions here and there"; a diagnosis that K. matter-of-factly agrees with: "I did neglect her," he says. "I would be happy if she returned, but then I would immediately start neglecting her again. That's how it is. When she was with me, I was always away on those wanderings that you ridicule" (307).

Kundera makes the point that Odysseus chooses the safe option: "he chose the apotheosis of the known (return)" instead of the "ardent exploration of the unknown (adventure)"; instead of "the infinite (for adventure never intends to finish), he chose the finite (for the return is a reconciliation with the finitude of life)" (Kundera 2002: 8). For Kundera, the "emotional power" of the "homeland" is "bound up with the relative brevity of our life, which allows us too little time to become attached to some other country, to other countries, to other languages" (121). K. stays wandering in a new language that wanders infinitely, enabling him to stave off finitude and return. The sounds and rhythms of the language are what signify in this world, what connects them all (except, perhaps, Amalia) in their quests, queries and stories.

The Castle has so often been read as a nihilistic book, written in the age of the end of God and ultimate meaning, with the loner and exile K. never reaching the Castle. From Brod's insistence that this was a novel about the search for salvation and the eternal exile of the Jew (Brod 1992) to more recent deconstructionist readings that see it as a perfect enactment of endlessly deferred meaning (Hillis Miller 2011), the novel is seen as a reflection of our own fruitless struggles toward any ontological or epistemological wholeness. What such readings tend to efface is the humor of the novel that is intrinsically tied into that moment of existential despair at the loss of immanence. A year or so before Kafka was writing his novel, Georg Lukács argued that irony was at the heart of the novel as a form, because it came to the fore as a literary form during the birth of modernity and, with it, the worries about a loss of God and ultimate meaning. The novelist returns "to the home of all things, [which] is merely the immanence of a surface that covers up the cracks but is incapable of retaining this immanence and must become a surface riddled with holes" (Lukács 1974: 92). The irony lies not only in a knowledge of the loss of God but also "intuitively speaks of past gods and gods that are to come" (92); in other words, the irony in the novel is not only aware of the illusions of ultimate meaning but also the inescapable need for humans to re-create gods and meaning – "the lost, utopian home of the idea that has become an ideal" (92).

Jeremias, the assistant, tells K. that the other assistant, Artur, is "filing a complaint" against K. at the Castle: "We are complaining," he says "that you cannot take a joke" (Kafka 1998a: 233). K. finally discovers why the assistants were sent to him in the first place; they were told that they did not need experience with land surveying, their actual job was to "cheer him up a bit" (234). "From what I hear," the Castle official told them, "he takes everything very seriously. He has come to the village and right away thinks this is some great event, but in reality it's nothing at all. You should teach him that" (234). As Jeremias tells him this, K. notices that Jeremias has aged and grown far more serious-looking; in the earlier chapters the assistants have been slapstick comedians, popping up and down behind Barnabas's back, scratching at the windows, giggling, smiling and laughing, a performance, it seems, intended to lighten up K., the "hermeneutic machine" and putative hero, to get him to stop his incessant questions, and to enjoy incessantly interpreting.

For, if there is a profound Lukácsian irony in the novel in the constant construction (through Castle stories) of slippery gods in the face of a lack of immanence, there is also a more gag-like humor in the unbearable length of the disquisitions. What drove Adorno crazy, those endlessly repeated conversations, should drive you crazy. "[D]oes the story bore you?" the council chairman asks K. after "interrupting himself" in the midst of a long, long story about a file traveling from Department A to Department B. "No," K. says, "it amuses me" (63). Kafka pokes his readers, or listeners – as Malcolm Pasley points out, Kafka had brought the manuscript "merely […] to the stage at which he could read aloud from it if occasion arose" (Kafka 1998a: 319), to laugh at themselves here, once we realize that we have become "hermeneutic machines" trying to work out what is meaningful and what is not in the long speeches the characters make. As a reader, we can choose to quickly skip over or speed read the council chairman's or Bürgel's considerations of K.'s case with the same guilty sense of not wanting to miss out on the important nugget of information that might make sense of this world, but the joke is on us: the strange, prolix lullabies make us laugh, make us throw our hands in the air, and make us think. The gag of seeming endlessness is a common slapstick trope – we think the joke is over, and feel that we can return to normalcy, but it goes on and on, at once unbearable, unbelievable and funny (think of the excruciating scene of the naked Borat wrestling with his naked sidekick in a scene that becomes an endless, squirming chase). Pasley's observation about Kafka's unusual punctuation being "merely" ready for reading aloud is key here, as it is useful to think of these speeches as being acted out and of the pace and rhythm this might require. The humor in the iterative acts in *The Castle* certainly attracted a writer like Václav Havel, who directly references the council chairman's story of the memo in his 1964 play *The Memorandum*, in which his characters embark on fast-paced, long and convoluted monologues and dialogues of apparent nonsense that end up commenting on how we use language and how language uses us (how we become won over and imprisoned by our own iterative acts). The Sirens are ourselves.

Momus

The humor of *The Castle* may also be found in the texts that underwrite some of its characters. Momus, Klamm's secretary, who demands to interrogate K., is something of a Havelian character, but his name references classical mythology; he is the "personification of carping criticism" (Swift 2003b: 609), placed in opposition to Athena's wisdom (and critical of her sandals! It is the only thing he can find to criticize). Yet it seems possible (given that Kafka, quite hilariously, was doling out parenting advice to his sister from Jonathan Swift – a man notoriously abandoned or kidnapped as a child – while writing *The Castle*) that Kafka's Momus arose out of a biting satire, Swift's *The Battle of the Books*, in which the books of the "Ancients" (Homer, Virgil, etc.) go into battle against the books of the "Moderns" (Milton, Dryden, etc.), a satire on the contemporary debate of the value of the two that is written in a mock-epic style with invocations to the Muses and goddesses disappearing "in a mist" (14). In Swift's satire, Momus, "the patron of the Moderns," flies to the goddess Criticism, a "malignant deity," (12) to urge her to save the Moderns.

While neither side wins – as part of the joke, the manuscript describing the battle is presented as a fragment with parts missing, and it ends incomplete – Swift is clear as to which side is the better. Whereas Virgil, the book, "appeared in shining armour" (15), his translated book, by Dryden, wears armor of "rusty iron" (16). In addition, Dryden's "helmet was nine times too large for the head, which appeared situate far in the hinder part … like a mouse under a canopy of state" (15–16) but he calls Virgil his "father" and argues that (since he is a translation of Virgil's work) "they were nearly related" (16) and proposes "an exchange of armour, as a lasting mark of hospitality" (16). But when he tries on Virgil's armor, its magnificence becomes a joke, "worse than his own" (16); they swap horses but "Dryden was afraid and utterly unable to mount (16). Swift satirizes Dryden's act of translation, as an act intended to crown his own greatness by wearing Virgil's "armour," something that ill-fits because the Moderns are not as great as their literary ancestors.

Kafka, of course, has borrowed Homer's armor, but via the lineage of the novel as a form, a form that has detoured via *Don Quixote* and in which the epic stance is no longer viable or even wanted, something of which Swift, in his satires, is well aware. The beauty that modernity offers is a beauty of disillusion, of Don Quixote's cardboard armor and his innate need to imagine it is not so. The heroics are laid bare, made fun of, but still utterly necessary to live humanly. Swift's own text that delights in making fun of the moderns is itself completely modern, as aware of its own constructedness and that of heroics; in a quite postmodern move – in order to pretend that the text is ancient – Swift deliberately fragments his text, declaring that parts of it are missing (and it does not really finish; we never find out who wins the battle).

Swift compares the constructed nature of modern writing with the naturalness of the Ancients using the classical metaphor about writing, of the bee making honey out of pollen in contrast with a spider weaving its web in the corner of the library. While the bee uses natural, good things to make its art, the spider constructs its web out of "dirt and poison" (10). The web is a "castle," the avenues of which

> were guarded with turnpikes and palisadoes, all after the modern way of fortification. After you had passed several courts, you came to the centre, wherein you might behold the constable himself in his own lodgings, which had windows fronting to each avenue, and ports to sally out upon all occasions of prey or defence (7).

It takes a "wandering bee" to disrupt things; the bee "alight[s] upon one of the outward walls of the spider's citadel" and "endeavoured to force his passage, and thrice the centre shook" (7–8). The bee ends up wrecking the web and the spider finds it nonchalantly "cleansing his wings and disengaging them from the ragged remnants of the cobweb"; the spider "swore like a madman": "Do you think I have nothing better to do (in the devil's name)," he shouts, "but to mend and repair after your arse?" He has "swollen himself into the size and posture of a disputant" (8), willing only to argue and not to listen; he sees himself as "a domestic animal" and the bee as nothing but "a vagabond without house or home" (8).

Swift's humorous metaphor (taking up the classical metaphor of the bee collecting honey) may have influenced a metaphor in *The Castle*, a strong, odd image (not unlike the description of Klamm as an eagle) of Frieda as a spider. Pepi, toward the end of *The Castle*, tells K. that Frieda trapped him, that "she was just sitting there in the taproom like a spider in its web, had threads everywhere that only she knew of" (Kafka 1998a: 289); "she [Frieda], the spider, has connections no one knows about," Pepi adds, "she now began to exploit those connections, K. gave her the opportunity to do so; instead of sitting with her and keeping watch over her, he hardly ever stays at home, wanders about, has discussions here and there" (303). K., in other words (apart from the Odysseus reference), seems here compared, humorously, to the classical bee; the irony lying in the fact that he does picks up the pollen of various conversations, without turning it into anything viable in terms of new knowledge. Swift's notion of the spider as a "constable himself in his own lodgings, which had windows fronting to each avenue" also seems to prefigure Klamm and the panopticon of *The Castle*.

In addition, Swift's subversive description, in this world, of the messengers of the gods, sounds similar to Kafka's world of messengers and copyists in the Castle offices:

> They travel in a caravan, more or less together, and are fastened to each other like a link of galley-slaves, by a light chain which passes from them to Jupiter's great toe; and yet, in receiving or delivering a message they may never approach above the lowest step of his throne, where he and they whisper to each other through a long, hollow trunk. These deities are called by mortal men accidents or events (Swift 2003b: 12).

Momus, of course, is in a way one of these Castle messengers, writing depositions that may never be seen by Klamm; he needs K.'s answers only to "fill in two or three gaps" in his "precise description of this afternoon" (Kafka 1998a: 113). He is part of this overtly textual world (like Swift's imagined Books battling each other) helping to inscribe it; "A lot of writing goes on here," K says, making Momus laugh. "Yes, a bad habit," he says, after which "the entire room became serious" as if what he had said "had exceeded his own comprehension" (110). He buries himself in his files, his texts, and writes, "and then there was not a sound in the room save for his pen" (110).

Tearing up the letter

The Castle is at least partially inspired by a translator. Milena Jesenská, with whom Kafka had just ended his love affair before writing the novel, haunts it in a wry cognizance of her effect on Kafka as a person as well as a lover. Critics have identified biographical keys in the novel to their relationship, beginning with Max Brod who schematically identified certain characters involved centrally and peripherally with the love affair. Ultimately, however, such readings have done little to open up either readings of the novel or a reading of another element central to the Kafka–Jesenská relationship: translation. While it is fascinating to suggest which characters might have a biographical counterpart (for instance, Boa suggesting that Sortini might be a "composite" of Kafka and Jesenská's husband, Pollak), in the end, what is most interesting about Jesenská as a possible inspiration for the novel – most notably, for two of the characters, Frieda and Amalia – is actually the question of communication and interpretation that was central to the Kafka–Jesenská relationship.

Brod, František Kautman and others read the Jesenská–Frieda analogy mostly via the sexual relationship depicted in the novel, which Brod sees as a "bitter caricature" (Brod 1992: 238) of what happened in real life. Kautman, quite correctly, warns against Frieda or Amalia being seen as just "=" to Jesenská, but still sees Frieda as being just a representation of Jesenská's "sensual, instinctual" side and Amalia as a representation of "her intellectual, socially compassionate essence" (Kautman 1968: 32). Kautman protests that Frieda cannot be a direct representation of Jesenská owing to repeated references to Frieda's lack of beauty (as Jesenská, at the time of the affair, was startlingly beautiful), but, of course, Amalia, too, is specifically noted as not being beautiful. In the novel, beauty is placed on the two of them as part of the objectification of women in the village; as Boa argues, they become currency in the patriarchal set-up of the Castle village (and the all-male Castle). What sets Amalia apart, in addition to her silence, is her unsettling gaze back (an unsettling gaze that Frieda too attains briefly at the end of the novel). Brod, and inadvertently Kautman, are, in effect, objectifying Jesenská in such analogies. The sexual scenes, which Brod finds unappealing and a result of Kafka's "skepticism and bitterness" toward Jesenská and the failed relationship (Brod 1992: 220), are both, in fact, unusual, anti-lyrical and subversive, and both speak to the question of communication and the body, foreignness and the home. They both end in an almost slapstick type of humor. This is no romantic, lyrical, fake representation of the sexual act, but a visceral conveying of the beauty of its messiness and incongruity.

Frieda is not just a sex object (although used as such, apparently, by Klamm); she navigates the world for K., literally becoming his interpreter in a scene with the schoolteacher. She, too, shows herself to be a "hermeneutic machine" in reinterpreting their relationship, via the landlady's opinions of K. – here both she and her protector, the landlady, act as interpreters of K. and his meaning – and how he has changed meaning – in their world. Brod suggested that the landlady was a portrait of "Milena's girl-friends who advised against the connection with Kafka," and, certainly, Kafka had a particularly difficult relationship with Staša Jílovská, who was also a translator, and who acted as a kind of gatekeeper to Jesenská and her emotions (220). What is interesting here is the duet of interpretation happening, the wry analysis of influence and reassessment as meaning shifts.

As the novel goes on, Frieda becomes more voluble in this voluble village; Amalia's silence is a rebuke to what she calls the "Castle stories" and their hypnotic effect on those who participate.[2] Her rebuttal of Sortini's advances is encapsulated in the act of tearing up his letter, an active disavowal of the iterative and textual imperative of the village. The ostracism of Amalia and her family is met with her silence and dignity, and it is this self-possession and independence that makes Kautman see Jesenská in her. Certainly, we can read Jesenská in her: the social ostracism Jesenská felt from her Czech family, her exile and sense of isolation in the talkative literary Vienna scene, and – like Amalia and her family – the consequent material losses, descending down from a very bourgeois existence in Prague to a hard-scrabble one in Vienna. Amalia as an outside observer, however, also displays wit about the length of the Castle stories, the propensity for falling for them, and K.'s weakness for women. Her meeting with Sortini – in which he "fixes his gaze" on her, plays out in silence like a silent comedy – the absolute opposite of an expected seduction scene – a silence that is only broken by Amalia's scream when she receives his lewd letter requiring sex. This silence, the gaze and the wit speak to Jesenská as a writer and translator of the foreign world – both Viennese and patriarchal – around her.

The two acts of sex with Frieda in the novel are acts of interpretation, even though – or perhaps because – they take place in silence: the first takes places under the beer counter among "puddles of beer and other rubbish" (Kafka 1998a: 41); we have seen this sentence before: "Hours passed there," Kafka writes:

> hours breathing together with a single heartbeat, hours in which K. constantly felt he was lost or had wandered farther into foreign lands than any human being before him, so foreign that even the air hadn't a single component of the air in his homeland and where one would inevitably suffocate from the foreignness but

---

[2] Kafka's Sirens are silent; in his short story "The Silence of the Sirens," the Sirens "have an even more terrible weapon than their song – namely, their silence (Kafka 2007: 128). But Odysseus, who has put wax in his ears and tied himself to the mast, "did not hear their silence"; he "was thinking of nothing except wax and chains" (128), or perhaps was only pretending to do so to fool the gods. In a letter to Robert Klopstock in 1921, Kafka noted that a letter Klopstock had received from a woman was akin to the "seductive voices of the night, this is how the sirens sang" (Kafka 1978: 310). Yet, he points out that the sirens were lamenting only for themselves: "We do them an injustice when we think they intended to seduce. ... They could not help it that their lament sounded so lovely" (310).

> where the meaningless enticements were such that one had no alternative but to go on and get even more lost (41)

The beautiful, lengthy sentence articulates in its length and clauses the flow of time and the rhythm (with all the repeated words: hours, foreign, air, lost) of the act itself. The notions of foreignness and homeland, wandering and being lost of course speak to K.'s wider predicament in this village, but it is also an apt description of translation – of bringing K. (wordlessly) into the language and locus of the village and the female realm. The sentence mirrors one – in its sense of temporality deliberately communicated through the lengthening of the syntax, and in its conveying of wandering and being lost but guided – that Kafka wrote to Jesenská regarding her translation of "The Stoker":

> your translation is faithful and I have the feeling that I'm taking you by the hand through the story's subterranean passages, gloomy, low, ugly, almost endless (that's why the sentences are almost endless, didn't you realize that?), almost endless (only two months, you say?) hopefully in order to have the good sense to disappear into the daylight at the exit (Kafka 1990: 20).

One of his comments on her translation regarded the word "Luft" – a word central to K.'s love-making with Frieda in this village where the "air" is different to that at home ("Heimatluft"). Kafka notes that the expression he uses to describe the "freie Lüfte" that blow about the Statue of Liberty "is a little more grand" than Jesenská's choice in Czech, "volný vzduch," but realizes that it is probably impossible to translate fully; "there's probably no alternative," he writes (13). In *Amerika*, of course, this "freie Lüfte" is indicative of Karl's arrival in the new world, a suggestion of freedom from any "Heimatluft."

The second time Frieda and K. have sex there is an equally long sentence describing it and again a repetition of words, seeking and pawing, that suggests a search for meaning and for illumination. They suddenly make love after disagreeing about the assistants and how Frieda acts toward them, and there is a sense that Frieda, who is "attempting to say something else" but cannot go on, is attempting to communicate the importance of the act of searching through the act of love:

> "I think you know what I mean," she said, clasping his neck and attempting to say something else, but she couldn't go on, and since the chair stood by the bed they stumbled over it and fell down. They lay there, but without abandoning themselves as fully as that time at night. She sought something and he sought something, in a fury, grimacing, they sought with their heads boring into each other's breasts; their embraces and arched bodies, far from making them forget, reminded them of their duty to keep searching, like dogs desperately pawing at the earth they pawed at each other's bodies, and then, helpless and disappointed, in an effort to catch one last bit of happiness, their tongues occasionally ran all over each other's faces (Kafka 1998a: 45–6).

If the first moment of sex was a kind of forgetting – of the homeland, a movement toward the foreign – here they are "reminded … of their duty to keep searching." The animality of the scene, "like dogs desperately pawing," is strangely beautiful, underscoring the amorphous borders between human and animal (a border K. crosses in the first scene where he "wanders farther into foreign lands than any human being before him" as if this is an un-human place) and the functioning of non-verbal communication: "they sought with their heads boring into each other's breasts" – the head here being used viscerally instead of metaphorically (and intellectually) to find meaning (alongside the interesting desexualization of the "breasts"); and "tongues" here become a physical rather than a verbal tool for "searching."

Both scenes are infused with melancholy, but end in comic relief (albeit an unsettling comedy): when K. and Frieda stand up from the beer puddles, they see the assistants sitting on the counter, "somewhat tired from the lack of sleep, but cheerful" (42). The assistants have been there all night watching; "This isn't easy work," one of them says, "that's for sure." "I need you by day," K. retorts, "not at night" (42). Directly after the second scene, "the maids come up" to the attic and one of them "out of pity … threw a sheet over them" (46). After a while K. "extricated himself from the sheet" and sees the assistants in the corner which "didn't surprise him" but what does is the landlady who was "sitting by the bed, knitting a sock, a small task ill-suited to her large frame" (46). The ridiculous lack of privacy contains a dark side of the panopticon of modernity but it is also a "comic poetry" (Kundera 1996: 52) – the nonchalant assistants yawning at the show, the maid throwing a sheet over them, the huge landlady knitting her sock over their covered bodies. There is nothing "bitter" in these love scenes; they are, as Milan Kundera put it, "a walk beneath the sky of strangeness. And yet that walk is not ugliness; on the contrary, it attracts us, invites us to go on still farther, intoxicates us: it is beauty" (49).

Frieda literally becomes K.'s interpreter soon after the second love scene, when she intervenes to prevent him from saying something he should not. "I'll speak to [the schoolteacher]" Frieda tells him, as K. shivers in his underwear, slapping himself to keep warm, "you need only be present, you don't have to say a word, and it will always be this way, you will never have to speak to him yourself, unless you want to, indeed I'm the only one who will be his subordinate, and even I shall be no such thing, for I know his weaknesses" (Kafka 1998a: 93–4). In becoming K.'s interpreter, Frieda undertakes the role of the "subordinate" so that K. will not feel so as the school janitor – a job the schoolteacher has been told to offer him and a considerable step down in K.'s eyes from the job of land surveyor. Yet Frieda sees the advantages of being an interpreter too, as she knows that she will just perform the position of a "subordinate" while being "no such thing, for I know his weaknesses"; it is a position of persuasion and manipulation. Frieda tells the teacher that "*we* accept the post" (94), an admission that shows her control over their fate but also that she is accepting a post, being professionalized, just as K. is. But the teacher insists that K. "says what he thinks," so Frieda turns to K. and tells him, "he accepts the post, don't you K.?" Because it is Frieda who has addressed him, K. says "Yes" back to her. The teacher only speaks to K. "alone" (95), trying to get a rise out of him, but Frieda tries to intervene, until finally K. bursts out in annoyance that he would be doing the teacher a favor by becoming the janitor; the teacher was "smiling, now that he had actually forced K. to speak" (95). K. exacts revenge, because the teacher takes umbrage that "you have all this time been negotiating with me, I keep staring and can hardly believe it, in your shirt and underpants." "'Yes,' K. exclaimed, laughing and clapping," and the teacher tries to barge out but is met by the maids squeezing into the room and he has to squeeze out between them (96).

Of course, it is Frieda who has been doing the "negotiation" while K. stands in his underpants trying to warm himself in front of the stove. She is trying to negotiate the terms and conditions, including pay, because she understands the local culture, and yet is not apparently successful because the teacher tries to impose his power by refusing to even consider the idea of pay. At the same time – and this is left unsaid – she achieves what she wants: for K. to secure employment and for them to secure a new home in the schoolroom. The scene uses the now clichéd comic trope of intralingual translation used to bypass dispute, in which everyone understands the language but are refusing to communicate except through a mediator who simply repeats what is said, except here we see what also goes on in translation: negotiation and protection. Only later in the novel does K. appreciate Frieda's discourse, when she tells him that she has returned to the taproom (and left him); it was "as if what she was saying was not important but beneath the words she was holding a conversation with K. and this was what was important" (246).

The disparity of interpretation and the possibility of multivalent and coterminous interpretations comes to the fore in the scene in which Frieda effectively breaks up with K. because she effects the landlady's interpretation of K. and their relationship alongside her own. Brod suggested that the landlady represented "Milena's girlfriends" because of the way the landlady guards Frieda, distrusts K. and meddles in the relationship; Kafka was quite open in his letters to Jesenská about his frustration and quite mordantly funny about having to mediate with her friends in Prague, particularly Staša Jílovská. "Staša is awful," he wrote (about Jesenská's best friend) to Jesenská:

> As you said, she is warm, friendly, beautiful, and svelte, but terrible. ... One shudders with horror at her as if at a fallen angel. I don't know what happened to her, probably her husband has extinguished her. She is tired and dead and doesn't know it. When I want to imagine hell I think about her and her husband (Kafka 1990: 83).

Kafka felt that Jesenská's friends in Prague lived in a kind of "underworld" when they talked about her, "speaking wearily about you who are alive" (163). "There truly is a sign above" Jílovská, Kafka wrote to Jesenská, "saying: 'Abandon hope all ye who enter here'" (86). Kafka seemed increasingly frustrated by Jílovská's advice about his and Jesenská's relationship; she "says practically the dumbest thing that can be imagined," he writes, but notes, "of course – this should not be forgotten – it is love through and through; she is holding out her arms to you even from her grave (85).

In a recent interview, Jílovská's daughter said: "My mother was not overly thrilled about their relationship, she had the feeling that it would not end well. Kafka idealized Milena terribly. He only saw her intellect and her modern, independent presence" (Sýkorová 2006: 17, my translation). Certainly, defensiveness and jealousy is part of his negative reaction; when Jesenská sends him a note Jílovská has sent her, he notes the "incredible accord" between "her and you" that is

> something practically spiritual, like someone who simply passes on what he has heard, something he alone was allowed to hear and understand (and his awareness of this fact is also significant, since it accounts for the pride and beauty of the whole). He himself doesn't do anything more than mediate, and remains virtually unmoved (Kafka 1990: 116).

Of the note, he says, "she's not even in the note, she's speaking for you" (116). This almost prophetic mediation is unsettling, as if a message can be unmediated, one person's voice directly and in an untouched manner re-voiced by another. Jílovská – unlike him – is "alone … allowed to hear and understand," something which seems to explain her attitude toward him. Nonetheless, he admires Jílovská only when she is actually trying to interpret something – a photograph Jesenská has sent Kafka: "Staša had a wonderfully beautiful moment as she studied your photograph, actually inconceivably long and very concentrated and silent and serious" (99). "I," on the other hand, Kafka writes, very K.-like, "was tired, empty, boring, deserving to be spanked, indifferent, and from the beginning all I wanted to do was go to bed" (99).

This moment with the photograph may have a parallel in the novel, when the landlady shows K. some things that have meaning for her, a shawl, a cap and a photograph of a messenger – her "mementos" from Klamm (Kafka 1998a: 79). The landlady asks K. to study the photograph, to interpret it, but "it wasn't easy to make anything out in the picture, for it was faded with age, broken in several places, crushed and stained" (77). K. correctly guesses it is a "young man" who he thinks is "lying down … on a board, stretching and yawning" which the landlady says is "quite wrong" and tells him to "take a closer look" (77–8). When he does, he realizes that the man is "doing a high jump" and the landlady is thrilled, because this is exactly what it depicts – a Castle messenger practicing, the very messenger Klamm "first summoned me with" (78). While the photograph has layers of meaning for the landlady which K. can only begin to decipher, he is also distracted, he "found it impossible to listen closely" because the assistants are hopping up and down outside, tapping at the window. "You misinterpret everything," the landlady tells him, "even the silence" (80).

After Frieda watches K. try to manipulate Hans Brunswick she tells him that he had only one goal with her: to reach Klamm, and that without that connection to Klamm she would be of no value. Since he will never meet with Klamm, their relationship is doomed. "I felt as though the landlady were sitting beside me," she says to him, "and explaining everything and I were trying with all my strength to push her away, but now I see clearly the hopelessness of such efforts" (158). The landlady has warned her about K.'s single-mindedness and, watching him in conversation with another, Frieda feels as if the landlady is "sitting beside" her, interpreting K.'s words in a way that Frieda has not before. "I couldn't always distinguish your opinion from the landlady's," K. says, and Frieda acknowledges that it is all the landlady's opinion, the first of her opinions that Frieda has ever "rejected" (156), but now believes is right. "Do make an effort sometime to listen to him properly," the landlady had told her, "not just superficially, no, really listen to him" (154), and she is finally listening to him via listening to the landlady. "Everything," K. says, when he hears the accusations, "everything you say is in a sense right, it is not wrong, only it is hostile" (158). Kafka gets to the heart, here, of interpreting and analyzing relationships in the present and in retrospect, from the inside and the outside, when the same facts and circumstances may change hue, depending on how and when you interpret them (and who interprets them). Frieda sees her and the landlady's interpretations happening at the same time, with (as K. notices later) the "blurred look of somebody trying with great difficulty to remember something" (246).

When Frieda leaves him and sets up home with Jeremias, K. understands why; she has "succumbed to the illusion" that "was nothing but moments, ghosts, old memories, mostly your past, your constantly receding former life" (253). She has returned to the Gentleman's Inn, to the landlady, to her past, all of which has a stronger pull than strangeness and an uncertain future; "we came together, each of us, from a completely different world," K. says (253). Jílovská, from Jesenská's past and Czech bourgeois milieu, offers Jesenská in her isolated exile something Kafka never can – a path back, which begins with Jílovská arranging translation work for Jesenská that brings Jesenská back to that Czech and Czech language milieu. The matriarchal power of the landlady, pulling Frieda back from her temporary exile, works within the patriarchal power of the Castle. In some senses, the paid translation work that Jílovská arranges gives Jesenská an entry into the still patriarchal literary world.

This is not to say that the landlady is all Jílovská (just as Frieda is not all Jesenská): the landlady is enormous, "a mighty figure" (3), and this size seems, perhaps, related to a comment Kafka makes in a letter to Max Brod about the landlady in the inn near where he is staying in the country with his sister Ottla, as he was writing *The Castle*. When he looks at her and Ottla in conversation, he says he "stood there like Gulliver listening to the giant women conversing" (Kafka 1978: 358). Gulliver arrives in the land of the Brobdingnags who are immense and also speak their own language, which he has to learn (thanks to the farmer's daughter Glumdalclitch); at one point he becomes the plaything of the Queen's Maids of Honour, these giantesses who sit him astride their nipples for fun (Swift 2003a: 111) and "strip themselves to the Skin" in front of him (110), just as the landlady dresses in front of him – "Hand me my skirt" she says to K. showing "no consideration" for him (Kafka 1998a: 86–7). The problem with the giantesses is that all the flaws in their bodies may be seen up close because they are so huge, "with a Mole here and there as broad as a Trencher, and Hairs hanging from it thicker than Packthreads" (Swift 2003a: 111). Gulliver realizes that the Lilliputian women seemed to have perfect complexions only because they were so tiny and he could not properly see them.

The photograph that Kafka showed Jílovská, and which she pored over in silence, was "a pitiful picture" (Kafka 1990: 91) with Jesenská's "lovely, poor eyes" (93), the "clear depths" of which can only tell the truth, whether or not it is what Kafka wants to hear (92). It makes him want to try "to look at the whole things from your point of view" he writes, from "that angle it looks strange" (92). The objectification of women in the Castle village, the patriarchal Castle gaze, is disrupted by Amalia, who gazes back with "her bleak gaze" (Kafka 1998: 188). This gaze is something that seems paralleled to Jesenská, who was an intellectual equal, who understood Kafka's work, who as his translator and his lover made him want "to excel in your eyes" (Kafka 1990: 91).

Amalia's troubles begin when the Castle official Sortini "fixed on Amalia" at the Firemen's Association festival. He is spectacularly ugly, "small, frail, pensive [...] all his wrinkles [...] spread out in fanlike fashion straight across his forehead and down to he bridge of his nose" (Kafka 1998a: 188); Amalia, who "certainly wasn't beautiful," suddenly becomes so, dressed almost for sacrifice in a white, lacy blouse and a necklace of garnets, originally from the landlady, but it is her "bleak gaze" that "went high up over our heads" that makes her family want to bow "down before her" (188). Not a word is spoken between her and Sortini; he indicates his desire by jumping over the shaft of the engine (a *double entendre*) to be near her, but the family "misunderstood" the gesture and move toward him; he waves them away with his hand. That is the seduction scene in total; Amalia is just "more silent than ever," which makes Brunswick convinced that she is "utterly, madly in love with Sortini" (191). Everyone agrees because they are "in a daze from the sweet Castle wine"; "all of us, except Amalia" and they fall into a "wine-induced sleep" (191). The next morning they are woken by Amalia's "screams" at the crude letter Sortini has sent, but only Olga gets up, in time to see Amalia tear up the letter and throw "the scraps in the face of the man outside" (192).

Kautman sees Jesenská in this Amalia, the "unbroken, morally unambiguous, single-minded being" (Kautman 1968: 31) who refuses to collaborate in patriarchal and political norms, though he writes in hindsight of Jesenská's immense courage and integrity during the war, and also, to some extent, in the shadow of her silence (due to her missing letters and, thus, her missing voice in the Kafka exchange). Certainly, however, Jesenská was showing her independence in the early 1920s (and her early 20s) by translating and writing in Czech while living in Vienna, ostracized by her Czech family and marginalized by the Viennese literary milieu to which her husband belonged. Members of that circle remembered her silence, her inability to function in the literary German-language tone of the café debates. Her immense literary activity from 1920 onward in Czech, however, enabled her to turn her back on that world, to not be an initiate but instead an observer.

Amalia's silence first appears to be a result of trauma, and there seems to be an allusion again to *The Odyssey*: the "wine-induced sleep" similar to Circe's potion with which she drugs Odysseus's men "to wipe from their memories any thought of home" (Homer 1997: 237) and turns them into swine, except for Eurylochus who "sensed a trap" and did not take part and he runs back to the ship but "he couldn't get a word out/Numbing sorrow had stunned the man to silence" (238). Odysseus has to go and rescue his men and is given help by the gods; Hermes, who "looked for all the world/like a young man sporting his first beard ... grasped me by the hand" (239) and gives Odysseus an antidote to the potion, otherwise "you won't get home yourself/you'll stay right there, trapped with all the rest" (239). K., of course, gets no potion, but the letters delivered by Barnabas.

Yet, Amalia is not completely silent and when she isn't she is witty and sharp. She teases K. about her sister who, she tells him, is in love with him. When K. starts talking about the enmity between her family and Frieda, she points out that it is not enmity, "only a slavish repetition of common opinion" (Kafka 1998a: 169) – language and the incessant conversations about her family have caused the situation, in other words. Her tearing up of the letter was the ultimate insult in this textual world. She will not say not goodbye to K. because she knows he will end up talking to Olga for a long time, she knows the appeal and power of the "Castle stories" and she teases K. about his fascination with them. She tells him a brief story about a villager who becomes obsessed with the Castle: "people feared for his ordinary faculty of reason," she says of this man, "since all his faculties were always up at the Castle" (205). In the end, it turns out that this man was in fact not obsessed with the Castle but with "the daughter of a scullery maid at the offices" (205). "I would like that man, I think," K. says. "As for your liking that man," Amalia quips, "I'm not so sure about that, but you might like his wife" (205). After her cheeky quip about K. as the new village *homme fatal*, she goes to bed and Olga mutters, "It isn't easy to understand exactly what she is saying, for one doesn't know whether she is speaking ironically or seriously, it's mostly serious, but sounds ironic." "Stop interpreting everything!" K. snaps.

K. was earlier taken with Amalia's smile; it makes her "silence eloquent and her strangeness familiar" (169), but their conversation about Olga and Frieda is almost wholly reported in the third person, until Amalia makes her point about Frieda's attitude to her family not being enmity but received opinion. She tells him he can always come to their house using "Barnabas's messages as a pretext" and says so in six short sentences. It is one of the shortest speeches a character delivers in the book, but "K. had never heard Amalia speak continuously at such length," Kafka writes, "it even sounded different from her normal speech, for it had a certain majesty" (169). While they have possibly had a long conversation that is only mostly reported second-hand, it rushes past (comparatively) in the novel; here Kafka is being cheeky, but K. is impressed – he claims to "understand [her] better" and tries to find "the right word" to describe her, "but he couldn't find it right away and made do with a rough equivalent" and calls her "good-natured" (170). He attempts to translate her into language but can only find this "rough equivalent"; within a page, Olga dismisses the idea that Amalia is good-natured and K. completely backtracks and claims "that the praise had actually been meant for her, Olga, but Amalia was so domineering that she not only appropriated everything said in her presence but that one was even willing to let her have all of it" (172–3). There is tragedy in Amalia's fate but also humor and a peculiar form of grace: she seems content to be outside the discourse of the "Castle stories" and to view the world with her "bleak gaze" and silence while becoming the de facto head of the family (this exile from the community is the only way she can).

The wry Amalia-like voice (when it speaks), the one no longer under any illusions about the "Castle stories" and the endless conversations, may be found in Jesenská's writing, particularly in an article called "The Café" that Jesenská wrote for the Czech newspaper *Tribuna* in August 1920. In "The Café" Jesenská shines her wry, "bleak gaze" at the eco-systems of literary cafés in Prague and in Vienna; cafés "with a rather strange existence that no one can understand until he penetrates it to the core, until he fills his lungs with its air" (Jesenská 2003: 64). The striking resonance of this language with that of *The Castle* (and, specifically, with the language of the first love scene between Frieda and K.) may be seen in other parts of the article, which suggests a kind of blueprint world for *The Castle*. The hierarchy is here, with "the great ones" at the top:

> Those who already have a name in the official world, those who are the pride of the café and whose pictures and caricatures hang on the walls of the bar; those who, when they arrive, sit like capitalists of the spirit behind a table and only a few are permitted to sit beside them (64).

The idea of these "great ones" (great artists, writers, etc.) having a name in "the official world" and whose pictures – like the castellan in *The Castle* – "hang on the walls of the bar" seems suggestive of the world of *The Castle* and its officials who "sit like capitalists of the spirit behind a table" (like Klamm) and who only allow those "few" who "are permitted to sit beside them" to come to them. In fact, as Kathleen Hayes points out, the phrase "capitalists of the spirit" is a direct reaction to something Kafka wrote in a letter to Jesenská about Franz Werfel a few months earlier. Jesenská insulted Werfel's corporeality, and Kafka wrote back in defense that "only these capitalists of airspace are immune from worry and insanity" (Hayes 2003: 18). Yet, there is a creative dialogue here; it is not just a one-way street of inspiration.

Under these "great ones" are the journalists of varying fame, "the crowd of writers" with "poems in their pockets" (these texts, like the letters and depositions being carried around) and "the crowd of castaways, the crowd of the strangest characters with the most mysterious of lives, people who will never get anywhere and will never manage to achieve anything, the bravely resigned and the quiet melancholics about whom the world does not know and never will know anything" (Jesenská 2003: 65). "In the café," she writes, "one lives, one idles and the hours pass … whoever once succumbs to the lazy, sluggish pace of life in these cafes will hardly ever get ahead" (66). Again, the language seems resonant – the "hours pass," again reminiscent of K. entering the foreign land of Frieda and the village – and the notion of Amalia's warning to K. not to succumb to the "Castle stories" seems prefigured here.

The café, like the village, has its own structure that supports these denizens: "The strangest thing of all," Jesenská writes,

> is the common life of the café, including the owner, the scorer, the waiters, the busboys, the old lady in the cloakroom, the old lady taking money at the toilets, all of them together, the entire community, its laws, its jargon, all that is so completely cut off from the rest of the world (66).

Whereas the power seemed located in the "great ones" of the "official world," the café runs on the labor of a myriad peripheral personalities, "the old lady taking money at the toilets," and is made up not only of "laws" but of "its jargon" – a language that constructs the "community" that "is so completely cut off from the rest of the world" (as the village appears to be).

Women play a role front of house also, and Jesenská's striking description of how they function as items of (decreasing) value in the café bears a real resemblance to the officials' treatment of women in *The Castle*. In the café:

The women who are brought along move gradually from table to table, either "for no reason," or because of marriage, infidelity, divorce. In the end they belong to the café; they lose their surnames and are called simply by their nicknames; they turn into friends. With the growing number of cigarettes smoked and the growing number of lovers, they lose their true femininity and become stale, boring, ugly (66).

To some extent this description is autobiographical, reflecting Jesenská's own anxieties at being branded simply Pollak's wife and of becoming less attractive and unwanted, but the notion that the women in "the end ... belong to the café" seems prescient to the women who seem to belong to the Castle (something Amalia resists and is expelled for) and who do, for the most part (excepting Mrs. Brunswick), "lose their surnames" (as Jesenská herself will do in the iconization of her as "Milena"). Frieda, passed from hand to hand – from Klamm to K. to Jeremias – is basically declared "stale, boring, ugly" by Pepi at the end of the novel. As a woman, writing this in 1920 about "infidelity, divorce" and "lovers," Jesenská is ahead of her time and, though describing a bohemian world, she argues it is inherently "bourgeois" in the article (65), thus suggesting that this use of women is simply a more emphatic version of women's fate in general. Yet, it seems also to encapsulate the fate women face in the world of *The Castle*, moving "gradually from table to table 'for no reason.'"

"Reading 'The Café,'" Kafka wrote to Jesenská in August 1920, "was like listening to Stein ["he is modest, respectful, very careful in his judgments and endowed with a subtle mind" (Kafka 1990: 156)], except you tell a story much better than he does; who else can tell a story so well?" (157). He admonishes her for wasting her story-telling talents on *Tribuna*, but tells her that while he

> was reading it I felt I was walking up and down in front of the café, day and night, year after year; every time a guest came or went I would peer in through the open door to check that you were still inside. Then I would resume the pacing and waiting. This was neither straining nor sad. And how could it be straining or sad to wait in front of a café when you are inside! (157)

Kafka's image of himself "pacing and waiting" outside of Jesenská's textual café, "neither straining nor sad" keeping an eye out for her, peering through the open door when guests enter or exit, exhibits his close gaze on her work and his quite visceral connection to it. The pace of the sentence, rocking back and forth, "up and down," "day and night," "year after year," "came and went," "pacing and waiting," "straining or sad," speaks too to the temporal tone of *The Castle*, its rhythm of hours passing, of succumbing, as they all do, to words, except for Amalia, this partial figuration of Jesenská.

Kafka fictionalizes his translator, but also her work.

sensibilities of two artists meet; and what role does a new social, cultural and historical context give to an adaptation of a classic text; and how do critics bring their own "interpretants" to understanding or reading these films?

Traditionally, film adaptations have been "described and evaluated on the basis of [their] adequacy to the literary text" (Venuti 2007: 26). As, in academia, these literary texts had more cachet than their filmic adaptations, and film studies, too, was seen as only an emergent discipline, the film adaptations were often read as necessarily inferior to the sacred literary text, especially canonical ones (26). More recent film criticism has argued for "adaptation as essentially a form of intertextuality" which is "necessarily transformative" of the literary text and a hermeneutic rather than a communicative reading of it, but has tended then to "privilege the film adaptation over the literary text it adapts" (26–7). Lawrence Venuti argues that in thinking about adaptations (via the lens of translation studies) as hermeneutic acts, it is necessary to think about the category of the "interpretant" – the formal and/or thematic mechanisms by which not only the filmmaker, but also the critics and viewers reinterpret the source text. The "shifts" made in the film adaptation are places from which "to elucidate the interpretative operation performed by the film" and, by extension, the filmmaker, the critic and the viewer (33). Rather than simply judging these "shifts" as sometimes being too radical, too unfaithful, too odd, Venuti argues that these are the loci of "interrogating" the film *and* its source text. "The interpretants deployed in a film adaptation," Venuti writes, "may be complementary, mutually reinforcing an overall interpretation inscribed in the prior materials, or disjunctive, resulting in opposing and even contradictory interpretations that may in turn be perceived differently by different audiences" (35). What is important is in thinking about "the new context [as] never simply interpretative, but potentially interrogative," an interrogation that "can invite a critical understanding of the prior materials as well as their originary or subsequent contexts" (38). Once this "interrogation is set going, it need not stop at the prior materials; they may in turn be used to probe the translation or adaptation, along with the cultural forms and practices that constitute it as well as the traditions and institutions to which it is affiliated" (38–9). In other words, instead of thinking of adaptation in terms of a kind of critical horse-race, judging one to be better (or faster!) than the other, Venuti suggests that a "mutual" (39) or "double" interrogation (40) between the source, literary, text and the film adaptation can open up readings of both. Instead of pointing out faults, the critic or viewer, Venuti argues, should analyze both the filmmaker's and their own responses to the "shifts" in form, tone or meaning.

It is an approach that can be especially fruitful when considering film adaptations of Kafka's work, which have generally been considered to be unsuccessful, despite being undertaken by some of the great filmmakers of the twentieth century (Welles, Fellini) and the leading auteurs of today (Michael Haneke, Steven Soderbergh, Straub and Huillet). As Martin Brady and Helen Hughes point out, a central problem lies in the pitfalls of over-visualization, the films being "conspicuously, even spectacularly, visual" (Brady and Hughes 2002: 227), thus responding quite "faithfully" or literally to Kafka's "strongly visual use of language" (i.e., a man changed into a bug) but not necessarily to the "restricted viewpoint of the protagonists" (228) or to the uneasiness of literally not

3

Adapting Kafka

In 1931, a 16-year-old actor took the stage in the new Gate Theatre in Dublin. He was playing the 50-year-old duke, Karl Alexander, in Ashley Dukes's stage adaptation of the Muirs's translation of Lion Feuchtwanger's *Jud Süss*. After uttering the line, "A bride fit for Solomon. He had a thousand wives, did he not?" there was a cry from the audience, "that's a black Protestant lie!" Thrown off, the young actor flubbed his next line and, to distract the audience, hurled himself into that audience, "and was greeted by an even greater ovation than he had received" after the first act (Callow 1996: 96). One of the theater's founders, Micheál Mac Liammóir, fumed in the wings as he watched all the glory go to the young actor, and none to his fellow actors, the playwright, the novelist. "[B]ack goes the big head," he wrote of the actor, "and the laugh breaks out like a fire in the jungle" (96). The Dublin audience was on its feet to herald a new star, an American teenager who had come to Ireland in search of J.M. Synge: Orson Welles.

Ten years later, Welles made and acted in his first film *Citizen Kane*, bringing to it influences he had learned about from Mac Liammóir and Hilton Edwards at the Gate: the new non-naturalistic German and Russian theater (109). He then brought his use of light, montage, camera angles and sometimes abstract settings, influenced by this theatrical and also German expressionist filmic tradition, back to Europe: in 1962, he filmed Kafka's *The Trial*. "It's a film inspired by the book," Welles said in an interview,

> in which my collaborator and partner is Kafka. That may sound like a pompous thing to say, but I'm afraid that it does remain a Welles film and although I have tried to be faithful to what I take to be the spirit of Kafka, the novel was written in the early twenties, and this is now 1962, and we've made the film in 1962, and I've tried to make it my film because I think that it will have more validity if it's mine (Welles 1962).

Welles mentions some of the issues that are central to what Roman Jakobson called "intersemiotic translation" (Jakobson 2000: 114) or the adaptation of a text from one semiotic realm (writing) to another (the visual): the fraught question of whether one even should be faithful to a original text in another medium; how much influence of the adaptor should be seen (and in Welles's case, heard); what happens when the seeing what is being described. Brady and Hughes quote Kafka's famous 1915 response to the illustration of an insect that his publisher, Kurt Wolff, wanted to put on the cover of "Metamorphosis." Kafka was worried that the illustrator "might want to draw the insect himself" (Kafka 1978: 114). "Not that, please not that!" he writes. "The insect itself cannot be depicted. It cannot even be shown from a distance" (114–15). Kafka's written representation of the insect is deliberately ambiguous; he shows himself reluctant for anyone to expressly represent it or interpret it, in so doing then influencing the reader.

Similarly, when "The Stoker" was published, Kafka also protested at the outdated image of an early nineteenth-century steamboat that Wolff put on the cover. "I was at first alarmed," he wrote. "I had after all presented the most up-to-date New York; in second place, the picture had an advantage over my story since it produced its effect before my story did, and a picture is naturally more concentrated than prose; and, thirdly, it was too pretty" (98). Kafka, clearly worried that the picture would influence how a reader might read the story, nonetheless thanks Wolff for it: "I feel my book has been definitely enriched by the print and that already an exchange of strength and weaknesses has taken place between picture and book" (98). This comment about "an exchange of strength and weaknesses" is illuminative; Kafka trusts that readers will react to the juxtaposition of this pretty, early nineteenth-century romantic view of a Brooklyn ferry with his written version of the depths and heights of an ocean liner, with all its hopes and restrictions, arriving on a very twentieth-century New York shore. It provides a "mutual interrogation" of the theme.

When writing "The Stoker," and throughout his writing career, Kafka was a moviegoer (Zischler 2003: 6), and recent criticism has been quite convincing in suggesting that the new technology of film – which Kafka seemed ambivalent about – influenced how he wrote; Duttlinger and Anderson provide nuanced readings of the filmic qualities of Amerika's narrative and its reconsideration of how we *see* in the modern world (Anderson 1992; Duttlinger 2007). "For Kafka," Hanns Zischler writes, "the almost demonic technological element challenges the way we have learned to see" and "confronts the author's powers of sight and writing with very great, agonizing demands" (Zischler 2003: 16). The cinema "works against the stillness of the gaze and generates less a living than a mechanical reality, an automated unease" (28). Yet, Zischler argues that Kafka's presentation of his bachelor travels with Max Brod in his *Diaries* (in the aborted co-written fictionalized travelogue *Richard and Samuel*) shows an artistic appropriation of this new "mechanical reality" in which he writes of a taxi ride that "hums along as mechanically as clockwork, like a projector. … Pure kinetic, cinematographic, and graphomatic pleasure" (39): Kafka is the camera. This kind of kinetic camera technique is evident in the opening of one of Kafka's last stories, *The Hunger-Artist* (1922), in which, in one long paragraph, the narrator performs a kind of vertiginous tracking shot from "the whole town" down through the "people" to the "season-ticket holders" to "the children" to the hunger-artist himself, in his cage "poking his arms through the bars" to the glass of water in his hands which he lifts, in the last word of the almost page-long paragraph, to "his lips" (Kafka 2008b: 252).

Brady and Hughes fear that cinema may be too obvious in its rendering of these (already cinema-infused) visuals, obliging the "reader-turned-viewer" to "observe how metaphors work differently from images" and to feel, ultimately, a little dissatisfied (Brady and Hughes 2002: 239). Yet, what is interesting about many of the films of Kafka's work lies exactly in their self-reflexivity about cinema and its visual metaphors; their self-conscious considerations of the auteur as a figure; and, finally, their engagement with an iconic Kafka. Orson Welles's *The Trial* (1962), Michael Haneke's *The Castle* (1997), Federico Fellini's *Intervista* (1987), Vladimír Michálek's *Amerika* (1994), Steven Soderbergh's *Kafka* (1991), and Peter Capaldi's *Kafka's It's a Wonderful Life* (1993) all appropriate Kafka's work quite forcefully. The directors not only imprint their own styles and interpretations on the source text but do so quite flagrantly, thus establishing and de-stabilizing their authority and, thus, foregrounding interpretation and form. The films, in dialogue with (rather than in competition with) the source texts, can open up rereadings of those source texts, and of how we visualize Kafka, as well as opening up rereadings of the films, unbound from an expectation of fidelity to an already-conceived idea of what a Kafka film should be.

The Trial

Welles's *The Trial* is probably "the most famous of all Kafka screen adaptations" (Brady and Hughes 2002: 231) but it has been seen as problematic from the start for being unfaithful (231) to Kafka textually and "in spirit." In terms of Welles's own œuvre, it is also often seen as being a weak film. But its flaws also open up interesting avenues in reviewing Kafka's *The Trial* and in thinking about film adaptation as a translation, with all the difficulties and complexities that implies. Most central, perhaps, is the question of narrative voice – the utter presence of Welles's voice in the film (he appears as the lawyer Hastler, but also dubbed ten other parts with his voice) in contrast to the almost intangible presence of the narrator in Kafka's novel. In addition, the question of the historical and cultural context looms large over Welles's film; for him, the tone and narrative necessarily had to change because the world had changed since Kafka wrote the novel. Specifically, Welles made K. less passive at the moment of his death because for him "the ending [of the novel] is a ballet written by a Jewish intellectual before the advent of Hitler. Kafka wouldn't have put that in after the death of six million Jews. It all seems very much pre-Auschwitz to me" (Welles 1962). Welles, rightly or wrongly, addresses the effect of historical knowledge on a text written unawares of that knowledge. Finally, and connected to this, is the issue of humor. While there are touches of humor in the film, the dark and paranoid tone is very different to the subtle and wryly humorous tone of the novel. Welles's film is a product of his own chiaroscuro style, but is also expressive of its time and, in many senses, articulated, even defined the way in which Kafka would be read (or not read) in the postwar era.

Martin Brady and Helen Hughes argue that "Welles's approach could be seen as the triumph of what we understand as the 'Kafkaesque' over Kafka himself" (Brady and Hughes 2002: 233), i.e. as a fundamental misreading of what Welles called "the spirit" of the work, basing the film instead on the iconology of Kafka and what he seemed to represent, especially post-Auschwitz. *The Trial* was not well received by British and American reviewers owing to "the unrelieved grimness of its moral tone" (McBride 1972: 141), as well as Welles's rewriting of the narrative to emphasize possible resistance to a totalitarian world. "Welles," Joseph McBride writes, "effectively adapted Kafka's narrative to the demands of his own moral universe" (141), making Josef K. "a Wellesian hero" (Cowie 1989: 175) who becomes increasingly more resistant to the power of the Court during the film ending with a defiant death (175). Rather than K.'s supplicant death in the novel, in which he dies "like a dog," that "implie[d] a defeatism that Welles cannot accept" (175) in the film, the guards throw dynamite into the quarry and K. attempts to throw it back at them. All we see is the explosion and a black mushroom cloud. "I couldn't put my name to a work that implies man's surrender," Welles said. "Being on the side of man, I had to show him in his final hour undefeated" (McBride 1972: 141). In doing so, Welles has been seen as "betraying Kafka who rejected the terminal meaning of closed allegory" in defining "the allegorical significance of his film by ending it with politically-charged image of a nuclear holocaust" (Adams 2002: 154).

Symbols of the war, the Holocaust and the Cold War permeate the film: the bleak Yugoslav landscapes, the then abandoned Gare d'Orsay, the bare-chested, starved court supplicants with numbers around their necks, Titorelli's striped pajama top, "the Gestapo-like torturer" in the whip scene (Naremore 1989: 208), the Cossack guard in the opening pinscreen version of the Before the Law parable. These "historical circumstances" (200) inform the tone of the film and the presentation of K.'s fate: Welles wants K. to fight back, so that "Kafka's ironic, impersonal vision of despair has been transformed into a Wellsian morality play" (198). K. still does not survive the impersonal powers of the Court but he resists them, refuses the demonic Advocate and the open-ended advice of the parable, brought up toward the end of the film by the Priest and the Advocate. There is little humor here: "Welles, having lived through an epoch where the torture chamber and the concentration camp became law, has, not unnaturally, a more bitter view-point than Kafka's" (Cowie 1989: 165). The obviousness of the Cold War, post-Holocaust allegory seems, at first glance, to limit the scope of the film, turning the narrative into "a vehicle for contemporary social satire" (202), leaving none of the central ambiguity of Kafka's novel (where we never find out what the Court is, and whether K. is or is not guilty of an unspecified crime).

Welles's interpretive heavy-handedness seems apparent from the outset. Not only does he place the Before the Law narrative at the beginning, he personally relates it in his distinctive voice "which, with its slightly drawling transatlantic accent and its rich timbre, could make the City Directory sound Shakespearian" (Naremore 1989: 262). He then appends a brief, exegetical coda to it that sets the tone of his film: "Welles pauses, then comments in a heavy, monitory voice, 'This tale is told during the story called "The Trial." It has been said that the logic of this story is the logic of a dream – of a nightmare'" (Cowie 1989: 155). He says "of a nightmare" in a kind of stage whisper that cuts to the un-blurring image of K.'s (Anthony Perkins's) head. Welles's disembodied narrator comes back at the end of the film, as we watch the mushroom cloud and Albinoni's plaintive *Adagio* surges, saying, "This film, *The Trial*, is based on a novel by Franz Kafka" and Welles names all the actors in the film (rather than textually acknowledging them in rolling credits. "I played the Advocate," he ends, "and wrote this film. My name is Orson Welles."

The vocal signature of Welles's name ending the film is indicative of the narratorial control (as the director) and the vocal control in the film – Welles not only co-starred as the Advocate, but dubbed the voices of "no fewer than eleven of the speaking parts" (176). In one major scene toward the end of the film Welles, playing the Advocate Hastler, debates his client Block, played by Akim Tamiroff but dubbed by Welles. He literally talks to himself. In the Cathedral scene, he dubs the Priest (played by Michael Lonsdale) who talks to K. alongside the Advocate (played of course by Welles). Among others, he also dubs the painter Titorelli (played by William Chappell). Although he uses different accents, the timbre of Welles's voice is unmistakable and it seems, at first, that this is a megalomaniacal move, Welles literally insisting on his voice being heard over Kafka's narrative, in sharp contrast to the elusive, barely present narrator in Kafka's novel who refuses to comment or give the reader much extra direction or information. When Welles appears bodily, however, something interesting happens. We don't initially see him, and then, because a flannel is over his face, it is difficult initially to understand what he is saying.

K. goes with his uncle to see the Advocate Hastler and is brought through a labyrinthine series of rooms, full of papers and candles. Leni brings K. and his uncle into a room which has a huge, baroque, gilded bed on a platform, and a figure is in the bed, invisible through cigar smoke. Just as the smoke begins to clear, Leni puts a flannel over Hastler's face, and although he speaks, it is hard to understand him; steam rises up from his chin. It is only when he hears Josef K's name that he snatches the flannel off and we see Welles's face and hear his clear, enunciating voice. He rises up from the bed and there is a shot, angled down from behind Hastler/Welles that makes him seem a giant looming over K. As James Naremore suggests, Welles "devised a typically theatrical entrance for himself," making Hastler, through all the smoke, steam, candles and lightening, "a demonic presence" (Naremore 1989: 209). The dramatic entrance, however, is slightly de-stabilized by the muffled voice and the dark comedy with the flannel. The flannel on his face makes him appear monstrous, his mouth inhaling the cloth, but he is also comic and mischievous; it does not stop him whispering into Leni's ear and grabbing her posterior.

As Jeffrey Adams points out, while "Welles does not miss an opportunity for a grand entrance" and "steals the show," his "larger-than-life presence" is "a campy, self-ironic image that draws its power from Welles's well-established fame" (Adams 2002: 149). The cinematic language of the scene references expressionist and silent cinema: "As if flirting with the silence of early cinema, Welles suppresses sound and speech, speaking his first lines from beneath the steaming towel, thus muffling them to the point of incomprehensibility while heightening the noirish visual effects" (149). The scene's "jokey self-consciousness" stages "the farce-like quality often found in Kafka's stories" (149) and certainly found in Kafka's *The Trial*. The scene from the novel in which K. has to interpret what the Italian businessman is saying but cannot because of his beard does not appear in the film, but the steaming towel is an equivalent motif right at the point when Welles's voice is united with Welles's body in the film.

The Trial was the first film since *Citizen Kane* (Welles's first film in 1941) over which Welles had complete artistic control, and it is possible to read his own voice in the mouths of other actors in the film as an articulation of a hermeneutic control. But the humor and self-consciousness in this initial scene with Hastler that highlights miscommunication is suggestive of a more self-conscious and self-referential attitude to the multiplicity of Welles's voices, emanating from a voice that was famous in its own right. The exaggerated nature of Welles's aural presence brings to the fore the question and the action of the auteur's interpretation. We cannot help but see and hear Welles's interpretations of the novel as he introduces and concludes the film, acts in it and over-dubs his actors, but there is a certain instability in so much presence. Asked about the variety of different readings of the novel and whether he chose a particular interpretation of it on which to base the film, Welles replied: "I think that a film ought to be, or a good film ought to be as capable of as many interpretations as a good book" and that he had to refuse to answer the question: "I'd rather that you go and see the film, which should speak for itself and must speak for itself. I'd prefer that you make your own interpretation of what you think!" (Welles 1962).

But Welles does seem to have imposed a strong interpretation on the text, leaving the viewers little space in which to make their own. James Naremore and Joseph McBride both point to Welles's de-contextualization of the Before the Law parable; by placing it at the beginning of the film outside of its comic context, it seems grim and prophetic of K. being unable to escape his fate, despite (in Welles's film) his heroic attempt to do so. When Welles comes back to the parable toward the end of the film, the long and funny exegesis of the parable – the discussion between the priest and K. in the Cathedral – is "edited down to a brief exchange" (153) with Welles in person, both as the character Hastler and as the hugely attenuated voice of the Priest. Hastler makes only one brief mention of "the commentators" and their view of the parable, saying that "the man came to the door of his own free will." K. dismisses the parable, saying that everyone has heard it all before and rejecting the seemingly obvious bleakness of the message Hastler implies (i.e., that humanity has no choice before its own fate and before the Court). Unlike the novel, in which K. completely accepts the priest's various commentaries and is oddly, and quite humorously, acceptant of his fate, K. in the film rebels, and does so in Welles's language rather than in Kafka's (most of this scene is entirely from Welles's own pen).

More interesting, perhaps, is what is going on visually. When Hastler tells K. very briefly what the commentators think, he is showing K. the pinscreen animation that we, as viewers, have seen at the beginning of the film. K., standing before a screen, also now stands before the pinscreen door on the screen behind him. On an obvious level he has become the man in the parable, and Hastler will tell him that the door is now closed for him. K., refusing to accept his fate, switches off the projector, leaving a shadow of Hastler/Welles in front of a blank screen. Hastler and K. then switch places and we see K. in full light in front of the blank screen also. Meta-cinematically, Welles is showing his own film (though the pinscreen was shot by Alexandre Alexeïeff and Claire Parker) inside his film, the actor switching it off. The authority and authenticity of the message, though seemingly hermetically reduced in the dialogue, is being challenged in visual language. Welles makes a determined interpretation of the Cathedral scene that the parable condemns man to a fate determined by a power above him, but that man can, and should, rebel, but he returns in person in his own film – in both body and voice – and still cannot effect complete and salutary meaning. The screen is blank; we can see the shadow of the director and the body of the leading man on it, but it is a space we have to interpret.

While the film appears to be full of symbols that seem very interpretable, partly because Welles was working in a slightly anachronistic film noir style, there are visual elements that are deliberately left ambiguous and undercut or de-stabilize the rather more obvious dialogue. A good example may be seen in the figure of the statue which looms over the Court supplicants: the huge statue, the arms of which are outstretched, is completely covered by a cloth. What, or who, does it signify? Christ? Stalin? One of the unnamed Court justices, or even the director himself (it might remind us, after all, of the flannel cloth on Hastler's face)? "Consistent with the allegorical ambiguity of Kafka's imagery," Jeffrey Adams writes, "it is not clear what this specter might signify" (Adams 2002: 148). The ambiguity of the image does remind us of the representations of Justice, described by K. in Kafka's *The Trial*, which have wings like Nike and remind him of the huntress Diana. Or even the Statue of Liberty at the beginning of *Amerika*, whom Karl sees with a sword.

The visuals are far more interesting and ambiguous in Welles's film than the language. Adams argues that, in at least a couple of scenes, Welles deliberately "flatten[s] the dialogue [...] rendering it nearly superfluous, so that the visual aspect becomes the primary focus and purveyor of meaning" (146). When K. goes to Titorelli's studio, the words are "spoken so rapidly and flatly that they are all but incomprehensible. Instead, our attention is drawn to the visual codes of film noir, which articulate the ineffable mixture of moods informing this scene" (151). Welles, as a cinematic translator, is not interested in translating Kafka's language to the screen, in fact is deliberately at times making it incomprehensible, but he is interested in transforming that language into his own "movie syntax" that Naremore argues is "as lucid and correct as Kafka's own prose. In *The Trial* it is the *mise-en-scène* which has become irrational" (Naremore 1989: 204–5). When an interviewer asked him if he did not "have any compunction about changing a masterpiece," Welles said no,

> Not at all, because film is quite a different medium. Film should not be a fully illustrated, all talking, all moving version of a printed work, but should be itself, a thing of itself. [...] So no, I have no compunction about changing a book. If you take a serious view of filmmaking, you have to consider that films are not an illustration or an interpretation of a work, but quite as worthwhile as the original (Welles 1962).

"The thing of itself" which is actually in dialogue with Kafka's novel is the style and *mise-en-scène* of the film rather than its linguistic content, which seems overly obvious and overly interpreted. Again, though, on a superficial level, the style of the film also appears quite obvious and even, for the time, passé. Welles chose to film a film noir in black and white after that style's heyday and, since Welles was regarded as a past master of that form, his choice to do so might be seen as "a narcissistic return to his glory days when he helped create a style that would become the signature of his auteur identity" (Adams 2002: 141). Welles's use of the idiom of film noir though seems to be a reflection on it, with "citations" (145) to that idiom, rather than an unquestioning use of it. The film is full of that idiom: the lighting, the *femmes fatales*, the overcoats and trilbies, the fog and smoke, the "dark city" atmosphere (146), the close-ups, and the "Freudian subtext" (152) of the images that might suggest the film is a sexual "psychodrama of a troubled bureaucrat" in which the images are "generated from the subconscious of the central character" (Naremore 1989: 205).

These myriad "allusions to film noir style and idiom suggest that Welles is at least as interested in playing with noir aesthetics as in recreating a classic of world literature" (Adams 2002: 144); Welles is thinking about the meaning of style while implementing it, and, in this way, "this emphasis on style rather than substance is consonant with the worldview both of Kafka and film noir" (144). Style is actually substance; if film noir subverts the "established codes of cinematic realism" (143), then using it in quite a self-reflexive manner established a "cinematic equivalent of that strange blend of nightmare absurdity and theatrical farce" (141) in Kafka's work where "unexpected violations of the conventions of literary realism create the hallmark absurdity" of his texts (143). A good example is K.'s escape from Titorelli's studio, when he runs through a passage made of wood planks which suddenly becomes a brick passage, perhaps a sewer, from which he emerges in front of the Cathedral. Adams argues that "the accelerated montage technique and elliptical editing in this sequence echo the labyrinthine narration of Kafka's novel" (153). The same may be said of K.'s journey through Hastler's labyrinthine house, or the chase up the spiral staircase toward Titorelli's studio (K. being chased by a horde of young girls).

Perhaps even more expressive than these images are the *texture* of the images and the repetition of them: slatted wood, the bricks, files and papers, the 750 Olivetti typewriters in K.'s office, the concrete slabs in the Zagreb high-rise apartments, Hastler's gilded bed, the decay of the Belle Epoque Gare d'Orsay, the decaying bodies of the Court supplicants and, of course, all the doors. These are almost tactile motifs (a tactilism used to a more emphasized effect by Jan Švankmajer, the contemporary Czech surrealist filmmaker, hugely influenced by Kafka). "I do try to keep the screen as rich as possible," Welles said, "because I never forget that the film itself is a dead thing, and for me, at least, the illusion of life fades very quickly when the texture is thin" (217). The visual texture of the film, the thickness of these images and repetitions may be set in dialogue with the texture of Kafka's prose, the recursive images and long sentences and paragraphs, and read as a way of translating the feel of these to the screen (rather than in terms of a literal translation of Kafka's words to Welles's dialogue). This visual texture works with the multiplicity of Welles's own voice, a consistent visual echo alongside a verbal one.

Micheál Mac Liammóir's fury at the teenage Welles stealing the show is consistent with the critical fury at Welles appropriating Kafka's voice for his own ends, but its very audacity and over-determined nature can open up readings of how to translate and adapt the specific and very verbal nature of Kafka's prose to the screen. The ubiquity of Welles's voice and the baroque nature of the visual images do not necessarily drown out or excise Kafka's voice, but can provide fertile avenues for thinking about narration, image, metaphor and meaning in Kafka's work. In other words, a clearly unfaithful version (whatever that may mean) can be as expressive as any form of literal one.

The Castle

Asked by a reviewer whether one of his films anticipated the events of September 11, Michael Haneke answered: "That's why I grew a beard. Because I wanted to be a prophet" (Foundas 2001). Haneke's rare flash of public humor underscores his rejection of didacticism and his move to place the viewer in a position of ethical decision-making, but also the seriousness with which his films are viewed and their lack of humor in general. Haneke's rigorous and hugely unsettling films deliberately instill a sense of "unpleasure" in the viewer, challenging the dominant mode of filmmaking as an escape and an inculcation into a passive culture of commodification and violence. "Haneke feels that audience members must be persuaded – or forced, if necessary – to contribute to a film's meaning themselves and to recognize their complicity in its psychological dynamics" (Brunette 2010: 7).

Haneke is one of the most celebrated contemporary art-film directors, winning the Palme d'Or at Cannes for *Amour* in 2012 and for *Das weiße Band: Eine deutsche Kindergeschichte*/*The White Ribbon* in 2009, the latter of which was also nominated for two Oscars and won the Golden Globe for Best Foreign Language Film in 2010. *The White Ribbon* takes place in a fictitious German village, Eichwald, immediately before the outbreak of World War I; the outbreak of acts of violence in the seemingly strictly moral Protestant community has been read as an investigation into the roots of Nazi violence. Haneke, who grew up in postwar Austria, criticized the propensity of Austrian culture to see itself as a victim of the Nazis rather than as a perpetrator, and Peter Brunette connects the "bitterness" and "the profound, never fully explained unhappiness" of his characters with this history and violence at a more universal level as it is manifested in a contemporary culture of material and ethical entropy (4). Haneke's utterly disturbing 1997 film *Funny Games*, in which a bourgeois family are mentally and physically tortured, then murdered in their country home by two young men – Peter and Paul – who insinuated themselves into the house, considers this material, entropic culture not only through the characters, but also through the viewer "by confronting them directly with their complicity in the cinematic production of desire and illusion" (Wheatley 2009: 78). He plays with the tension between the desire to see the family survive with our desire for violence and suspense, frustrating our need for easy catharsis and making the viewer think about the manipulation of mainstream cinema, the "pleasure-driven conventions [of which] obscure the ethical void at the heart of its narrative structures and forms" (87).

In 1997, the year that *Funny Games* was released, Michael Haneke directed a television film of *Das Schloß*/*The Castle*, starring three of the same actors who starred in *Funny Games*: Ulrich Mühe, Susanne Lothar and Frank Giering (all of whom, incidentally, died tragically young; Mühe and Lothar were married). Haneke does not include *The Castle* in his filmography, saying that he is "very clear about the distinction between a TV version and a movie" (Foundas 2001), but it was released as a Haneke film on DVD in the US in 2007 "only after Haneke's growing reputation made that a financially astute move" (Wheatley 2009: 11). It should be added that Ulrich Mühe is prominently displayed on the back of the DVD and his huge success in Florian Henkel von Donnersmarck's 2006 Oscar-winning film *Das Leben der Anderen/The Lives of Others* also presumably added to the cachet of the film.

Haneke makes the distinction between a film adaptation of a novel (such as his 2001 adaptation of Elfride Jelinek's 1983 *Die Klavierspielerin/The Piano Teacher* as *La Pianiste*) and a television adaptation of a novel. "Films for TV," Haneke argues, "have to be much closer to the book, mainly because the objective of a TV movie that translates literature is to get the audience, after seeing this version, to pick up the book and read it themselves" (Foundas 2001). Haneke firmly rejects *The Castle* as a film worthy of being in his filmography because of its perceived fidelity to the novel; whereas he altered the structure and tone of *The Piano Teacher*, he felt that he "serve[d] audience expectations" with *The Castle*, and thus "TV can never really be any form of art" (Foundas 2009). He "would not have dared to turn *The Castle* into a movie for the big screen; on TV, it's OK, because it has different objectives" (Foundas 2001).

Haneke's *The Castle* is, in a way, remarkably "faithful" to the plot (such as it is) of Kafka's novel. Yet, as his interviewer Scott Foundas points out, it is "a distinctly personal interpretation that remains quite faithful to the events of the source material" (Foundas 2001). Because it was a TV film, Haneke felt he had to be faithful in order to entice viewers to read the book, rather than confronting them, as he does in his "big screen" movies; yet his auteurial style is very evident in the film and elements of this auteurial style are very much in dialogue with Kafka's narrative form and its awareness of and dialogue with Kafka's putative readers. While Haneke feels that his TV movie panders to "audience expectations," his signature use of "black shots" in between scenes, a technique critics see as essential to his ethical cinema (pauses that force the viewer to think), appear all through *The Castle* and are a cinematic engagement with or translation of the profusion of texts and their interpretation in the novel and the constant bringing into view of the act of reading in the novel (just as the act of viewing is brought to the fore in the film). In addition, his disruptive and uncharacteristic use of a narrator opens up the presence of the narrator in the novel.

K. arrives in the village, dressed like a contemporary hiker – woollen hat, anorak, rucksack – and walks into a provincial village bar. The opening title shot is of a pretty, old-fashioned and stylized map of a mountain village that, as the camera pans back, covers the smoky glass of the worn bar door. The actual villagers and the bar inside present a modern but, at the same time, out-of-date picture (Haneke capturing the odd mishmash of styles in places where time does not impinge as forcefully); an old-style radio plays a kind of Bavarian folk tune that is immediately switched off. What K. first sees (shot from his POV) are two black coats and two black homburgs on pegs by the door, that look almost lifelike, a filmic reference to the darker side of his assistants – played with broad comedy – and perhaps to the guards in *The Trial*. The bar stops and everyone looks at K. but he is given a mattress for the night, and there is a believable realism in the stranger/hiker coming into a village pub, his presence being noted and frozen out at the limits of hospitality. As he falls asleep, the screen goes black.

He is woken up (as in the novel) by Schwarzer who phones the Castle; the Castle initially tells him there is no land surveyor but then the phone rings and it tells him that there is. The camera cuts to K. who sneaks a look out from under the covers and the screen goes black again. The next scene opens with K. walking through the snow and meeting the teacher and schoolchildren; the teacher tells him not to speak about the Count and the screen goes black. The next shot is a snowball hitting a window; K. is lost and he is reluctantly invited into Lasemann's house which is almost completely dark inside except for a small window shining light onto Mrs. Brunswick. K. is physically thrown out by Lasemann and Brunswick, who tell him that they have "no need for guests." The screen goes black. The next shot is a head shot of two young, comically hapless looking men, bobbing up and down expectantly like children: they are K.'s new assistants, though they tell him they are also his old assistants and salute him, which, as he thinks about his time in the Army, makes him laugh. The screen goes black.

On the face of it, Haneke takes a straightforward approach, roughly following the events of *The Castle* and the "actors adopt the codes of the most unremarkable realism – which conveys the sense that everything is normal" but, as Jean Cléder writes, "the black screens brutally segment the scenes (violating the rule of classic montage) and insidiously corrode the continuity of the narrative" (Cléder 2007: 508, my translation). The black screens open up "temporal cavities" and disrupt any sense of "cause and effect" (508). The realism in the scenery, the clothes, the acting are juxtaposed with slight diegetic irrealism; but more than this, the short fades to black to function interrogatively. They provide a brief space to consider the mystery in each scene: who is this K.? Why is he surprised that the Castle agrees he is the land surveyor? Why does the schoolteacher speak French? Why can't we see the Castle they talk about? Why is he being physically removed from Lasemann's cottage? Why couldn't we see properly inside the cottage? Who are these assistants? Why do they claim to be the "old assistants" when they clearly aren't? These are questions left unanswered in the novel, leaving the reader to think, and Haneke is attempting to do the same visually in his editing of the film and in the use of his signature black screens. "Only in fragmentation can we tell a story honestly," Haneke said. "Showing the little pieces and the sum of these little pieces opens up a little bit the chance for the spectator to choose and to work with his own experiences (Brunette 2010: 43).

Such fragmentation extends to identity; as Peter Brunette notes, "our experience of other people is incomplete and fragmentary as well" (43). In traditional realist narrative, an omniscient narrator may help us gain some insight into K. and into the workings of the village that might fill in the "temporal" and existential "cavities." In fact, fairly unusually for a Haneke film (*The White Ribbon* is an exception), there is a narrator (voiced by Udo Samel) who does give us some background information about K., so, for instance, when the assistants salute him, the narrator tells us that it reminds K. of being in the Army. However, something odd occurs: the narrator then tells us that K. "laughed" a moment before K. laughs on screen. This subversive use of what feels like an omniscient narrator continues through the film; when K. meets the schoolteacher, he asks him if he knows the Count – "I suppose you know the Count," the teacher answers him: "How should I?" and, before he has finished saying this, the narrator's voice speaks over him, saying "How should I? said the schoolteacher." The narrator then tells us that the schoolchildren go silent, even though this is evident from the film itself. Similarly, later on in the film, as K. invites Olga and Amalia to visit him in the schoolroom, the narrator tells us that K. is inviting them as we can still hear K. doing just that.

In another instance, the narrator tells us something that could easily be portrayed on film but is not. K. telephones the Castle and from "the mouthpiece came a humming, the likes of which K. had never heard on the telephone before. It was as though the humming of countless childlike voices – but it wasn't humming either, it was singing, the singing of the most distant, of the most utterly distant, voices" (Kafka 1998a: 20). In the film, the narrator describes this siren-like humming (which the Chairman uses as proof of the improbability of connecting with the Castle) while we watch K. standing with the phone to his ear. Although we have heard noise from the phone (the emphatic "no!" given to the two assistants when they ask if K. can go to the Castle), now we hear nothing, except what the narrator tells us.

Haneke does two important things here: it is more than possible to sonically convey an odd humming sound that might be ethereal and disturbing but, in many ways, not providing it aurally is more unsettling (the viewer has to decide what the sound sounds like); and second, the music of the sound is tied into the words. Haneke, in giving primacy to Kafka's language, perhaps only does so because (as he says in interviews) this was a TV version rather than a film adaptation. Yet, in doing so, he heightens the disjunction (very much in his auteurial style) between the narrator and K., and between normalcy and mysteriousness in the language of the novel. Similarly, Haneke portrays K. and Frieda's first meeting and sexual encounter in the taproom quite faithfully in diegetic terms – K. hides beneath the counter, Frieda bends down and kisses him while telling the landlord that K. is not there, they fall into each other's arms – but then the narrator comes in and tells us that they rolled around in beer puddles (though there is no visual evidence of this) and, when he starts narrating the passage which describes their love-making, the camera fixes on a door, barely seen in the darkness, with a semicircular window over it, through which the light barely breaks. During the long, fixed shot, he says: "Hours passed there, hours breathing together in a single heartbeat, hours in which K. constantly felt he was lost …," and so on. The murky shot of the door is unremarkable but works in conjunction with the beautiful language that is far less obvious than any clichéd shots of sexual embraces that might not convey the strangeness, the sense of getting lost, other than through purely sexual escape. The length of the shot is indicative, too, of Haneke's style and what Catherine Wheatley identifies as part of his ethical filmmaking; a long take can lead "the spectator to examine the image visually on an aesthetic and intellectual level, rather than to 'scan' the image mentally in order to place it within the context of the narrative [...] the extended duration of the image, coupled with the lack of narrative drive, creates an awareness in the spectator themselves *as a spectator*" (Wheatley 2009: 93, italics in original). She quotes Haneke saying that when "time becomes manifest in a film, it disturbs the spectators who are used to a fast pace"; they first "react with irritation, then they are bored and finally annoyed" (93). This, he argues, is "the classic sequence of the defensive position" but if the viewer is "confronted in picture and sound" then the "contents *once again will become felt*, instead of being merely registered" (93).

There is an affinity here with Kafka's narrative style – the endless sentences and paragraphs, recursive motifs and so on – with perhaps one difference. Of *Funny Games*, which was released the same year as *The Castle*, Haneke said that he wanted to "'rape the viewer into autonomy' by confronting them directly with their complicity in the cinematic production of desire and illusion," which emphasized passivity and the consumption of violence (78). For Haneke, this is a political issue, a cinematic move against the pacifying of the spectator and their complicity in this pacification and relinquishing of personal and moral responsibility (tied into his reaction to Austrian history and Nazism). Kafka, though, pushes the reader from irritation to boredom to annoyance to humor, an extra step not found generally in Haneke's films. Kafka's humor works, to some extent, as a human form of grace, a moment of insight (that can become a mechanism of self-awareness and criticism but in a much more subtle fashion than Haneke's "rape"). An example of a dialogue between the two aesthetics may be seen in K.'s conversation with the Chairman in Haneke's film.

In the novel, the Chairman explicates at almost unbearable length the procedure by which the village and the Castle discussed the possibility of a land surveyor ("Am I boring you?" he cuts in on his own monologue at one point). One might assume that Haneke, here, could employ a long, static take that would convey this unbearable length, but instead he produces a scene that, while quite long in terms of the rest of the film (at around ten minutes), cuts between shots of the Chairman, K., the Chairman's wife Mizzi and the assistants, Artur and Jeremias, so that the scene emphasizes the encounter as much more of a dialogue and also emphasizes and enhances the humor in the scene. In Haneke's film, the Chairman, who is not in bed but in a wheelchair with a towel on his head and mismatched blankets on his lap – visually unimpressive as a superior, but the towel might remind us of Hastler's flannel in Welles's *The Trial* – tells K. immediately that a land surveyor is not needed but decides to tell him the history of the debate and to show him the official document that proves his statement. He asks Mizzi to look for it and the camera pans to the very murky interior of the rundown cottage. "It must be down at the bottom. The bottom!" We can barely see the cupboard, until Mizzi opens the door and all the files fall out and the camera stays on her as the Chairman continues speaking; then saying to her that the file will have "Land Surveyor" on it "underlined in blue." "It's too dark in here," she says, and the camera pans back to the Chairman. Then the assistants ask to come in because "it's too cold" outside and the Chairman tells them they can help with the files; they walk in with an awkward childish style and fall into the files, and we hear them giggle as the Chairman tells K. that he should not be tired of his assistants and that it is significant that he has been assigned them. "Not much thought went into their assignment," says K. with an utterly deadpan face.

As the Chairman continues with the story, we can hear laughing and giggling and rustling; occasionally the camera pans back to the assistants and Mizzi moving the cupboard, lifting it, sifting through the files, although it becomes more apparent that the file is not necessary (as it contains the story the Chairman is actually telling). He says this to Mizzi and asks her to bring the torch and to read Klamm's letter (K.'s proof that he was hired); as she comes back the torchlight wavers here and there on K.'s unresponsive body, but while she reads the letter the camera pans back to the assistants who are shouting "Hura! Hura!" like children and putting the cupboard back on its feet. "Mizzi shares my opinion," the Chairman says, even though we have not seen her read the letter or speak to him (she does, as in the novel, transform the letter into a paper boat). The Chairman offers to "report" to the Castle, but K. declines help, only wanting his "rights." Mizzi wheels the Chairman backward out of the scene; the assistants run to the door and Artur whistles cheekily in impersonation of the wintry wind outside.

The scene opens with Mizzi piling blankets in the space between double casement windows to keep the snow and the cold out, and in some sense this is suggestive of what Haneke does with his adaptation. The master of "emotional glaciation" here adds warmth with the humor that is present but perhaps less pronounced in the novel. While the content of the conversation in the film points to hopelessness – K. remarks on his position as "insoluable" and has a beleagured and downtrodden look, though the Chairman thinks it is not (Klamm's letter offers surety to stay in the village) – the slapstick antics of the assistants break into the endlessness of the Chairman's explanation, and produce exasperation rather than desperation on the part of K. Haneke engages with the filmic aspect of the scene – the comic duo in Kafka's work that has its roots in Yiddish theater and silent film (and the two are connected). They approach the physical manifestation of the Castle's ontology – the endless, messed-up files – with childish joy and humor, as if already aware, before the Chairman says so, that the file is not needed. Haneke provides entertainment here over discomfort.

Compare the assistants in this scene to the duo, Peter and Paul, in *Funny Games* – one of whom (Peter) was played by Frank Giering in the same year as he played Artur. Peter and Paul (Arno Frisch) seem courteous, if odd, when they first arrive at Anna (Susanne Lothar) and Georg's (Ulrich Mühe) but turn out to be murderous psychopaths and cheeky and playful at the same time, comparing themselves (while they hold hostage, torture and murder a family) to Tom and Jerry and Beavis and Butthead. Haneke told the two young men, Giering and Frisch, to act as if they were in a comedy, and the couple who are eventually murdered as if they were in a tragedy; "when you put the two together," he said, "it's horrible because there are no more rules" (Brunette 2010: 65). The cheeriness of the two, the lack of motive, the games, jar horribly with the acts, psychological and physical, they commit. Haneke wanted to make a statement about the consumption and commodification of violence in film, and the audience's complicity in it; he wanted to make, he said, an "anti-Tarantino" film, luring the audience into wanting violence and then making them understand the consequence of that desire for pleasure (Wheatley 2009: 98).

Peter and Paul are a far darker pair than Artur and Jeremias, but both pairs arise from the tradition of the slapstick duo. In the novel, though, there is a slight mysteriousness about that slapstick nature: Jeremias confronts K. and tells him Artur has gone to complain to the Castle that K. "cannot take a joke" (Kafka 1998a: 233). Jeremias has clearly been acting the role of the hapless young assistant, because now, to K., he "seemed older, wearier, more wrinkled, but with a fuller face, even his gait was completely different from the assistants,' which was nimble, as though their joints were electrified; he walked slowly, limping slightly, elegantly infirm" (233). He tells K. that they were employed to "cheer him up a bit" because K. "takes everything very seriously" (234). In the film, Jeremias tells K. that Artur has gone to complain, but the assumption is that it is K.'s violence toward them (throwing them out of the schoolroom), and the reason for their service is not mentioned. Rather than acting out the role, Jeremias remains a young, quite hapless man, a joke himself. Artur and Jeremias are comic relief for the audience rather than a melancholic and perhaps malevolent one for K. (comedy without a modicum of the "grandeur of tragedy" (Kundera 1996: 105)).

Their comedy can lead to obfuscation and Haneke uses the assistants in similar ways to the narrator, especially in connection to physical texts in the film. The camera shows the text of the first Klamm letter, cutting between it and K. and the assistants craning over his two shoulders; with Klamm's second letter we do not see the physical text but both K. and the assistants read out the contents at the same time so that they become somewhat muddled, with the three voices not quite in sync. K. gives Barnabas (André Eisermann) a verbal message to send back to Klamm, and Barnabas repeats it. Again the two assistants also repeat the message so that it comes across somewhat garbled, and turn the serious communication into comedy. It reflects, of course, the miscommunication in the novel and the foregrounding of communication as performance as well as Haneke's auteurial interest in miscommunication: "We talk and talk," he said in an interview, "but we don't communicate" (Brunette 2010: 39) though he "subscribe[s] to the notion that communication is still possible, otherwise I wouldn't be doing this. I cannot make comedies about these subjects," he adds, "so it is true the films are bleak" (6–7). Haneke thinks communication is possible through form, through an insistence that the spectator participate in making meaning, in interpreting images and sound, much as Kafka's texts demand the same of the reader. Here, though, we see one of Haneke's signature themes actually in something of a comedy, or at least a deft excavation of the comedic potential of Kafka's novel.

Part of the audience's work is in developing the characters for themselves. Haneke eschews the portrayal of any psychological background or reasoning for his characters. In *Funny Games*, Paul tells the terrified family that Peter had a terrible childhood, and then laughs and says in fact "he's a spoiled little shit," thus initially appearing to give a standard, expected reason for Peter's violent behavior toward the family and the viewers, but then immediately pulling the rug from under their feet (making us aware of our own rationalizations and perhaps the lazy thinking behind them). "Because their motives are unpredictable," Peter Brunette writes, "they become even more frightening" (60). The mysteriousness behind their behavior, behind them, makes the audience have to work for meaning, and perhaps realize that they might not finally ever understand it. It is not only the antagonists who are somewhat two-dimensional in their psychological background; we get no real insight into the context of the victims either. As with almost every Haneke film, the protagonists are called Georg and Anna (or, in the French-language films, including the recent *Amour*, Georges and Anne), "as if to emphasize a kind of Eisensteinian 'typage' rather than a specificity of individualized character that doesn't really interest him" (11). Haneke's films are not uninterested in individualized characters, but rather demand that the audience participate in imagining those characters, much like Kafka. We do not get any more of K.'s identity than one initial, and only one or two fleeting memories of his past (his wife and child; standing on the wall of the cemetery); as Mark Harman pointed out, Kafka excised other details that may have given a rounder psychological portrait of his protagonist. As a result, the reader does not know why K. is in the village, what his real past is, whether he is lying: the question the characters most ask him, "What do you want?," is something that the readers do too, without much help from the narrator (asking it of K. and of themselves).

The result is a somewhat self-enclosed world with its own rules that become more apparent only in the reading or the viewing of a work; one that may remain, however, as murky as Kafka's and Haneke's interiors. In both cases this is not a result of a kind of playful modernism or postmodernism (as arch as, say, Lars von Trier's *Dogville* – it is perhaps closer to his *The Kingdom*) but an understanding of how the self and communities produce such self-enclosed worlds. In this aspect, Haneke's *The Castle* resembles his 2009 film, *The White Ribbon/Das weiße Band: Eine deutsche Kindergeschichte*. *The White Ribbon* takes place in an unnamed German village, where odd acts of sabotage, torture, kidnapping and murder occur – a result of the children's reactions to the strict (and hypocritical) rules of the adults. This film, too, has a narrator, the schoolteacher who is remembering the events that took place just before World War I, but from the vantage point of a time after World War II. The simmering violence and hypocrisy of this small community is rearticulated, *means* differently, with the hindsight of the rise and fall of the Third Reich. The insularity of the village, its rhythms and rules, speaks to that of *The Castle* – where the villagers are complicit, if not generative, of the modes and rules of behavior. In Kafka's novel K. sees the Castle, but cannot get to it; he sees Klamm once through the peephole in the taproom (though Klamm, according to the other characters, has a protean appearance); in Haneke's *The Castle* we never see either the Castle or Klamm and this solidifies, in a way, their irrelevance to how the village K. walks into works. The notion of personal moral responsibility, so pregnant in all of Haneke's work, permeates the structure Kafka provided; it comes with loaded meaning for an Austrian filmmaker working with the knowledge of World War II.

Haneke is known for the abrupt, unexpected final shots. In some cases – as with *Caché/Hidden* (2005) – the final frame can radically change what viewers have come to assume through the film and unsettle them. Haneke wants his viewers to leave the cinema uncomfortable and challenged, rather than to reaffirm an easy closure or pleasant transit back into a real context. Haneke ends a film that is explicitly about miscommunication – *Code inconnu/Code Unknown* (2000) with a deaf child signing but without subtitles (a circular end to the film which begins in a classroom of deaf children playing charades – but at the beginning their sign-language is subtitled: "Alone?" being the first guess of one of the classmates). For Haneke, realism is just about this: walking in on conversations, on lives, walking out again mid-sentence. It is fiction – literature, films, art – that presents an aestheticized version of this messy, non-omniscient reality. Kafka's unfinished conclusion, mid-sentence, of *The Castle* is thus perfect for Haneke's end. We see K. walking with Gerstäcker through the stinging snow and the screen fades to black mid-sentence. It is, again, the narrator speaking, but this time describing something that is not happening on screen – K. is still journeying toward Gerstäcker's house in the snowstorm, the eternal journey, but, according to the narrator, he has arrived and sees Gerstäcker's mother with her book. She looks up and "she said …." Fade to black.

Amerikas

In his "Introduction" to his new 2012 translation of *Der Verschollene/The Man Who Disappeared*, Ritchie Robertson notes how cinematic the novel is and what a paradox it is that "filmmakers have shown less interest in *The Man Who Disappeared*" [*Amerika*] than in Kafka's other two novels (Roberston 2012a: xxvi). Robertson mentions Jean-Marie Straub and Danièle Huillet's 1984 film version of *Amerika*, *Klassenverhältnisse/Class Relations*, noting rightly its "slow and stiff" movement and how the "sense of space evoked by Kafka's panoramic descriptions is lost" (xxvi). The claustrophobic film is perhaps most interesting in its politicized reading of Kafka's novel (indicated by the title). The undercurrent of social critique exists in the novel, but is not necessarily its heart; however, the rather dour film does enable some engagement with that element of critique, and also its misreading of the novel's comic and cinematic tone allows a consideration of why that tone is important to understanding the novel. "It is surely time," Robertson concludes, "for a director to appreciate Kafka's cinematic effects and retranslate them to the screen" (xxvi–xxvii).

In fact there are two other film versions of *Amerika* that are important and worth considering: Federico Fellini's 1987 mockumentary film about making and not making a film version of *Amerika*, *Intervista/Interview*; and Vladimír Michálek's 1994 Czech film, *Amerika*. Michálek's film focuses on the early part of the novel, especially Karl's time at his Uncle Jakob's, and is a very interesting reconsideration of Kafka in the light of the then recent Velvet Revolution, the end of communism and arrival of capitalism – and, of course, the end of censorship on Kafka's work. Out of all the translations of Kafka's work to screen, Fellini's would seem, at first glance, to be the least faithful; even an attempt not to make an adaptation as Fellini, within the film and meta-filmically, explicitly, fails to make a film version of the novel. Yet there is a fascinating collision of technique and motifs that speaks to the structure and tone of Kafka's novel.

Cine-mendacity

In *Intervista* (1987), Federico Fellini tells a Japanese documentary crew, via an interpreter, about a dream he had just had: his disembodied hands grope around in the dark and, while his body would usually just fly up, "being older, heavier, I had trouble getting off the ground." He does fly up through fog and sees a building which he thinks at first is a prison or a nuclear bomb shelter, but then recognizes as the Italian film studio he loves, Cinecittà. As he tells them this, they are actually standing on the lot at Cinecittà; dawn hasn't broken yet and two cranes extend upward with arc-lights shining at each other. He is there to make a film of Kafka's *Amerika* and, toward the end of *Intervista*, we see him film two scenes from the fragments at the end of the novel: Brunelda's bath-tub scene and the fragment of Karl pushing a concealed Brunelda in a bath chair toward a brothel. But most of *Intervista* is taken up with a day on the set, being followed by the Japanese crew, auditioning, making sets, walking through other filming, and making a second film about Fellini's own past (as he tells the Japanese crew about it), specifically his first visit to Cinecittà as a callow youth to interview a famous actress. He takes a detour to Anita Ekberg's house with Marcello Mastroianni (who is filming a detergent commercial as Mandrake the magician), where Mastroianni and Ekberg watch their most famous scenes from Fellini's seminal *La dolce vita* (on a bedsheet conjured up with Mastroianni's fake wand), filmed over a quarter of a century before. Their aging faces and bodies watching their younger, iconic selves is almost unbearably moving; a trick of light conjuring up their past selves.

Kafka's *Amerika*, Fellini said in an interview, was "a pretext [*pretesto*] to tell what a director's day is like, what his relationship is like with the camera, the crew and the actors" (DVD interview). A pretext, a pretense to talk about film, and *Intervista* has mostly been read as a love letter to Cinecittà, "a manifesto about the craft that goes into actualizing" film, "a summation of Fellini's views on the nature of the cinema itself, on its craft, and on its future" (Bondanella 2002: 146). It was Fellini's penultimate film in a fifty-year movie career that spanned a golden age of European cinema; Fellini's joke to the Japanese documentary crew that he was unable to fly in his dream "being older, heavier" directly references the beginning of *8½* (1963), in which his *alter ego*, Guido (Marcello Mastroianni), is stuck in traffic and flies up, having to be pulled down with a rope tied to his leg. Fellini journeys back to his past and to the past of cinema, aware of the mortality of both. He chooses as his "pretext" a novel of youth, about a teenage boy traveling forward perhaps to his future, perhaps to his death, written as the first long prose piece of a young writer.

Kafka was "one of Fellini's favorite authors" (Bondanella 1992: 206) and his influence may be seen in a film like *8½* which switches consistently from reality to dream and memory, but his influence on *Intervista* has not been commented on, with his novel regarded only as a "pretext" or pretense; "the references to *Amerika* in *Intervista*," Peter Bondanella writes, "exist for the sole purpose of presenting an unmade film" (206). This "unmade film" in *Intervista* is a reference to Guido's unmade sci-fi film in *8½* and the scaffolding for the spaceship is visually referenced at the end of *Intervista* in one of the closing sequences with a row of scaffolding holding cameras and lights over an "American street." However, *Amerika* is an important pre-text for *Intervista*: not only do we see Fellini (as himself) filming a couple of scenes from the novel, but he also engages with motifs and images in the novel, as well as the narrative style of a novel that is so located in cinematic movement and modernity.

Fellini rejected the idea that a filmmaker should adapt literary texts in the normal sense, suggesting that such an approach was "poisonous" (Fellini 1976: 100). Instead, the director "has to identify with the feeling, the atmosphere, and the various characters, as well as with the objects […] I don't believe the author can speak very confidently about what he's done. At the most he can talk about how he did it, about the craft he used to translate it" (DVD interview). Fellini not only shows himself filming two scenes from *Amerika*, but he explores the auditioning process for them. His crew go out on a subway train to look for Bruneldas and the camera fixes on a variety of larger women and the variety of unexpected beauty in their faces (a beauty given by the cinematic gaze); as the train comes into the Cinecittà stop, a poster adorns it in multiple iterations and it is a poster of an utterly symmetrical model's face. In contrast, as two of the women exit the train, one of them pulls the other's Elvis T-shirt down over her corpulent belly warning her that she is messing up his face.

Faces, Fellini writes, are "the human landscape of the film" (Fellini 1976: 104). During auditions he sees

> five or six thousand faces, and it is precisely these faces which suggest to me the behaviour of my characters, their personalities, and even some narrative sections of the film. I look for expressive, characterful faces for my film – faces which immediately say everything by themselves as soon as they appear on the screen (104).

We see interviews with potential Bruneldas (one crying because her "accent is wrong. But you say I play a foreigner"); others rejected because they're not blonde, or angry because they may have to be naked in the bath-tub scene. Various Bruneldas are eventually dressed in identical orange Edwardian dresses and tested in a soft armchair for the bath-tub scene. "You're familiar with the character?" Fellini asks one of them. "You told me before," she says. "A former singer, of ample proportions, overbearing, childish, gluttonous, self-pitying, complaining …" Fellini says. "It's hot," she answers.

"He should have used Ekberg," one the crew mutters. "He didn't ask her," another one answers, but they voice exactly what the viewer was thinking. Having just returned from Anita Ekberg's house, and watched her watching her past self – her past iconic beauty now transformed into a Wagnerian statuesque presence, aged and knowing with a kind of toughened nostalgia – she seems perfect for the role. We realize that Fellini has not just included her in this film as a homage to his own previous work and to the nature of memory and film, but also as a variation on character. What fascinates Fellini about Kafka's Brunelda is her identity as one composed of her former glory – the artifice of the stage clinging to her present reality.

Part of Brunelda's character, in Kafka's novel, is our inability to see her. Karl's first sight of her as he looks up to her balcony is obscured – she is covered by a red parasol.

When he, Delamarche and Robinson wait outside in the corridor for her to let them in, Delamarche has to peek through a keyhole: "I can't quite make her out," he says, "the blinds are drawn" (Kafka 2002a: 150). When the men are allowed in, Brunelda is lying in the dark and Karl cannot fully see her because he "had eyes only for her double-chin"; "why is he staring at me like that?" she asks (151). The bath-tub scene is funny because she is obscured again with undergarments and limbs appearing now and then; in the final fragment (which we watch being filmed in *Intervista*), Brunelda covers herself with "a large grey cloth" (197) as she is wheeled out in the bath chair. At the same time her life has been about spectacle and being seen, the inflation of which is denoted in her huge size and sexuality. Fellini is intent on seeing her from different angles, from the past and from the present.

In another variation of Brunelda earlier on in the film *Intervista*, Fellini recounts – and also shoots – a scene from his own past. As a very young reporter, he travels to Cinecittà to interview a star actress Katia (Paola Liguari). When he enters her trailer, he sees her vaguely through the glass door of a shower (a reference to the later bath-tub scene) and waits for her to come out to the pink-quilted innards of the trailer. He waits with two older men, a comic duo, who are discussing the Kama Sutra and giggling about its names for the genitals: yoni and lingam. Rubini (a young Fellini, played by Sergio Rubini) asks her a couple of facile questions as she is made up for her role in a historical B-movie as a Maharaja: "Write only what I say," she admonishes him, "word for word." Fellini films his own memory (as he tells it to a documentary crew in a film in which it is all a fiction) and connects it to Kafka's Karl, Brunelda and the comic duo (albeit sinister) of Delamarche and Robinson. We pull back and see the wooden outside of the trailer set and Fellini in his director's chair being asked about what kind of Karl he wants. His assistant director later says he "wanted a delicate, spiritual face, yet full of life. Because the star in Kafka's *Amerika* is just a kid."

Karl's adolescent journey is connected to that of Fellini's younger self. Fellini films the tram journey to Cinecittà (from the center of Rome to its outskirts), but instead of showing the journey as if it were real, he shows himself and his crew looking for old trams, looking for the old station and finding it in disrepair, re-creating it in another building. The trams are also created, half open so that the cameras can be mounted on them; we transfer then into a "realistic" version of the journey but the tram passes stereotypical singing peasants (iconicized by the then fascist regime), elephants, Native American warriors, a huge waterfall – all entirely unrealistic in the suburban journey through Rome. "Fellini's re-creation of the distance his younger self travels stretches across not only distance but also the imagination" (Bondanella 2002: 150). Fellini/Rubini sees the world with an innocent wonder, thus, like Karl, de-stabilizing it, questioning what reality is – and finally ending up in a place where the boundaries of reality are both questioned and re-created, in Cinema City/Cinecittà. If Karl sees the Statue of Liberty with a sword and a bridge between New York and Boston, then the suburbs of Rome can have its elephants and Native Americans; Fellini like Kafka questions the borders between imagination, dream and reality, and how we see the world beyond an empirical evidential immediacy.

Rubini is the outsider, the immigrant to this new world of cinema; if Karl's de-stabilizing sight unearths the fictions of modern American reality, Rubini arrives in an obviously fictional world of cine-mendacity. The real Sergio Rubini is filmed being made up and one of the assistants asks him what character he is playing: "Some nice little character" he shrugs as Fellini watches him being transformed into Fellini's younger self. Fellini insists they paint on a pimple to get him into character, to make him feel as embarrassed and vulnerable as Fellini had before the beautiful star. "There's even a young Fellini!" an Italian interviewer notes in the DVD extras, and a grizzled, tired-looking Fellini quips back: "The young Fellini is what you see now" but there's a truth in it; having seen this "little too personal film" it is clear that the young Fellini is carried around in his "older, heavier" version.

Four young Karls are presented to Fellini at the beginning of the film; he had told the Japanese documentary crew that he might be late "if traffic delays me" – a reference to the opening shot of the traffic jam in *8½* but also to the endless traffic in *Amerika* – and reassures them that his assistant director will help them. The next shot is of his A. D. (played by Fellini's actual A. D. Maurizio Mein) talking to them in the morning, explaining that it is "really heroic" to remain an assistant, "something against nature, a man who decides to stay an adolescent forever." His humorous embrace of the anti-heroic state of being the assistant rather than the director is listened to by the Japanese crew, but not translated by their interpreter (who interprets everything Fellini says). Fellini arrives and his A. D. points out a boy beside Fellini's assistant: "Shall I pick out some of these for a test?" he asks and the camera pans along a group of *actual* adolescents. "Giancorso, Alfredo, Antoine," his assistant says, "and a surprise – I bet you can't. ..." The last androgynous "boy" turns around. "He's a girl," Fellini immediately guesses, and the girl introduces herself as "Sophie." "Are you French?" Fellini asks in Italian. "I'm English," she replies in English.

Sophie appears again, in costume as Karl, as Fellini prepares to film the bath-tub scene. "We've looked at dozens of boys for Karl," his A.D. says, as Sophie looks at herself in a stage mirror, flanked by a couple of women in identical Brunelda costumes. The shot pans to another "Karl" in an identical gray suit and pom-pom tie, to whom Sophie goes over, as Maurizio Mein explains that: "We went to schools, special academies, religious institutes. Fellini wanted a delicate, spiritual face, yet full of life." A boy, not in costume, bends down, flirting with Sophie, and she turns to the camera and smiles. "Because the star in Kafka's 'Amerika' is just a kid" Maurizio says as Sophie whispers into the other "Karl"'s ear. Maurizio has to make his decision and asks them to "make the same gestures. When I say get up, you both get up." They stand up. "Okay now. The same gesture, in unison. Fix your pom-poms and adjust your hair. Smile, look at the camera." The two fix their pom-pom ties and muss up their hair, giving half-embarrassed smiles and looking nothing alike. The bath-tub scene (which Fellini is preparing and casting for as the set is being moved around the studio) in Kafka's novel begins with Robinson shouting at Karl to "Get up! Get up!" as the usually laconic Robinson rushes around in order to show Karl how to be a servant. It is a performance for Robinson, he is acting out being a servant to instruct Karl, just as Brunelda's bath-time is a performance, a leftover from her stage career. Here, Maurizio orders "Karl" (both of them) to "get up" to see if they too will fit the bill; it is a meta-reference to the scene that they will play, and commenting on the performative nature of the scene from the novel.

The scene shifts to Fellini (off screen) talking via a megaphone to the various Bruneldas, who are all dressed in similar orange dresses, and getting them positioned on the movie set, Brunelda's boudoir (the viewer looks at the set from the viewpoint of the director; we can see it is a set). He tests a Brunelda and then asks for the "Delamarche pair" to be brought on set; two men with moustaches, one in a dressing-gown, walk on set and the camera pans to "Karl" and "Robinson" on a bundle of sheets watching them; Fellini (still off screen and via the megaphone) asks what the name of the actor playing Robinson is (Cruciani), and then tells him to eat his sardines. He asks for the first Delamarche's name (Carniti) and asks him to smile at Brunelda and the others. "Twirl your moustache," he orders, then asks him to smooth his hair and look at the camera: "A seductive look, the look of a scoundrel." Robinson is gulping down sardines: "I know they're disgusting," Fellini says, "but your character loves sardines." Robinson licks his fingers. As the two Delamarches lead Brunelda to the bath-tub "like a big baby doll" Fellini keeps giving instructions to Robinson: "You go on eating sardines. ... Pour the oil into the palm of your hand. ... Lick your fingers, you really lust for sardines. ... You're insane about sardines! ... Take another one. Bravo! Bravo!"

The whole scene is gestural; although Fellini asks Robinson to "say your line" we cannot hear it, as Fellini guides the actor via megaphone and develops the characters through the broad strokes of vaudevillian gestures. The only dialogue in the scene is Fellini's; "Karl" – the boy who was measured against Sophie – watches it unfold, looking at the unseen Fellini and the unseen viewer, saying nothing. Fellini actively engages with the gestural nature of Kafka's novel; not only Karl's de-stabilized and de-stabilizing sight (his innocent and immigrant viewing of his new habitus), but also Robinson's gnawing hunger and thirst, his constant animal-like ingestion, through the novel, of food and drink. Fellini takes the image of sardines straight from the novel; when Karl and Robinson are forced out on the balcony of Brunelda's apartment, Robinson pulls out "an already opened but still rather full sardine tin spilling oil" (Kafka 2002a: 154), some bread and a perfume bottle:

> which seemed to contain something other than perfume because Robinson pointed it out with particular gusto, and smacked his lips, to Karl. "You see Rossmann," said Robinson, consuming one sardine after another, and from time to time wiping his hands on a woollen cloth that must have been left out on the balcony by Brunelda: "You see, Rossmann, you need to put some food aside like me, if you're not to starve. You know, I'm an outcast. And if you're treated like a dog the whole time, you end up thinking that's what you are" (154).

Robinson explains to Karl how he has been abused by Brunelda and Delamarche, how he was locked out on the balcony and whipped by Delamarche at Brunelda's urging, and Karl cannot understand at all why he would stay (other than because of a strange sexual attraction to Brunelda), nor how this explanation might be an incitement for Karl to become their servant too. Robinson asks him how he thinks he might leave (Karl does not understand that he is imprisoned) as he "chiseled out the soft part of the bread and was carefully dunking it in the oil in the sardine can" (155). He tells him they cannot enter the apartment unless Brunelda and Delamarche ring for them, "keeping his mouth as wide open as he could while eating the oily bread, and catching the oil that dripped from the bread in his other hand, and using it as a reservoir, dunked the rest of the bread in it from time to time" (155).

Robinson is both comic and sinister, an animalized vaudevillian, voracious and pathetic. But, as he recounts to Karl how they met Brunelda, we discover that behind this is a man who is starving and desperate; his loyalty to Brunelda is sealed by a "whole bowl of soup" (157). His actual hunger is connected to a metaphysical and sexual hunger; when he first sees her, he "could have licked her all over. I could have gobbled her up" (157). She is, as it turns out, the divorcee of "a chocolate manufacturer" (158); her money comes from food. By the end of the bath-tub fragment, Karl and Robinson, having procured a breakfast for Brunelda from the leftovers at the apartment house, are accused of having "already breakfasted on the way somewhere" (192); nevertheless, she "fed Karl a handful of crumbs by way of reward" (193). Karl, comically, seems to succumb to Robinson's sexually charged debasement.

Fellini recognizes how central the visual act of eating and slurping is to an understanding of Robinson's character; we see the actor, in a cut-away shot, now caressing Brunelda's shoulders as she lies in the bath (her legs are draped out of the bath onto Delamarche's shoulders): "And you, Cruciani," Fellini shouts through his megaphone, "lick your lips like a greedy dog." He takes the small detail – easily missed in a reading of the novel, but very telling – and constructs the visual character through it. These small details are dotted around his set: Karl lies back on what looks like a bundle of sheets, a visual reference to Kafka's description of him lying down on "many different sorts of curtains [that] had been thrown on to one great heap" from where he looks at Brunelda with "staring eyes" (Kafka 2002a: 152). Earlier in the film, in one of the meta-filmic moments, a man cycles past one of the studios almost completely covered in bandages, and is heckled by a couple of men standing outside who suggest it is the result of his wife's anger, but it also references the slapstick end of "The Robinson Episode" chapter, when Robinson is beaten up by the lift boys and left on the street, "head, face and arms all swathed in bandages" (138) with "unsightly bandages of old rags which the lift-boys had completely swaddled him in, evidently for a lark" (139). Pedestrians rush past him on the sidewalk and "people regularly hurdled athletically over Robinson's body" (139).

Delamarche and Robinson, like Brunelda and Karl, have characters who are variations of them through the rest of the film. When Fellini's camera focuses on the Delamarche, whom he asks to "twirl your moustache," the actor turns to the camera and he seems a younger version of Mandrake the magician – the rakish Marcello Mastroianni dressed in a magician's costume, moustache and slicked-back hair, for the detergent commercial. Mastroianni first appears on a crane that lifts him up to a window of an office, in which Fellini and his crew are examining old black-and-white photos of America and Americans. They see a sheet appear and balloons: "What's going on?" Fellini asks as Mastroianni appears in a fog of dry ice. "Hi there boys!" Mastroianni says. "The usual headaches. ... Run out of money. ... Worse still? Sexual problems? Forget your woes! Mandrake's here! Two taps of his stick and up comes your dick!" He points his wand at them and the crane starts descending. "I'll see you downstairs!" As they walk out, they walk into a commercial being filmed for "Smack" detergent, with a group of women in white leotards and white sheets singing "Rub, rub, rub away dirt" to a bored director. Sergio Rubini is standing there and Fellini asks Mastroianni if he has met him. The aging Mastroianni looks at Rubini skeptically: "The young Fellini? Couldn't I have played him for you?" It is an in-joke, of course, because he already has in 8½, only it was 25 years earlier. He looks appreciatively at a young woman there, Antonella, and asks if she is one of Fellini's girlfriends, but Fellini just nods and turns to her and tells her he's heard she plays "the sax very well. I have an idea for the finale."

In mentioning the "finale" Fellini references the last chapter of *Amerika* and the Theater of Oklahoma, in which Karl is greeted by "the sound of many trumpets" and sees "a hundred women dressed as angels in white cloths" (Kafka 2002a: 203). These "angels" are advertising the Theater's job drive (though Karl feels they put more people off), and here we have – though only four – women in white dancing and singing in another commercial, with a reference to the "sax" and the "finale" evoking those trumpets. Antonella and Sergio turn up later in the bath-tub scene playing the sax and piano and appearing as the sets are moved – first, "Stormy Weather" (which sets the scene for the stormy and rainy "American street" scene) and then "Yes sir, that's my baby" which gets all the Bruneldas dancing a kind of Charleston. Mastroianni, appearing and descending in the crane, also references the novel – when Karl returns the bandaged Robinson to the suburbs, he first sees Delamarche up on Brunelda's balcony, and Delamarche has to come down to save him from the policeman's demands for identification papers.

Fellini steals Mastroianni and Rubini off the set to go for a drive in the country to reunite, unbeknownst to them, Mastroianni and Anita Ekberg. Again, Fellini mixes references to *Amerika*: both Karl's ominous visit to Pollunder's country house, and Karl arriving at Brunelda's apartment. When they arrive at Ekberg's house, the Villa Pandora (having been guided there by a priest on a motorcycle), she will not let them past her gates, just as Delamarche, Robinson and Karl cannot go into Brunelda's apartment when Karl arrives until Brunelda verifies that it is Delamarche outside. Here, Fellini has to identify himself via an intercom at the gates: "It's Federico," he says, "I've brought some friends. Can't you open up?" When they drive in, she comes to greet them as if she has just emerged from the bath-tub, with an orange towel wrapped around her head and an orange bathrobe, her three guard dogs barking around her. "What does she need dogs for?" Mastroianni marvels. "She's stupendous, like a gladiator."

The orange colors identify her, of course, with the auditioning Bruneldas; Mastroianni's flirtation with her and their pairing off, as well as his younger avatar who auditions for Delamarche by twirling his moustache, connects to the two as a variation on Brunelda and Delamarche. Like Brunelda and Delamarche, the two actors are past their glory days, and the humor and vulnerability that Fellini evokes from them plays with notions of age and youth. "Marcello, you are still so handsome!" the excited Ekberg says as she embraces him, then stroking his cheeks she adds: "Where are the scars?" "What scars?" he says, surprised. "Then they lied to me," she says. "I heard you had a minimum of three face-lifts." Mastroianni takes it well: "No, not yet. Still too soon. Maybe when I'm 80." "You're nearly there, my love," Ekberg quips.

The Ekberg "country house" episode is bitter-sweet, a variation itself on Fellini's exploration of film that both halts time and marks it. Mastroianni, as Mandrake the magician, waves his wand, a white sheet appears and some iconic scenes from *La dolce vita* play. Fellini cuts back and forth to the aging, and slightly ravaged, Mastroianni and Ekberg watching their celluloid selves, over a quarter of a century earlier, where they are sharp, defined and iconically beautiful. "There are many questions I'd like to ask," Mastroianni says to the teary-eyed Ekberg. "Do you have any schnapps?" he adds, after a pause. "Fuck you, Marcello," she laughs.

Mastroianni acts rakishly as he asks about the phone immediately upon entering Ekberg's house, telling someone on the other end that he's "at the hospital." "How can you tell so many lies," Ekberg teases. It is a re-enactment of Marcello Rubini's constant search for phones in *La dolce vita*, and his phone call to one of his lovers from the hospital where his girlfriend is recovering from a suicide attempt (the result of his inconstancy). Even being in a country house with a group of people is a reference to the film and the famous orgy scene at the end, when Rubini seems to have chosen to live the life of a hack rather than a writer. Yet, it also references Pollunder's country house in *Amerika* (especially the drive there), and the rakish, slightly sinister resurrection of Marcello Rubini touches on Delamarche.

Fellini's variation here on Brunelda and Delamarche, though, humanizes the characters. Brunelda is ensconced high up in an apartment building, but, as Delamarche remarks, "that has its advantages too. We very rarely go out, I go around in my dressing-gown all day, it's all very cosy. Of course, we're too high to be troubled by visitors'" (Kafka 2002a: 149). Karl wonders where they would get visitors from, this couple and their suspicious set-up. Here, Ekberg remains behind locked gates, barring entry, as if her past and her present should be kept untouched. In *Amerika*, Brunelda the opera singer no longer sings because the "neighbours have stopped her singing," Robinson says, "but no one can stop her from shouting" (164). He adds, "when you're least expecting it … she suddenly sits bolt upright, bangs the sofa with both hands, so that she disappears in a cloud of dust" (164). Ekberg's acting career, based as it was on her statuesque beauty, results in the necessity of her aging self to be behind gates. Fellini opens up the gates, but also allows her to disappear "in a cloud of dust"; that is, through the screen of the past. Mastroianni's Delamarche, too, is humanized, ravaged and heavily made-up as a rake for a soapsuds commercial that promises to "rub, rub, rub away at the dirt."

Doubles and comic duos/trios proliferate; in the car journey to Ekberg's house (referencing Pollunder's and Karl's journey), there are three Fellini's in the back seat: Fellini himself, Sergio Rubini (who plays the young Fellini in *Intervista*) and Mastroianni (who played the young Fellini, as Marcello Rubini, a quarter of a century earlier). Fellini is obscured most of the time by a large plant in the front seat, a present for Ekberg. After Fellini complains about Mastroianni smoking, the latter asks Rubini if he objects. Rubini answers that he does not smoke or drink, and the shocked rake asks him if he at least likes women. Rubini, embarrassed, assents but adds, with unnerving innocence, that "Frankly, what I like best is jerking off." "Good solution," Mastroianni says in English, because, he adds in Italian, it is a creative act, it "stimulates fantasy … and I'd say it develops a novelist's turn of mind." Mastroianni then adds, "My experiences, for example, were like installment novels. Always new characters, who introduced other new ones. 'Meet my sister. This is my cousin. …'" and, as he does so, applies some eye drops to his eyes. He then, suddenly, looks out of the car and we see a shot of an aqueduct: "Where are we going?" he asks, startled.

Mastroianni explicates the structure of the film, in the apparently free-flowing movement between scenes, between films and between past and present, but also the novel – Kafka's novel – and the supposition that this randomness in fact replicates the way life is, rather than a clear linear narrative or trajectory of the kind imposed by traditionally narrative cinema or fiction. The intermittent nature of the tableaux and scenes in *Amerika* is also a function of Karl's immigrant sight, his way of viewing that disrupts American reality. It is a technique that Kafka appropriated from Dickens's "installment novel" *David Copperfield* (and his child's view and innocent interrogation of the adult world). Mastroianni applying the eye drops changes the vista from city to country, from Roman traffic jams to the Roman past.

The trio and duo variation is clear in the scene in which Sergio Rubini is being brought in through the studio to see the star. As he enters, the three Alsatian guard dogs (who were running around when Fellini arrived in present-day Cinecittà at the beginning of the movie; Ekberg also has three guard dogs) run in; when he comes out there are three cleaners sweeping as if they have been metamorphosed. He and the star's assistant stop at the door of one of the sound stages and he sees two stage-hands up on swing stage scaffolds painting an immense blue sky for "a super-colossal production" (six years later Fellini's coffin would be placed under that set for his funeral). Both their backs are to us; "Hey Cesare," one says to the other. "What is it?" "Why don't you go and fuck yourself?" The assistant notes the pimple on Rubini's nose and tells him to use bread and milk to get rid of it. "Hey Cesare," we hear, "I was thinking." "What?" "Why don't you go and fuck yourself?" The assistant starts moving out, and Rubini hesitates. "Hey Cesare," the stage-hand says again. "Uh-huh?" "You know who I ran into, Old Snotty. You know what he said?" "No." Rubini turns to go out. "Why don't you go and fu.…" The juxtaposition of the gorgeous pastoral blue set with the earthy foul-mouthed painters, suspended aloft in the fake sky, interspersed by Rubini's innocent wonder and laughter, presents a lovely revelation not only of the mechanics (and the magic of those mechanics) of film but also of comedy (the repeated phrases and comic timing).

The swing stage scaffolds the painters stand on are themselves visual motifs of the film that speak to the novel. In the film, there are the cranes at the beginning, on which cameras and lights are placed, that allow for the dream sequence of flying over Cinecittà, and the scaffolding that lines the "American street" in one of the final scenes, again for the cameras and the lights. That scene visually references the scaffolding for the spaceship in Guido's putative sci-fi movie in *8½*, but also the profusion of balconies as a motif in *Amerika*. The high-rises of this new world have these liminal additions, both part of the outside world and the inside apartment, that radically alter the view of the denizen.

When he arrives at his uncle's, Karl is warned that some "new arrivals" end up "stand[ing] on the balcony for days on end, staring down into the street like lost sheep" (Kafka 2002a: 29). "Seen from above," the street:

> appeared to be a swirling kaleidoscope of distorted human figures and the roof of vehicles of all kinds [...] penetrated by a mighty light, that was forever being scattered, carried off and eagerly returned by the multitudes of objects, and that seemed so palpable to the confused eye that it was like a sheet of glass spread out over the street that was being continually and violently smashed" (28–9).

The suburbs in which Brunelda lives consist of high-rise apartment blocks with endless balconies. Karl and Robinson are forced out of the apartment to sleep on the balcony, a physical articulation of their being "outcasts." Again, the balcony is a place from which sight and light are confused. Brunelda squeezes Karl against the balcony and forces him to look through her opera glasses at an election rally, but "he could see nothing at all" (169). The rally is full of light, from the "lanterns on long poles" (166) which some in the crowd carry to the "car headlamps with extremely powerful light, which they ran slowly up and down the buildings on either side" and which, though it didn't affect Brunelda's balcony, "on the lower balconies you could see the people whom it brushed hurriedly shielding their eyes with their hands" (167).

Mark Anderson notes "the cinematographic quality of these passages" (Anderson 1992: 119) and "the constantly shifting, discontinuous, self-improvising quality of images," a spectacle that "undermines and deterritorializes this vision of 'America'" (118). Kafka, he argues, engages with the new, shifting medium of film to think about how it might change how and what we see, a new "phenomenological description of the act of seeing" (121). "Image, frame, light, movement" Anderson adds, "are the constitutive ingredients for Kafka's presentation of 'America'" in which nothing is "still or familiar" (121). What Kafka investigates via Karl is something that connects with some central concerns of Fellini the filmmaker: the primacy of light, of investigating the imaginary as a reality – as equal to the "real" world – and the insistent movement of people and things, but not necessarily the camera.

"I believe in light," Fellini writes, "and light is what I use, what my imagination needs" (Fellini 1976: 165). But it is not a "real" light: "My light will never be sunlight," he writes. "I believe in constructing daylight" (165). *Intervista* begins with the headlamps of Fellini's car and ends with two arc lights trained on a studio floor. "And I hear the words of an old producer," Fellini says in voice-over. "What? Without the faintest hope, or ray of sunshine. Give me a ray of sunshine, he would beg, at the end of each film. A ray of sunshine." The hope is film itself, with its man-made illumination that lays bare the sets; the cinema is "a way of interpreting and remaking reality, through fantasy and imagination," Fellini writes, showing how the border between reality and fiction is more porous than accepted (111). For him there is no such thing as "cinéma-vérité" only "cine-mendacity": "A lie is always more interesting than the truth," he said. "Fiction may have a greater truth than everyday obvious reality" (100).

The cranes and arc lights at the beginning of the film allow Fellini to re-create a dream in which he flies over Cinecittà; the studio comes into view as a fog clears, but it is only later in the film that we see it is a scale model, so that Fellini "revealed the artifice of his craft and falsified it, as well" (Bondanella 2002: 147). But just as light and Karl's de-stabilizing sight produces what Anderson calls "'America'" (i.e., an America in inverted commas, a fictionalized America that draws attention to the fictions that create the "real" America), Fellini foregrounds artifice and place. "Will you shoot Kafka's *Amerika* in America?" the Japanese journalist asks, just after his crew is asked to "keep their light out of" the bath-tub scene. In answer, Fellini asks for the studio doors to be opened and Karl wheels Brunelda out of the studio into daylight and into the "American street," a muddy field in Cinecittà lined with scaffolding that holds up cameras and lights. "Test scene," he says, "Karl in the American street pushing Brunelda in the wheelchair towards the whorehouse." "Where's the whorehouse?" someone asks. "How should I know? The atmosphere is good. This is the light I wanted." In some senses he gets to the heart of Kafka's fictional America in this scene, based on a fragment which equally gives no sense of where Kafka is or where he is going, only that he is pushing Brunelda, who is covered with a grey cloth, to "Enterprise No. 25" (Kafka 2002a: 200) in which "the artificial palms [were] only slightly dusty" (201). Kafka's image of America is based on images – photographs – of America, and photographs and photographic sight are central to the novel. Here, in Fellini's "American street," blown-up photographs of Americans from that period are dotted along the street: a rabbi, men in top hats, women in Edwardian dress and a dapper African-American man, elegantly attired in a top hat. Karl, of course, in the final chapter of the book, will rename himself "Negro."

Fellini, like Kafka, has no intention of presenting a real America, but in thinking about fictionality and place and the nature of reality as it is mediated through the imagination and sight (whether human or technological). Fellini chose not to work in America, in Hollywood, but stayed in the "Italian Hollywood," Cinecittà, and *Intervista* is, among other things, a tribute to the studio in the year of its fiftieth anniversary (Bondanella 2002: 143), which, for Fellini, was "not merely a physical place where I work, a place that cannot be exchanged for another place or abolished altogether, but a kind of mental and psychological dwelling-place, the very means of expression for me" (Fellini 1976: 111). The studio holds Fellini's memories and he re-creates through film his introduction to Cinecittà as a journey into the imagination and the power of artifice and fiction. Real places are just as intangible and unreal: Fellini writes about his shock at returning to his hometown Rimini after it was devastated during the war, and his further shock at returning to it when it was rebuilt and thriving; it became an "unknown Rimini" (40). To re-create the Rimini he knew from his youth, he filmed in Ostia; it became "a filmic reconstruction of the town in my memory, into which I can penetrate – how shall I put it? – as a tourist without being involved" (33). The artifice of Cinecittà, the "cine-mendacity," allows him to travel as a tourist to the real, as it is constituted in imagination and memory.

By 1987, Fellini was no tourist to Cinecittà; he had worked there for almost fifty years, but he returns to that initial discovery of the studio in *Intervista* when, Karl-like, he sees this new world for the first time and he does so as a result of a group of people who are also foreigners to this world: the Japanese film crew. They are there to produce a fly-on-the-wall documentary of Fellini's work day. Fellini wants to explain to them why and how he makes films and how his love affair with the movies began, but, though he talks directly to them via a female interpreter, and answers questions, he turns to film and cinematic language to enable them to understand his origins. Like Karl, they are actual foreigners arriving in a new place; in initiating them into this world via Sergio Rubini, another outsider and Fellini's younger self, he tries to convey the haphazard beauty of this world.

"Have you read Kafka's *Amerika*?" Fellini asks two young men who are presented to him as possible candidates for Karl. They laugh nervously. "If all goes well," he says, "you'll have to read it." Fellini had clearly read the novel closely and produces a film that is actually an intricate engagement with the motifs and themes of the novel, as well as its narrative style (which is connected to those motifs and themes). *Amerika* is not simply a hook for Fellini to explore the idea of an unmade film, but is a text that he inter-views. *Intervista* [Interview] is staged around a couple of obvious inter-views: that between the Japanese journalist and Fellini, and Fellini's memory, via his avatar, Sergio Rubini, of his interview with the star, that served as his introducion to Cinecittà. Fellini referred repeatedly to the "little film/filmetto" as "a pleasant chat among friends," meaning his crew, his viewers, but also with his past self and, finally, with Kafka.

Metropolis and the velvet hangover

The ocean liner, in which Karl Rossman travels to America, appears at the beginning of Vladimír Michálek's 1993 film, *Amerika*. At first glance, in a cut-away shot, it seems uncomfortably clear that the ocean liner is a model. It is soon followed by a shot of the ship arriving at the Manhattan skyline, where there is clearly no attempt to pretend this is a real ship arriving at a real harbor; it is deliberately a model arriving at a skyline that is far too futuristic for the 1912 setting and does not even correspond to iconic images of the New York skyline. Once Karl lands in America and is housed at his Uncle Jakob's vast art deco palace, none of the outdoor shots are presented as in any way real. Instead, these huge, sharp-edged buildings are a clear visual reference to Fritz Lang's 1927 film *Metropolis*. The obvious fakeness of the scenery is possibly a result of a limited budget, but the result allows the director to both reference a cinema heritage, and the unreal, invented "Amerika" of Kafka's novel. As one reviewer wrote, "there's no attempt to treat the story realistically, and the film boasts a lovely art-deco-inspired theatrical look with painted skyline backdrops and mattes of overpowering urban landscapes" (Gaydos 1994: 40).

Amerika, Michálek's first feature, was not a huge success, but he became one of the emergent filmmakers of the post-Velvet Revolution period in the Czech Republic, with critically acclaimed and popular films such as *Je třeba zabit Sekal/Sekal Has to Die* (1997) and *Babí léto/Autumn Spring* (2001). The 1990s and 2000s were a quite fertile time in Czech filmmaking, with a mixture of a talented young generation of filmmakers coming of age (Jan Svěrák – who won an Oscar in 1997 for *Kolja*; Saša Gedeon; Jan Hřebejk) and the continuing work of the New Wave generation (those who stayed and those who returned from internal or external exile) such as Jan Němec, Ivan Passer, Vladimír Černý, Jiří Menzel, Věra Chytilová (and, in Hollywood, of course, Miloš Forman) and Jan Švankmajer. However, this period in Czech film, following the fall of communism, was dubbed by Robert Buchar the "sametová kocovina"/"velvet hangover" in a book of that name (2001) because the era following the Velvet Revolution in 1989 was seen as a mixed period due to the sudden marketization of film, the loss of an obvious political theme, and some nostalgia for the golden era of Czech film in the 1960s (that was abruptly attenuated after the Soviet invasion in 1968 and the period of communist normalization). "Now materialism is more materialist than Marxism," Věra Chytilová remarked. "Before, the ideology of propaganda ruled, now the ideology of money rules" (Buchar 2001: 46, my translation).

Chytilová, like Menzel, had been allowed to work after the invasion under conditions of censorship but within a state-subsidized system. In 1993, the main film studio, Barrandov, was privatized (71) and private funding had to be sought to make films. With new freedom to film any story they might want, filmmakers discovered that there were other types of pressures and there was a worry that the mixture of commercial pressures (especially making commercially viable films in a language spoken by only ten million people) and the lack of an overarching subject (as filmmakers had had during the Prague Spring in the 1960s) might provide an entropic atmosphere, especially for young filmmakers. "I take [the new generation] seriously as creators, as artists," the veteran director Antonín Maša said, but "I have the impression though that they have nothing to say" (17, my translation). Filmmakers did have the subject of the last turbulent half century, with some of the most successful films revisiting the communist era (*Kolja*, *Pelíšky*) and World War II (*Musíme si pomohat*, *Tmavomodrý svět*), and Czech literature (Michálek's next film was an adaptation of Jakub Deml's *Zapomenuté světlo* and his 2000 film, *Anděl Exit*, an adaptation co-written with Jáchym Topol of Topol's novel *Anděl*).

Michálek's *Amerika* reflects this period in its adaptation of Kafka's novel – Kafka who, of course, had only newly been un-banned after 1989 (the film acknowledges that it is "inspired by Kafka's *Amerika*" and lists the 1990 edition of Josef Čermák's translation in the titles). The film starred A-list Czech actors: Martin Dejdar (Karl), Oldřich Kaiser (Delamarche), Jiří Lábus (Uncle Jakob and Karl's father) and Pavel Landovský (Robinson), a famous dissident actor (and friend of Václav Havel's) who had recently returned from political exile in Austria. The question of emigration and exile was a central one at this time, as émigrés were returning and families re-calibrating after the large waves of emigration during, before and after the war and following the Soviet invasion in 1968. Karl's emigration to America was, in fact, a timely subject, as was his immersion in the wealthy and hard-hearted capitalist world of his Uncle Jakob; Michálek's film veers between a memory of the totalitarian past and anxiety about the capitalist future.

The majority of the film centers around Karl's relationship with his Uncle Jakob (which only takes up the opening three chapters of the novel), a billionaire businessman who lives in a giant skyscraper, the interiors of which are brutalist art deco, immense open spaces that diminish the few people who inhabit them. The exteriors are all painted, obvious scenery that clearly references *Metropolis* in its expressionist-futurist style. Karl himself made the decision to go to America: the film opens with him being questioned by his father (Jiří Lábus, who also plays Uncle Jakob) and affirming his decision. When he arrives at customs, the guard – a model of communist bureaucrat efficiency tells him he cannot enter, but a gloved hand – that of Uncle Jakob's chauffeur – tells the guard that everything is fine. He arrives at his Uncle's skyscraper and enters a monumental room with a desk and his Uncle Jakob at the end. "I also felt trapped in the old world," his Uncle – identical, of course, to his father – says. He brings him to his new bedroom, another vast space, with a basketball hoop, and filmed through a blue filter, and they move out to the balcony and look out at a vast, stylized set of a futuristic (for the expressionest era) city. "There is nothing but work, work, work," his Uncle tells him at breakfast ("My father says the same," Karl answers. "Not at all," his Uncle retorts).

His Uncle Jakob has hit on a scheme to make even more money; he will set up vast water pumps and sell water to the people. "But it belongs to everyone," Karl says of the water. "It belongs to ones who claim it," his Uncle says. "I'll be able to provide water everywhere," his Uncle adds later. "To give or to sell?" Karl asks innocently, receiving a black look back from his Uncle. Pollunder, Green and Mack are business associates who meet to discuss this new scheme; Karl is put to work in one of the pump rooms; we see him take lunch in front of one of the pistons, a cinematic reference to Chaplin's *Modern Times* (in which the factory owners come up with a scheme to mechanically feed the workers that goes comically awry). Mack promises to introduce Karl to his friends, including his lover, Klara, a vulpine heiress obsessed with music. She invites Karl to a concert where some drummers play; after the concert the musicians thank Karl's Uncle Jakob for his support and ask for another donation – he pulls out his checkbook. Meanwhile, Karl makes a secret assignation with Klara and they meet at a bar, the "Sahara," down in the underbelly of the city, at the docks, where the clientele look like extras from *Cabaret* (an obvious reference to the Weimar period of Lang's film).

Michálek's emphasis on the Uncle Jakob episodes in the novel underscores the element of social critique in Kafka's novel and puts it front and center, also because he puts the novel in dialogue with *Metropolis*, in which the city is divided between the heavenly over-world of Joh Frederson and the privileged sons and the underworld of the workers, the worlds of the brain and the hands that the prophetic Maria wants to join via a mediator, the heart (in the shape of Frederson's son, Freder). In the end (when the evil robot version of Maria is destroyed), the workers do unite with Frederson via the mediation of his son, whereas, of course, in Kafka's novel Karl is unceremoniously dumped by his capitalist Uncle, as he is in Michálek's film, only to be saved (from the murderous hands of Delamarche and Robinson) by the stoker (Jiří Schmitzer).

Given that the film was released four years after the end of communism and in the beginnings of a market economy in and "Westernization" of the Czech Republic, when state entities – including the film studio where the movie was made – were being privatized, the vision of the cabbalistic capitalists selling back to the populace what they already own seems marked and, perhaps, cynically prescient. That the drummers have to play for the wealthy and then immediately ask them for more donations fixes the film's sensibility in this new era of commercialized art. At the same time, although *Metropolis* has attained the status of an art-house film, it was itself a commercial product, "one which was to crown Germany's challenge to Hollywood as an international maker of films" though it nearly bankrupted UFA, the German studio (Gunning 2000: 53). Lang was enthusiastic about the notion of film as a universal language (a possibility in the era of silent movies), and Tom Gunning connects this aesthetic interest with Maria's recounting of the Tower of Babel story "as an allegory for this new universal language of silent cinema" (56). Maria tells the story in order to connect the workers with the boss – the boss who has the vision, the "brain" to see a magnificent Tower (the model of which in the film is based on Pieter Brueghel's painting of the Tower) but does not have the "hands" to do it; all they need, she suggests, is "a mediator" – "the heart." As she recounts the story in front of an exhausted crowd of workers, inspiring hope in them (and in Freder, who is there disguised as a worker), Lang shows images of her story which, however, ends in violence, the slavish workers revolting against their visionary boss, so that the "visual emblems" are not an "inert translation of a verbal moral" but act as "a site for the play of opposed energies," undercutting Maria's idealism (61). *Metropolis* ends – despite the workers' revolt (at the behest of the "machineman" robot of Maria, made by the evil inventor, Rotwang) – with a reconciliation between the boss Frederson, and the workers via the mediation of Freder. "*Everyone* hates this ending," Gunning remarks (78); "this ignorant old-fashioned balderdash!" H. G. Wells sputtered in a contemporary review (Wells 1927).

Neither Kafka, nor Michálek, provide either hubris or reconciliation; in both novel and film, Karl is definitively exiled from the upper echelons of "Amerikan" society. In the novel, the break is unexpected and absurd. But in the film, it follows something of the pattern of Freder's rebellion against his father. As Gunning points out, Freder takes three voyages into the underworld: the first time he sees the Moloch machine; the second time he dresses and works as a worker; and the third time he goes to the catacombs and sees Maria preach about the Tower of Babel (and falls in love with her, her purity and idealism); each "voyage calls into question his father's power" (63). Similarly, in Michálek's film, Karl travels to and works in the factory; he exchanges clothes in the underworld bar, the Sahara, with the stoker; and he ends up, twice, at Tereza's (Kateřina Kozáková) apartment – she is the barwoman at the Sahara, but in her khaki explorer get-up is remarkably pure (and bears some resemblance to Brigitte Helm who played Maria in *Metropolis*). While she does not preach about the Tower, there is a poster in her apartment for the "Oklahoma Theater" clearly influenced by Brueghel's style with some hellish figures at the bottom, but up top, paradisical fields and rivers and a small truck, with a man and a woman, its full beams on. Right at the end of the film, Karl returns to Tereza's apartment and hears trumpet playing from outside; when he enters she is lying on her bed, wearing white and playing a trumpet:

"Angels in Oklahoma have to, don't they?" she says. And the parting shot is of the two of them in the back of a 1930s pick-up heading, in true road movie style, through the empty desert, somewhere.

Michálek embraces the free-spirited beat version of America, while having Karl definitively reject the "Masters of the Universe" version which, in the film, conforms to the oligarchic and panopticon-like communism, from which Czechoslovakia had just emerged. Karl is followed by his Uncle's spy (also a reference to the Thin Man in *Metropolis*) who produces a "quarterly report" on Karl, telling his Uncle, in front of a business meeting, that Karl had consorted with Klara in the Sahara pub, had not gone to riding or banking lessons, and, worst of all, had been "kind to strangers around the harbor." "I thought I could do what I wanted in my free time," Karl protests. "You work for me twenty-four hours a day," his Uncle retorts. H.G. Wells's problem with *Metropolis* lay in its assertion that mechanization would turn workers into "drudges" when he felt it would do quite the opposite: "the efficient industrialism of America has so little need of drudges," he wrote, as an example, "that it has set up the severest barriers against the flooding of the United States by drudge immigration. Ufa knows nothing of such facts" (Wells 1927). But, of course, all Karl finds (in Kafka's novel) is that the "efficient industrialism of America" needs exactly those drudges (the lift boys, the "Negro: technical worker"), just as communism had.

The film, at its end, evinces a Czech romanticism with America – the 1960s being a golden era nostalgically in the Czech Republic and associated with a similar cultural era in the US – but it also evinces a clear-eyed knowledge of the actual emigrant experience embodied in Karl's tumble into the underworld of American society and in the figure of the stoker. In the novel, the stoker appears in the opening chapter (published as a story, "The Stoker") in which Karl discovers an odd camaraderie with the working-class figure, trying to defend his rights, then abandoning him though weeping at the thought. Here, the stoker does not appear until the middle of the film, and then saves Karl twice: first, in providing a place to live, and then bringing him back to the shack when Robinson and Delamarche have beaten Karl up and left him to die. The stoker is a kind of Hrabalian figure: a huge drinker and apparent wastrel who nevertheless is a beacon of humanity compared to the frozen, monumental world of the wealthy capitalists (Schmitzer, in fact, played one of the lead roles in Jiří Menzel's 1980 film version of Bohumil Hrabal's *Postřižiny/Cutting it Short*). His waterside shack is a mess, but is covered in sepia photographs: family photographs, landscapes and the odd pornographic picture. Tereza's apartment is similar, covered in photographs and posters (including the "Oklahoma Theater" poster), in direct contrast to the bare, marble walls of the over-world. These photographs, like the photographs in the novel, connect the immigrants to their past world, portable mementoes of a previous identity (and, as Duttlinger argues, they emblematize the photographic style of the novel's narrative). Apart from the photographs, all the stoker has in the shack is his rabbit, Ferdinand, that he kills and cooks in order to give back Karl his strength at the end of the film. When Karl tells him that he intends to return home (his Uncle had given him some money and a return ticket to Hamburg), the stoker looks wistful when he hears the name of his home city: "I never thought I'd die elsewhere from Hamburg," he says, and collapses, seemingly dead from drink. Karl packs his rucksack and, just before he leaves, he checks to see if the stoker is alive. The stoker moves, and Karl takes out his ticket and leaves it on the table for him. Karl, we find out in the next shot, has chosen to go West with Tereza, but there is a poignancy (perhaps wishful, and in a sometimes deliberately cold film) in the figure of the immigrant for whom the American dream has not worked and who is still inextricably tied to his homeland.

That Karl finds his happy ending (in contrast to the more ambiguous one of the novel) with Tereza at least promises some sense of freedom, albeit perhaps illusory – when he asks Tereza whether the Oklahoma Theater actually exists, she shrugs and replies it would be nice if it did – and kindness in the harsh "Amerikan" world. In the novel, Theresa is also a haven for Karl (they learn English together, and he leaves his suitcase with her – we never see her or it again, but it is an unfinished thread in the narrative), and a clear reference to Dickens. Theresa recounts her mother's story to Karl in all its cruel and Dickensian detail, a story of immigrant failure and destitution. In the film, however, Tereza exudes bohemian independence in her silent kindness behind the bar, her acceptance of all, including Karl, and in her downtown, bare brick wall studio apartment. Her past is encapsulated in the photographs on the walls and her simple (and, like Maria in *Metropolis*, prophetic) dream in the poster of the Oklahoma Theater. Tereza, as opposed to Maria, does not see a universal language being mediated between the workers and the bosses: her dream is one of independence, in going West.

Not all of the characters in the underworld are good: Michálek's Robinson and Delamarche have little of the slapstick element they have in the novel: here they are crooks and murderers, who also turn out to be the two guards in *The Trial* who have stabbed K. Karl drunkenly fights the stoker in the Sahara bar and thinks he has killed him; Robinson offers him sanctuary at Brunelda's apartment, but knowing that Karl is Jakob's nephew and hoping, in fact, to demand a ransom. Brunelda (Libuše Tomanová) goes against type: she is painfully thin and, like Klara, quite vulpine, with overly red lips and slick black hair. When Karl bathes her, she comes on to him, goading him "to find the soap" as it moves around her body, but Delamarche returns (having tried to get money from Jakub and having been attacked by his dogs) and savagely beats Karl up, swearing that Karl will now be his slave because he's "a filthy murderer." Cowed in a corner, Karl listens to Robinson tell a story around the kitchen table, replete with beers, that seems to be a drunken, entertaining tale, told with initial good cheer, but that soon becomes identifiable as the ending of *The Trial*. "Then the two in black took him to a sandpit," Robinson starts:

DELAMARCHE: A quarry. ...
ROBINSON: You're right. ... A quarry in Batrvos. ... He smelled something but he didn't know what. ... And the guys took off his coat and suit and put them on a stone. But the most interesting thing was that he didn't show any resistance. He just. ...
DELAMARCHE: Doe-eyed.
ROBINSON: Then they took out that big knife. ... Who brought it?

DELAMARCHE: I did.

ROBINSON: You gave it to me. I gave I back to you. You were boasting that you'd gut him. You gave it back to me. As we were passing the knife, he reached out for it, as if he wanted to kill himself.

DELAMARCHE: Yeah (laughs and looks at Karl). Come here. ... Come here ... come here ... get a knife out. ... (Karl takes a knife out of the drawer.) Stab yourself! Stab yourself! Stab yourself! Stab! Stab yourself! Stab! Stab!

Karl is holding the knife to his neck but he stops and points it at the screaming Delamarche and then escapes, throwing the knife to the ground. When he gets to the street, he finds himself in a blind alley with Robinson at the end of it. Turning, he sees Delamarche, who knocks him unconscious with a crowbar. Thinking him dead, they walk off. "The stab-yourself game works every time," Robinson says.

The scene is beautifully modulated by Michálek, moving from the bonhomie of Robinson's story, allowing the viewer to connect the story he tells with Kafka's other novel, to a frightening, psychopathic conclusion – the change begins in the small movement from the third person: "Then they took out that big knife. ... Who brought it?" to the first person: "I did." It is a nuanced move from the comic to the horrific that shows the all-too-easy slippage between the two, from being distanced from horrific acts to being part of them.

It reflected reality. "The man waited beside some stone balustrade of the bridge," Eda Kriseová writes:

> and then attacked him. They started to wrestle. He wanted to throw Pavel over the balustrade of the bridge, so Pavel hooked his leg around the balustrade. The man jumped on his leg and broke it. It cracked like a branch, Pavel says. Because the man was pounding Pavel's face with his fists, it was clearly a matter of life or death and he thought he would have to kill the man. He took out a knife he always carried and knocked the man out with the shut knife. Blood spurted out and the body of the State Security man slackened (Kriseová 1993: 166).

Thus Kriseová describes why Pavel Landovský, the famous Czech actor playing Robinson, and giving this rendition of the last scene of *The Trial*, had to go into exile in Austria in 1979 (and not return for the next decade). The dark remnants of the communist regime clearly mark this version of Robinson and Delamarche, since it seemed to make the darker aspects of Kafka's work come true. More frightening, perhaps, is that these two murderers are nascent capitalists too: they want to ransom Karl and, when they discover he has no value, only then does the "stab-yourself game" become worthwhile.

Anxieties about the past and coming social orders permeate the film, that in some ways takes sanctuary in film itself: the only escape is the final scene, an iconic cinema trope of America and its endless desert landscape and highways, and the film is also in constant dialogue with a high watermark of early European cinema. The fictional (cinematic) version of America (also via *Metropolis*'s skyscrapers) references the fictionality (and cinematic scope) of the "Amerika" in Kafka's novel. The influence of silent cinema and slapstick, gestural narrative imprinted itself on the novel; the choice of *Metropolis* as a reference for Michálek's film perhaps makes sense. Adorno, writing to Benjamin, commented that he thought it telling that Kafka's death coincided with the death of silent cinema (Zischler 2003) – three years before *Metropolis* was filmed – because of the affinity between the two. Sound, of course, changed the ascendancy of European cinema because of the more difficult question of translatability (the intertitles of silent film were easy to change and insert); Lang's hopeful "Tower of Babel" scenario, a universal language of cinema, became harder in commercial terms when sound was involved. Lang, of course, because of the rise of Nazism (his ex-wife and co-creator of *Metropolis*, Thea Harbou, became a committed Nazi) left for Hollywood and filmed in English in the commercial capital of film – the "mediator" was not so much the "heart" as physical and linguistic translation.

Michálek, working in a new era of free expression, with material "inspired by" a newly un-banned Prague author, understands – and considers in the film – the relationship between the hand and the brain, the work and the money, because he is a filmmaker working in a minor language that only ten million people speak (thus the potential viewership in the original language is relatively tiny). Market capitalism is not necessarily regarded in the film as innately equated with freedom, but brings with it its own strictures and underbelly. In some ways, Michálek's adaptation of *Amerika* has more in common with Kafka's own conception of the Tower of Babel in his story, "The Great Wall of China." In the ongoing, endless building of a wall full of gaps, apparently intended to keep the unseen northerners out and to protect the unseen emperor (who may be a succession of emperors), who sends messengers who cannot escape the palace, and the unseen, slightly fanciful Beijing, one academic claims that the wall was once the foundation for the Tower of Babel. The narrator is puzzled, since the wall is not round and would not logically be the right shape for the foundations, the "weakness" of which the academic claimed was the "principal" reason the Tower collapsed – not God or human pride. If the Wall was only a "spiritual" foundation, the narrator asks, why build the Wall at all? The "addled minds" obsessed with reasoning about the Wall (and the Tower) were "seeking to rally as much as possible around a single purpose. Human nature, giddy at heart, a thing of flying dust, cannot be fettered; if it fetters itself, it will soon go mad, begin to rattle its chains, and tear to pieces wall, chain, and itself, scattering them to the winds," the narrator thinks (Kafka 2007: 116). The human propensity to fetter itself to one system or another, to inculcate itself into systems of power, to rally around "a single purpose" because it is "a thing of flying dust" is articulated in the film and its metatext, a narrative of escape: emigration, escape from wealth, poverty, servitude, from the Czech past and the Czech future.

Kafka-ish

"I've tried to write nightmares," Kafka says to Dr. Murnau in Steven Soderbergh's *Kafka* (1991) "– and you've built one." Dr. Murnau (Ian Holm) is a mad scientist up at the castle who is "trying to come up with a more efficient person" by lobotomizing and killing people. Meanwhile, he's also torturing anarchists trying to overcome him, including Gabriele Rossman (Therese Russell) and Kafka's friend Eduard Raban. Kafka (Jeremy Irons), viewing a victim trapped in a giant machine in a giant hall with his skull opened to a giant microscope, knows what to do: having at first refused to write propaganda for the anarchists, once he found all of them dead in an attic full of skylights, he decided to come to the castle with a suitcase full of their leaflets. He finds a bomb inside. He throws it.

Kafka was an unmitigated flop.

The *New York Times* complained that the film was only a shallow pastiche, a "Kafka-ish" work written with "the blinding optimism of a sophomore who expects his five-page outline for a novel to win a National Book Award"; it was "Kafka meets Indiana Jones" (Canby 1991). It seemed to be a pastiche of Kafka's work (with characters named after those in different novels and stories – Gabriele Rossman after Karl Rossman in *Amerika*; Eduard Raban after the protagonist of "Wedding Preparations in the Country"; Bürgel after the castle official in *The Castle*; Inspector Grubach after Frau Grubach in *The Trial*, etc.), and a pastiche of older films and film genres (Dr. Murnau after F.W. Murnau, whose Count Orlac from *Nosferatu* is also referenced), especially German Expressionist films and film noir. The "lustfully layered metatext" (Ritzer 2011: 146) seemed to reference Kafka's work and his life in a scatter-shot manner among references to myriad films, from *Metropolis* to *The Wizard of Oz* to *The Third Man* and Welles's *The Trial* in "a postmodern pastiche" in which "Every scene is overlaid by memories about other scenes, from other movies, from other characters, from other worlds" (151).

First reactions to the film sensed it was too willfully clever, too superficial, and too self-aware in its cool postmodern referentiality. *Kafka* was only Soderbergh's second film; he had shot to fame as a film "wunderkind" (Palmer and Sanders 2011: 1) three years earlier with his indie film, *sex, lies, and videotape* (1989). That film won a Palme d'Or at Cannes and was a commercial success. Soderbergh was only 26 when he made it, inviting critical comparison with Orson Welles, who made *Citizen Kane* at the same age. *Kafka* seemed a complete departure in tone and size; it was a big-budget film with big stars such as Jeremy Irons and Alec Guinness, and seemed to contain none of the same putative auteur voice or style of the first film. In retrospect, however, this lack of an overarching auteurial style has become a stamp of Soderbergh's filmmaking. He moves consistently between big Hollywood movies and indie films (making *Bubble*, for instance, after *Ocean's Twelve*, or releasing *The Girlfriend Experience* the same year as *The Informant!*). Jeffrey Adams argues that Soderbergh chose a kind of anti-style, choosing different styles depending on the material in hand, rather than imposing an auteurial voice on every film (Adams 2011); he also argues that Soderbergh very deliberately chose not to do so with *Kafka*, as a rejoinder to Welles's *The Trial*, who, in that film, "exploits every opportunity to seize authorial control, staging a tour-de-force of auteurist adaptation" (Adams 2011). Adams suggests that Soderbergh was in a kind of oedipal struggle with Welles, deliberately seeking out "an earlier ancestry" and revisiting the "early cinematic traditions" of film noir and German expressionism to "veer away" from Welles. In doing so, he "attempts to erase the figure of the autonomous, visionary auteur" (Adams 2011).

Yet Welles's *The Trial* is an "undeniable touchstone for the movie" (Wood and Duncan 2002: 30) and Soderbergh includes clear visual references to Welles's film; for instance, the anarchists' headquarters, the dilapidated state of which is lit by skylights, resembles the then abandoned Gare d'Orsay which Welles used for various shots in *The Trial*. In addition, one of the main filmic intertexts is *The Third Man* (1949), both in theme and style, a film that starred Welles. When Kafka moves through an underground tunnel to get to the castle in *Kafka*, Soderbergh references both *The Trial* (when K is running away from Titorelli) and *The Third Man* (Welles's escape as Harry Lime through Viennese sewers). *Kafka* and *The Third Man* start with a similar premise: the disappearance and apparent death of a friend; Harry Lime's fake death is an attempt to escape being caught for diluting penicillin and selling it on the black market which resonates in Dr. Murnau's medical experimentations in *Kafka*.

The extravagant overdetermination of film references in *Kafka*, paradoxically, gives it depth, as an extended conversation with varieties of film language, a "cinema as cinephilia" (Ritzer 2011: 150), through which the young filmmaker "sought to explore the formal possibilities of film grammar" (Wood and Duncan 2002: 7). This reflexivity and "seemingly endless fascination with the medium itself" in fact, James Wood argues, became one of the signatures of Soderbergh's style (21). The film's insistent referentiality results in "artificial visual images" that, Ivo Ritzer argues, enable the film to "dramatically" depart "from Hollywood's style of illusionist transparency" (Ritzer 2011: 152), thus politicizing the pastiche in questioning "Hollywood's bourgeois realism" (152).

Part of the "artificial" style in the film that challenges any sense of commercial "bourgeois realism" is Soderbergh's decision to use both black and white and color. Most of the film takes place in black and white, a deliberate reference to the eras of German Expressionism and film noir. When Kafka enters the castle, through a filing cabinet, the film suddenly explodes with color; when he leaves, the film returns to black and white. The castle episode – with the mad Dr. Murnau and his giant machine – is the most fantastical and dream-like episode in the film; in making the oneiric part of the narrative in color, Soderbergh reverses "the standard visual coding" of dream (often in black and white, whereas "reality" is in color) "as a counter-cinematic technique" (Adams 2011). In doing so, he returns to the early days of color film – for instance, *The Wizard of Oz* (1939), in which Dorothy's real life in Kansas bookends the film in black and white, whereas her dream of Oz is in vivid Technicolor. At this point, audiences did not "regard color films as displaying a realist aesthetic, but as expressing a sense of magic and fantasy" (Ritzer 2011: 148). The "rubiginous and red-tinted compositions" (148) in the castle scenes are exaggerated and "sensual/sensational" (147) and deliberately not mimetic, thus bringing into question what reality is.

This surprising and knowingly artificial use of color does become something of a signature in Soderbergh's films (think of the color-coding in *Traffic* or, to a lesser extent, in *The Girlfriend Experience*, or the flatness and hardness of color in the *Oceans* franchise). But it is also a visual translation of a formal quality of Kafka's work: the breakdown of strict barriers between the dream and the real, and his constant return to the oneiric quiddity of everyday life. As Jeffrey Adams suggests, the sudden and unexpected use of color in *Kafka* is a means of "transposing a Kafkaesque disruption of viewer expectations" (Adams 2011) – its textual equivalent might be, for instance, Georg Bendemann's walk from his sunlit room (and apparent normalcy) in his apartment to his father's room bathed in darkness (where things start to become uncertain). "Kafka's prose is full of subjunctives," Ritzer writes, "and Soderbergh tries to transfer his verbal phrasing to the screen" (Ritzer 2011: 152); the blatant unreality of the color sequence is one means of doing so.

Kafka enters the castle via the subterranean passage reminiscent of the sewers in *The Trial* and *The Third Man*; it begins in the cemetery and the entrance is shown to him by the stonemason Bizzlebek (Jeroen Krabbe). Bizzlebek, an admirer of Kafka's stories, is a stand-in for Max Brod, something that becomes evident in this scene. He opens up a large gravestone, a cenotaph, and indicates to Kafka that he should get in. "Don't get stuck," he says. "Not a chance," Kafka says, "I'm the thinnest person I know." Kafka starts going down, but he pops back up, and stands half-emerged from the gravestone. It is a visual reference to Federico Fellini's *8½* – a dream sequence in which Guido's parents come back to him and, movingly, he brings his dead father to a grave and he chats with him as his father stands half in it. In the Kafka scene, there is a knowing conversation between Kafka and Bizzlebek. "You appreciate my writing," Kafka says and asks Brod to do him a favor. "Another one?" Bizzlebek quips. "If I don't see you later – go to my house and find my notebooks – and destroy them. All my manuscripts – just burn them. Please." "What an extraordinary request," Bizzlebek says. "It's my last and final one." "Then its authority is in doubt." "A true friend would do it," Kafka says. "Not necessarily," Bizzlebek says. "A *wife* would."

It is a not particularly subtle reference to the real Kafka's request to Brod to burn his papers, a request Brod did not fulfill. But the visuals and the tone are interesting. The half-buried Kafka is talking about his legacy and the shot jokes about how that legacy has been shaped (Bizzlebek is a sculptor as well as a stonemason) and how a half-entombed, half-bodily Kafka might speak to our sense of the iconic "Kafka." One of the main reasons the film was badly received among American reviewers was "the widely-held consensus ... that Soderbergh had reduced a hallowed literary icon to mere cinematic ornamentation for a retro-styled thriller" (Adams 2011). The film was better received in Europe, something Soderbergh ascribes to viewers in Europe being "more open than in the States to the liberties we took; they are less protective of Kafka's image" (Adams 2011). American critics seemed to want a reverent portrayal both of Kafka and of the Kafkaesque (rather than the Kafka-ish). Yet the portrayal of Kafka in the film is not simply a playful and irreverent portrait, but it is also an inquiry into the process of iconicization: "Kafka is already a myth," Oanig Kerguen writes. "He shows in a way the artificiality of the myth 'Kafka' ... Soderbergh uses this evanescent and unreal presence of the author and his work as a lesson in working through the alphabet of the 'Kafkaesque,' while at the same time reading and rewriting the myth and all it evokes" (Kerguen 2007: 490, 496, my translation).

Kafka survives the castle and the film ends with a closing shot of Kafka at his desk framed by a window frame, as Jeremy Irons – who has a passing resemblance to photographs of Kafka – suddenly looks exactly like one of those iconic representations. The film ends as it begins with a voice-over of "Kafka" reading a letter to his father, but it eschews and plays with the wording of Kafka's famous letter to his father which has conditioned so many of the readings of his work.

The scriptwriter, Lem Dobbs, asserts that "Kafka was not a biopic" because of the impossibility, "the awful burden and straightjacket of 'the truth'" that hangs over any writer reproducing the biography of any person (Dobbs 2010). Especially when the truth of Kafka and who he really was is already contested, already to some extent a fiction. Thus, "it is 'Kafka' we see in Kafka; it is not Kafka: it is a virtual character, not the representation of a historical personage" (Ritzer 2011: 155). Film scholars, in reassessing the film, are in agreement that it is "[e]mphatically not a biopic" (Wood and Duncan 2002: 12), a deliberate anti-biopic, with a "postmodernist anti-biography approach to producing a biography of sorts for the Prague-born writer" (Palmer and Sanders 2011: 3). It neither attempts to produce "a straightforward biography of the Czech writer nor an adaptation of his fiction" (Baker 2011: 7), but is instead a performative investigation of "what the word – and by extension the man – Kafka means to us" (Adams 2011).

In being deliberately unfaithful to the iconic image, the film asks how faithful to Kafka that given image is and lays bare the processes that create fictions about him. As Jeffrey Adams argues, "the free adaptation that characterizes Soderbergh's *Kafka* reveals the performative aspect of adaptation" itself; it is a "dialogical analysis which examines how meaning is produced via an intertextual dialectic in which models and their copies mutually define and augment each other" (Adams 2011). The film, at times apparently silly and irreverent in its portrayal of Kafka, might lead the viewer to question why, and why their image of Kafka seems to diverge from it. Adams also argues that there is no reason why Soderbergh's film should "be accepted as true or faithful to Kafka" especially since Kafka's own writing suggests he "was not interested in 'faithful' representations of reality" (Adams 2011). Kafka's de-stabilization of the everyday, in other words, is being honored in some sense by the de-stabilization of the iconic image of Kafka. In any case, the film does seem to question the acts of re-representation, adaptation and the virtue of fidelity.

American reviewers felt that the film did not capture the nightmarish mood of Kafka's work, possibly because of the irreverent, and sometimes easily missed, humor of the script even though the kind of deadpan humor attempted in the film is in the spirit of Kafka's writing. "One fools around with Franz Kafka's lucid prose and dread visions at one's own peril," Vincent Canby wrote in the *New York Times* (Canby 1991), but Kafka's "dread visions" and "nightmarish moods" (Adams 2011) are also absurd and often funny. Even newspaper reports from the filming of Kafka – a news item because Soderbergh was filming in the newly liberated and post-communist Czechoslovakia – pigeon-holed the expected mood of Kafka and his work; it is a "thriller based on the life of a writer whose pessimism and prophecies of motiveless horror and regimentation made him persona non grata for a regime that all too often resembled his terse, nightmarish tales," Ann McIlvoy wrote in the London *Times* (McIlvoy 1990); Steve Kettle in the *Toronto Globe and Mail* wrote that it was a film based on "Kafka's novels, such as *The Trial* and *The Castle*, [that] depict futile searches for salvation in a nightmarish world" (Kettle 1990).

Yet, in some ways, the deadpan humor of both the script and the visuals is the most faithful element of the film; the problem is that critics' and perhaps viewers' expectations were based on a postwar and Cold War image of Kafka and his work. The visual joke of Kafka standing in the grave is underscored by the deadpan humor: he is not afraid of getting stuck because he's "the thinnest person I know." When he asks for a favor, Bizzlebek/Brod is incredulous: "Another one?" The fundaments of the *iconic* biography are consistently treated with irreverence. Bizzlebek/Brod snaps back that "A *wife* would" burn the manuscripts, humorously referencing Kafka's indecision about marriage, his lover Dora Diamant destroying his manuscripts in Berlin, as well as Brod's wifely role. Earlier in the film, Kafka meets Anna (a kind of Felice Bauer figure) who says she visited his parents, assuming he would be there. He tells her that he's moved out and is surprised she is surprised he left the parental home. He says he "wrote repeatedly" that he would. The iconic image of Kafka never leaving home is, of course, not quite true, but he certainly did write about the notion, and Lem Dobbs, in the script, pokes fun at the Kafka of the *Diaries* and *Letters* who often performs his suffering.

Suffering itself is a joke in the film. Kafka is promoted and given two assistants, Ludwig (Keith Allen) and Oskar (Simon McBurney). The two are based on Artur and Jeremias in *The Castle*, but also the two guards, Franz and Willem in *The Trial*. "It's not too bad working here," Ludwig says. "You don't think," Kafka answers, "it's a horrible double life from which there is probably no escape but insanity?" Ludwig and Oskar exchange "perplexed" glances. "No," says Ludwig. The assistants, as in the novels, are a comic duo, albeit tinged with hints of horror. In fact, Dobbs initially wrote the two as "supernatural beings" and envisaged the script as a "Kafkaesque horror tale" in which the assistants were the "raison d'etre" who "lay at the heart of the mystery" and who, at the end of the film, would jump "on the boat to go to 'Amerika'" – a scene that was filmed, but cut. He wanted them to be "memorable monsters" like Frankenstein or Dracula, and, though much of the material was cut, Dobbs asserts that "their casting and performances, are the most faithful to my original script and vision" (Dobbs 2010). But they are comic monsters – insisting that they are identical twins when they look nothing alike – and come complete with visual gags: one of them unspools a paper from his typewriter and it goes straight into the other's typewriter. They morph into Kafka's guards later in the film, however, in order to bring him to the castle and probably death, absurdly walking breast-to-breast almost as one being (just as Kafka describes it in *The Trial*).

Dobbs – who has since worked again with Soderbergh on the quite commercially successful *The Limey* (1999) as well as *Haywire* (2011) – was hugely critical of the final film because of the changes to the script, including the loss of many "biographical scenes" that were "lost from the get-go, which contributes to the overall shallowness of the film and its hero" (Dobbs 2010). This is perhaps a response to the critical failure of the film, but it speaks too to the natural process of filmmaking, and the director's translation of the script to the screen. It also speaks to the unreadiness of critics to counter or accept a serious film that plays with certain iconic figures (though this seems to be changing with B-movie-type films such as *Abraham Lincoln: Vampire Hunter*). Dobbs's concept of a comic horror, foregrounding the assistants, to some extent parlays with Kafka's own interest in minor characters and their centrality to the overall narrative, however fleeting they seem.

Soderbergh's film is by no means perfect, but its critical pigeon-holing as a failed attempt to get to the heart of the real Kafka, as opposed to a deconstruction of the "reel" Kafka, the iconic Kafka that the critics themselves are beholden to, needs to be examined. The critical reluctance opens up questions of what Kafka we expect, want and desire, and why – questions that Soderbergh poses in the film.

Local hero

Franz Kafka's It's a Wonderful Life (1995) was born out of a "slip of the tongue" (Adams 2009). Peter Capaldi, an actor, was somewhat frustrated by a plateau in his career and wanted to write a script, and when his wife, another actor Elaine Collins, referred to Frank Capra's 1946 classic film *It's a Wonderful Life* and called Capra Kafka, Capaldi thought: "There it is right there. That's a gag that we could make into something" (Adams 2009). Capaldi "adored the Monthy Python sketches" and the influence of Python's absurd sketches is evident in the film that went on to win an Oscar for Live Action Short (Millar and Bendoris 1995). It was the first Scottish film to win an Oscar in over thirty years; there was far more interest in the film's Scottish identity following that Oscar win than in the subject itself.

Franz Kafka's It's a Wonderful Life is an elongated sketch about Franz Kafka (Richard E. Grant) trying to write the first sentence of "The Metamorphosis" but keeps getting stuck when it comes to imagining what kind of object Gregor Samsa might transform into. He looks around his gothic garret – a clock? A banana! The color film changes into a sepia-tinted, flickering homage to Georges Méliès's silent films from the very early 1900s, with Gregor Samsa (Crispin Letts) struggling underneath his bedclothes, only to throw them off and find that he is, in fact, a giant banana rolling about the bed.

Kafka is constantly interrupted when he gets to that last word of the opening sentence: "a gigantic …?" by Woland the knifeman (Ken Stott), whose overcoat is stuffed full of knives and who is looking for his friend "Jiminy Cockroach" ("Times are hard," he adds in answer to Kafka's quizzical look); and Miss Cicely (Elaine Collins) and her girls' dancing school downstairs. At one point he his interrupted by a delivery from Max Bunofsky's joke shop – Mrs. Bunofsky (Phyllis Logan) appears with a giant insect costume, but finds it is the wrong address. Still, she asks Kafka if he wants anything from the shop. "No thank you very much," Kafka says. "I don't like jokes," but he takes a balloon animal that he bursts when he closes the door.

The giant insect costume, of course, gives him an idea for his first sentence and, just as he begins to write it down, he squashes a cockroach. Kafka is horrified he has killed the animal and Woland accuses him of murdering his friend Jiminy and pulls out a sharpened knife. He is saved by Miss Cicely and her girls (all in Edwardian dress) who bring him presents: jars tied with bows full of cockroaches and various insects. Mrs Bunofsky arrives with a cockroach in a jar that Woland claims to recognize as Jiminy. "I didn't realize I had so many friends!" Kafka exclaims. "I think perhaps you've just become a little anal," Miss Cicely says. "Please call me F.," Kafka replies. Kafka, Woland, Bunofsky, Miss Cicely and the girls break into a rendition of "Hark the Herald Angels Sing" as snow comes down outside the window. The film ends with a sepia-tinted Gregor, his human face and small cockroach legs ensconced in a pillow, singing "Ah! Sweet Mystery of Life."

That Kafka is helped by his neighbors and they sing a Christmas carol of course nods to Capra's film. It is a deliberately absurd and kitsch end with the lonely, miserable writer in his garret surrounded by neighborly love and saved from death by jars of bugs, prettily presented with pink ribbons. The archetypal happy end is both cloying and dream-like, a desire rather than a reality. It opens up questions about our kitschification of Capra's film, seen as a heartwarming holiday staple, a prevailing view somewhat at odds with the darkness in a film about thwarted ambition, suicide and unchecked capitalism. It challenges our notion of the iconic Kafka, turning his angst into a schmaltzy acceptance of the sweet mystery of life and, in doing so, in presenting an improbably content Kafka also makes us question the improbably discontent Kafka. The film opens with a shot of a gothic castle-type structure that is quite obviously a model, cartoon-like, a "lair" that made Janet Maslin see the film as "more Tim Burton" than Kafka or Capra (Maslin 1995). The cartoonish style of the castle and the cartoonish view of the city from Kafka's garret frames a Kafka that we might suspect is not real either, even if or *because* he seems to conform to all the clichés viewers may have of him: a miserablist; isolated and full of artistic angst in his artistic attic.

The juxtaposition of a writer taken so seriously, with absurd and clearly comic situations – the balloon animal, a giant banana, a knifeman and his cockroach friend, a group of girls dancing "the Kangaroo Hop" jumping up and down like beribboned squirrels – evokes Monty Python and their surreal match-ups between the deadly serious and the absurd (for instance, the Philosophers' soccer game). The Pythonesque surrealism is connected to Kafka's oneiric narratives. When Kafka knocks on Miss Cicely's door to complain about the music her girls are dancing to, she asks him, "Is this a real conversation or an imaginary one?" "An imaginary one," he answers. "Thank goodness!" she says, "It's a wonderful party."

Nevertheless, he follows Miss Cicely in to see an array of delightful young women in costumes designed by Hazel Pethig who Capaldi notes in an interview "had done all the Monty Python TV shows" (Adams 2009). For the "insect head singing" Pethig introduced him to Val Charlton who had worked on special effects for "*Time Bandits* and *Brazil* and stuff like that," i.e. films by the ex-Python Terry Gilliam (Adams 2009). The film was made on a budget of just £30,000 and Capaldi felt it was largely due to Pethig's and Charlton's "ethos, a creativity about them that I felt was very interesting, and one could see it in the *Python* movies" that translated into an imaginative set and visual tone (Adams 2009). "They were interested in being arty," Capaldi said, "trying to make things look good, and in literally hand-making effects. I love people where, at the end of the day, they'll pick up a paintbrush and paint clouds" (Adams 2009).

Capaldi was shocked when *Franz Kafka's It's a Wonderful Life* was nominated for an Oscar; he was "grateful our wee film's gone this far," he said in an interview, but "To be honest, the film is just a pile of gags put together in a way that is, hopefully, a stylish and imaginative way" (Donegan 1995). Capaldi's self-deprecating description of the "wee film" speaks to the influence of the surreal chains of *Python* sketches and Terry Gilliam's aesthetic sensibility but also nudges the slapstick and putative vaudevillian nature of Kafka's writing (think of Robinson rolled up in bandages in *Amerika* and the cop chase that follows, or Klara's ju jitsu on Karl). If Capaldi teases the angst of the tortured artist, turning that angst into giant bananas, kangaroos and insect costumes, so does Kafka, whose narrators display ironic and sly views of their artists: of Josefine, of the Hunger-Artist; of the officer and his machine in the penal colony. Capaldi's humor, like the Pythons', is far more broad and obvious, but its roots are similar to those of Kafka's (certainly in his interest in the broad gestures of Yiddish theater).

The central "gag" in the film revolves around the one thing that readers might associate with Kafka: the insect, cockroach, bug. It is the one emblem that readers might know about before coming to Kafka's writing, or might associate with the name Kafka without having read any of the work – as the *Glasgow Herald* reminded readers (with reference to Capaldi's film: "Frankie Kafka, you might remember, wrote about the bloke who woke up one morning and found he had turned into a giant insect" (Bell 1995). As it is a cultural touchstone, Capaldi can invent a gag about it: everyone has heard about the man turned into the insect. At the same time, in dealing with it humorously, Capaldi also quite seriously questions the accretion of cultural iconicity; we all know the crux of the story, but few are interested in what it may mean, or try to affix an absolutist reading of the insect as a sign – it's the Freudian child, the Jewish "vermin," the disabled body, the animal consciousness, etc. The constantly changing visuals of Gregor as metamorphosed in his bed in the film – giant banana, kangaroo, giant insect, cockroach – de-stabilize the iconic status of the cockroach image and poke fun at the horror of the image, or rather, the perceived horror of the image. The story, of course, is full of humor, not least in Gregor's matter-of-fact reaction to his transformation and the initial simple joy of his new body in which he can cling to the ceiling. As viewers of the film we can feel comfortable that we know the cultural reference, but at the same time the film quite subversively plays with that comfortable knowledge.

While *Kafka* garnered a great deal of publicity once it won an Oscar, there is very little interest in the subsequent reviews and news information, however, about Kafka and his work: the contents of film itself are barely referred to. Some mention the film's [["odd sensibility" and "twisted, surreal" humor, that it is a "surreal, black comedy" (Laing 1995)]]; others dutifully refer to its picture of the "German author" or the "Czech" but, despite (or because of) the Oscar, the narrative is simply about the success of the product. There is an interesting element to the journalistic reaction (there is almost no academic reaction) to the film in that the central narrative about the film's success is connected to its national genesis. "A Scottish Kafka, shunned by the London Film Festival," one headline read, "is in line for an Oscar" (Donegan 1995). The Scottishness of the film is something that is mentioned and considered in almost all of the articles on the Oscar nomination and win.

A central reason for this is that *Kafka* was the first Scottish film to win an Oscar in thirty years – the last one had been *Seawards the Great Ships* (1960), a Scottish documentary that won an Oscar in 1962 – and *Kafka* was funded by the brand-new Tartan Fund, set up by BBC Scotland expressly to promote Scottish film. That *Kafka* won a BAFTA as well as an Oscar, and was among the first two Scottish films nominated for Sundance, was a boost to the new fund and its efforts: "Win or lose," Lawrence Donegan wrote in the *Guardian* just before the Oscars, "Capaldi's success underlines the emergence of a Scottish film industry" (Donegan 1995). In fact, the BAFTA for Kafka led to the BBC increasing the value of the Tartan Fund (Lappin 1994).

There was real pride in Scotland that the film was nominated for an Oscar and the fact that Capaldi would bring a "touch of tartan" to the red carpet (Donegan 1995). In a phone call to Richard E. Grant after hearing the news, Capaldi told Grant that "people are apparently 'going nuts [in Glasgow], as I am the only Scotsman since Sean Connery to be nominated'." "You brilliant bloody bastaaaard!" Grant yelled back (Grant 1995). What was important to the Scottish media was that this was a "purely Scottish film" (Laing 1995), i.e., that it had been written and produced by a Scotsman and contained Scots actors. The success of *Kafka* might bring more of this: "Scotland's hills and cities could be alive to the sound of indigenous film crews rather than the accents of Hollywood or Pinewood on location," *Scotland on Sunday* enthused (Mowe 1994). Alex Salmond, leader of the Scottish National Party and currently Scottish First Minister, noted Capaldi's "remarkable" *Kafka* and suggested it was an example of the "new and exciting films" being developed by the "pioneering Tartan Shorts programme" and the Scottish Film Production Fund, these "brave bodies and individuals trying to encourage film" native to Scotland (Salmond 1994). Salmond, in his article "Invasion of the Body Snatchers," sees it as only a small, bright light in a native industry dominated by Hollywood and the British, and advocates for a national Scottish film industry which should take its cues from small European national industries, such as the Irish one, advocated by then Irish Culture Minister (and now President) Michael D. Higgins. "[W]arn Hollywood," the *Glasgow Herald* announced after Kafka's nomination, that "the Jocks are coming" (Laing 1995).

Once nominated for the Oscar, however, *Kafka* started being identified in the British media as a "British" film. "It doesn't star Hugh Grant and it only cost £30,000 to make," the London *Evening Standard* wrote, "Yet among the British films nominated for an Oscar at next month's award ceremony is a 25-minute surreal comedy about a man who is transformed into an insect" (Delgado 1995). "Now, at last, the British really are coming to Hollywood," cried the *Evening Standard* in another article later that month. "Despite Hugh Grant's failure to get onto the best actor list […] we virtually lead the field for short films, the traditional breeding ground for British film-makers […] two of the five live action short films are British [i.e., including *Kafka*]" (Roberts 1995). The failure of Hugh Grant to be nominated for *Four Weddings and a*

Funeral seems slightly mitigated by the nomination of this British "surreal comedy" with the other Grant which arose out of a "breeding-ground for British film-makers" (Roberts 1995). Philip French, film critic for the *Observer*, rolled his eyes at the fact that "more than one British newspaper concentrated almost exclusively upon the British nominees" for Oscar but "to put in my own chauvinistic oar," he adds:

> I hope the British cinematographer Roger Deakins wins an Oscar for *The Shawshank Redemption* and that Peter Capaldi wins the Best Live Action Short Film for *Franz Kafka's It's a Wonderful Life* which has one of the best titles of all time and gave me more laughs than *Four Weddings and a Funeral* (French 1995).

The interesting national tensions evident from Scottish and English media appropriations of the film reflect the complex apportioning of art to a particular national culture, as well as the importance of art to a definition or expression of such national cultures. Kafka was largely funded by the British Broadcasting Company, albeit through their Tartan Fund, and contained English as well as Scottish actors. In addition, many of those Scottish actors live and work in England because of the anglo-centerism, even London-centerism, of the British culture industry. This includes Capaldi and his wife Elaine Collins (who starred in the film) who live in London, "a city he describes as a difficult place for Scots to break into mainstream work and where a sense of not quite belonging is all pervasive" (*Sunday Times* 1995). Capaldi wrote *Kafka* "in frustration"; he was "chippy about not being English" as he was finding it difficult to find work as a Scottish actor: "I just kept thinking there is no market for me, so I would become this other thing ... a young, English, middle-class man. But that didn't work either, because there's plenty of those" (Gilbert 2011).

When asked what he thought "the impact of the award" would be on the "Scottish film industry" after winning the Oscar, he said, "I would hope it means that there will be greater confidence" in Scotland in terms of filmmaking, but he also posited it as a release from Scottish identity, at least as it was defined in England:

> One of the very, very exciting things I have found here in L.A. is that no one talks to you about being Scottish. Whereas, if you are in London and you are trying to put films together and be a film-maker, there is a kind of unspoken sense that, if you are Scottish, you have something to overcome or else you cannot really do that project (Laing 1995).

Capaldi was offered a Hollywood contract after winning the Oscar (that would fall through) and he felt it was a release from the condescending attitude toward his Scottishness that he found in London. "Here (in LA) they talk to you completely as a film-maker," he said. "No one has once said to me 'What's it like in Scotland' or 'My, what a lovely accent you have.' It is wonderful" (Laing 1995). What seemed to irk Capaldi was an English sense of Scottishness, not Scottishness itself, which was a more complex identity for Capaldi, who is the grandson of an Italian immigrant. Although he "does not make much of his lineage," his first short film, which he wrote and starred in, *Soft Top Hard Shoulder* (1993), centered on a Glaswegian Italian (*Sunday Times* 1995). Capaldi has shot to fame again as an actor, the foul-mouthed (and Scots)

Malcolm Tucker, in a BBC TV (and now Netflix) series *The Thick of It*, written by a fellow Glaswegian of Italian heritage, Armando Iannucci.

Capaldi was heralded as a "local hero" in Scotland after *Kafka*'s success (Millar and Bendoris 1995) – a reference to his first major acting role in the 1983 Hollywood film set in Scotland and starring Burt Lancaster, *Local Hero*. Yet no one focused on how a complex, local and extra-local sense of Scottish identity might be in dialogue with the contents of the film: instead, it was judged quite superficially in terms of being a national product (whether Scottish or, once internationally successful, British). Given Capaldi's candor about the "frustration" of having to become something else, "a young, English, middle-class man" in order to become an actor and his subsequent decision to write this film as a way out of the stasis, the film may be read as an engagement with that frustration, with necessary and multiple metamorphoses, with alienation – but all of this through the lens of humor. Capaldi makes the iconic version of Kafka comical, Pythonesque, but there is also a modicum of self-deprecation here, a consideration of his own ridiculous frustration and perceived suffering. Capaldi's Kafka finds himself saved by a rag-tag community, and the obviously kitsch and exaggerated saccharine end seems to be Capaldi poking fun at a romantic wish for some form of inclusion that may or may not exist, but when it comes, it comes with jars full of creepy-crawlies. Capaldi admitted to the *Telegraph* that he had "a black response to everything"; his interviewer suggests that this "gallows humour" is an "in-built advantage" of "Scotsmen," something with which, she writes, her "friendly interviewee [...] placidly agrees" (Paton 2011). Capaldi seems patient with the stereotyping, but the humor is, finally, a personal response to his own experiences partially defined, ironically and Kafka-ishly, by having national identity forced upon him.

A member of the public, writing in the *Glasgow Herald*, noted that what was being elided in the celebrations for the Tartan Oscar was any celebration of the fact that it was for a *Scottish* film that did not portray the Scots in any stereotypical way. It looked outward and internationally, not obsessed with defining or re-defining what Scottishness was. "Missing, but not missed," Paul Foy wrote, "were the now almost obligatory ex-Barlinnie inmate with a heart of gold; scenes of domestic violence [...] mental abuse added to physical in the form of alcohol or drug abuse [...] down-and-outs who we are supposed to see as being as heroic as characters from ancient mythologies" (Foy 1995). He saw the "surreal comedy" with its "influence from ... alien cultures" mixed with Capaldi's "peculiarly Scottish sense of humour and perspective" was "a positive way forward for Scottish culture" something that could be appreciated at home and beyond "this land of self-stifled potential." He compared Kafka to the work of the cartoonist Bud Neill who drew a cartoon strip that followed the adventures of cowboys in Arizona who spoke in Glaswegian demotic.

Odd as it sounds, in fact the film began life as a kind of cartoon. Richard E. Grant became involved in the project when he found "the whole film storyboarded like a comic book" in Capaldi's study (Grant 1995). After his wife mistook Kafka for Capra, it "trigger[ed] Peter's lightbulbs and started him writing his own version of how *Metamorphosis* might have come about. He accompanied his words with drawings and started to ferret out funding. With each rejection, he literally went back to the drawing-board and sketched in more of what the film would look like" (Grant 1995). Grant's description of Capaldi's process (Capaldi studied at the Glasgow School of Art) is suggestive of Kafka's writing process in the film, a process that is continually changing, interrupted, absurd and necessary.

"As Gregor Samsa awoke from uneasy dreams he found himself transformed in his bed into a gigantic ...."; Richard E. Grant gets to the near-end of that sentence several times in the film, screws up his face on screen, then screws up paper and tosses it to the ground. That famous opening sentence, one of the most famous of the twentieth century, is easily filled in by an audience who, if they know anything, know it's an insect. Thinking back to the point when Kafka might not have known what the metamorphosis was is a starting point for Capaldi in thinking about how non-inevitable art might be, how tentative and searching it is during its genesis. How funny it can be if it fails.

Capaldi was wheeled backstage at the Oscars to face the world's press. "Peter Capaldi just won an Oscar for *Franz Kafka's It's A Wonderful Life*. Are there any questions?" the PR person asked. "And" Capaldi remembered, "it's just, like, tumbleweeds. Not even any British press. Not even the *Edinburgh Chronicle* or anything like that. Nobody wanted to talk to me" (Adams 2009). Almost immediately, however, he was acclaimed in the Scottish and English press on grounds of national pride, rather than on grounds of an aesthetic inquiry that touched on art, film and literature. Forgotten, too, though, even within this narrative of national pride, was that the sentence the film was predicated on, this famous opening line of twentieth-century literature, was Scottish too. Kafka may have struggled to find his "Ungeziefer," but it was a couple from Shetland and Orkney who worked on finding the "insect."

4

Interpreting Kafka

Even our demystifications of Kafka are full of mystery.
Zadie Smith (Smith 2009: 61)

Transreading

In his "Introduction" to Joyce Crick's new translations of Kafka's stories, Ritchie Robertson points to the difficulty of translating particular words in the story, "Josefine the Singer, or The Mouse-People," including the heavily, culturally and historically laden term "Volk" and the description of the activity that the mice *Volk* do: "pfeifen," which "usually translated as 'pipe' or 'whistle', is not the normal word for the squeaking of a mouse" (Robertson 2012b: xxix). Both Robertson, and Crick in her "Note on the Translation," go into some detail about the difficulties of conveying "Volk" and why Crick chose "people" to translate it, "which is suitable enough for the range required by 'Josefine'" and why she, on occasion translated it as "nation" because "it accommodates readings that take into account the nationalisms, Zionist and Czech, which most preoccupied Kafka and his circle" (Crick 2012: xliii). In addition, she notes Kafka's use of the cognates "völkisch" and "Volksgenosse" which she found "were more intractable" and "which both, notoriously entered Nazi discourse." She translates as "national" and "fellow," "renderings," she feels that were "consequently weaker" because of the inability to fully translate all the loaded meanings of the terms (xliii).

Crick's modesty bears a hint of the anxiety that might be felt by readers of translations, that they may be missing all the meanings of a story because of what gets lost in translation, what is both untranslatable and seemingly absolutely germane to an understanding of a text. But her "Note" exemplifies why it is important to face down such anxieties, to problematize them, not simply to understand the contextual meanings – social, historical and linguistic – of the source-language text, but also to understand these difficulties and untranslatable elements as a nexus through which we can begin an interrogative reading of the text.

Central to the story of "Josefine" is the question the narrator keeps asking as to whether she is actually singing or not, whether what she produces is the exact same sound as that which the normal, everyday mice produce. The narrator goes back and forth on whether it is song (*Gesang*) or a whistle/pipe/squeak (*Pfeifen*) that she produces: "Ist es denn berhaupt Gesang? Ist es nicht vielleicht doch nur ein Pfeifen?" (Kafka 1946: 269). We never find out whether she actually produces *Gesang* or *Pfeifen* – we get to decide whether or not she does sing, and whether or not it is even important, whether her performance is as or more important than the sounds she produces. What is often more overlooked is the performance of the narrator, who tries to pin down and describe the sound she makes, and in doing so produces his/her own sound, who makes the text itself sing, or pipe, or whistle, or squeak.

Different translators have chosen different ways of translating "pfeifen": Crick, Malcolm Pasley (Kafka 1992: 221) and the Muirs (Kafka 1971: 129) opt for "piping"; Michael Hofmann for "whistling" (Kafka 2008b: 265) and Stanley Corngold for "squeaking" (Kafka 2007: 95). Corngold adds a footnote to his choice of "squeaking": "The German word translated throughout this story as 'squeaking' is *pfeifen*, which, for human beings, means 'whistling'" (95). Corngold's footnote and Robertson's introduction both alert the reader to a choice having been made by the translator: either, as Robertson and Crick decide, to translate the unusualness of the German term (as applied to mice), or, in Corngold's case, to insist on the normalcy of the sound that the narrator suspects Josefine the mouse is producing. Michael Hofmann, taking the first course, also deliberately applies the sound associated with "human beings" to the mice people. That Kafka was dying as he wrote the story, physically unable to speak because of a tubercular larynx, aware of his own body's "wheezing" (Robertson 2012b: xxxi) and whistling, may account for this human animal "pfeifen."

The diverse translations – and the translator's or editor's address to the possibility of diverse interpretations – of this one word provide gateways to reading the story. Rather than arguing which translation might be closer to Kafka's intent (did he hear whistling or squeaking or piping mice?), in fact a consideration of all these possibilities (a gift that translation gives us) allows us to read or imagine – even better, *to hear* – the story in slightly varied ways. For "Josefine" is a story that, above all, should be heard; a story written by a dying writer condemned to silence, that is not just about music and its relation to the everyday, but is itself a form of textual music, full of intersecting melodies, of which the word "pfeifen" is one. Whether it is translated as piping, or squeaking, or whistling, the repetition of the word is integral to the story's soundscape.

The opening four paragraphs of the story in fact contain four melodies based on four words, moving one to the other: music, song, whistling and nutcracking/Musik, Gesang, Pfeifen, Nüsseknacken (underscored by other repetitions – some excluded due to space considerations here – but we can see below: leben, hören, Kunst, lieben, unsere, nicht, nur, vielleicht, Volk).

Unsere Sängerin heißt Josefine. Wer sie *nicht gehört* hat, kennt *nicht* die Macht des **Gesanges**. Es gibt niemanden, den ihr **Gesang** *nicht* fortreißt, was um so höher zu bewerten ist, als *unser* Geschlecht im ganzen **Musik** *nicht liebt*. Stiller Frieden ist uns die *liebste* **Musik** [...] wie es die **Musik** ist [...] das Verlangen nach dem Glück haben sollten, das von der **Musik** *vielleicht* ausgeht. *Nur* Josefine macht eine Ausnahme; sie *liebt* die **Musik** und weiß sie auch zu vermitteln; sie ist die einzige; mit ihrem Hingang wird die **Musik** – wer weiß wie lange – aus *unserem Leben* verschwinden.

Ich habe oft darüber nachgedacht, wie es sich mit dieser **Musik** eigentlich verhält. Wir sind doch ganz un**musik**alisch; wie kommt es, daß wir Josefinens **Gesang** verstehen [...] die Schönheit dieses **Gesanges** so groß ist [...] müßte man vor diesem **Gesang** zunächst [...] Im vertrauten Kreise gestehen wir einander offen, daß Josefinens **Gesang** als **Gesang** nichts Außerordentliches darstellt.

Ist es denn überhaupt **Gesang**? Trotz *unserer* Un**musik**alität haben wir **Gesang**süberlieferungen; in den alten Zeiten *unseres Volkes* gab es **Gesang** [...] Eine *Ahnung* dessen, was **Gesang** ist, haben wir also, und dieser *Ahnung* nun entspricht Josefinens *Kunst* eigentlich nicht. *Ist es denn überhaupt* **Gesang**? Ist es nicht *vielleicht* doch *nur* ein **Pfeifen**? Und **Pfeifen** allerdings kennen wir alle, es ist die eigentliche *Kunst*fertigkeit *unseres Volkes* [...] Alle **pfeifen** wir, aber freilich denkt niemand daran, das als *Kunst* auszugeben, wir **pfeifen** [...] daß das **Pfeifen** zu *unsern* Eigentümlichkeiten *gehört*. Wenn es also wahr ware, daß Josefine *nicht* **singt**, sondern *nur* **pfeift** und *vielleicht* gar, wie es mir wenigstens scheint, über die Grenzen des *üblichen* **Pfeifens** kaum hinauskommt – ja *vielleicht* reicht ihre Kraft für dieses *übliche* **Pfeifen** nicht einmal ganz hin [...]

Es ist aber eben doch *nicht nur* **Pfeifen**, was sie produziert [...] ein wenig auffallendes **Pfeifen**. Aber steht man vor ihr, ist es doch *nicht nur* ein **Pfeifen** [...] Selbst wenn es *nur unser* tagtägliches **Pfeifen** ware [...] Ein **Nuß** auf **knacken** ist wahrhaftig keine *Kunst*, deshalb wird es auch niemand wagen, ein Publikum zusammenzurufen und vor ihm, uhm es zu unterhalten, **Nüsse knacken**. Tut er es dennoch und gelingt seine Absicht, dann kann es sich eben doch *nicht nur* um bloßes **Nüsseknacken** handeln. Oder es handelt sich um **Nüsseknacken** [...] und daß uns dieser neue **Nußknacker** erst ihr eigentliches Wesen zeigt, wobei es dann für die Wirkung sogar nützlich sein könnte, wenn er etwas weniger tüchtig im **Nüsseknacken** ist als die Mehrzahl von uns (268–71).

Our singer's name is Josefine. No one who has not heard her knows the power of **song**. There is no one who is not enraptured by her **song**, which is all the more remarkable as our people are not overly **music**-loving. The dearest **music** to our ears is peace and quiet [...] something as remote from the rest of our lives as **music** [...] a yearning for the felicity that perhaps is provided by **music**. In all this the only exception is Josefine; she loves **music**, and is capable of transmitting it too; when she is gone, **music** will disappear – perhaps for ever – from our lives.

I have often pondered this matter of **music**. We are completely a**music**al; how is it, then, that we understand Josefine's **song** [...] the beauty of her **song** is such. [...] Among ourselves, we openly admit that Josefine's **song** qua **song** is nothing out of the ordinary.

> Can it even be described as **song** at all? For all our lack of **musi**cal sense, we have a tradition of **song**; in former times our people used to have **song**; our legends tell of it, and some of our old **songs** have been preserved, even though none of us is able to sing them. But we at least have an intimation of what **song** is, and Josefine's art does not really accord with it. Can it be described as **song** at all? Might it not just be a form of **whistling**? And **whistling** is something with which we are all familiar, **whistling** is the true aptitude of our people. [...] We all **whistle**, but it wouldn't occur to any of us to claim it as an art, rather we **whistle** thoughtlessly, without even noticing it, and there are many of us who don't even know that **whistling** is among our characteristics. If it were true, then, that Josefine doesn't **sing**, but merely **whistles**, and perhaps as it appears to me at any rate, barely exceeding the normal limits of **whistling** – yes, perhaps her strength is not sufficient for normal **whistling**. [...]
>
> It isn't just **whistling** that she makes [...] nothing besides a perfectly ordinary **whistling** [...] more than a **whistling**. [...] Even if it is nothing more than our common or garden **whistling**. [...] **Cracking a nut** is really not an art form, and so no one will dare to call an audience together and entertain it by **cracking nuts**. If he does it nevertheless, and does so successfully, then it must be a matter of something more than merely **cracking nuts**. Or is it **cracking nuts** [...] it took this new **nutcracker** to reveal its true nature to us, and it can even help his demonstration if he is a little less proficient at **nutcracking** than the rest of us (Kafka 2008b: 264–6).

The narrator's long rumination on whether Josefine sings or not, and what might represent song or not, and whether her performance is what matters rather than what she utters, turns back on itself, moves from the personal to the collective and back again. We cannot hear Josefine sing or whistle/pipe/squeak, so we cannot decide or judge whether or not she does so, just like the narrator who is re-performing the sound in words – translating music to text but at the same time musicalizing that text. Michael Levine points to a similar effect in another Kafka story, "Forschungen eines Hundes"/"Investigations of a Dog":

> Tellingly, the reader of Kafka's text has no sense of what this ravishing music actually sounds like. Indeed, its incompatibility is such that we know it only through the immediate effect it has on the young dog and, less directly, through the swelling rhythms, anaphoric repetitions, surging clauses, and fanfare-like blasts of the long-winded sentence in which the effects are described. Such a description implies that the music, which had so overwhelmed the narrator in his youth, still remains very much in the ear of the adult, dictating the cadences of his speech, giving shape and measure to his phrases, and uncannily setting the tone of his life-long investigations (Levine 2008: 1054).

The way in which the narrator does this in "Josefine" mimics the recursive nature of rumination, but moves forward at the same time, one melodic word shuttling through the text until it reaches another melodic word. That pfeifen/whistling/piping/

squeaking and Nüsseknacken/nutcracking are all, to some extent, onomatopoeic and enhance the importance of sound and performance here in the story: the translator's choice of whistling/piping/squeaking is, as such, also a choice of euphonic texture.

The narrator's movement from exalted song and music via whistling to nutcracking seems wry and ironic, as he/she imagines how anything might become art as long as it is performed. The audacious suggestion that nutcracking might be put on stage is enacted and put on the stage in the narrator's soundscape – he/she performs the sound in the text. And of course by the 1920s, when the story is written, nutcracking had already been high art for over thirty years via Tchaikovsky's ballet, an adaptation of E. T. A. Hoffmann's story "The Nutcracker and the Mouse King." Hoffmann's story includes a battle between the nutcracker – come to life – and the mouse people, headed by the Mouse King and Mouse Queen, the latter of whom had magically metamorphosed into the Princess who had to be transformed back by a nutcracker. In "Josefine" the mice people are constantly embattled; her concerts are the "scant intervals between battles [where] the people dream" (Kafka 2008b: 275) but "such gatherings have been the object of surprise attack by the enemy, and not a few of us paid for our attendance with our lives" (276). The enemy (in Hoffmann's story, the nutcracker, but unnamed in "Josefine") may have been lured by Josefine "who, perhaps even, by her whistling, showed the enemy where to go" (276).

The sound of nutcracking had also played on Kafka's mind in terms of language, specifically when writing to Milena Jesenská, equating to the sound of the Czech verb *nechápu*/I don't understand:

> A strange word in Czech and even in your mouth it is so severe, so callous, cold-eyed, stingy, and most of all like a nutcracker, pronouncing it requires three consecutive cracks of the jaw or, more exactly, the first syllable makes an attempt at holding the nut, in vain, the second syllable then tears the mouth wide open, the nut now fits inside, where it is finally cracked by the third syllable, can you hear the teeth? (Kafka 1990: 21)

Josefine makes a "demand" that is "rejected" (in paragraphs that repeat these two words) by the mouse folk: she wants to give up work in order to sing. When her demand is rejected, she decides to punish them by curtailing her singing style, specifically her use of coloratura as she sings. The narrator, with deadpan irony, tells us that s/he does not even know what coloratura is and therefore can hear no difference, but, at the same time, the narrator enacts a textual coloratura by repeating the term (this time, of course, coloratura is an Italian term that remains untranslated in the musical lexicon, making it more straightforward lexically and euphonically to translate, from the German "koloratura" to the English "coloratura"). Thus, when the narrator reports Josefine making a diva-like fuss over whether she might curtail her coloratura, s/he presents us with four short sentences that repeat the word in quick succession. "Apparently, she has already acted on this threat," the narrator then says, and "coloratura" is repeated three more times but not in as quick succession, as if it is truly disappearing and the narrator, too, is tapering off in his/her coloratura:

Thus, for instance, a rumor was put about that Josefine would *curtail* her **coloratura** *passages*, if she were not given her way. I don't know anything about **coloratura**. I have never noticed any **coloratura** in her *singing*. But now Josefine wants to *curtail* her **coloratura** *passages*, not cut them entirely, but shorten them. Apparently, she has already acted on this threat, though to my ears there was never any difference from previous renditions. *The people listened* as ever, without saying anything about the **coloratura** *passages*, and their response to Josefine's *demand* remained similarly unchanged. Incidentally, there is something at times very delicate in Josefine's frame and indisputably in her thinking. So, following each performance, as if her decision regarding the **coloratura** *passages* struck her as being too tough on *the people* or too abruptly taken, she has *announced* she would soon *sing* them again in their entirety. But after the next concert, she thought again, and it really was the end for the great **coloratura** *passages*, and they would not be taken up in her repertoire until a *decision* was passed in her favour. Well, *the people disregard* these *announcements* and *decisions* and revised *decisions*, just like an adult *disregards* the chatter of a *child*, in a spirit of mingled benevolence and unconcern (Kafka 2008b: 280).

So wurde zum *Beispiel* das Gerücht verbreitet, Josefine beabsichtige, wenn man ihr *nicht* nachgebe, die **Koloraturen** *zu kürzen*. Ich weiß *nichts* von **Koloraturen**, habe in ihrem *Gesange* niemals etwas von **Koloraturen** bemerkt. Josefine aber will die **Koloraturen** *zu kürzen*, vorläufig *nicht* beseitigen, sondern nur *kürzen*. Sie hat angeblich ihre Drohung wahr gemacht, mir allerdings ist kein Unterschied *gegenüber* ihren früheren *Vorführungen* aufgefallen. Das *Volk* als Ganzes hat *zugehört* wie immer, ohne sich über die **Koloraturen** zu äußern, und auch die Behandlung von Josefinens *Forderung* hat sich *nicht* geändert. Übrigens hat Josefine, wie in ihrer Gestalt, unleugbar auch in ihrem Denken manchmal etwas recht Graziöses. So hat sie zum *Beispiel* nach jener *Vorführung*, so als sei ihr *Entschluß* hinsichtlich der **Koloraturen** *gegenüber* dem *Volk* zu hart oder zu plötzlich gewesen, *erklärt*, *nächstens* werde sie die **Koloraturen** doch wieder vollständig *singen*. Aber nach dem *nächsten* Konzert besann sie sich wieder anders, nun sei es endgültig zu Ende mit den großen **Koloraturen**, und vor einer für Josefine günstigen *Ent*scheidung kämen sie *nicht* wieder. Nun, das *Volk hört über* alle diese *Er*klärungen, *Ent*schlüsse, *Ent*schluß̈änderungen *hinweg*, wie ein *Er*wachsener in Gedanken über das Plaudern eines *Kindes hinweghört*, grundsätzlich wohlwollend, aber unerreichbar (Kafka 1946: 287–8).

Kafka's wryly funny passage, with the diva stamping her foot and using one of her few weapons to curtail her coloratura, that is – at least on the narrator's part – a perfectly useless weapon because no one can hear that coloratura, is beautifully underscored by the music of the passage itself. The tone-deaf narrator both denies and produces coloratura, but in a matter-of-fact, deadpan and ironical manner, divesting the act of its sense of ultimate showmanship, of postured trilling.

Kafka finished the story, his last, in the spring of 1924, just before he received the diagnosis of tuberculosis of the larynx. "I think I began to investigate that animal squeaking at the right time," he told his friend Robert Klopstock, who added, "I didn't have the courage to ask him to let me read it. That same evening he told me that he felt an odd burning in his throat whenever he drank certain beverages, especially fruit juices, and said he was worried that his larynx might also be affected" (Kafka 1978: 495). The diagnosis produced the "most fearful day of disaster," Brod wrote in his diary (Brod 1992: 204).

Kafka died in June. "In the last few weeks," Brod writes,

> he was ordered to speak as little as possible. He used therefore to communicate with us by writing messages on slips of paper, a few of which are in my possession. On one of them he writes, "The story is going to have a new title, 'Josefine the Songstress – or The Mice-Nation.' Sub-titles like this are not very pretty, it is true, but in this case it has perhaps a special meaning" (205–6).

The mice-folk, or mice-nation (depending on how one might translate Volk), articulate themselves via the narrator, who textually sings of Josefine's song or un-song (her whistling, piping, squeaking). The subtitle may have "special meaning" because they are as important in the soundscape as their diva performer Josefine; it may have "special meaning" because language is equated to music and gives Kafka a voice just as he begins to suspect disease in his larynx. Two things are perhaps important: first, Kafka brings up the question of "special meaning" and does not explain what it is; second, he produces a story full of sounds – even though it is just a set of black marks on a page – just before he himself lapses into silence.

Or is that all just too pat, too meaningful? Can we escape Kafka when we discuss his work? Can we learn as much from the translations of Kafka's texts as we can from the "translation" of Kafka's biography?

The death and "translation" of the author

Max Brod's trip to Kafka's deathbed is full of significant detail: "the whole journey," he wrote, "lay under the shadow of death" (207). As he leaves his house he is told that a young man in the apartment below is dying; when he gets on the train, a woman is dressed in mourning clothes and talks of her dead husband; when he gets to the clinic, Dora Diamant, Kafka's lover, "whispered to me that that night an owl had appeared at Franz's window. The bird of death" (208). When they bury Kafka in the Prague suburbs at 4 p.m. on June 11, 1924, they return to the town center and find that the famous Town Hall clock stopped at 4 p.m., "its hands were still pointing to that hour" (209).

The drama of coincidence, Brod's wrestling of it into significance, speaks to his grief, to his urgent need to resurrect his friend. "I came to feel the necessity of bringing my incomparable friend to life in a living work of art [...] as an epic figure," Brod writes about his novel *The Kingdom of Love*. "Above all, I wanted to bring him to life for myself in this new way. So long as I lived in this book, in working at it, he was not dead, he still lived with me" (63–4). Brod repeats this need for resurrection in a biography written in 1937 about a little-known author, quoting extensively from passages in his novel in order to explain who Kafka was and why Kafka's personality was inextricably linked to his work: "admirers of Kafka who know him only from his books," he writes, "have a completely false image of him. They think he must have made a sad, even desperate impression in company too" (39). "The category of sacredness (and not really that of literature)," he writes a few pages later, "is the only right category under which Kafka's life and work can be viewed. By this I do not wish to suggest he was a perfect saint [but] one may pose the thesis that Franz Kafka was on the road to becoming one" (49).

That Kafka's putatively saintly life exemplified the message of his work – its search for ultimate human Truth – becomes ossified when Brod returns to the biography and adds to it in 1947, by which time, he notes, "one can hardly survey the gigantic essay literature that is concerned with Kafka" and which contains "very many absurdities and contradictions" (213). By now, Kafka's art shines with "a pure light" with "its religious depth and power to convert" (213). Kafka longed "for intimate fusion with the pure, the Divine"; "he was wholly striving for the highest ethical pinnacle a man can attain – a pinnacle which in truth scarcely can be attained"; his "efforts were directed toward inner perfection, toward a stainless life" (214). Brod's exasperation with misunderstandings over Kafka's work, with critical emphasis on style over substance, moves him to a sweeping statement: "If humanity would only better understand what had been presented to it in the person and work of Kafka it would undoubtedly be in a quite different position" (213).

Brod, of course, writes this last sentence two years after the end of the war, post-Holocaust. Brod had escaped Prague on the last train out of Nazi-occupied Czechoslovakia "carrying a suitcase stuffed with Kafka's papers" (Batuman 2010); Kafka's three sisters were murdered in concentration camps. If Brod had written his novel and then the biography to bring his friend back to life, in 1947 the stakes were larger. Kafka and Brod had become close friends because of the death of Brod's childhood friend, Max Bäuml. In his biography, Brod has to quote from his novel to elucidate the new intensity of his friendship with Kafka after Bäuml's death: "Will you ... fill his place for me?" the Brod character (Kristof) asks the Kafka character (Garta) with bathetic hesitation (Brod 1992: 65). After Kafka's death, after the Holocaust, the textual Kafka would have to do, would now have to "fill [Kafka's] place for me."

The image of Brod carrying his Copperfield-Rossman "box," his suitcase full of Kafka's papers from Prague to Palestine, is suggestive of religious translation: both the translation of holy relics and the translation of chosen biblical figures and saints to heaven without death. Brod never entirely revealed the contents of the case during his lifetime and presided over the relics of Kafka's manuscripts (as did his executrix, his secretary, and then her daughters), as if they were the remains of his now sainted friend. From the publication of Brod's novel onward, Brod produced what Milan Kundera has called "a veritable artillery attack" (Kundera 1996: 40) of work presenting his image of Kafka and underlining the notion that, to understand the work, it was necessary to understand the man. Due to the initial pre-war meager reaction to Kafka, Kundera argues that Brod "realized that he would have to undertake a real and long war." This meant "presenting it, interpreting it" in prefaces to Kafka's works and in four books of interpretation, including the biography of Kafka. In doing so, he turned Kafka into "*der religiöse Denker*," a saint and a prophet (40).

The emphasis on Kafka's life was underscored by Brod's preferential treatment of Kafka's biography, his letters and aphorisms over his stories and novels (and editing the novels to fit this image), thus setting the tone, in Kundera's eyes, for Kafka criticism. Brod "created Kafkology," Kundera writes (42), a field of study that reduces Kafka to the Kafkaesque, a translated vision of the work balanced on an iconicized picture of the author, whether as a suffering artist, a suffering son, a suffering Jew or all of the above. For Kundera, it all began with *The Kingdom of Love*:

> the whole image of Kafka and the whole posthumous fate of his work were first conceived and laid out in this simpleminded novel, this garbage, this cartoon-novel concoction, which, aesthetically, stands at exactly the opposite pole from Kafka's art (38).

Kundera is not alone; as Elif Batumen writes, the "received image of Brod in Kafka studies is a well-meaning hack who displayed extraordinary prescience, energy and selflessness in the promotion of his more talented friend" but who "understood nothing" of the work (Batumen 2010). "The problem is not solely Brod's flat-footed interpretations of Kafka's work," Zadie Smith writes, "it's his interventions in the text themselves" (Smith 2009: 59). Smith points to Brod's editing of *The Trial* to make it feel "like a journey towards an absent God [...] because Brod placed the God-shaped hole at the end" in deciding to make the "In the Cathedral" chapter the penultimate one. Brod's "common sense" approach completely misunderstood Kafka's "uncommonness" (59). "It is important," Adam Thirlwall writes, "when reading Kafka, not to read him too Brodly" (Smith 2009: 60).

Brod's editorial practices – there were "1,778 unexplained textual variations" between the 1925 and 1935 editions of *Der Proceß* and his revision of "works that Kafka himself had proof-read" (Durrani 2002: 212) – made postwar scholars question Brod's claim of authenticity for the texts; these "editorial failings were magnified in the eyes of those who objected to his religiously coloured interpretations. [...] His views were too prescriptive" (212). The Kafka-shaped hole in Brod's life, his apparent need to translate his melancholia into what Kundera calls a "Saint Garta" iconology, affected how the works were edited, Brod's physical control of the manuscripts (initially denying scholarly access to them), and his paratextual work introducing Kafka – his "veritable artillery attack" on the literary world. Eventually scholars would gain access to the manuscripts and re-edit the works, but Brod's early influence not only constructed this saintly picture of Kafka, translating him into a sanctified realm, but also initiated a metholodology of interpretation that placed the author (or a translated image of the author) at its heart in a period of literary criticism – whether New Criticism, Barthesian structuralism or Foucauldian post-structuralism – that promoted the effacement of the author in coming to any hermeneutical understanding of the text. In some ways, it was a fated meeting between Brod's iconicized Kafka and a textualized notion of authorship.

The curious twilight of humor

Famously, Brod announced Kafka's genius in 1907 in the Berlin weekly *Die Gegenwart*, "thus offering to the public the name of a writer a single line of whose had not been printed at the time" (Brod 1992: 62), listing this unpublished writer alongside Franz Blei, Thomas Mann, Gustav Meyrink and Frank Wedekind. The 24-year-old Kafka, Brod notes, "wrote me a letter full of humor about this 'carnival-like' first appearance before the public [...] 'Very well, so I have had one dance this winter after all,' Franz mocked" (62). Kafka's cheeky skepticism and his indulgence of his friend, who himself dismisses his act as "high spirits" and "a little joke" (62), point to brief glimpses of a more nuanced portrayal and understanding by Brod of his friend in his biography.

When Brod writes that "admirers of Kafka who know him only from his books have a completely false image of him. They think he must have made a sad, even desperate impression in company too" (39), he emphasizes that what is missing from not knowing Kafka leads to a misunderstanding that he was "one of the most amusing of men I ever met" (39–40). Brod continues:

> There was no end to our joking and laughing – he liked a good, hearty laugh, and knew how to make his friends laugh too. [...] The fact that from his books, and above all from his diary, such a totally different, much more depressing, picture may be drawn than when it is corrected and supplemented by the impressions one can add from living with him day by day – that is one of the reasons that persuaded me to write these memoirs. The portrait-from-life of Kafka that remains in the memory of our circle stands alongside his writings, and demands to be taken into account in any final judgment of him (40).

Brod's urgent sense that the "picture" of Kafka the reader might gain "from his books, and above all from his diary" has to be "corrected and supplemented" by a "portrait-from-life" Kafka leads him to write the biography in order to convey Kafka's warmth and humanity and, most especially, both Kafka's humor and how an understanding of that humor might open up the work. Yet each time Brod emphasizes Kafka's humor, and the necessity of understanding that before judging the tone of his work he inevitably connects it to a sacred or sanctified Kafka. His endeavor thus becomes paradoxical: at once, trying to convey Kafka's warmth and humanity and trying to sanctify him as a pure and saintly figure. Thus, Brod argues that Kafka's interest in rightness and truth is:

> Immediately bound up with this interest is a pervading irony. Even in the most gruesome episodes in Kafka's writings (*In the Penal Colony*, "The Whipper" – chapter v of *The Trial*) stand in a curious twilight of humor, an investigator's interest and tender irony. This humor, which is an essential ingredient of Kafka's writing (and of his manner of living), points to the meshes of reality and to the divine existence beyond (49–50).

Brod's lovely turn of phrase, the "curious twilight of humor" in Kafka's work, gets to the heart of it, is its "essential ingredient," that "tender irony" in the work that makes it anything but nihilistic and depressing and hopeless. But the humor cannot rest alone, it cannot just point "to the meshes of reality"; it has to point, in Brod's overarching theological schema, "to the divine existence beyond."

Kafkology: Kafka "translated"

In 1946, Angel Flores published a large edited volume of Kafka criticism called *The Kafka Problem*, containing forty essays of varying lengths, including ones by Albert Camus, W.H. Auden and Max Brod. The first essay is a "biographical note" by Kate Flores "based largely" on Brod's biography (Flores 1963b: 1), which had not yet been translated into and published in English. Kate Flores quotes verbatim at points from Brod's biography, but her portrait of Kafka, condensed into nineteen pages, notably excises any mention of humor. Instead Kafka is presented as "tormented" by his father, living in "meek terror" of his schoolmasters (3), the "hopelessness" of his early writing (3), the "sense of guilt of which he seems to have been always conscious" (4); "Mutilated, suffering human beings stared him in the face every day" at work in the insurance company (6); he saw his writing as "worthless" (8) and his "monotonous, hateful work" at the office was "an almost insuperable obstacle to his writing" (8); having to write at night was "a practice which cost him his health" (8); Felice Bauer "tormented him for five years on the question of marriage" (10); he lived in a "torturing abyss" (10); he "lived more alien than any stranger" (13); like Stifter, he "suffered incurable illness[es]; and each faced a bitter conflict between his art and his profession. Kafka's struggle, however, reached an unparalleled intensity" (15).

Kate Flores distills Brod's Kafka – humorous but toward a vatic and religious end – into a poet of pain and torment, whose personal "struggle" was "unparalleled" in its "intensity," as if he were an *übermensch* of misery and despair. At the same time, several contributors explicitly reject Brod's religious interpretation of Kafka and his work as simplistic and reductive, but maintain a religious reading albeit through Kierkegaard (including Flores herself). The Kierkegaardian – and implied existentialist – move creates a sense of Kafka as a thinker rather than a novelist in his Kierkegaardian path from aesthetics to ethics to the religious, and all the angst that journey might contain. (Kafka did read Kierkegaard but seemed more interested in a biographical similarity – i.e. in their love lives – than in responding novelistically to him (Kafka 1964: 230).) What is important is the subtle distillation of Brod's argument: that knowing Kafka is essential to understanding his work (hence *The Kafka Problem* begins with the "biographical note" and several short memoirs of Kafka), but what is known about him is quickly being shaped to fit into how his work is read and how the world has changed. In his introduction to the book, Angel Flores notes the post-World War II "intensified interest" (Flores 1963b: xi) in Kafka, a writer who was previously "established" but whose reputation was "confined almost entirely to rather snobbish circles" (x). He attributes this to two things: "the revival of interest in Existentialism and Kierkegaard" and the European world of the late 30's and early 40's with its betrayals and concentration camps, its revolting cruelties and indignities [that] bore a remarkable resemblance to the world depicted by Kafka in the opening decades of the century. History seems to have imitated the nightmarish background evoked by the dreamer of Prague. Readers who at almost any other historical period might have dismissed Kafka's works as far-fetched and inconceivable now recognized in them their own familiar world (xi).

Kafka, in other words, was the right writer for the right time. If Brod's grief made him translate Kafka into a somewhat sanctified angel of teleological literature (somewhat sanctified because he still admitted the "twilight of humor" in the work), early postwar criticism served to translate him, from a collective grief, into a darker angel of eschatological literature (albeit with what Albert Camus, in Flores's collection, called the hope of absurdity).

This, before all of Kafka's work had been translated into English and digested in itself by an Anglo-American readership.

The Kafka Problem was reviewed by the *New York Times* in December 1946, and the reviewer, Richard Plant, notes the paradox of the publication of this large volume of Kafka scholarship being published "before the general public has had a chance to study extensively the works with which they deal" but hopes that "perhaps" the "contributors' efforts will help to bring Franz Kafka the American public he deserves." He ends his review skeptical that the critical works might help bring Kafka to the American public, placing his faith rather in its contemporary relevance to the immediate post-World War II context. "Our age, so it appears, is no longer so remote from the precisely controlled nightmares of this poet from Prague. His stories of punishment in search of a crime seem to correspond more and more to the deep anxiety into which our world has thrown us" (Plant 1946).

To emphasize the point, there is a line drawing of Kafka at the center of the review – before the iconic images of Kafka were staple – that shows a brutish squiggle of a man, square-jawed, jutting forehead, bulbous nose, Cold War eyebrows, a shock of Beckettian hair, and a mouth open in despair at an untouched wine glass and its shadow. If Hermann Kafka had dated Brunelda, it may have looked like *this* Franz. The drawing (printed in *The Kafka Problem*) is *by* Kafka not *of* Kafka but the assumption that it is a self-portrait reflects "the deep anxiety into which our world has thrown us," providing an identikit of an artist under the thumb of totalitarianism. Still, it is actually a refreshing change from the iconic image of Kafka, seemingly emaciated, hollow-cheeked and down at the mouth, the "brooding face of Kafka [that] has become the icon of the K.-myth" (Hawes 2008: 5). This iconic photo of Kafka, taken shortly before his death, was retouched by the German publishers, Fischer, in the 1950s "to give Kafka's eyes the desired gleam" of prophecy (5).

Saint Garta

"To hell with Saint Garta!" Milan Kundera declares (Kundera 1996: 53), attacking Max Brod for turning Kafka into the saint, Richard Garta, in Brod's novel, *The Kingdom of Love*. "The words 'saint,' 'saintly,' 'mythological,' 'purity,' are not a matter of rhetoric [in the novel]; they are to be taken literally" (39). Kundera blames Brod's portrait for the "widely held" vision of Kafka today (37); a Kafka who is "the patron saint of the neurotic, the depressive, the anorexic, the feeble; the patron saint of the twisted, the *précieuses ridicules*, and the hysterical" (45). What Kundera leaves out in his list is the seemingly paradoxical positioning by Brod of Kafka as a Jewish saint. Even before Kafka's death, Brod compared him to an angel in a 1921 *Neue Rundschau* article, an angel who "writes, alongside the general tragedy of mankind, in particular the sufferings of his own unhappy people, homeless, haunted Jewry" and does so "without the word 'Jew' appearing in any one of his books" (Brod 1992: 135).

Stephen Dowden, in his excellent study of how literary criticism of *The Castle* has reflected the historical and social contexts of the critics, poses some interesting evaluations of how Kafka's Jewishness was emphasized or de-emphasized depending on time and place. "The Holocaust," he writes, "conditioned his reception in obvious ways" as he was "partly understood as a voice representing the last generation of intellectual Western European Jewry, and therefore an unimpeachable witness against the bestiality of Nazism" (Dowden 1995: 4). In postwar West Germany, Günther Anders saw the "Kafka plague" as a "phony means of absolution": "The idolization of Kafka," he wrote, "dissolved the fact that millions of his kinsmen had been murdered" (33).

This postwar reckoning met with an increasing critical interest in identity studies; "this concern with ethnic roots ... underlies the turn to figures like Kafka who wrestled with these issues," Dowden writes, underlining that "the critic's contemporary setting is the context that really counts because it decides which issues of the past are the ones worth thinking about" (98). Critics, of course, are reading Kafka through the lens of the Holocaust he (thankfully) did not live to see himself, and thus some readings become loaded with the language of prophecy; as J. Hillis Miller wrote recently about the last scene of *Amerika*, "it almost seems as though Kafka must have had some occult telepathic premonition of what the genocide would be like" and he explicitly argues for these and other scenes of "premonitions of Auschwitz" in Kafka's work (Miller 2011a: 65). A little more reasonably, Walter Sokel, who suggests "Description of a Struggle" has "an amazingly prophetic ring" to it (in terms of the Holocaust), argues that "Kafka was first-rate seismograph of his place and time, which indicated the future because it sounded the depth hidden in the present" (Sokel 1999: 838), i.e., that: "Living under the double threat of German racism and Czech pogromic populism, the Jews of Prague lived with an undertow of anxiety, a siege mentality of which, even though few admitted it, Kafka's nightmare fiction has become the eloquent testimonial" (841).

What is not parsed out in such readings – and what needs to be – is the difference between the work and its context, and the work and our context. Hillis Miller is right in suggesting that the final scene of *Amerika*, in which Karl and the others are herded, luggage-less, onto the train to an undetermined location, cannot *but* remind us of, as Michael Hofmann writes in his preface, the "Judentransporte" because we live in the post-Holocaust age. But Kafka did not, and I think this is vital to understand when we talk about what has for so long been designated his "nightmare fiction." In other words, we see the nightmare world that the world became and therefore impute his work with our own experiences. This is not to say that Kafka's experiences with anti-Semitism and his acute sense of otherness as a Jew and as a relatively assimilated Jew did not affect his work, but to extrapolate prophecy from this speaks to our own need for an individuated understanding of suffering in the Holocaust. It also innately connects his work only with suffering, emanating only from a sense of alienation from dominant and hostile cultures, thus making his prose "nightmare fiction." If we come to the work with such parameters, it may be all that we see: the horror of what was to come.

Josefine and Jewishness

Mark Anderson more persuasively contextualizes Kafka's final story in the anti-Semitic times in which he lived; "a few months before writing 'Josephine,' he witnessed the anti-Jewish pogroms that swept through the streets of Berlin, pointing to events to come" (Anderson 1992: 215). He argues that the story, written in a "political register" (215), responds to contemporary anti-Semitic theories of music and gender, specifically the writings of Richard Wagner and Otto Weininger and Karl Kraus (the latter two were Jewish) in which Jews, like women, were seen as inherently unmusical, speakers of a bastard and contaminating language, "*mauscheln*, literally, 'to speak (German) like Moses' and which was interpreted as a sign of the Jew's 'inhuman,' 'deceptive' nature" (197). Kraus "single[d] out the degraded 'musical' intonation of their speech, 'the chant-like intonation with which they conclude their business deals [and] which obligingly accompanies the sound of rolling coins'" (203). Kraus's "dogmatic, fanatical" language with its "utter lack of humour" (211) is turned on its head, Anderson argues, in Kafka's literalization of the racist stereotypes in *Josefine the Singer*: "Anti-Semites treat Jews like animals or disgusting vermin; Kafka takes the street metaphor literally," thereby subverting the racist discourse in making it absurd (204–5). He also invents a "fictional version of Mauscheldeutsch," Anderson writes, "what one might term their 'Mäusedeutsch'" (205).

By "Mäusedeutsch" Anderson suggests that the narrator's slyness, his/her shifting of positions, is an appropriation of the racist discourse of a deceitful language, the "slippery 'mouse' language" is "the *mauscheln* of a people 'who love slyness beyond everything'" (207): we never find out who the narrator is (or what gender); we are not sure if this narration is apparently textual or oral; we never find out if Josefine is really singing or not. Because we see Josefine from the inside view of the mouse folk, "the animals are given the human status denied them by the racial stereotype" (211). Whereas, Anderson argues, Kafka was worried about an "ethnic accent" in his writing, in this story, "he makes this ethnic sign of difference the subject of the narrator's musings, attempting to explain how an almost inaudible voice can have such an 'enormous influence' on his audience" (216). His "political weapon" is "understatement, the voice of the animal, the woman, the Jew ... the music of 'Mäusedeutsch,' his own particular variation of the *Mauscheldeutsch* castigated by anti-Semites as the mark of Jewish difference" (216).

Anderson locates the representation of Mäusedeutsch in identity and theme – the figure of the mouse, the woman, the Jew – but not in the language, not in the actual "music of 'Mäusedeutsch.'" The celebration of the "almost inaudible voice" of Yiddish in the persona of Josefine is achieved through the bravura performance of the narrator in his/her muscular, propulsive and exuberant voice. This is not, as Deleuze and Guattari famously suggested, an "arid" language (Deleuze and Guattari 1986: 19); prose that articulated Kafka's "own *patois*, his own third world, his own desert" (18), inflected with Prague German or Yiddish or *mauscheln*; it is a mode of using the German language, a narrative style that is decisively and insistently present. In a famous letter to Brod, Kafka wrote that *mauscheln* "bookish German [Papierdeutsch] and pantomime [*Gebärdensprache*]" (Kafka 1978: 288) (or "paper German and sign language"). Those writing with an awareness of it, or tied to it, exhibit:

> a sensitive feeling for language which has recognized that in German only the dialects are really alive, and except for them, only the most individual High German, while all the rest, the linguistic middle ground, is nothing but embers which can only be brought to a semblance of life when excessively lively Jewish hands rummage through them.

That is a fact," he adds, "funny or terrible as you like" (288). While he chooses not to employ it, he does "rummage" through the "paper German," aestheticizing its normalcy, making music out of the subject of non-musicality.

The "far from trustworthy" narrator (Baer 2010: 146) has often been read as a silencer of Josefine, deliberately undercutting her art so that "instead of being told, Josefine's story becomes negatively inscribed in the failure of the narration" (Norris 1983: 368); "the narration constitutes a bestial gesture that marks the trajectory from signification to its obliteration, from remembering to forgetting" (367). Yet, as Andrea Baer points out, the whole story is a remembering, an inscription of Josefine, that cannot "be forgotten now that it has been recorded and relayed to the reader" (Baer 2010: 146). The narrator does not fail in his/her narration but provokes the reader, in his/her unreliability and slyness and "challenges some of his audience's most basic assumptions about Josephine's performance, such as the song's musicality and production of sound. It is thus left up to the reader to decide what she will or will not believe about this text" (140). Nearly all of those writing on the story, though, focus on what the narrator says (and the illogicality of it), not on *how* he/she says it.

At one point in the story, silencing and silence are brought to the fore: a "naughty little thing" in the stalls starts whistling when Josefine is performing and the audience hiss and whistle to silence the child-mouse, not perhaps because she is interrupting Josefine but rather the mice folk's silence as they listen to Josefine; unusual because they too whistle all the time. The contradictions – is Josefine actually singing? Is her whistling the same as the child's? Is it the same as the mice folk's whistling? Why are they silent when they should be whistling as they are happy? – are all about sound or the absence of it in a text that, because it is written, is silent, and yet, in the narrator's constant repetitions and recursiveness, full of sound:

> As *whistling* is one of our unthinking habits, one might have supposed that such *whistling* carries on in Josefine's auditorium too; her art *cheers* us up, and when we are *cheerful* we *whistle*; but her listeners do not *whistle*, rather they are as quiet as mice; we are as *silent* as if we had secured the yearned-for peace and quiet, which our *whistling* keeps from us. It is her *song* that enraptures us, or is it not perhaps the festive *silence* surrounding that feeble little voice? There was one occasion when some naughty little thing started innocently *whistling* during Josefine's *singing*. Well, it was no different from what we were hearing from Josefine herself; there on stage the still bashful *whistling*, for all her routine, and here in the stalls the mindless childish *whistling*; it would surely not be possible to mark a difference between them; and yet we quelled the disturbance with angry *hisses* and *whistles*, even though there was no need for it, because she would have crept away in fear and shame anyway, as Josefine emitted her triumphal *whistle* and was quite beside herself with her outspread arms and neck stretched till it would stretch no further (Kafka 2008b: 267).

It is not only Josefine and the child who are making sounds, whistling, but also the audience hissing and whistling, and, most of all, the narrator is speaking of these whistles and songs and hisses and "festive silence"; the "unthinking habit" of sound. The last sentence – the story of the "naughty little thing" stretches from "Well, it was not different" to "it would stretch no further" – Josefine's physical act of dominant presence replicated by the narrator, being acted out viscerally in the prose which, like her neck, is being stretched out further and further. The thematic questions of what sounds are art (what makes the child's whistling different from Josefine's "bashful whistling"?) and what sounds are actually desired (the "yearned-for peace and quiet," "the festive silence" or Josefine's "triumphal whistle"? Or are the first only possible with the second?) are there in order to produce the musical tone of the text and its narrator.

The audience are "as quiet as mice"/"mäuschenstill" (272), a cheeky re-metaphoricization of the mice, who are presented as literal rather than figural vermin, that interrogates a familiar, even clichéd simile. Are mice, in fact, quiet? The narrator distances him/herself from the listeners just here, saying that "they" are as quiet as mice but after the semicolon reverts back to the collective: "we are as silent as if we had secured the yearned-for peace and quiet"; moving from an observer of the listeners to becoming a listener, the narrator is in fact speaking all the time and neither "silent" nor, like all the other mice, who whistle and hiss, "as quiet as mice." The rummaging through language is not an inflected language and not a silencing but a song, a turning and stretching of language into an artistic act. We spend the story wondering whether or not Josefine sings or whistles, whether or not she is an artist or a fake, when all the time we are listening to the music the narrator inscribes.

Music

In discussions of *Josefine*, critics often point out Kafka's own sense of unmusicality, from a line in a letter to Milena Jesenská: "Do you know that I am completely unmusical," he wrote to her in June 1920, "more completely than anyone I have ever known?" (Kafka 1990: 48). For Stanley Corngold, Kafka has to repress music to write, and places "his resistance to music at the origin of his own writing" (Corngold 2011: 175); for John Hargraves, in *Josefine*, Kafka uses "his own musical blind spot convincingly to portray an attitude toward (an) art, an attitude which was reflected in his own family history" (Hargraves 2007: 330), i.e., it reflects his father's ambivalence toward his writing and its worth. The language of his work reflects this "musical blind spot": "Kafka's spare Prague German," he writes, "is in a way the very antithesis of a musical style" (321).

Corngold notes that another scholar, Ronald Speirs, wrote to him to remind him of another comment in Kafka's *Letters to Milena*: "The translation of the concluding sentence is very good," he wrote to Jesenská,

> Every sentence, every word, every – if I may say so – music in that story is connected with the "fear." It was then, during one long night that the wound broke open for the first time (Kafka 1990: 173–4; Corngold 2011: 191–2).

Speirs and Corngold both agree, however, that this "Musik," and Kafka's admission of it, is unique to *The Judgment* which was "a quite exceptional experience of writing in his œuvre … something close to the *Poésie pure* he dreamt of" (Speirs in Corngold 2011: 192). The entire comment which Kafka makes to Jesenská is as follows:

> The translation of the concluding sentence is very good. Every sentence, every word, every – if I may say so – music in that story is connected with the "fear." It was then, during one long night that the wound broke open for the first time and in my opinion the translation catches this association exactly, with that magic hand which is yours (Kafka 1990: 173–4).

> Die **Übersetzung** des Schlußsatz**es** ist sehr gut. In **jener** Geschichte **hängt jeder Satz**, **jedes** Wort, **jede** – wenn's erlaubt ist – Musik mit der 'Angst' **zusammen**, damals brach die Wunde zum erstenmal auf in einer langen Nacht und diesen **Zusammenhang** trifft die **Übersetzung** für mein Gefühl genau, mit **jener** zauberhaften Hand, die eben Deine ist (Kafka 1952: 214).

Look at how the two sentences (in German; three in Philip Boehm's translation) are constructed. The first brief sentence: "Die Übersetzung des Schlußsatzes ist sehr gut" – a straightforward statement about the last sentence of *The Judgment*, but one full of sibilance. The second sentence is beautifully calibrated, beginning with "jener Geschichte"/"that story" and concluding with "jener zauberhaften Hand"/"that magic hand"; what "hängt … zusammen"/"connected" literally "hung together" returns (as does the mention of the translation in "die Zusammenhang trifft die Übersetzung" with "mein Gefühl genau"/"my feelings exactly." The repetition of "every" heightens the language while talking about language – and importantly, pausing – think of those em dashes – to connect that language with "Musik": "jeder Satz, jedes Wort, jede – wenn's erlaubt ist – Musik." "Every sentence, every word," "every music" in the story "is connected with the 'fear'": "Musik mit der 'Angst' zusammen, damals …" – the consonance connects the idea here. Similarly we see assonance in his description of the "long night" in which he wrote the entirety of *The Judgment* that serves to lengthen out the statement: "erstenmal auf in einer langen Nacht." Kafka is not using poetic or ornamental language per se, but *the way he uses it* introduces rhythm, melody, music.

The sentence he refers to is the famous ejaculatory one – Kafka said to Brod: "Do you know what the last sentence means? When I wrote it, I had in mind a violent ejaculation" (Brod 1992: 126). Georg Bendemann, having been judged to die by his father, throws himself in the river: "At that moment, a quite unending flow of traffic streamed over the bridge" (50)/"In diesem Augenblick ging über die Brücke ein geradezu unendlicher Verkehr" (68). Jesenská translated this as: "Právě v tomto okamžiku převalilo se přes most takřka nekonečné proudění" (Kafka 1923: 372)/"Exactly at that moment an unending flow rolled over the bridge." It is impossible to translate all the connotations of "Verkehr" – the sexual traffic as well as vehicular, but what Jesenská chose to do was to introduce alliteration of a plosive "p" and consonance of the rolled and emphasized "ř" to strengthen the effect: "**Pr**avě v tomto okamžiku **př**evalilo se **př**es most takřka nekonečné **pr**oudění." Her magic hand, indeed.

"Read a few sentences of Kafka aloud," Brod wrote in a review in 1921,

> and your tongue and your breath will feel a sweetness never experienced before. The cadences, the breaks, seem to follow mysterious laws; the little pauses between phrases have an architecture of their own, a melody is heard that has its roots in other material than that of this earth. It is perfection, simply perfection. … But it is perfection on the move, on the march, at the double, even (Brod 1992: 131–2).

Forgiving Brod his sweetnesses and perfections for a moment, he does make a salient point about the melody and "kinetic aspect" (Corngold 2011: 172) of the "cadences, the breaks … the little pauses between phrases" that propel the prose to "move, [be] on the march, at the double, even." Brod argues that this melodious "architecture" is connected to Kafka's lack of ability when it came to music: "Kafka, as if to compensate for the remarkable gift he had of musical speech, had no talent for pure music," Brod wrote, noting that this unmusical aspect of Kafka was similar to other writers "whose verse or prose bears all the characteristics of good music in its rhythm and dynamic" but because of this he "expends all his musical energy on speech" thus with no room "left for the world of musical sounds" except of course in his writing (Brod 1992: 115).

To return to his famous sentence in which he tells Jesenská that he is unmusical: "Do you know that I am completely unmusical, more completely than anyone I have ever known?" (Kafka 1990: 48)/"weißt Du eigentlich, daß ich vollständig, in einer meiner Erfahrung nach überhaupt sonst nicht vorkommenden Vollständigkeit unmusikalisch bin?" (Kafka 1952: 60). The sentence comes in parentheses in a letter about a dream he had about Jesenská (a dream of meeting her before they physically meet in Vienna);

what makes him think of telling her this (the connection: "Zusammenhang") is the dialogue he remembers from the dream, his language:

> I was holding your hand and now an insanely quick conversation began, all short sentences went bang bang bang and lasted almost without interruption throughout the dream. ... Instead of a greeting I said quickly, in response to something in your face: "You imagined me differently." You replied: "Frankly I thought you'd be a little more *fesch* [dapper, elegant]" (actually you said something even more Viennese, but I forgot what).
>
> These were the **first two phrases** (on which subject it occurs to me: Do you know that I am completely unmusical, more completely than anyone I have ever known?) but with that everything had been decided; what more could there be? (Kafka 1990: 48).

> ich hielt Deine Hand und nun begann ein unsinnig schnelles, kurtsätziges Gespräch, es ging klapp klapp und dauerte bis zum Ende des Traums fast ununterbrochen. ... Ich sagte statt einer Begrüßung, schnell, durch irgendetwas in Deinem Gesicht dazu bestimmt: "Du hast mich Dir anders vorgestellt," Du antwortest: "Wenn ich aufrichtig sein soll, ich dachte, Du wärest fescher" (eigentlich sagtest Du einen noch wienerischeren Ausdruck, aber ich habe ihn vergessen).
>
> Das waren die **ersten zwei Sätze** (in diesem Zusammenhang fällt mir ein: weißt Du eigentlich, daß ich vollständig, in einer meiner Erfahrung nach überhaupt sonst nicht vorkommenden Vollständigkeit unmusikalisch bin?), nun war ja damit im Grunde alles entscheiden, was denn noch? (Kafka 1952: 60).

The lexical connection between the dream dialogue and the discussion of unmusicality is with the word "Satz" which means both "sentence"/"phrase" and a musical "movement": the "first two phrases," the two short "klapp klapp"/"bang bang bang" sentences that Kafka remembers from the "insanely quick conversation" make him think of music – or, rather, unmusic. What he thinks of is the uncomfortable rhythm and tempo of this dream conversation, in which his anxieties about meeting Jesenská – her husband is in the dream as Kafka holds her hand – are articulated in her immediate dismissal of him as not being as "fesch" as she thought, not what she imagined. Again, there is real melody in his description of this frightening "klapp klapp" conversation; the speed is relayed through the language not only onomatopoetically but also through consonance: "Deine Hand und nun begann ein unsinnig schnelles." Kafka's aside in parentheses about being "unmusikalisch" serves also to slow down the panicky syntax – a self-deprecating time out from the anxiety that also attempts to put off what seems decided in the dream: her rejection.

"The most horrible thing about the conversation was not the words," Kafka adds, "but the underlying tone, the senselessness of it all, also your continuous, unspoken argument: I don't want to come. So what good is it to you if I do come?" (Kafka 1990: 49). He watches her in the dream but "your words were all I cared about" and though she seems physically different, less attractive in a "masculine" suit, he remembers "a phrase from one of your letters: 'dvoje šaty mám a přece slušně vypadám'" (Kafka

1952: 61)/"I have two dresses and I still look well" but in Czech "mám" and "vypadám" rhyme – he calls it her "verse" and it makes him like her clothes in the dream better. The anxiety from her Viennese German and the reassurance from her Czech show Kafka even in his dream world (a dream that enabled him to sleep because he had to wait for it to end, it held him "by the tongue") thinking about – and replicating – the sounds and variances of language.

He has a second dream the next day, also about her speaking:

> We were sitting next to each other, and you were warding me off, not angrily but in a friendly way. I was very unhappy. Not because you were warding me off, but because I was treating you like some mute woman, ignoring the voice that was speaking out of you directly to me. Or perhaps I wasn't ignoring it, but just unable to answer. I left more disconsolate than in the first dream (Kafka 1990: 50).

> Wir saßen neben einander und Du **wehrtest** mich **ab**, nicht böse, freundlich. Ich war sehr unglücklich. Nicht **über** die **Abwehr**, sondern **über** mich, der ich Dich behandelte wie eine beliebige **stumme** Frau und die **Stimme überhörte**, die aus Dir **sprach** und gerade zu mir **sprach**. Oder vielleicht, **ich hatte** sie **nicht überhört**, aber **ich hatte** ihr **nicht** antworten könnten. Trostloser als im ersten Traum ging ich fort (Kafka 1952: 66).

Kafka's anxieties about miscomprehension, about not listening to hear when in physical proximity to her, about not being able to answer what she says is built up again with melodious resonances: of "Abwehr(en)," "über," "überhören" "sprach," and the near homophones "stumme" and "Stimme." The passage is replete with words about communication and sound: voice, speech, muteness, hearing, answering. It seems, in some ways, to have textual consanguinity with *Josefine* in its ambiguity about the language coming out of this dream – Jesenská and the listener's doubts about his own reactions to and recognition of that language. In the first dream, Kafka sees her first coming toward him – she "remained something bluish-white, flowing, ghostlike" – "You had also spread your arms out, but not to stretch; it was more a ceremonial gesture" (Kafka 1990: 48), as if, like Josefine, she was about to whistle.

Josefine, the translator

Or do you really think that a home has any other function than to protect and protect and protect an individual from the world and mainly from his internal mirror?

Milena Jesenská, "The Devil at the Hearth" (Jesenská 2003: 109).

Only in passing does František Kautman suggest that Jesenská may have influenced the depiction of Josefine (Kautman 1968: 33). Jesenská was still in touch with Kafka, after he had moved to Berlin with Dora Diamant; the tone of his much less frequent letters are still affectionate if shorn of the passion of those at the height of their affair in 1920, and he is still reading and reacting to her writing, her journalism, particularly her article, "The Devil at the Hearth," published in January 1923. In it, Jesenská decried the illusions of marriage and the mistaken and illusionary equation of happiness with it. For Jesenská, "it is the task of marriage to tolerate the essence of the other and to tolerate it in such a way that the other person feels justified in being the way he is"; the function of a home is "to protect and protect and protect an individual from the world and mainly from his internal mirror" (Jesenská 2003: 109). The promise given in a marriage should be: "I won't let them get you" (109). The "talent for happiness" like "a talent for singing, for writing" comes from within, not from illusory love (110). Kafka responded to the article with a set of cheeky playlets imagining a marriage between an angel and Jewry: both the angel and the Jews quote Jesenská, but completely misunderstand each other, because, he jokes, "it's inevitable that Jewry will twist the words of the angel whenever possible" (Kafka 1990: 230). Kafka, though, argues that there "are no unhappy marriages, there are only incomplete ones and they are incomplete because they were made by incomplete human beings" (231).

That Kafka immediately converts Jesenská's notions of marriage into the parameters of community, with an ironic twist, and her central notion of a relationship as a core protection for fallibility (what Kafka picks up as the "incomplete human beings"), seems to speak to the mice folk's ambivalent but essentially protective relationship to Josefine, who is flawed as an artist and a mouse, yet still a part of their community, protected from the world (even if she occasionally seems to put them in danger when she whistles and attracts their unnamed enemies and wants to "spit" on their "protection" (270)) and from her own "internal mirror." Josefine thinks and acts like a singer and the community allow her to think it, even as they harbor doubts because she refracts their internal mirror: her whistling allows them a community of silence; their focus on her lets them escape introspection about their own lives – they can laugh at her rather than at themselves.

While not a fictionalization of Jesenská (but perhaps a response to her writing), Josefine, who has been read consistently as one of Kafka's misunderstood artist figures, is also, to some extent, a translator figure. The anxiety in the story of whether she elevates the whistling to singing, whether she is a "genuine vocal artist" with "this tiny voice, this tiny achievement," her "feeble whistling," speaks to doubts about the authenticity of translation as an art – as she attempts to turn the whistling into performance (Kafka 2008b: 272). The narrator wonders if this "alleged artistry" (265) is not just the same as their own workaday whistling. But at the time he/she thinks there is something different: "here was something produced from the larynx that one had never heard before, and that we are not really even equipped to hear, something that Josefine and only she equips us to hear," the narrator says: "Can it even be described as song at all?" (265). Josefine's sounds seem completely familiar – perhaps exactly the same as those the "naughty little thing" produces during Josefine's performance – or even weaker; nonetheless, there is something strange about what she produces, something "one had never heard before" or perhaps something "we are not really even equipped to hear": it takes Josefine to equip them to hear. The narrator is both fascinated with these strange sounds, unsure about them, unsure whether they are familiar or strange, and wondering whether they have to be trained to understand them. It is their whistling, but not quite.

The narrator suspects that Josefine is all performance; her body and attitude are more central than the sound she emits. Her body is a core element that gives meaning to the whistling; "it is part of understanding her art," the narrator says, "not merely to hear her but to see her as well" (266). But she is also the "embodiment of delicacy, really strikingly delicate even in our people" (266), a "frail creature, quivering alarmingly" (268) but she has attitude, she is pert, conceited, diva-like. And when she performs, "only the very young among us have any interest in the person of the singer, they watch in astonishment as she curls her lips, as she expels the air between her cute incisors, swoons in admiration of the notes she herself produces" (275). What her performances do, however, is bring the community bodily together. Skeptical of her performance at first, as she sings, "body warmly pressed against body" (268); "it's as if the limbs of each individual relaxed, as if each anxious veteran were finally able to stretch out in the big warm bed of the people" (275). Often we think of the non-corporeality of the translator, but Josefine seems all body, all gesture – a form of translation that eschews language or goes beyond it – she communicates protection and community while seemingly also (through sound) placing the mice folk in danger (by exposing them to their enemies, who may presumably speak another language). She brings the mice close to foreignness but at the same time lets them re-identify as a community.

"Translators as embodied subjects are not only points of intersection of language, culture and textual and oral memory," Michael Cronin writes, "they are also implicated in hierarchies of discourse and power" (Cronin 2000: 135). Their material existence signs a form of difference (in Josefine's case, perhaps in terms of gender – her fragility – and her – faked – limping) which makes them "vulnerable" but also allows "the translator to speak as an active subject of change rather than as a passive agent of discursive function" (135). Although the narrator claims that Josefine will be "forgotten" when she physically disappears, her presence engenders the narrator's tale and the construction of his/her own music.

Having seemingly failed, the narrator in fact has translated the melody into his/her own language. In the penultimate paragraph of the story, the narrator wonders whether the "people will get over her loss" and whether they will able to be together "in complete silence" without her performance. Yet in articulating this loss and in speaking about silence, the narrator creates a beautiful, layered passage full of euphony, motifs and musical breath:

> Soon the time will come when her last **whistle** sounds and falls **silent**. She is a little episode in the never-ending story of our **people**, and the **people** will get over her loss. It won't be easy for us; how will our assemblies be possible in complete **silence**? Then again, were they not **silent**, even with Josefine there? **Was** her actual **whistling** noticeably louder and livelier than in our **memory** of it? **Was** it ever more than a **memory**, even while she was alive? **Was** it not rather the **people** in their wisdom valuing Josefine's song so highly, because in such a way, it was impossible for them to lose it? (Kafka 2008b: 282).

> Bald wird die Zeit kommen, wo ihr letzter **Pfiff** ertönt und **verstummt**. Sie ist eine kleine Episode in der ewigen Geschichte unseres **Volkes** und das **Volk** wird den Verlust überwinden. Leicht wird es uns ja nicht werden; wie werden die Versammlungen in völliger **Stummheit** möglich sein? Freilich, waren sie nicht auch mit Josefine **stumm**? **War** ihr wirkliches **Pfeifen** nennenswert lauter und lebendiger, als die **Erinnerung** daran sein wird? **War** es denn noch bei ihren Lebzeiten mehr als eine bloße **Erinnerung**? Hat nicht vielmehr das **Volk** in seiner Weisheit Josefinens Gesang, eben deshalb, weil er in dieser Art unverlierbar war, so hoch gestellt? (Kafka 1946: 290).

The words "Volk" and "stumm" are repeated through the passage, as well as "Pfeifen" and "Erinnerung" – people, silence, whistling and memory. As the narrator wonders what will happen, whether there was silence in the first place, and whether the song they heard was itself a communal memory, he/she asks a set of rhetorical questions, giving the passage a certain rhythm, punctuated by the repeated "War" and question marks. The questions are rhetorical because the narrator is answering them, in the musical manner in which he/she asks them. The euphony of the repeated motif words is supported by consonance and assonance – the repeated "v" and "w" sounds and, for instance, the repeated "e" which slows down the opening of the sentence: "Sie ist eine kleine Episode in der ewigen Geschichte unseres" which inscribes her into that story or history (Stanley Corngold translates "Geschichte" as "history" as do the Muirs; Joyce Crick as "story"); a sentence that then speeds up with the "v"/"w" consonance: "**Volkes** und das **Volk** wird den Verlust überwinden" when the narrator really wants to insist that her disappearance will not be a loss.

Look at what does get translated: Hofmann translates the repetition of the key terms: whistle, silence, people, memory, but also the euphony of the passage. Thus, we see the "e" assonance in the same sentence as above: "She is a little episode in the never-ending story of our people." Other translators also convey this assonance: "brief episode in the eternal history" (Kafka 2007: 107); "small episode in the eternal story" (Crick 2012: 79–80); "little episode in the endless history" (Kafka 1992: 236), translating "ewig" as "eternal" or "endless" – Hofmann's choice of "never-ending" speaks to the lengthening out of the sound and the pace of the sentence. All the English translations introduce sibilance into the passage in place of the German "v"/"w" repetition; Hofmann's first three sentences, for instance, are replete with it:

> Soon the time will come when her last whistle sounds and falls silent. She is a little episode in the never-ending story of our people, and the people will get over her loss. It won't be easy for us; how will our assemblies be possible in complete silence?

The sibilance is the whistling, the sound of it at least, translated into the narrator's language, his/her "story" (emphasized in Hofmann's translation with the repetition also of the "w": "will come when her last whistle"). When the narrator thinks about the sound of the whistling, he/she introduces another example of consonance: "War ihr wirkliches Pfeifen nennenswert lauter und lebendiger" (with resonance around it:

"wirkliches"; "als" "Lebzeiten"; "als"; "bloße") that Hofmann translates as: "Was her actual whistling noticeably louder and livelier" with an emphasis on that "l" consonance: "actual," "whistling," "noticeably," "while," "alive" and in the key terms "silence" and "people." As do other translators:

> Was her real piping truly any louder and livelier than our memory of it will be? Even when she was still alive, was it anything more than a mere memory? (Crick 2012: 80).

> Was her actual squeaking notably louder and livelier than the memory of it will be? Even during her lifetime was it every more than a mere memory? (Kafka 2007: 107–8).

> Was her actual piping notably louder and more lively than the memory of it will be? Was it even in her lifetime any more than simply a memory? (Kafka 1992: 236).

> Was her actual piping notably louder and more alive than the memory of it will be? Was it even in her lifetime more than a simple memory? (Kafka 1971: 376).

The translations vary slightly, but each translator is aware of the euphony, choosing to address it in slightly different ways: "truly" or "notably" or "noticeably"; "louder and livelier" or "louder and more lively" or "louder and more alive." The then insistent repetition of the "m" – "more than a mere memory," "more than simply a memory" – signals the act of inscribing a memory that "will be" – the odd conjunction of past and future shows both being made in the present, the "story" or "history" being written by the narrator in words and in sound.

Reading the various translations together along with the translators' prefaces and footnotes opens up how we read the story of an unnamed narrator translating Josefine's song into language and narrative ("geschichte"). They raise questions of untranslatability – how to translate "Volk" and the strangeness of words in the original – mice that emit a "Pfiff" – and the different translatorial choices that ensue. Looking at those different choices can open up our reading of the piece: the different translations of "ewig" as "never-ending," "endless" or "eternal" are all part of capturing the euphony of the sentence but also the differences may bring us back to the question of the word choice in the original, given its use in the German term "der ewige Jude" or "the wandering Jew" which might resonate in "der ewigen Geschichte unseres." Thinking about the choice of "story" or "history" for "Geschichte" opens up the central theme in the story that is locked into its narrative mode – how communal stories are made by both the community itself and others. The "loss" of Josefine's song will be overcome because it was never lost; we hear that in the narrator's narration in German and in English. While some connotations, some untranslatable resonances might disappear like Josefine and be "forgotten," in fact, like Josefine, they are not; they are present in the choices that the translators make – we, as readers, just need to be aware of that process and the results.

Bibliography

Adams, Jeffrey. 2002. "Orson Welles's *The Trial*: Film Noir and the Kafkaesque." *College Literature*, 23.9: 140–57.
—2011. "Soderbergh's Kafka: In Retrospect." *Post Script*, 31.1: 26.
Adams, Sam. 2009. "Interview. Peter Capaldi." *A.V. Club*, July 23. http://www.avclub.com/articles/peter-capaldi,30792/
Adorno, Theodore. 1981. *Prisms*. Cambridge, MA: MIT Press.
Allen, Kirsty. 1996. "Introduction." Willa Muir, *Imagined Selves*, v–xiii. Edinburgh: Canongate.
Alter, Robert. 2005. "One Man's Kafka." *The New Republic*, April 25: 31.
Anderson, Mark (ed.). 1989. *Reading Kafka. Prague, Politics, and the Fin de Siècle*. New York: Schocken.
—1992. *Kafka's Clothes. Ornament and Aestheticism in the Hapsburg Fin de Siècle*. Oxford: Oxford University Press.
Arrojo, Rosemary. 2002. "Writing, Interpreting and the Control of Meaning." In *Translation and Power*, Edwin Gentzler and Maria Tymoczko (eds), 63–79. Amherst: University of Massachusetts Press.
Baer, Andrea. 2010. "Performative Emotion in Kafka's 'Josephine, the Singer; or, the Mouse Folk' and Freud's 'The Creative Writer and Daydreaming.'" In *Kafka's Creatures. Animals, Hybrids, and Other Fantastic Beings*, Marc Lucht and Donna Yarri (eds), 137–156. Lanham, MA: Lexington Books.
Baker, Aaron. 2011. *Contemporary Film Directors: Steven Soderbergh*. Chicago: University of Illinois Press.
Baker, Mona. 2006. *Translation and Conflict: A Narrative Account*. London and New York: Routledge.
Batumen, Elif. 2010. "Kafka's Last Trial." *New York Times Magazine*, September 22. http://www.nytimes.com/2010/09/26/magazine/26kafka-t.html
Beckett, Samuel. 1990. *The Complete Dramatic Works*. London: Faber and Faber.
—1994. *Molloy. Malone Dies. The Unnamable*. London: John Calder.
Bell, Anthea. 2009. "Note on the Translation." In *The Castle*, trans. Anthea Bell, xxix–xxxi. Oxford: Oxford World Classics.
Bell, Ian. 1995. "Readers Sent Barking Up the Wrong Tree." *Glasgow Herald*, March 15.
Bernheimer, Charles. 1977. "Symbolic Bond and Textual Play: Structure of The Castle." In *The Kafka Debate: New Perspectives for Our Time*, Angel Flores (ed.), 367–84. Staten Island, NY: Gordian Press.
Berthoff, Warner. 2009. "Kafka Again." *Sewanee Review*, 117.3: 499–502.
Bhabha, Homi. 1994. *The Location of Culture*. London and New York: Routledge.
Binder, Hartmut. 1976. *Kafka-Kommentar zu den Romanen, Rezensionen, Aphorismen und zum Brief an den Vater*. Munich: Winkler.
Boa, Elizabeth. 1996. *Kafka: Gender, Class, and Race in the Letters and Fictions*. Oxford: Oxford University Press.

Böhme, Hartmut. 1977. "Mother Milena: On Kafka's Narcissism." In *The Kafka Debate: New Perspectives for Our Time*, edited by Angel Flores, 80–99. New York: Gordian Press.

Bondanella, Peter. 1992. *The Cinema of Federico Fellini*. Princeton, NJ: Princeton University Press.

—2002. *The Films of Federico Fellini*. Cambridge: Cambridge University Press.

Borges, Jorge Luis. 1970. "Kafka and His Precursors," trans. James. E. Irby. In *Labyrinths. Selected Stories and Other Writings*, 234–6. London: Penguin.

Bowman, Martin. 2000. "Scottish Horses and Montreal Trains: The Translation of Vernacular to Vernacular." In *Moving Target. Theatre Translation and Cultural Relocation*, edited by Carole-Anne Upton, 25–33. Manchester: St. Jerome.

Brady, Martin and Hughes, Helen. 2002. "Kafka Adapted to Film." In *The Cambridge Companion to Kafka*, Julian Preece (ed.), 226–41. Cambridge: Cambridge University Press.

Brearton, Fran. 1999. "An Interview with Michael Hofmann." *Thumbscrew*, 13 (spring/summer). http://www.poetrymagazines.org.uk/magazine/record.asp?id=8095

Brod, Max. 1992. *Franz Kafka. A Biography*, 2nd edn. New York: Da Capo Press.

Brunette, Peter. 2010. *Michael Haneke*. Urbana, CH and Springfield: University of Illinois Press.

Buber-Neumann, Margarete. 1977. *Milena: The Story of a Remarkable Friendship*, translated by Ralph Manheim. New York: Schocken.

Buchan, James. 2009. "The Path of Least Resistance." *Guardian*, March 6. http://www.guardian.co.uk/books/2009/mar/07/alone-in-berlin-hans-fallada

Buchar, Robert. 2001. *Sametová kocovina*. Brno: Host.

Butler, Christopher. 2004. "Joyce the Modernist." In *The Cambridge Companion to James Joyce*, Derek Attridge (ed.), 67–86. Cambridge: Cambridge University Press.

Byatt, A.S. 2013. "Review: The Emperor's Tomb." *Guardian*, January 25. http://www.guardian.co.uk/books/2013/jan/25/emperors-tomb-joseph-roth-review

Cabada, Ladislav. 2010. *Intellectuals and the Communist Idea: The Search for a New Way in Czech Lands 1890–1938*, trans. Zdeněk Benedikt. Lanham, MD: Lexington Books.

Callahan, Clare. 2009. "'I Do Not Want the Judgment of any Man:' The Unstable Animal–Human Boundary in Linguistics and Kafka's 'A Report to an Academy'". In *Of Mice and Men: Animals in Human Culture*, Nandita Batra and Vartan Messier (eds), 81–91. Newcastle: Cambridge Scholars Publishing.

Callow, Simon. 1996. *Orson Welles. The Road to Xanadu*. London: Vintage.

Canby, Vincent. 1991. "Jeremy Irons as the Writer with a Day Job." *New York Times*, December 4. http://movies.nytimes.com/movie/review?res=9D0CE2DC1338F937A35751C1A967958260&emc=eta1

Capaldi, Peter. 2001. *Franz Kafka's It's a Wonderful Life and Other Strange Tales*. DVD. Directed by Peter Capaldi and others. Los Angeles, CA: Vanguard Films.

Černá, Jana. 1988. *Kafka's Milena*, trans. Gerald Turner. London: Souvenir.

Chamberlain, Lori. 1992. Gender and the Metaphorics of Translation. In *Rethinking Translation. Discourse, Subjectivity, Ideology*, Lawrence Venuti (ed.), 57–74. London and New York: Routledge.

Christianson, Aileen. 2007. *Moving in Circles: Willa Muir's Writings*. Edinburgh: Word Power Books.

Cléder, Jean. 2007. "Pour la transmission de pouvoirs empruntés: lecture cinématographique des textes de Franz Kafka." In *Sillage de Kafka*, edited by Philippe Zard, 497–510. Paris: Éditions Le Manuscrit.

Coetzee, J. M. 2001. *Stranger Shores. Literary Essays*. New York: Penguin.
—2007. *Inner Workings: Literary Essays 2000–2005*. New York: Penguin.
Corbett, John. 1999. *Written in the Language of the Scottish Nation. A History of Literary Translation into Scots*. Clevedon: Multilingual Matters.
Corngold, Stanley. 1996. "Kafka's The Metamorphosis: Metamorphosis of the Metaphor." In *Franz Kafka. The Metamorphosis*, Stanley Corngold (ed. and trans.), 79–107. New York: Norton Critical Edition.
—2002. "Kafka's Later Stories and Aphorisms." In *The Cambridge Companion to Kafka*, Julian Preece (ed.), 95–110. Cambridge: Cambridge University Press.
—2004. "Kafka and the Dialect of Minor Literature." In *Debating World Literature*, Christopher Prendergast (ed.), 272–90. London and New York: Verso.
—2011. "Musical Indirections in Kafka's 'Forschungen eines Hundes.'" In *Franz Kafka. Narration, Rhetoric & Reading*, Jakob Lothe, Beatrice Sandberg and Ronald Speirs (eds), 170–95. Columbus: Ohio State University Press.
Cowie, Peter. 1989. *The Cinema of Orson Welles*. New York: Da Capo Press.
Crick, Joyce. 1981. Kafka and the Muirs. In *The World of Franz Kafka*, J.P. Stern (ed.), 159–74. New York: Holt.
—2012. "Note on the Translation." In Franz Kafka, *The Hunger Artist and Other Stories*, trans. Joyce Crick, xli–xliv. Oxford: Oxford World Classics.
Cronin, Michael. 2000. *Across the Lines: Travel, Language, Translation*. Cork: Cork University Press.
—2003. *Translation and Globalization*. London and New York: Routledge.
Damrosch, David. 2003. *What is World Literature?* Princeton, NJ and Oxford: Princeton University Press.
Deleuze, Gilles and Guattari, Félix. 1986. *Kafka. Towards a Minor Literature*, translated by Dana Polan. Minneapolis and London: University of Minnesota Press.
Delgado, Martin. 1995. "Kafka, an Oscar and the Cockroach." *Evening Standard*, February 16: 14.
Demetz, Peter. 2008. *Prague in Danger. The Years of German Occupation, 1939–45: Memories and History, Terror and Resistance, Theater and Jazz, Film and Poetry, Politics and War*. New York: Farrar, Straus & Giroux.
Derrida, Jacques. 2002. "The Animal That Therefore I Am (More to Follow)," translated by David Wills. *Critical Inquiry*, 28.2: 369–418.
Dickens, Charles. 2012. *David Copperfield*. New York: Vintage Classics.
Dobbs, Lem. 2010. "The Dan Schneider Interview 21: Lem Dobbs." http://www.cosmoetica.com/DSI21.html
Donegan, Lawrence. 1995. "A Scottish Kafka, Shunned by the London Film Festival, is in Line for an Oscar." *Guardian*, February 16: 10.
Dowden, Stephen D. 1995. *Kafka's Castle and the Critical Imagination*. Columbia, SC: Camden.
Durrani, Osman. 2002. "Editions, Translations, Adaptations." In *The Cambridge Companion to Kafka*, Julian Precce (ed.), 206–25. Cambridge: Cambridge University Press.
Duttlinger, Carolin. 2007. *Kafka and Photography*. Oxford: Oxford University Press.
Elphinstone, Margaret. 1997. "Willa Muir: Crossing the Genres." In *A History of Scottish Women's Writing*, edited by Douglas Gifford and Dorothy McMillan, 400–15. Edinburgh: Edinburgh University Press.
Fellini, Federico. 1976. *Fellini on Fellini*, trans. Isabel Quigley. New York: Delacorte Press.

—2005. *Intervista*. DVD. Directed by Federico Fellini. New York: Koch-Lorber Films.
Findlay, Bill. 2004. *Frae Ither Tongues*, Bill Findlay (ed.). Clevedon, OH: Multilingual Matters.
Fletcher, John and Bradbury, Malcolm. 1991. "The Introverted Novel." In *Modernism: A Guide to European Literature, 1890–1930*, James McFarlane and Malcolm Bradbury (eds), 394–415. London: Penguin.
Flores, Angel. 1963a. In *The Kafka Problem*, Angel Flores (ed.). New York: Octagon Books.
Flores, Kate. 1963b. "Biographical Note." In *The Kafka Problem*, Angel Flores (ed.), 1–19. New York: Octagon Books.
Florian, Josef. 1993. *Vzájemná korespondence*. Prague: Documenta.
Foundas, Scott. 2001. "Decade: Michael Haneke Talks 'Code Inconnu' and 'The Piano Teacher.'" *Indiewire*, December 4. http://www.indiewire.com/article/decade_michael_haneke_talks_code_inconnu_and_the_piano_teacher
Foy, Paul. 1995. "Capaldi's Oscar." *Glasgow Herald*, April 1: 14.
Franzen, Jonathan. 2012. *Farther Away: Essays*. New York: Farrar, Straus & Giroux.
French, Philip. 1995. "Hanks but no Hanks." *Observer*, February 19: 5.
Gaydos, Steven. 1994. "*Amerika (Czech Republic)*." Variety. July 18–July 24: 40.
Gifford, Douglas. 1997. *Contemporary Fiction I: Tradition and Continuity*. In *A History of Scottish Women's Writing*, Douglas Gifford and Dorothy McMillan (eds), 579–603. Edinburgh: Edinburgh University Press.
Gilbert, Gerard. 2011. "Peter Capaldi: 'People ask Me to Tell Them to #@*! Off.'" *Independent*, April 9. http://www.independent.co.uk/news/people/profiles/peter-capaldi-people-ask-me-to-tell-them-to--off-2264021.html
Gilligan, Vincent, Gould, Peter and Mastras, George. 2010. *Breaking Bad*. "Kafkaesque." Season 3, Episode 9. First broadcast May 16 by AMC. Directed by Michael Slovis.
Grant, Richard E. 1995. "Arts Diary." *Observer*, February 26: 6.
Gray, Ronald. 1977. "But Kafka Wrote in German." In *The Kafka Debate: New Perspectives for Our Time*, edited by Angel Flores, 242–52. Staten Island, NY: Gordian Press.
Greve, Anniken. 2011. "The Human Body and the Human Being in 'Die Verwandlung.'" In *Franz Kafka. Narration, Rhetoric & Reading*, edited by Jakob Lothe, Beatrice Sandberg and Ronald Speirs, 40–57. Columbus: Ohio State University Press.
Gross, Ruth. 2010. "Report to the Academy." *German Quarterly*, 83.4: 410–11.
Gunning, Tom. 2000. *The Films of Fritz Lang*. London: British Film Institute.
Haneke, Michael. 2002. *Code Unknown*. DVD. Directed by Michael Haneke. New York: Kino International.
—2006. *Funny Games*. DVD. Directed by Michael Haneke. New York: Kino International.
—2007. *The Castle*. DVD. Directed by Michael Haneke. New York: Kino International.
—2009. *The White Ribbon*. DVD. Directed by Michael Haneke. Los Angeles: Sony Pictures Classics.
Hargraves, John. 2007. "Kafka and Silence: An Alternate View of Music." In Franz Kafka, *Kafka's Selected Stories*, Stanley Corngold (ed. and trans.), 321–33. New York: Norton Critical Edition.
Harman, Mark. 1993. "Joyce and Kafka." *The Sewanee Review*, 101.1: 66–84.
—1996. "'Digging the Pit of Babel': Retranslating Franz Kafka's *Castle*." *New Literary History*, 27. 2: 291–311.
—1998a. "H. and K.: A Translator's Story." *The Sewanee Review*, 106.2: 374–9.

—1998b. "Terminal Fantasies: Beckett and Kafka." In *That Other World. The Supernatural and the Fantastic in Irish Literature, Vol II*, Bruce Stewart (ed.), 177–87. Gerrards Cross: Colin Smythe.
—1998c. "Translator's Preface." In Franz Kafka, *The Castle*, trans. Mark Harman, xiii–xxiii. New York: Schocken.
—1999. "'At Least He Could Garden': Beckett and Kafka." *Partisan Review*, 66.4: 574–9.
—2008. "Translator's Preface." In Franz Kafka, *Amerika: The Missing Person*, xv–xxxiii. New York: Schocken.
—2012. Interview with Michelle Woods, February 10.
Hawes, James. 2008. *Why You Should Read Kafka Before You Waste Your Life*. New York: St. Martin's Press.
Hayes, Kathleen. 2003. *The Journalism of Milena Jesenská*. New York, Oxford: Berghahn Books.
Heaney, Seamus. 1990. *New Selected Poems 1966–1987*. London: Faber and Faber.
—2002. "Edwin Muir." In *Finders Keepers. Selected Prose 1971–2002*, 246–56. London: Faber and Faber.
Heller, Peter. 1977. "On Not Understanding Kafka." In *The Kafka Debate: New Perspectives for Our Time*, edited by Angel Flores, 24–41. Staten Island, NY: Gordian Press.
Hockaday, Mary. 1997. *Kafka, Love and Courage. The Life of Milena Jesenská*. Woodstock, New York: The Overlook Press.
Hoffmann, E. T. A. 1967. "Nutcracker and the King of Mice." In *The Best Tales of Hoffmann*, E. F. Bleiler (ed.), 130–82, trans. Major Alexander Ewing. New York: Dover.
Hofmann, Michael. 2001. *Behind the Lines. Pieces on Writing and Pictures*. London: Faber and Faber.
—2002a. "Translator's Introduction." In Joseph Roth, *The Radetzky March*, v–xvi. London: Granta.
—2002b. "Introduction." In Franz Kafka, *Amerika: The Man Who Disappeared*, vii–xiv, Translated by Michael Hofmann. New York: New Directions.
—2004. "Afterword." In Gert Hofmann, *Lichtenberg and the Little Flower Girl*, 240–5. New York: New Directions.
—2008. "Introduction." In Franz Kafka, *Metamorphosis and Other Stories*, vii–xv, trans. Michael Hofmann. New York: Penguin Classics.
—2009. "Michael Hofmann Responds." *Poetry Magazine*. December 30. http://www.poetryfoundation.org/poetrymagazine/letter/238454
—2010. "*Why Translation Matters* by Edith Grossman: Review." *Daily Telegraph*, May 15. http://www.telegraph.co.uk/culture/books/bookreviews/7719866/Why-Translation-Matters-by-Edith-Grossman-review.html
—2012. Interview with Michelle Woods, January 22.
Homer. 1997. *The Odyssey*, trans. Robert Fagles. New York: Penguin Classics.
Huillet, Danièle and Straub, Jean-Marie. 2007. *Klassenverhältnisse*. DVD. Munich: Film & Kunst.
Inghilleri, Moira and Harding, Sue-Ann. 2010. *The Translator*. Special Issue: *Translation and Violent Conflict*, 16.1.
Jakobson, Roman. 2000. "On Linguistic Aspects of Translation." In *The Translation Studies Reader*, edited by Lawrence Venuti, 113–18. London and New York: Routledge.
Janouch, Gustav. 1985. *Conversations with Kafka*, trans. Goronwy Rees. London, Melbourne and New York: Quartet Books.

Jesenská, Milena. 1996. *Milena Jesenská zvenčí a zevnitř*. Prague: Nakladatelství Franze Kafky.
—2003. *The Journalism of Milena Jesenská. A Critical Voice in Interwar Central Europe*, Kathleen Hayes (ed. and trans.). New York and Oxford: Berghahn.
Jirásková, Marie. 1996. *Stručná zpráva o trojí volbě. Milena Jesenská, Joachim von Zedwitz a Jaroslav Nachtmann v roce 1939*. Prague: Nakladatelství Franze Kafky.
Joyce, James. 2000. *Ulysses*. London: Penguin Classics.
Kafka, Franz. 1920. "Topič." *Kmen*. April 22: 61–72.
—1923. "Soud." *Cesta*, December/January, 369–72.
—1946. *Erzählung*. New York: Schocken
—1952. *Briefe an Milena*. New York: Schocken.
—1960. *The Great Wall of China. Stories and Reflections*, trans. Willa and Edwin Muir. New York: Schocken.
—1962. *Amerika*, trans. Willa and Edwin Muir. New York: Schocken.
—1964. *Diaries 1910–1923*, trans. Joseph Kresh, Martin Greenberg and Hannah Arendt. New York: Schocken.
—1968. *Dopisy Mileně*, trans. Hana Žantovská. Prague: Academia.
—1971. *The Complete Stories*, trans. Willa and Edwin Muir and Tania and James Stern. New York: Schocken.
—1978. *Letters to Friends, Family and Editors*, trans. Richard and Clara Winston. London: John Calder.
—1990. *Letters to Milena*, trans. Philip Boehm. New York: Schocken.
—1992. *The Transformation and Other Stories*, trans. Malcolm Pasley. Harmondsworth: Penguin.
—1994. *Der Verschollene (Amerika)*. Frankfurt am Main: Fischer.
—1996. *Franz Kafka. The Metamorphosis*, trans. Stanley Corngold. New York: Norton Critical Edition.
—1998a. *The Castle*, trans. Mark Harman. New York: Schocken.
—1998b. *The Trial*, trans. Breon Mitchell. New York: Schocken.
—2002a. *Amerika: The Man Who Disappeared*, trans. Michael Hofmann. New York: New Directions.
—2002b. *Das Schloß*. Frankfurt am Main: Fischer.
—2006. *The Zürau Aphorisms of Franz Kafka*, trans. Michael Hofmann. New York: Schocken.
—2007. *Kafka's Selected Stories*, Stanley Corngold (ed. and trans.). New York: Norton Critical Edition.
—2008a. *Amerika: The Missing Person*, trans. Mark Harman. New York: Schocken.
—2008b. *Metamorphosis and Other Stories*, trans. Michael Hofmann. New York: Penguin.
—2009. *The Castle*, trans. Anthea Bell. Oxford: Oxford World Classics.
—2012. *A Hunger Artist and Other Stories*, trans. Joyce Crick. Oxford: Oxford World Classics.
Kautman, František. 1968. "Kafka a Milena." In *Dopisy Mileně*, 7–34. Prague: Academia.
Kerguen, Oanig. 2007. "Kafka au 'service' du film de genre: emprise et reprise du mythe 'kafkaïen' dans Kafka de Steven Soderbergh." In *Sillage de Kafka*, Philippe Zard (ed.), 485–96. Paris: Éditions Le Manuscrit.
Kettle, Steve. 1990. "Soderbergh Cashes Ticket in on Czech Author Kafka." *The Toronto Star*, October 25: B4.

Knight, Stephen. 2008. "Metric Conversion: Why poet Michael Hofmann Stopped 'Wreaking Destruction' on his Family in Verse." *Independent*, May 25. http://www.independent.co.uk/arts-entertainment/books/features/metric-conversion-why-poet-michael-hofmann-stopped-wreaking-destruction-on-his-family-in-verse-832527.html

Kramsch, Claire. 2008. "Multilingual, Like Franz Kafka." *International Journal of Multilingualism*, 5.4: 316–32.

Kriseová, Eda. 1993. *Václav Havel. The Authorized Biography*, trans. Caleb Crain. New York: St. Martin's Press.

Kundera, Milan. 1993. *The Art of the Novel*, trans. Linda Asher. New York: HarperPerennial.

—1996. *Testaments Betrayed*, trans. Linda Asher. London: Faber and Faber.

—2002. *Ignorance*, trans. Linda Asher. New York: HarperCollins.

Laing, Allan. 1995. "Scottish Film Wins Oscar Nomination." *Glasgow Herald*, February 15: 3.

Lappin, Tom. 1994. "Extra Funding for 2nd year of Tartan Shorts from BBC." *The Scotsman*, July 14.

Levine, Michael G. 2008. "'A Place So Insanely Enchanting': Kafka and the Poetics of Suspension." *MLN*, 123.5: 1039–67.

Lewis, Philip. E. 1985. "The Measure of Translation Effects." In *Difference in Translation*, Joseph F. Graham (ed.), 31–62. Ithaca, NY and London: Cornell University Press.

Lewis, Wyndham. 1965. *The Apes of God*. London: Penguin.

Licari, Rosanna. n.d "Michael Hofmann in Conversation with Rosanna Licari." Stylus Poetry Journal. http://www.styluspoetryjournal.com/main/master.asp?id=923

Light, Alison. 2008. *Mrs. Woolf and the Servants. An Intimate History of Domestic Life in Bloomsbury*. New York, Berlin, London: Bloomsbury.

Lothe, Jakob, Sandberg, Beatrice and Speirs, Ronald. 2011. "Introduction: Narration and Narratives in Kafka." In *Franz Kafka. Narration, Rhetoric & Reading*, Jakob Lothe, Beatrice Sandberg and Ronald Speirs (eds), 1–21. Columbus: Ohio State University Press.

Lukács, Georg. 1974. *The Theory of the Novel*. Cambridge, MA: MIT Press.

Lutz, Alfred. 2009. "Letter to the Editor." *Poetry Magazine*, December 30. http://www.poetryfoundation.org/poetrymagazine/letter/238422

Maier, Carol. 2006. "The Translator as Theorôs: Thoughts on Cogitation, Figuration and Current Creative Writing." In *Translating Others (Volume 1)*, Theo Hermans (ed.), 163–80. Manchester: St. Jerome.

Marková-Kotyková, Marta. 1993. *Mýtus Milena*. Prague: Primus.

Maslin, Janet. 1995. "Making the 'Invisible' Clearly Visible." *New York Times*, November 29. http://www.nytimes.com/1995/11/29/movies/film-review-making-the-invisible-clearly-visible.html

McBride, Joseph. 1972. *Orson Welles*. New York: Viking Press.

McCulloch, Margery Palmer. 1997. *Fictions of Development 1920–1970*. In *A History of Scottish Women's Writing*, Douglas Gifford and Dorothy McMillan (eds), 360–72. Edinburgh: Edinburgh University Press.

McDowell, Edwin. 1987. "Random House to Buy Schocken Books." *New York Times*, July 9. http://www.nytimes.com/1987/07/09/books/random-house-to-buy-schocken-books.html

McIlvoy, Ann. 1990. "Film Maker Raises Kafka's Ghost in Old Prague." *The Times*, October 26.

Mellown, Elgin. W. 1964. "The Development of A Criticism: Edwin Muir and Franz Kafka." *Comparative Literature*, 16. 4: 310–21.

Michálek, Vladimír. 1994. *Amerika*. VHS. Directed by Vladimír Michálek. Warner Home Video.

Millar, John and Bendoris, Matt. 1995. "Scots Oscar Hope Keeps his Cool; Peter Capaldi Talks About His Academy Award." *Daily Record*, February 16: 15.

Miller, J. Hillis. 2011a. *The Conflagration of Community. Fiction Before and After Auschwitz*. Chicago, IL: University of Chicago Press.

—2011b. "The Sense of an Un-Ending: The Resistance to Narrative Enclosure." In *Franz Kafka. Narration, Rhetoric & Reading*, Jakob Lothe, Beatrice Sandberg and Ronald Speirs (eds), 108–22. Columbus: Ohio State University Press.

Mitchell, Breon. 1998. "Translator's Preface." In *The Trial*, trans. Breon Mitchell, xv–xxvi. New York: Schocken.

Mowe, Richard. 1994. "Short Cuts to Hollywood People the Highlands." *Scotland on Sunday*, August 7.

Muir, Edwin. 1963. *The Structure of the Novel*. London: Hogarth Press.

—1967. *Essays on Literature and Society*. Cambridge, MA: Harvard University Press, 2nd edn.

—1990. *An Autobiography*. Saint Paul, MN: Graywolf Press.

Muir, Edwin and Muir, Willa. 1966. "Translating from the German." In *On Translation*, edited by Reuben Brower, 93–6. New York: Oxford University Press.

Muir, Willa. 1965. *Living With Ballads*. New York: Oxford University Press.

—1968. *Belonging*. London: Hogarth Press.

—1996. *Imagined Selves*. Edinburgh: Canongate.

—Willa Muir Archive. St. Andrews University.

Nabokov, Vladimir. 1982. *Lectures On Literature*. San Diego, London and New York: Harvest.

Naremore, James. 1989. *The Magic World of Orson Welles*. Dallas: Southern Methodist University Press.

Nekula, Marek. 2003. *"... v jednom poschodí vnitřní babylonské věže ..."/Jazyky Franze Kafky*. Prague: Nakladatelství Franze Kafky.

Neumann, Gerhard. 2011. "The Abandoned Writing Desk: On Kafka's Metanarratives, as Exemplified by 'Der Heizer'." In *Franz Kafka. Narration, Rhetoric & Reading*, Jakob Lothe, Beatrice Sandberg and Ronald Speirs (eds), 81–93. Columbus: Ohio State University Press.

Neumann, Stanislav. 1920. "Poznamká." *Kmen*, April 22: 72.

—1921. "Poznamká." *Kmen*, March 3: 587.

Norris, Margot. 1983. "Kafka's Josefine: The Animal as the Negative Side of Narration." *MLN*, 98.3: 366–83.

—2010. "Kafka's Hybrids: Thinking Animals and Mirrored Humans." In *Kafka's Creatures. Animals, Hybrids, and Other Fantastic Beings*, Marc Lucht and Donna Yarri (eds), 17–31. Lanham, MD: Lexington Books.

Ormsby, Eric. 2001. *Facsimiles of Time: Essays on Poetry and Translation*. Erin, ON: Porcupine's Quill.

Palmer, R. Barton and Sanders, Steven M. 2011. "Introduction." In *Philosophy of Steven Soderbergh*, R. Barton Palmer and Steven M. Sanders (eds), 1–9. Lexington: University of Kentucky Press.

Pasley, Malcolm. 1998. "Afterword to the German Critical Edition." In *The Castle*, trans. Mark Harman, 318–21. New York: Schocken.

Paton, Maureen. 2011."Peter Capaldi on The Ladykillers: Why I'm Happy Being Mr Angry." *Telegraph*, November 1. http://www.telegraph.co.uk/culture/theatre/theatre-features/8863090/Peter-Capaldi-on-The-Ladykillers-Why-Im-happy-being-Mr-Angry.html

Plant, Richard. 1946. "Punishment in Search of a Crime." *New York Times*, December 8. http://query.nytimes.com/mem/archive/pdf?res=F20D12FE3A5D177A93CAA91789D95F428485F9

Politzer, Heinrich. 1966. *Franz Kafka: Parable and Paradox*. Ithaca, NY: Cornell University Press.

Preece, Julian. 2002. "The Letters and Diaries." In *The Cambridge Companion to Kafka*, Julian Preece (ed.), 111–30. Cambridge: Cambridge University Press.

Provan, Alexander. 2009. "An Alienation Artist: Kafka and His Critics." *The Nation*, March 2. http://www.thenation.com/article/alienation-artist-kafka-and-his-critics?page=0,2

Raoul-David, Jacqueline. 2012. *Kafka in Love*, trans. Willard Wood. New York: Other Press.

Reyes, Alina. 2000. *Nus devant les fantômes*. Paris: Éditions J'ai lu.

Ritzer, Ivo. 2011. "Philosophical Reflections on Steven Soderbergh's Kafka." In *Philosophy of Steven Soderbergh*, R. Palmer and Steven M. Sanders (eds), 145–58. Lexington: University of Kentucky Press.

Roberts, Alison. 1995. "Glorious 18 Lead the March on Hollywood; How Britain's Army of Oscar Hopes Lines Up." Evening Standard, February 21: 16.

Robertson, Ritchie. 1987. *Kafka. Judaism, Politics, and Literature*. Oxford: Clarendon Press.

—2012a. "Introduction." In Franz Kafka, *The Man Who Disappeared*, xi–xxvii, translated by Ritchie Robertson. Oxford: Oxford World Classics.

—2012b. "Introduction." In Franz Kafka, *The Hunger Artist and Other Stories*, xi–xxxix, translated by Joyce Crick. Oxford: Oxford World Classics.

Ross, Maggie. 1983. *Milena*. London: Collins.

Salmond, Alex. 1994. "Invasion of the Body Snatchers." *Glasgow Herald*, August 11: 15.

Samuelson, Arthur H. 1998. "Publisher's Note." *The Trial*, trans. Breon Mitchell, vii–xiv. New York: Schocken.

Self, John. 2008. "Gert Hofmann: Lichtenberg and the Little Flower Girl." *Asylum*. http://theasylum.wordpress.com/2008/10/18/gert-hofmann-lichtenberg-and-the-little-flower-girl/

Shenker, Israel. 1956. "Moody Man of Letters: A Portrait of Samuel Beckett, Author of the Puzzling 'Waiting for Godot'." *New York Times*, May 6: 1, 3.

Sholz, Anne-Marie. 2009. " 'Josef K von 1963 …': Orson Welles' 'Americanized' Version of The Trial and the changing functions of the Kafkaesque in Postwar West Germany." *European Journal of American Studies*, 1. www.ejas.revues.org/7610

Shreve, Gregory M. and Angelone, Erik. 2010. *Translation and Cognition*. Amsterdam, and Philadelphia, PA: John Benjamins.

Simon, David. 2008. *The Wire*. "–30-." Episode 10, Season 5. First broadcast on March 9th on HBO. Directed by Clark Johnson.

Simon, Sherry. 1996. *Gender in Translation: Cultural Identity and the Politics of Transmission*. New York: Routledge.

Smith, Zadie. 2009. *Changing my Mind. Occasional Essays*. London: Hamish Hamilton.

Soderbergh, Steven. 1992. *Kafka*. VHS. Directed by Steven Soderbergh. Miramax Home Video.

Sokel, Walter H. 1999. "Kafka as a Jew." *New Literary History*, 30.4: 837–53.

Soukup, František. 1912. *Amerika: řada obrazů amerického života.* Prague: Práva lidu.
Straus, Nina Pelikan. 1996. "Transforming Franz Kafka's Metamorphosis." In *Franz Kafka. The Metamorphosis*, Stanley Corngold (ed.), 126–40. New York: Norton Critical Edition.
Sunday Times. 1995. "Direct Route Shows Peter's Soft Heart, Hard Head." February 19.
Sussman, Henry. 1977. "The Court as Text: Inversion, Supplanting, and Derangement in Kafka's *Der Prozeß*." *PMLA*, 92.1: 41–55.
Swift, Jonathan. 2003a. *Gulliver's Travels.* London and New York: Penguin.
—2003b. "The Battle of the Books." In *Major Works*, 1–22. Oxford: Oxford World Classics.
Sýkorová, Jasná. 2006. "Fotil jsem Fučíka." *Lidové noviny*, July 29: 17–18.
Theim, Jon. 1995. "The Translator as Hero in Postmodern Fiction." *Translation and Literature*, 4: 207–18.
Thwaite, Mark. 2005. "Michael Hofmann." *Ready Steady Book.* http://www.readysteadybook.com/Article.aspx?page=michaelhofmann
Tymoczko, Maria. 2007. *Enlarging Translation, Empowering Translators.* Manchester: St. Jerome.
Venuti, Lawrence. 2007. "Adaptation, Translation, Critique." *Journal of Visual Culture*, 6.1: 25–43.
—2008. *The Translator's Invisibility. A History of Translation* (2nd edn). London and New York: Routledge.
Vondráčková, Jaroslava. 1991. *Kolem Mileny Jesenské.* Prague: Torst.
Von Flotow, Luise. 1997. *Translation and Gender. Translating in the "Era of Feminism".* Manchester: St. Jerome.
—2012. "Upgrading the Downgraded." *The Iowa Review.* The Iowa Review Forum on Literature and Translation. http://iowareview.uiowa.edu/?q=page/upgrading_the_downgraded
Wagnerová, Alena. 1996. *Milena Jesenská.* Prague: Prostor.
Wallace, David Foster. 2006. *Consider the Lobster and Other Essays.* New York, Boston, London: Back Bay Books.
Welles, Orson. 1962. "Orson Welles on *The Trial*." http://www.wellesnet.com/trial%20bbc%20interview.html
—1999. *The Trial.* Chatsworth, CA: Image Entertainment.
Wells, H.G. 1927. "Mr. Wells Reviews a Current Film." *New York Times* April 17. http://query.nytimes.com/mem/archive/pdf?res=F50B16FC3F5415738DDDAE0994DC405B878EF1D3
Wheatley, Catherine. 2009. *Michael Haneke's Cinema. The Ethic of the Image.* New York, Oxford: Berghahn Books.
Wirkner, Alfred. 1976. *Kafka und die Außenwelt. Quellenstudien zum "Amerika"-Fragment.* Stuttgart: Ernst Klett.
Wolf, Michaela and Fukari, Alexandra (eds). 2007. *Constructing a Sociology of Translation.* Amsterdam, and Philadelphia, PA: John Benjamins.
Wood, Jason and Duncan, Paul. 2002. *Steven Soderbergh.* Harpenden: Pocket Books.
Woods, Michelle. 2006. *Translating Milan Kundera.* Clevedon, OH: Multilingual Matters.
—2012a. *Censoring Translation: Censorship, Theatre and the Politics of Translation.* London and New York: Continuum.

—2012b. "Framing Translation: Adolf Hoffmeister's Comic Strips, Travelogues, and Interviews as Introductions to Modernist Translations." *Translation and Interpreting Studies*, 7.1: 1–18.

Yeats, William Butler. 1983. *The Poems of W.B. Yeats*, Richard J. Finneran (ed.). New York: Macmillan.

Zischler, Hanns. 2003. *Kafka Goes to the Movies*. Chicago, IL, and London: Chicago University Press.

Index

Abraham Lincoln: Vampire Hunter 233
Adams, Jeffrey 196, 198, 228, 230, 231
Adorno, Theodore 1, 2, 175, 177, 227
Albinoni, Tomaso 195
   Adagio 195
Alexeïeff, Alexandre 197
Allen, Keith 232
Alter, Robert 73, 85, 92, 93
Anders, Günther 253
Anderson, Mark 150-1, 152, 193, 218, 219, 254, 255
Apollinaire 10, 28, 99
Arrojo, Rosemary 143
Attridge, Derek 110
Auden, W. H. 251

Baer, Andrea 255
Barthes, Roland 118, 249
Bartók, Béla 10, 99
Batumen, Elif 249
Bauer, Felice 232, 251
Bäuml, Max 248
Beavis and Butthead 205
Beckett, Samuel 4, 80, 84, 85, 87, 88, 96-104, 117, 252
   Malone Dies 97, 98, 100
   Molloy 84
   Trilogy 80, 84, 85, 97
   Waiting for Godot 100
Begley, Louis 79
Bell, Anthea 103, 104
Bell Jar, The 124
Benjamin, Walter 3, 227
Benn, Gottfried 113, 122
Bernhard, Thomas 105, 119
Beyer, Marcel 125
Bhabha, Homi 82
Binder, Hartmut 150-1, 153
Bishop, Elizabeth 120
Blei, Franz 250

Boa, Elizabeth 14, 180
Boehm, Philip 257
Böhme, Hartmut 14
Bolaño, Roberto 89
Bondanella, Peter 209
Borges, Jorge-Luis 89, 105
Bowman, Martin 58
Brady, Martin 192, 193, 194
Braque, Georges 10, 99
Brecht, Bertolt 107, 123
   Good Person of Sichuan, The 123
Broch, Hermann 66
Brod, Max 3, 7, 8, 9, 16, 23, 42, 45, 64, 67, 72, 73, 74, 75, 88, 91, 96, 100, 107, 176, 180, 181, 184, 186, 193, 230, 232, 247-51, 252, 253, 255, 258
   Kingdom of Love, The 67, 247, 249, 253
Brueghel, Pieter 223
Brunette, Peter 200, 202, 206
Buber-Neumann, Margerete 29, 37, 40, 41
   Kafkas Freundin Milena/Milena 37, 40
Buchar, Robert 221
Büchner, Georg 119
Budin, Stanislav 38, 39
Bunyan, John 72
   Pilgrim's Progress, The 72
Burney, Frances 59
Burton, Tim 234
Buzzatti, Dino 123
   Tartar Steppe 123
Byatt, A. S. 111-13

Cabaret 222
Callahan, Clare 143
Camus, Albert 251, 252
Canby, Vincent 231
Capaldi, Peter 10, 194, 233-9
   Kafka's It's a Wonderful Life 10, 194, 233-9
   Soft Top Hard Shoulder 237

Čapek, Karel 28, 51
Capra, Frank 233, 234, 238
    It's a Wonderful Life 233
Celan, Paul 120–1
Čermák, Josef 221
Černá, Jana 13, 37, 41, 43
    Adresát Milena Jesenská/Kafka's Milena 37
Černý, Vladimír 221
Chaplin, Charlie 222
    Modern Times 222
Chappell, William 196
Charlton, Val 234
Christianson, Aileen 47, 49, 66
Chytilová, Věra 221
Cléder, Jean 202
Coetzee, J. M. 5, 72, 75, 84–6, 88, 90, 91, 93, 95, 96, 109–13, 124, 127
Collins, Elaine 233, 237
Congreve, William 59
    Way of the World 59
Connery, Sean 236
Corbett, John 58
Corngold, Stanley 31, 32, 33, 96, 114, 116, 139, 140, 141, 143, 174, 242, 257, 248, 263
Crick, Joyce 57, 58, 59, 74, 116, 241, 242, 263
Cronin, Michael 262

Damrosch, David 75, 88, 89, 95, 96
Deakins, Roger 237
Dejdar, Martin 221
Deleuze, Gilles and Guattari, Félix 4, 7, 96, 139, 255
Derrida, Jacques 130
Diamant, Dora 232, 247, 260
Dickens, Charles 75, 123, 148, 149, 151, 153, 154, 155, 158, 217, 225
    David Copperfield 10, 83, 149–51, 153–9, 166, 217, 248
Dobbs, Lem 231, 232, 233
Döblin, Alfred 37
Donegan, Lawrence 236
Don Quixote 178
Donne, John 102
Donnersmarck, Florian Henkel von 201
    Das Leben der Anderen/The Lives of Others 201

Dowden, Stephen 9, 253
Dowie, John Alexander 163
Dryden, John 178
Durrani, Osman 72
Duttlinger, Carolin 151, 193, 224

Earle, Steve 1
Edwards, Hilton 191
Eisermann, André 206
Ekberg, Anita 209, 210, 215, 216, 217
Elphinstone, Margaret 66, 78

Fallada, Hans 105, 124
    Alone in Berlin 105
Fastrová, Jarmila 16
Faulkner, William 4
Fellini, Federico 10, 124, 192, 194, 208, 209–20, 230
    8½ 209, 210, 212, 215, 217, 230
    Intervista/Interview 10, 194, 208, 209–20
    La Dolce Vita 209, 216
Felsteiner, John 120–1
Feuchtwanger, Lion 46, 56, 66, 69, 191
    Jud Süss 50, 56, 191
Findlay, Bill 58
Flores, Angel 251, 252
    Kafka Problem, The 251, 252
Flores, Kate 251
Florian, Josef 15, 16
Foer, Jonathan Safran 89
Forman, Miloš 221
Foundas, Scott 201
Four Weddings and a Funeral 236, 237
Franzen, Jonathan 89
Freud, Sigmund 126
Frisch, Arno 205

Gedeon, Saša 221
Gibian, George 41
Giering, Frank 201, 205
Gilliam, Terry 234
    Brazil 234
    Time Bandits 234
Gilligan, Vince 9
    Breaking Bad 9
Gogol, Nikolai 119
Gonne, Maude 107

Grant, Hugh 236
Grant, Richard E. 233, 236, 237, 238, 239
Gravity's Rainbow 88
Greve, Anniken 144
Guinness, Alec 228
Gunning, Tom 223

Haas, Willy 37
Hamburger, Michael 121, 122
Haneke, Michael 10, 192, 194, 200–8
  Amour 200, 207
  Caché/Hidden 207
  Code Inconnu/Code Unknown 207
  Das Schloß/The Castle 194, 200–8
  Das Weiße Band: Eine deutsche Kindergeschichte/The White Ribbon 200, 202, 207
  Funny Games 200, 201, 204–7
  La Pianiste/The Piano Teacher 201
Harbou, Thea 227
Hargraves, John 257
Harman, Mark 4, 5, 7, 26, 61, 72, 73, 74, 75, 79–104, 137, 207
Hauptmann, Gerhart 51
Havel, Václav 177, 178, 221
  Memorandum, The 177
Hayes, Kathleen 189
Heaney, Seamus 75, 107, 109
  "Dream of Jealousy, A" 107
Heller, Peter 1
Higgins, Michael D. 236
Hoffmann, E. T. A. 245
  "Nutcracker and the Mouse King, The" 245
Hoffmeister, Adolf 38
Hofmann, Gert 105, 108, 119
  Lichtenberg and the Little Flower Girl 105
Hofmann, Michael 1, 2, 3, 5, 7, 26, 30, 31, 32, 33, 61, 62, 63, 83, 104–27, 143, 166, 242, 254, 263, 264
Hofmannsthal, Hugo von 119
  Andreas 119
Holitscher, Arthur 151, 152, 163, 166
  Amerika Heute und Morgen 151
Holm, Ian 227
Homer 10, 99, 167, 169, 178
  Odyssey, The 10, 99, 168–72, 176, 187

Hrabal, Bohumil 224
Hřebejk, Jan 221
  Musíme si pomahat 221
  Pelíšky 221
Hughes, Helen 192, 193, 194

Iannucci, Armando 238
  Thick of It, The 238
Irons, Jeremy 228, 230

Jakobson, Roman 191
Jelinek, Elfride 201
Jenny, Zoe 124
Jesenská, Milena 6, 7, 10, 13–44, 133, 168, 180–90, 245, 257–61
  "Café, The" 6, 10, 188–90
  "Devil at the Hearth, The" 260, 261
  "Letters of Eminent People, The" 44
  "Slovíčka"/"Little Words" 34–6
Jílovská, Staša 15, 16, 38, 40, 181, 184–6
Joyce, James 4, 10, 75, 80, 81, 96, 99, 163, 168
  "Anna Livia Plurabelle" 99
  "Dead, The" 81
  Finnegans Wake 96, 99
  Portrait of the Artist as a Young Man, A 15, 99
  Ulysses 16, 96, 99, 163, 168
Joyce, Michael 96
Jünger, Ernst 105, 126
  Storm of Steel 126
Jungk, Peter Stephan 105, 122

Kafka, Franz
  Amerika/Der Verschollene 10, 13, 26, 45, 47, 58, 59–65, 78, 79, 81, 82, 90, 91, 105, 106, 107, 110, 119, 122, 123, 125, 138–9, 140, 145–66, 182, 193, 198, 208, 209–20, 221–7, 235, 253
  Aphorisms 1, 45, 59, 105, 249
  "Before the Law" / "Vor dem Gesetz" 130, 134, 135, 195, 197
  "Burrow, The" 127, 143
  "Business Man, The" / "Kupec" 16
  Castle, The / Das Schloß 4, 5, 6, 9, 10, 27, 40, 41, 45, 49, 66, 67, 68, 69, 72, 73, 74, 76, 78, 79, 80, 81, 82, 84,

85–104, 115, 167–90, 200, 201–8, 228, 232, 253
Contemplation 16, 23, 133
Country Doctor, The 114
Diaries 78, 88, 153, 193, 232
"Excursion into the Mountains, The"/"Výlet do hor" 16
"Great Wall of China, The" 114–18, 127, 227
Great Wall of China and Other Pieces, The 45, 57, 59
"Hunger Artist, The" 193, 235
"In the Penal Colony" 45, 144–5, 235, 250
"Investigations of a Dog"/"Forschungen eines Hundes" 244
"Josefine, the Singer" 99, 235, 241–7, 254–64
"Judgment, The"/"Das Urteil"/"Soud" 16, 28–34, 99, 119, 133, 257, 258
Letters to Milena/Briefe an Milena Dopisy Mileně 6, 13, 16–24, 26, 29, 36, 37, 40, 41, 42, 257
"Men Running Past, The"/"Ti, kteří běží mimo" 16
"Message from the Emperor, A"/"Eine Kaiserliche Botschaft" 114–18
"Metamorphosis, The" 16, 23, 40, 104, 105, 106, 114, 119, 127, 140–2, 174, 193, 233, 238
"On Parables" 130, 134
"Plight of the Bachelor, The"/"Neštěstí mládence" 16
"Poseidon" 167
"Report to an Academy, A"/"Zpráva pro akademii" 16, 142–4
"Silence of the Sirens, The" 99, 181–2
"Stoker, The"/"Der Heizer"/"Topič" 6, 13, 14, 16, 23, 24–8, 34, 36, 42, 119, 133, 153, 159, 182, 193, 224
"Sudden Walk, The"/"Náhle procházka" 16
Trial, The/Der Proceß 3, 4, 7, 16, 19, 23, 45, 49, 67, 72, 78, 90, 129–38, 143, 191–200, 202, 225, 226, 228, 232, 249, 250
"Unhappiness"/"Nesťastný" 16, 20
Way Home, The"/"Cesta domů" 16
"Wedding Preparations in the Country" 228
Kafka, Irene 96
Kafka, Ottla 186
Kaiser, Oldřich 221
Kaus, Gina 34, 37
Kautman, František 37, 41, 43, 180, 181, 260
Keegan, Paul 122
Kerguen, Oanig 230
Kettle, Steve 231
Keun, Irmgard 126
Kierkegaard, Søren 175, 251
Kleist, Heinrich von 79, 96
Klopstock, Robert 181–2, 247
Kmen 6, 16–17, 24, 26
Koeppen, Wolfgang 105, 122
Kozáková, Kateřina 223
Krabbe, Jeroen 230
Kramsch, Claire 7, 144
Kraus, Karl 254
Kriseová, Eda 226
Kundera, Milan 4, 5, 8, 9, 10, 14, 27, 64, 70, 89, 92, 94, 95, 99, 102, 119, 139, 166, 176, 183, 248, 249, 253
Kvapilová, Anička 40

Lábus, Jiří 221, 222
Lancaster, Burt 238
Landauer, Gustav 37
Landovský, Pavel 221, 226
Lang, Fritz 220, 222, 223, 227
Metropolis 220, 222, 223, 224, 226, 227, 228
Ledig, Gert 105
Letts, Crispin 233
Levine, Michael 244
Lewis, Philip 152
Lewis, Wyndham 48–9
The Apes of God 48
Liblická conference 37
Light, Alison 78
Liguari, Paola 211
Local Hero 238
Logan, Phyllis 233
Lonsdale, Michael 196
Lothar, Susanne 201, 205
Lowell, Robert 109

Lukács, Georg 176–7
Luxemburg, Rosa 25, 37

MacDiarmid, Hugh 55
Macgregor, Robert M. 47, 59
Mac Liammóir, Micheál 191, 199
Mann, Thomas 91, 119, 250
Marková-Kotyková, Marta 15–16, 29, 33, 43
Marquez, Gabriel García 89
Maša, Antonín 221
Maslin, Janet 234
Mastroianni, Marcello 209, 214, 215, 216, 217
May, Karl 107
McBride, Joseph 195, 197
McBurney, Simon 232
McIlvoy, Ann 231
Mein, Maurizio 212
Méliès, Georges 233
Menzel, Jiří 221, 224
    Postřižiny/Cutting it Short 224
Meyrink, Gustav 135, 250
    Golem, The 135
Michálek, Vladimír 10, 194, 208, 220–7
    Amerika 10, 194, 208, 220–7
    Anděl Exit 221
    Babí léto/Autumn Spring 220
    Je třeba zabít Sekal/Sekal Has to Die 220
    Zapomenuté světlo 221
Middleton, Christopher 122
Miller, J. Hillis 136, 138, 167, 253
Milton, John 178
Mitchell, Breon 3, 4, 90, 136
Monty Python 233, 234, 235, 238
Mühe, Ulrich 201, 205
Muir, Edwin 2, 3, 5, 9, 31, 32, 33, 44–52, 55–60, 64, 65, 69, 71–6, 83, 84, 85, 88, 89, 90, 91, 92, 115, 116, 143, 191, 242, 263
    Autobiography 50, 52
    Structure of the Novel, The 50
Muir, Willa 2, 3, 5, 6, 7, 9, 31, 32, 33, 44–79, 83, 84, 85, 88, 89, 90, 91, 92, 115, 116, 143, 191, 242, 263
    Belonging 44, 45, 47, 48, 49, 54
    Imagined Corners 45

Mrs. Muttoe and the Top Storey 45, 65–72, 74, 76
Mrs. Ritchie 45
Usurpers, The 45, 49, 50, 55
Woman: An Inquiry 44, 45, 75
Müller, Herta 105
Murnau, F. W. 228
    Nosferatu 228
Musil, Robert 10, 91, 99

Nabokov, Vladimir 110
Naremore, James 196, 197
Národní listy 14, 24, 34, 38
Neill, Bud 238
Nekula, Marek 7
Němec, Jan 221
Neumann, Gerhard 138, 140
Neumann, S. K. 16, 23, 24, 25

Ormsby, Eric 91, 92, 93
Ovid 109, 123

Parker, Claire 197
Pasley, Malcolm 4, 45, 88, 100, 177, 242
Passer, Ivan 221
Paul, Aaron 9
Peguyu, Charles 37
Perkins, Anthony 195
Peroutka, Ferdinand 38
Pethig, Hazel 234
Phillipe, Charles-Louis 37
Phillips, Adam 126
Plant, Richard 252
Plato 8
Politzer, Heinz 151
Pollak, Ernst 15, 25, 34, 38, 40, 180, 190
Preece, Julian 21, 24
Přítomnost 38, 39, 42
Proust, Marcel 91
Pujmanová, Marie 40

Raoul-David, Jacqueline 6, 36
    Kafka in Love 6, 36
Reyes, Alina 42
    Nus devant les fantômes 42
Richardson, G. K. 159
Richter-Bernburg, Melanie 93
Rilke, Rainer Maria 121

Index

Ritzer, Ivo 229, 230
Robertson, Ritchie 151, 208, 241, 242
Ross, Maggie 42–3
　Milena 42–3
Roth, Joseph 105, 106, 109–12, 113, 122, 124, 127
　Emperor's Tomb, The 109–12
　Hotel Savoy 106
　Radetzky March, The 127
Royo, Andre 1
Rubini, Sergio 211, 212, 215, 216, 217, 220
Rushdie, Salman 89
Russell, Therese 228

Salmond, Alex 236
Samel, Udo 202
Schiffrin, André 90
Schmitzer, Jiří 222, 224
Schocken publishers 79, 85, 90, 91, 93
Schulz, Gustav 37
Scott, Walter 83
Seawards the Great Ships 236
Seinfeld 88
Shawshank Redemption, The 237
Sheltering Sky, The 123
Simon, David 1
　Corner, The 1
　Wire, The 1
Sinclair, Upton
Smith, Zadie 241, 249
Soderbergh, Steven 10, 192, 194, 227–33
　Bubble 228
　Girlfriend Experience, The 228, 229
　Haywire 232
　Informant!, The 228
　Kafka 10, 194, 227–33
　Limey, The 232
　Ocean's Twelve 228, 229
　sex, lies, and videotape 228
　Traffic 229
Sokel, Walter 253
Soukup, František 10, 150–1, 152, 153, 160–6
　Amerika: řada obrazů amerického života 10, 150–1, 151, 160–6
Speirs, Ronald 257
Stamm, Peter 105

Steele, Richard 59
　Tender Husband 59
Steiner, George 72
Sterchi, Beat 122, 124
Stifter, Adalbert 96, 251
Stott, Ken 233
Straub, Jean-Marie and Huillet, Danièle 192, 208
　Klassenverhältnisse/Class Relations 208
Stravinsky, Igor 10, 99
Süskind, Patrick 105, 122
Sussman, Henry 133
Švankmajer, Jan 221
Svěrák, Jan
　Kolja 221
　Tmavomodrý svět 221
Swift, Jonathan 10, 104, 168, 178–80, 186
　Battle of the Books, The 10, 168, 178–80
　Gulliver's Travels 186
Synge, J. M. 191

Tamiroff, Akim 196
Tarantino, Quentin 205
Tchaikovsky, Pyotr Ilych 245
Thackeray, William 59, 75
　Vanity Fair 119
Third Man, The 228, 229, 230
Thirlwall, Adam 249
Tóibín, Colm 79
Tolstoy, Leo 37
Tom and Jerry 205
Tomanová, Libuše 225
Topol, Jáchym 221
　Anděl 221
Tribuna 15, 16–17, 37, 188, 190
Tucholsky, Kurt 122

Underwood, J. A. 91

Venuti, Lawrence 10, 152, 192
Virgil 178
Voliva, Wilbur Glenn 163, 164
Vondráčková, Jaroslava 15–16, 25, 38
Von Flotow, Luise 79
Von Trier, Lars 207
　Dogville 207
　Kingdom, The 207

Wagner, Richard 254
Wagnerová, Alena 15–16, 29, 34, 35, 36, 38, 40
Wallace, David Foster 130, 140
Walser, Robert 79
Wander, Fred 105
Webern, Anton 10, 99
Wedekind, Frank 250
Weil, Jiří 40
Weininger, Otto 254
Welles, Orson 10, 191, 192, 194–200, 204, 228, 229
  Citizen Kane 191
  Trial, The 191, 194–200, 204, 228, 229
Wells, H. G. 223, 224
Wenders, Wim 105

Werfel, Franz 37, 189
Wheatley, Catherine 203
Wizard of Oz, The 228, 229
Wodehouse, P. G. 123
Wolff, Kurt 159, 193
Woolf, Virginia 75
  Orlando 15
Woolf, Leonard and Virginia 45, 75

Yeats, Georgie 107
Yeats, William Butler 107–8
  "Towards Break of Day" 107–8

Žantovská, Hana 37
Zischler, Hanns 193